'I[...] insights, clarit[...] nd honest wit, it's h[...] imagine a more e[...] ok[...] about. As in the best TV itself, you find yourself learning something new with almost no effort.' *Observer*

'Richly detailed, as profoundly nostalgic as Findus Crispy Pancakes.' *Daily Mail*

'Moran's achievement is remarkable ... extensive research is lightly worn.' *Independent*

'Joe Moran's affectionate and erudite chronicle of our nation's love affair with TV achieves the impossible – it is scholarly AND accessible. It is a compelling account of a golden age and reminds us that today's age of plenty has diluted the cultural impact of TV.' Michael Grade

'You will find a lot to love. Impeccably researched ... *Armchair Nation* treats television with proper seriousness.' *New Statesman*

'Joe Moran is a superb elegist of the mundane ... his book is packed with glorious details.' *Country Life*

'At last! The view from the sofa. A history of television that reflects the lives of those who watch it – and that means pretty well all of us. Informative, evocative, funny, moving, sometimes even startling, Joe Moran, Britain's premier historian of the everyday, has pulled it off again.' Juliet Gardiner

'A warm, witty cultural history of television ... a compelling and surprising patchwork of the nation through its viewing habits and rituals ... timely and hugely entertaining.' *Time Out*

'Quite wonderful, an original piece of social history and beautifully written. It reveals a seated country, something [...] never happened before. There is nothi[...]

'All that time we were watching television Joe Moran was thinking about it. This wonderful book is packed with stories and characters, shot through with Moran's customary affection for the ordinary and the overlooked. A beautiful study of that flickering box that keeps us enthralled.' Sam West

'A scholarly, accessible and illuminating history of the everyday.' *Lady*

'A quite brilliant history of a now lost world of British terrestrial television, *Armchair Nation* is as warm and friendly as an old valve set and, correspondingly also crackling and humming with new insights and fresh research.' Travis Elborough

'Terrific … both erudite and highly entertaining.' Simon Hoggart

'Joe Moran is the most perceptive and original observer of British life that we have.' Matthew Engel

JOE MORAN is Professor of English and Cultural History at Liverpool John Moores University and contributes regularly to the *Guardian* and other newspapers. His previous books include *Queuing for Beginners* and *On Roads*, which was longlisted for the Samuel Johnson Prize.

Armchair Nation

An Intimate History of Britain in Front of the TV

Joe Moran

P

PROFILE BOOKS

This paperback edition first published in 2014

First published in Great Britain in 2013 by
PROFILE BOOKS LTD
3A Exmouth House
Pine Street
Exmouth Market
London EC1R 0JH
www.profilebooks.com

1 3 5 7 9 10 8 6 4 2

Typeset in Sabon by MacGuru Ltd
info@macguru.org.uk

ISBN 978 1 84668 392 3
eISBN 978 1 84765 444 1

In memory of my grandmother,
Bridget Moran (1915–2010),
who lived half her life without television

CONTENTS

SWITCHING ON

The worst fate that can befall me is to be stranded in a town without a television set.

Matt Monro[1]

In Scandinavia they call it 'the war of the ants'. We had a black-and-white television set with a tuning dial like a radio, and every time you switched channels you encountered this snowstorm of static, which, if you squinted a bit, resembled black ants scurrying round a white floor. Since we also had an indoor aerial and lived in a valley in the foothills of the Pennines, the television, even when it was meant to be tuned into a channel, could still blight a favourite programme with these random bursts of electromagnetic noise. Switching on the television was not an action to be taken lightly, like flicking a light switch or turning on a tap. There was something fragile and precarious about the way the radio waves had to be picked out of the air, converted into electrons and fired across the cathode ray tube towards the phosphorescent screen – to make, if you were lucky, a moving picture, and if you weren't, this atmospheric fuzz.

Television in our house was rationed, to half an hour a day. This law was policed inadequately, especially by our merciful mother, but its gesture to austerity was probably a blessing, for without it I would have watched television all the time. I was nearly two when, in January 1972, the telecommunications minister Christopher

Chataway brought an end to the last vestige of postwar rationing. The three channels, BBC1, BBC2 and ITV, would no longer be limited to 3,330 hours each per year, but could broadcast for as long as they liked. The age of plenty this decision ushered in, which coincided with the arrival of colour TV in most homes (but not ours), is now recalled as a lost age of one-nation television in which the same programmes were watched and loved by huge and diverse audiences, a diasporic national community loosely assembled in 19 million living rooms.

Children were the most voracious viewers. 'As a child growing up in the early 1970s,' the author D. J. Taylor has written, 'I watched television in the way that a whale engulfs plankton: gladly, hectically and indiscriminately.' The audiences for after-school television were huge (although also fickle, halving when the clocks went forward in the spring as children abandoned it for outdoors). Eighty per cent of British children watched *Scooby Doo*, a cartoon series in which a gang of teenagers and a cowardly Great Dane drove round in a van solving mysteries, invariably involving petty criminals disguised as ghosts. With this possible exception, children's TV radiated that well-meaning ethos of healthful activity and curiosity about the world that also informed organisations like the Puffin Club for young readers and Big Chief I-Spy's tribe of spotters. 'What would make me happiest,' said Monica Sims, head of children's programmes at the BBC about her viewers, 'would be if they went away.'[2]

This ethos inspired programmes like *Why Don't You ... Switch Off the Television Set and Go and Do Something Less Boring Instead?*, which showed children how to make computers from index cards and knitting needles, or build their own hovercraft; *Vision On*, an inventively visual show for deaf children, which received about 8,000 artworks each week from mostly non-deaf children hoping to be displayed in its gallery; and the collective rituals of the BBC's flagship children's programme, *Blue Peter*, whose pioneering correspondence unit invited viewers to write in with good programme ideas, the reward for which was a coveted shield badge. The letters suggested a keen sense of ownership over the programme. 'Dear Peter,' wrote nine-year-old Ronald from Falkirk to the presenter Peter Purves, 'I liked when you tried to ride a killer whale. I would like to see you try to skin dive and kill a shark. I have liked everything that *Blue Peter* has done especially that fort that Val made from lollypop sticks.'[3] These participatory rituals – tutorials on how to create forts from lollypop sticks or dachshund draught excluders from ladies' tights and old socks, and charitable appeals for silver paper or milk bottle tops which mysteriously converted into inshore lifeboats or guide dogs for the blind – seemed to be saying implicitly to us that we were not just a statistical aggregate of lots of individual viewers, but a virtual community, an extended family brought together twice weekly in front of the set.

Much of the television meant for adults also seemed to share this incantatory quality, this rhetorical conjuring up of collective life. The teatime magazine programme *Nationwide*, a *Blue Peter* for grown-ups which called itself 'Britain's nightly mirror to the face of Britain', corralled the nation into imagined togetherness by segueing from discussions of the IMF bailout to film inserts about Herbie the skateboarding Aylesbury duck. The consumer show *That's Life* was a similarly strange miscellany of high street vox pops, funny newspaper misprints and interviews with eccentrics who had invented udder warmers for cows or trained their pet dogs to say 'sausages'. But surely the oddest collective ritual came on Saturday afternoons between the half-time football scores and the classified results on ITV's *World of Sport*, when Dickie Davies introduced the wrestling. 'Ideally, every bout should tell a little tale,' wrote the wrestler Jackie Pallo in his revealingly titled memoir, *You Grunt, I'll Groan*.[4] In each match, the two wrestlers would suffer their share of being held in a headlock that had them slapping the canvas in mock agony, before the baddie, usually identifiable by his leotard, lost – a narrative so simple it could be understood with the sound turned down.

As I have since discovered, there were regular tabloid exposés about the wrestling, so the millions of viewers who did not know it was faked must simply not have wanted to know. The French critic Roland Barthes once observed that wrestling was not a sport at all, but a moral drama in which the audience looked for 'the pure gesture which separates Good from Evil, and unveils the form of a Justice which is at last intelligible'.[5] It did not matter that the result was fixed, only that good was seen to triumph.

Luke Haines's 2011 album, *Nine and a Half Psychedelic Meditations on British Wrestling of the 1970s and Early '80s*, made while his father was ill as a way of remembering watching *World of Sport* with him, captures perfectly this sense of the wrestling as its own weird, beguiling and wholly unironic world. Haines recorded the album in his living room with a cheap 1980s keyboard, interweaving old footage of *World of Sport* moments such as Kendo Nagasaki (aka Peter Thornley from Stoke) being ceremonially unmasked at Wolverhampton Civic Hall in 1977 with fantasies like the sackcloth-wearing, wild-bearded wrestler Catweazle's false teeth flying out of the TV and landing at Haines's feet. The wrestling was an extreme example of what was true of most television when I was growing up: it demanded total immersion in its symbolic universe, for looking at it with an outsider's eye would break the spell and render it meaningless and ridiculous. Television performed a mostly benign confidence trick, convincing us that we believed the same things and were part of the same armchair nation.

This belief in a Pax Britannica of three-channel television, when everyone sat in front of the same programmes, is largely a myth – and like many myths it says as much about our current preoccupations as it does about the television we watched a generation ago. It is partly a lament for the seemingly lost capacity of multichannel television to create shared moments of empathy and understanding. This belief is part of a wider sense that the nation once possessed a common culture that has now fragmented, a persistent idea in British cultural history running all the way from *Piers Plowman* to T. S. Eliot. Nostalgia being a malleable emotion, each age produces its own version of this myth: many blamed television itself for destroying older forms of communal life when it arrived in most homes in the 1950s. 'If there is one thing certain about "the organic community",' the cultural critic Raymond Williams once wrote, 'it is that it has always gone.'[6]

In memories of television, nostalgia often mixes with condescension. It is customary to belittle the experience of watching early TV, in a way that perhaps I have also been guilty of in my own recollections, above. The set took ten minutes to warm up. The screen was as small as a postcard. And when it wasn't switched on, the TV was hidden away guiltily behind a double door like a triptych, or modestly covered with an antimacassar. It was a time, according to the journalist A. A. Gill, summarising this orthodoxy, 'when the whole world was in 405 lines, took two minutes to warm up and vanished into a white dot at 11 p.m. after a vicar had told you off'.[7] We like to think of early television watchers as naïfs, responding with wide-eyed amazement to what seem to us absurd or antediluvian programmes, from dull monochrome panel shows to the Saturday afternoon wrestling. Thus we unconsciously patronise the viewers of the past, as if we were colonialists wondering at the strange habits of a remote tribe.

This mixture of nostalgia and condescension fails to convey how rich and deep the history of British television is, much of it now surviving only as listings. Even in its early years, when broadcasts took up just a few hours a day, the relentlessness of daily television, combined with the fact that it was mostly live and unrecorded, meant there was far too much of it to enter the sorting house for shared memories. Leafing through old copies of the *Radio Times* and *TV Times* is a melancholy activity, an entry into a lost world of spent effort, used-up enjoyment and forgotten boredom. Most television, to which talented, energetic people devoted months or years of their lives, has left momentary imprints on our retinas and slightly less momentary imprints on our brains before vanishing into the uncaring ether.

Any history of watching television inevitably becomes a meditation on the nature of collective memory, for a programme that millions once watched but which has now faded into the atmosphere like a dream is a neat encapsulation of the elusive quality of memory itself. The most banal TV from the past can be extraordinarily evocative. Numerous websites exhaustively dedicate themselves to collating and curating the old connective tissue of television, from continuity announcements to channel idents; there is even a group of devotees that meets every Easter in Leominster to share their enthusiasm for the design aesthetic and incidental music of the television test cards. But most television remains forgotten, and those bits that are remembered are often surrounded by wishful thinking and selective amnesia. What is remembered and forgotten is as revealing as the 'real' history of watching television, which is ultimately too vast and unrecorded to be told.

Here, for instance, is one piece of both collective and selective memory. On Saturday 13 November 1965 at 11.19 p.m., on the late night satire show *BBC-3*, the host, Robert Robinson, asked the critic and literary manager of the National Theatre, Kenneth Tynan, if he would stage a play in which there was sexual intercourse. 'Oh, I think so certainly,' replied Tynan, before adding as a seemingly casual afterthought, 'I mean I doubt if there are very many rational people in this world to whom the word "fuck" is particularly diabolical or revolting or totally forbidden.' This, at least, is the gist of what Tynan said; it was live TV and no one was writing it down. Tynan's stammer, *Private Eye* said cruelly, had created the first thirteen-syllable four-letter word in history.[8] The studio audience briefly inhaled its collective breath and the discussion carried on regardless.

The moment was too late for the Sunday newspapers but Monday's were filled with righteous anger. William Barkley of the *Daily Express* called it 'the bloodiest outrage I have ever known' and accused Robinson of wearing a 'lecherous leer' after the word was uttered. Barkley, who had stayed up with his family to watch *BBC-3*, said it was the first time he had ever heard the word used by 'an adult male in the presence of women'. His wife switched off the television straightaway and said to their 28-year-old daughter, 'It's time you went to bed.' Mary Whitehouse, of the newly formed National Viewers' and Listeners' Association, said Tynan should have his bottom smacked. 'The BBC should restrict its time to those communicators who are acting from *noble* motives, if the word still has meaning amid the indifference and irresponsibility thrust down our unwilling throats,' wrote eight students from the University of Essex Union. 'If it is incapable of fulfilling this task, the service should cease to demoralise the nation by closing down.'[9]

Anonymous letters to Tynan were more sinister: 'You will soon have the sack and my friends and I will be waiting for you to give you the best licking that you have ever had for your behaviour. So be careful and don't walk alone. We are waiting for you … you disgraceful blighter.'[10] Read like this, from the perspective of our apparently liberal and enlightened present, the story runs along familiar lines, gently amusing us that something which today would barely turn a hair once caused such consternation.

But the story is more complicated than it at first appears. Although Tynan is routinely cited as the first person to use the F-word on British television, it had actually been used at least twice before. In June 1956 the playwright Brendan Behan employed it liberally on *Panorama* during an interview with Malcolm Muggeridge. No viewers protested, perhaps because Behan's diction was severely impaired by drink, although hundreds rang to complain that they could not understand his Dublin accent. A few years later, just after Ulster Television had begun in 1959, the man with the Sisyphean task of painting the railings on Stranmillis Embankment alongside the River Lagan in Belfast appeared live on its teatime magazine programme *Roundabout*. The interviewer, Ivor Mills, asked if it was ever boring painting the same railings all year round. 'Of course it's fucking boring,' the man replied.[11]

The channel's managing director, Brum Henderson, waited anxiously for the inescapable tsunami of complaint to arrive at the studios. In the event, not a single viewer, even in this deeply religious region in which play swings were padlocked on Sundays, rang or wrote in. It is a reminder to historians to display humility in making judgements about the past, for there are things about even our most immediate ancestors that we will never know or understand. Were the viewers of *Roundabout* simply not paying attention or half-asleep, or did they think the word was such an unlikely thing to hear on a teatime broadcast they assumed they were hallucinating? Is it even possible that, without the collective prompting of other offended people, they were not offended at all?

We do know this: many viewers admired Kenneth Tynan for what one called his 'four-letter courage'. A Manchester student, Bronwen Lee, wrote to offer 'moral support in your splendid action against the self-righteous philistines'. A Harlow Labour councillor, Avril Fox, was moved to arrange a meeting of anti-Mary Whitehouse viewers in the Cosmo pub, Bloomsbury. The Cosmo Group against censorship, announced a few days later on the *Guardian* women's page, soon had a membership of 500, including clergymen, housewives, a general and 'one or two Wing Commanders' – the RAF, according to Fox, being especially anti-Whitehouse. Letters of support poured in from 'villages and places like Guernsey, with one anguished cry from Neath'. In the country, Fox argued, television played a greater part in people's lives and they were fiercely opposed to censorship.[12]

Tynan probably meant to create a reaction. He claimed he had only used an old English word as it came up in the conversation, and to have edited himself would have been patronising to the viewer. Since he wasn't really answering the question, this seems disingenuous. Robert Robinson thought he had 'grabbed at notoriety like a child', and the author Kingsley Amis felt he was 'just showing off'.[13] The BBC issued a qualified apology, pointing out that the word had been used on live TV in a serious discussion, and the controversy died a quick and natural death with no one losing their job over it.

A year before Tynan's use of the F-word, John Krish had made an affecting film documentary, *I Think They Call Him John*, which followed a widowed ex-miner living alone in a new London high-rise flat. The film shows him silently pottering round one Sunday, feeding his budgie, cooking two sausages and a potato for lunch, staring out of the window. Then, towards the end, as dusk descends on the flats, John switches on the television and his face is mirrored in the screen as he sits down on a hard-backed chair and waits for the sound, which comes on in the middle of an ad break: 'For whiteness that *shows*, she can depend on *Persil*.' After the break comes Beat the Clock, the section of *Sunday Night at the London Palladium* in which couples could win washing machines and fridges for playing silly games like bursting balloons with needles attached to their noses. John unwraps a boiled sweet and pops it in his mouth. 'I *knew* you were an Ada!' cries the instantly familiar voice of Bruce Forsyth, through audience laughter. 'As soon as you walked on there, I said, that's an Ada ... Oh we do have fun! You have sixty seconds to do this little bit of nonsense, starting from ... hold on, hold on, Ada, if you're going to make a farce of the whole thing ...' John takes out an ironing board and glumly irons a shirt for no one in particular while the programme carries on, his one-sided encounter with Bruce Forsyth being his only human interaction that day.

Despite its veneer of fly-on-the-wall authenticity, the film was actually a set-up: a public service documentary made on behalf of the Samaritans, with Krish calling out careful instructions to his subject. And yet it still seems to me to convey something important and often unspoken about watching television. The elderly widower in Krish's film had the most minimal relationship possible with Bruce Forsyth; he happened to be in the same room when Forsyth was on the television, which happened to be switched on. The TV audience is a momentary collective like this, an insubstantial gathering across millions of living rooms which anyone can join by making the rudimentary commitment of turning on the set.

But collective memories of watching TV tend to home in instead on those moments, such as Tynan's use of the F-word, when viewers took offence or were otherwise angered, excited or rapt by television. Indeed, the only continuous record of viewers' responses deals precisely with these reactions. The BBC was the first television company to begin logging viewers' calls in a 'duty log', not always enthusiastically. 'We must deal with telephone enquiries,' said the BBC's Chief Television Liaison Officer in the early 1950s. 'For goodness sake, why must they ring? Why can't they let us get on with our job of putting programmes on the air?'[14]

When the Television Duty Office moved to the fourth floor of the new Television Centre in White City in the 1960s, the operation became more professional and less obviously irritated by its callers. While two TV sets, one tuned to BBC1 and the other to BBC2, chattered away continually in one corner, the small group of shift-working duty officers scrawled down summative points from calls, before transferring them to two typewriters, one for each channel. In the 1980s the duty log became a cut-and-paste, word processed document, until it was outsourced, at the end of the millennium, to a private company working from a Belfast call centre. All commercial TV stations are also now required by law to keep duty logs.

Duty logs provide a complete record of what was shown on television, including any late runnings and last minute changes, so the police and lawyers regularly use them to check the alibis of suspects who say they were at home watching TV when a crime took place. Alongside the large number of calls from people who clearly phone just to talk to someone (nicknamed 'lonely hearts' by the duty officers) they supply a random stream of consciousness about television, although certain things – cruelty to animals, criticism of the royal family or the union flag being flown upside down – will reliably create a reaction. Most calls are simple requests for information about the name of an actor or incidental music, but there are also compliments and, of course, complaints: some sane and reasonable, others idiosyncratic and contrarian and communicated in that tone of suffocating earnestness, pained self-importance and pointless anger that will be familiar to anyone who reads internet message boards.

Just as it would be unwise of future historians to read the anonymous comments on websites as expressions of the collective mentality of our era, it would be equally unwise of us to pore over the duty logs in search of typical viewers. Most of us are not moved to ring up a stranger to let them know what we think about what we are watching. After a few false starts, the English language settled on the word 'watch' to describe what people do in front of televisions. But 'watch', which shares its origins with 'wake' and conveys associations of keenly looking and keeping guard, is not always the right word to denote our relationship to the TV set. Much viewing is absent-minded or indifferent, and even the intense feelings that the TV generates are usually fleeting and soon forgotten. Television's greater significance in our lives surely stems from its slowly accrued habits and rituals, the way it mingles with our other daily routines and comes to seem as natural as sleeping and waking.

Britain's single time zone and its small number of channels have meant that television, in its ways of talking to its viewers, has assumed that it represents 'the private life of the nation state', to use the critic John Ellis's phrase.[15] But viewers in Lerwick or St Helier have watched television with a different eye and ear to those in London (except during the substantial part of television's history when they were not able to watch it at all). Television has served as a distorted mirror through which to reflect on what defines the nation, and the nation's margins. So I have tried to tell the story that follows through the voices of those who have watched television in different parts of the islands, without presuming the existence of some imagined, scattered, national community brought together in front of the set. This book is mostly about individuals in specific places, usually but not always sitting in living rooms, watching TV and reflecting on what they see.

Yet I have also found that there is another kind of armchair nation – not perhaps the united, countrywide family that primetime television assumes it is addressing, but a more improvised community of viewers, formed wordlessly and unconsciously through collective habits and behaviours. Aerials and satellite dishes spring up silently on roofs, living-room curtains close, streets and roads empty of people and cars, the tills in public houses are stilled and the boiling of kettles synchronises across the nation – all because people are watching television. Precisely because it is so fragile and intangible and demands so little of those who belong to it, the armchair nation can create a sense of commonality among people who may have little else in common. And perhaps this collective habit of watching TV, which has taken up so much of our waking lives, can tell us something about who we are and what matters to us.

LONDON
COLISEUM
CHARING CROSS, W.C.
Managing Director - - Sir OSWALD STOLL
Manager - - WILLIAM AGNEW
2.15 - 5.15 - 8.15
THE NEW
RADIO SENSATION
TELEVISION
THE BAIRD BRITISH
INVENTION
FIRST TIME IN
ANY THEATRE
2.15 - 5.15 - 8.15

2

A WAKING DREAM

There are words which are ugly because of foreignness or ill-breeding (e.g. television).

T. S. Eliot[1]

'Oxford Street ... is a forcing house of sensation,' wrote Virginia Woolf in an essay for *Good Housekeeping* magazine in 1928. 'The great Lords of Oxford Street are as magnanimous as any Duke or Earl who scattered gold or doled out loaves to the poor at his gates. Only their largesse takes a different form. It takes the form of excitement, of display, of entertainment, of windows lit up by night, of banners flaunting by day.'[2] Woolf often shopped at Selfridge's, at the street's western end. From the moment you entered on the ground floor, with its heady perfume counter designed to disguise the bouquet of horse manure and other noxious gases from the street outside, Selfridge's was meant to be a profusion of scents, sights and sounds. It displayed Louis Blériot's plane on its lower ground floor the day after his cross-channel flight in July 1909, and Ernest Shackleton's twenty-two-foot boat, the *James Caird*, on its roof in February 1920.

The American owner, Harry Selfridge, was looking for another attraction to celebrate the opening of his western extension and the store's sixteenth birthday. On a tip-off, he visited John Logie Baird's Soho workshop and asked him to come and demonstrate his new invention. And so, one Wednesday morning in March 1925, in the electrical department on the first floor, this diffident-looking man in wire-rimmed glasses set up an odd contraption in one corner, assembled from such items as old cycle lamps, coffin wood and a biscuit tin (Rich Mixed), at the end of which was a rapidly spinning disc and a 'danger' sign. 'The House of Selfridge has always gone out of its way to encourage other pilgrims on the Road of Progress,' announced Callisthenes, Selfridge's column in *The Times*. 'And this picturesque apparatus with its cardboard and its bicycle chain is in direct succession to Blériot's gallant monoplane and Shackleton's brave boat.'[3]

Television was a dream long before it was a fact. This Greco-Latin word, coined in French and borrowed by the English language in 1907, means 'far sight'. Television was meant to defeat distance, to show events happening at the same time somewhere else. For centuries people had fantasised about the instantaneous journey of sound and vision across space. For St Augustine, the epitome of this incorporeal, telepathic communication was the angel, a word that means 'messenger'. The holiest mortals were also thought to have this power. Clare of Assisi, the founder of the Franciscan order of Poor Clares, was supposed, from her convent sickbed in Christmas 1252, to have watched midnight mass in the Basilica of St Francis a few miles away, projected on to the wall of her room. In 1958, Pope Pius XII declared this miracle to be the first television broadcast and named Clare the patron saint of television.

In a world that takes instant communication as read, we forget how much our ancestors worried about everything being so far away from everything else and obsessed about the annihilation of distance. The early moderns often longed for some form of miraculous overcoming of the rootedness of the human body and the tiresomely dispersed physical world. 'If the dull substance of my flesh were thought, Injurious distance should not stop my way,' writes the lovelorn poet of Shakespeare's 44th sonnet. Shakespeare's contemporary, Robert Greene, invented a 'magic mirror' for spying on others in his *Honorable Historie of Frier Bacon and Frier Bongay* (c. 1592). Someone at the BBC must have noted this work's prophetic quality because in

1953, when the corporation broadcast an 'Elizabethan night' imagining what television would have been like in 1592, the centrepiece was a performance of Greene's play.

The harnessing of electricity revived this long-nurtured dream of instantaneous contact. The unstated ambition of modern media, the American philosopher John Durham Peters argues, has been to 'mimic the angels by mechanical or electronic means'.[4] In the late nineteenth century, new inventions like telegraphy, the telephone and the phonograph had a near-mystical aura. The popular imagination linked them with those other late Victorian obsessions, mesmerism and telepathy, for they too seemed to fulfil the desire for an angelic communion, breaking down the painful distance between self and other. Einstein's discovery that the speed of light was the fastest thing in the universe, on any earthly scale as good as instant, gave the dream a new impetus. Television was sometimes called 'seeing by electricity', and a moving human face reproduced at the speed of light on a screen seemed a form of miraculous double presence, unlike the dead shadows of the cinema, which simply recreated something that had once been but was no more. The earliest television viewers compared what they saw to visitations and apparitions. In the late 1920s, when engineers noticed that a duplicate radio signal could create a displaced, repeated image on the television screen, they naturally called it a 'ghost'.

During the week of its sixteenth birthday celebrations, a million people came through Selfridge's doors. Baird's demonstration was just one attraction in a series of exhibitions including a Japanese garden and displays of the earliest gramophone, first editions of Dickens and Queen Victoria's old stockings. Sales assistants on the first floor handed out leaflets to shoppers: 'The apparatus here demonstrated is, of course, absolutely "in the rough" ... The picture is flickering and defective, and at present only simple pictures can be sent successfully; but Edison's first phonograph rendered that "Mary had a little lamb" in a way that only hearers who were "in the secret" could understand and yet, from that first result has developed the gramophone of today ...'[5]

At first, television asked a large imaginative leap of its viewers. Baird demonstrated his machine to small crowds, who looked through a cardboard viewfinder, rather as one might view a coin-operated telescope on the end of the pier. The four-by-two-inch screen displayed a quivering silhouette of simple shapes like the letter 'H' printed in white on black card, broadcast from a few feet away. 'It was a little disappointing really,' recalled Elisabeth Wood, then a schoolgirl, sixty years later, 'because there were black lines sort of wiggling across it. And it jumped up and down. And then we all clapped rather politely but we were all rather frightened of television. We believed if they could make this film they could see into our houses.' An eighteen-year-old South African music student, Margaret Albu, was coerced into viewing the demonstration by her mother. 'The invention had the effect which all mechanical things have on me and gave me a feeling of bewilderment and nausea,' said the young woman (who would later marry its inventor).[6] Giving three demonstrations a day for three weeks to queues of shoppers who seemed politely interested rather than astounded, Baird came down with nervous exhaustion and spent several weeks in bed.

But Harry Selfridge was sufficiently impressed that, on 20 February 1928, he invited Baird to open the world's first television department at his store. The Baird 'Televisors', encased in mahogany cabinets and priced at £6 10s. 1d., sold sluggishly compared to the electric gramophones and self-winding watches that went on display the same day. Shoppers seemed most excited about the Photomatons, the new photo-me-booths installed at the head of the escalators in the Bargain Basement, where they queued in their hundreds, sat on stools and received, a few minutes later, a strip of photos for a shilling. But Selfridge, an early adopter of new technology, knew which was the more exciting development. 'This is not a toy,' he said of television. 'It is a link between all peoples of the world.'[7]

The BBC, its energies directed at the still young and growing medium of radio, was a reluctant television broadcaster. 'The impression is of a curiously ape-like head, decapitated at the chin, swaying up and down in a streaky stream of yellow light,' said a BBC report of a demonstration at Baird's tiny studio in Long Acre, Covent Garden, in September 1928. 'I was reminded of those human shrunken heads favoured by such persons as Mr M. Hedges [the explorer F. A. Mitchell-Hedges]. Not even the collar or tie were visible, the effect being more grotesque than impressive ... The faces of those leaving the show showed neither excitement or interest. Rather like a Fair crowd who had sported 6d. to see if the fat lady was really as fat as she was made out to be.'[8] The Post Office engineers present were less dismissive, and asked the BBC to allow Baird to use its transmitter, conveniently located on the roof of Selfridge's, for more tests. And so on 30 September 1929, at 11.04 a.m., after a fifteen-minute radio talk entitled 'How I Planned My Kitchen' by Miss Sydney M. Bushell, the BBC transmitted an experimental programme, broadcast simultaneously on radio and television.

Images from the BBC's first scheduled television programme travelled by landline from Baird's studio at Long Acre, Covent Garden to the Selfridge's transmitter, from where they were radiated on carrier waves. After speeding silently and invisibly along a diagonal line south-east, over the oblivious shoppers and pedestrians of Regent Street and the intricate alleyways of Soho, they arrived back at Long Acre, where a small crowd of invited guests watched them on a screen about an inch and a half long and half an inch wide. The Yorkshire comedian Sydney Howard delivered a comic monologue, Lulu Stanley sang 'He's tall, and dark, and handsome' and Baird's secretary, Connie King, sang 'Mighty Like a Rose'. Each of the performers had to sit on a typist's chair to meet the gaze of the scanning beam, with the tiny Miss King raised on a pile of telephone directories. The pictures and sound could not yet be synchronised and so each person was televised in silence and then repeated themselves in front of a microphone. Asked after the broadcast how many people had seen it, Baird guessed there were nine of his televisors dotted around

London and about twenty built by intrepid amateurs from scratch: twenty-nine in all.[9]

People were fascinated, in a way that we would also be were we not inured to it through habit, by this strange phenomenon, the radio wave, which could race through all intervening obstacles and show distant events at the moment they were occurring, undetectable without that magical deciphering machine, a wireless or television receiver. One of the radio wave's great charms was that, unlike the telephone or the telegraph, it radiated to no one in particular. The earliest term for viewers was 'lookers in', which, like the radio term 'listeners in', suggested they were eavesdropping on something not meant solely for their eyes and ears.

The word 'broadcasting', which radio borrowed about a hundred years ago from the farmer's term for scattering seeds over a wide surface rather than neatly in rows, carried the same connotations of chance. Anyone with a televisor could tune in and pluck these animated images out of apparently empty space. The low frequency microwaves on which this primitive television was broadcast travelled vast distances, even though the transmitter was weak. One day in the autumn of 1929, a young Bessarabian engineer, Boris Alperovici, sat in a darkened room in a villa in the volcanic peaks of Capri, at a workbench surrounded with radio and TV equipment. He had read about Baird's broadcasts in a technical journal and had straightaway ordered two sets from England, one to pick up sound and the other vision. At first he could not get the sets past Italian customs because they did not recognise such a thing as television; but after much cajoling, they let them travel by boat from Naples to Capri. Alperovici assembled them in his radio workshop at the villa and waited for the tests to start. The first thing he saw, on a screen slightly bigger than a postage stamp spewing ugly red light from the cathode ray, was Gracie Fields. Twenty-three years later, Alperovici and Fields married, after Fields's nephew had knocked on his door in Capri, where Fields had a villa, and asked if he could fix his aunt's radio.[10]

This story, told to the *TV Times* in 1955, may be a case of the wish fathering the thought. Perhaps Alperovici wanted to believe his future wife was the first thing he saw on a television in 1929, although she did appear in some early broadcasts, some of which reached even further than Capri. On the island of Madeira, off the north African coast, W. L. Wraight, an amateur English engineer and member of the newly formed Television Society, built an aerial from copper tubing, installed it on top of his house in the island's capital, Funchal, and got fairly good pictures from the mast over 1,500 miles away on top of Selfridge's, at least between September and April when atmospheric conditions allowed. Although the images came without sound, Wraight declared himself delighted 'that such small items as teeth, buttons, cuff links, roller skates, and the dividing line between studio background and floor have all been quite easily distinguishable'.[11] More remarkably, Funchal sits in a natural amphitheatre to the south, facing the Atlantic, so the television signal had managed to make it over the island's volcanic mountains.

Even those a few streets away from Baird's studio felt the thrill of pulling a picture out of the air. 'I must thank you very warmly for the television instrument you have put into Downing Street,' the prime minister Ramsay MacDonald wrote to Baird after the first synchronised sound and vision broadcast in March 1930. 'What a marvellous discovery you have made! When I look at the transmissions I feel that the most wonderful miracle is being done under my eye … You have put something in my room which will never let me forget how strange is the world – and how unknown.'[12]

The novelist Anthony Burgess later claimed to have seen one of these early broadcasts: Luigi Pirandello's *The Man with a Flower in his Mouth*, the first television play, shown on the afternoon of 14 July 1930. To the strains of Carlos Gardel singing 'El Carretero', the play opened in an all-night café. A businessman who had missed the last, midnight train began talking to a stranger sipping a mint frappé. 'Death has passed my way and put this flower in my mouth,'

the stranger told him. He was dying of an epithelioma, a cancerous growth on his lip. He began evoking scenes of quotidian life which suddenly felt precious now he would soon no longer be able to witness them. 'Helps me to forget myself,' he said of his new habit of staring into shop windows, an unconscious allusion to the future power of television. 'I never let it rest a moment – my imagination! I cling with it … to the lives of other people.'

It was a bleak choice of play for this momentous broadcast, but its avant-garde minimalism – with only two speaking characters, lots of soliloquys and a twenty-minute running time – helped to conceal the medium's imperfections, particularly the fact that the televisable area was so small that only one actor could appear at a time. 'It was certainly startling, as well as helpful to the dialogue, to be able to see their every expression – even to the lifting of the eyebrows,' noted the *Daily Mail*. 'We even saw the gestures of their hands – although we had to sacrifice their faces for the time being.' The *Manchester Guardian*'s reporter had to apologise to his readers for being unable to file a review. He had missed the entire broadcast, having arrived at the head of the queue to watch the Selfridge's televisor just as it was fading out.[13]

As Anthony Burgess often reminded people, his hero James Joyce referred to television in *Finnegans Wake* as a 'bairdboard bombardment screen' and a 'faroscope', terms which convey the interwar excitement about the cathode ray's capacity to reveal visions of faraway things. (Burgess misremembered it as the more melodious 'bairdbombardmentboard'.) Although highbrow in most of his other tastes, Burgess remained generous about television all his life. 'A compulsive viewer who will sit guiltily in front of test-cards and even *This Is Your Life*,' he wrote on taking over as the *Listener*'s television critic in May 1963, 'I groan my way towards palliation of the guilt – the penance of dredging words out of my eyeballs.'[14]

Burgess actually felt little guilt. As *Listener* critic he watched no more television than he did normally, staying up all Friday night to write his column. In November 1963, after returning from a holiday in Morocco, he wrote that it was easy 'to indulge the romantic delusion that the life of goatherds, beggars, Marrakesh buskers, and Tangier junkies is *real* life, and that the British evening with television and chestnuts is a sort of substitute. Nonsense, of course – a mixture of sentimental Rousseauism and snobbish xenomania ... The Moors would be better off looking at [the soap opera] *Compact* than at nothing.' Burgess remained unafflicted by the snobbery about television that suffused British intellectual life when it became a mass form in the 1950s, perhaps because he had been excited about it in its embryonic form. In later life, he became a fan of Benny Hill, calling him 'one of the great artists of our age', and at Hill's memorial service in 1992 it was he who gave the eulogy.[15]

In fact it seems unlikely that Burgess saw the Pirandello on television as he claimed, especially since he wrongly dated it to 1932.[16] In the summer of 1930 Burgess was a thirteen-year-old schoolboy called John Wilson, and there were unlikely to have been many Baird televisors in the poor area of Moss Side, Manchester, where he lived with his parents above a tobacconist's shop. In any case, the broadcast was on a Monday afternoon, a school day, and the studious Burgess was an unlikely truant. He either embellished the truth as a novelist might or, more likely, rewrote it in his memory as people are wont to do with such an ephemeral activity as television viewing. The Inner London Education Authority reconstructed the broadcast in 1967; perhaps it was this that he saw.

It is, however, highly likely that Burgess listened to the first television programmes, for they were broadcast on the BBC's radio wavelength. As an avid reader of the *Radio Times* and the *Listener*, he would certainly have known about television, and he had built his own crystal radio set to hear Sir Adrian Boult's BBC Symphony Orchestra. After trying and failing to use his bed's wire mattress as an aerial, because it was full of fluff, he bought aerials that reached to his bedroom ceiling; he could then pick up stations as far away as the continent, listening to them on his headphones before drifting off to sleep.[17] So when the BBC began supplementing its mid-morning television broadcasts with late-night ones on Tuesdays and Fridays, after the radio programmes had ended, he would have picked them up. These early television programmes had far more listeners than viewers. Tap dancing was a popular feature because, although early television screens could not really cope with such frantic motion, listeners appreciated the sound of dancers' feet.

Among those who did see the Pirandello play were an invited audience of VIPs, including Guglielmo Marconi, the pioneer of long-distance radio, who just before 3.30 p.m. on the Monday afternoon were winched up the outside of Baird's Long Acre studio on a rickety open-air goods hoist with no railings. On the roof, they stood under a canvas canopy in front of a five-foot-high television, composed of 2,000 tiny incandescent bulbs spaced an inch apart, so the screen looked like a giant honeycomb. Each bulb lit up in turn to give the light and shade of the picture. Halfway through, the bulbs became so hot that they started to melt the screen's edges. A panic-stricken note was sent from the roof to the studio below, where Baird said, 'Tell them to go on, and let it melt.'[18]

One of the viewers on the Long Acre studio roof was the booking agent of the nearby London Coliseum. On his recommendation, Sir Oswald Stoll, the Coliseum's owner, hired the giant television for a fortnight's run at the theatre, starting on 28 July 1930, showing it during intervals. As the lights went down in the auditorium, a master of ceremonies stood at the side of the stage with a telephone in his hand. On the widest proscenium arch in London, the giant television looked rather small. A human face appeared on screen, broadcast from the Long Acre studio a few streets away. 'Would any member of the audience like to ask a question of the speaker?' asked the MC. 'Tell him to put his hand up,' cried someone from the darkness of the stalls. The MC telephoned this instruction to Long Acre and the speaker raised his hand to his chin. More interactive experiments followed. The Lord Mayor of London, on screen, asked his wife in the audience what time dinner would be and she replied, by phone, 'eight o'clock'. The 'Charming Belles in Harmony', Helen Yorke and Virginia Johnson, performed a duet with Yorke on stage and Johnson on screen. 'There was a kind of rustling effect all over the screen,' wrote *The Sphere* magazine, 'but through it one could distinctly make out the features of one well known personage after another. One could not only hear them speak, but see their lips moving.'[19]

The highlight of the run was the sixty-year-old music hall comedian George Robey, the 'Prime Minister of Mirth', doing a turn on the Coliseum stage, then running to nearby Long Acre while Baird showed a Robey film talkie and then, a little out of breath, appearing on television on the Coliseum big screen. It helped that Robey's trademark costume – a bald-fronted wig, red nose and heavily blacked eyebrows – was easily viewable and his 'whiplash diction', in Laurence Olivier's appreciative phrase, carried his voice through the theatre from the set.[20]

Television thrived among these big crowds. In June 1932 several thousand people at the Metropole Cinema near Victoria Station watched the Epsom Derby on a screen ten foot high by eight foot wide. Baird had shown the same race a year earlier, witnesses recording that 'a good imagination was required' and the horses and riders looked 'like out-of-focus camels'. But this broadcast was more successful: the Metropole audience could see the bookmakers' tic-tac hand signals and the horses rounding Tattenham Corner and flashing past the finish, though not even the announcer could tell who had won. Baird's assistant, Tony Bridgewater, said that this time 'you could at least tell they were horses'. Baird took a curtain call afterwards to cries of 'Marvellous! Marvellous!', receiving a bigger cheer than the Derby winner, which turned out to be April the Fifth.[21]

In *Brave New World*, published that year, Aldous Huxley imagined a different future for television, in the 'Galloping Senility' ward of the sixty-storey Park Lane Hospital for the Dying. 'At the foot of every bed, confronting its moribund occupant, was a television box. Television was left on, a running tap, from morning till night,' he wrote. The dying Linda was watching the semi-finals of a tennis championship with an expression of 'imbecile happiness', while 'hither and thither across their square of illumined glass the little figures noiselessly darted, like fish in an aquarium, the silent but agitated inhabitants of another world'. Huxley himself never owned a set and, interviewed in 1959, said that television was 'a sort of Moloch which demands incessant sacrifice ... the people who write for it just go quietly mad'.[22] His idea of television as an opiate of the masses in *Brave New World* was to become a familiar literary trope. In Pete Davies's Huxleyan novel, *The Last Election* (1986), set in a Britain of the near future ruled by the Money Party, a cable TV channel distracts the unemployed masses from their inevitable death by involuntary euthanasia with the narcotic of twenty-four-hour snooker.

Now that Huxley's vision has hardened into cultural cliché, we have to return to 1932 to realise how prescient it was, for when he wrote *Brave New World*, television was not an ambient presence, our relationship to which has become, in the novelist Ian McEwan's words, a 'casual obsession which is not unlike that of the well-adjusted alcoholic'.[23] As an occasional public spectacle, it seemed to have more in common with older traditions of shadow theatre, magic lantern displays or the panoramas and dioramas of the Regency and Victorian periods – sound and light shows with moving canvases of London or scenes from literary works, often featured during intervals of plays, just as Baird's giant television set had been at the Coliseum.

The BBC's experimental television broadcasts, coming from Broadcasting House, received scant attention. There were no schedules or listings so on four nights a week, a scattering of viewers tuned in at 11 p.m., not knowing what they would see. It might be Vic-Wells ballet dancers, the Rotherham comedian Sandy Powell saying 'Can you hear me, mother?', or Sally the Seal, brought to the studio in a large open Daimler and escorted up in the lift just so she could blow a saxophone and waggle her flippers for the camera. The press paid little notice unless there was a potential controversy. 'Apparently the BBC had no objections to pyjamas,' the *London Evening News* reported in November 1934, 'for I learned today that [the comedian George] Harris will do an act called "I Never Slept a Wink Last Night" prancing round the television studio in pyjamas and trying to shave himself by the light of a flickering television scanner.'[24]

The fossil record for this part of television history was non-existent until 1981, when a young amateur computer enthusiast, Donald McLean, borrowed a BBC LP from Harrow Library, *We Seem To Have Lost The Picture*, narrated by the comedian John Bird and made five years earlier to commemorate forty years of BBC television. At one point Bird introduced a rasping sound effect which he called 'Baird's brain-damaging buzz-saw', an eight-second, 78 rpm recording from the old experimental television broadcasts, discovered in the BBC archives. These broadcasts were transmitted on medium wave, a low enough frequency to be audible. Radio listeners in the early 1930s were familiar with this harsh buzzing sound, the auditory trace of the television picture itself, accompanied by the rhythmic thuds of the locking signal trying to keep it on the screen. 'That is what your face sounds like,' Baird told them. Fortuitously, McLean had just written some software to transfer sound waves from a tape deck to his home-made computer. One weekend, squatting on the floor of his spare bedroom in Northolt, he managed to turn Baird's brain-damaging buzz-saw into a waveform traced out in green ink on an oscilloscope. He wrote some more software to unravel the data and plot it as a picture and there, on his computer, appeared a reincarnated television image: the blurred head and shoulders of a Charlie Chaplin lookalike.[25]

Fifteen years later, McLean was given a disc. Some unknown archivist living in Ealing in the early 1930s had used one of the home audio recording machines which had just come on the market, with a 78 rpm cutting lathe like a gramophone, to record one of the television broadcasts. McLean once again tweaked his computer software to turn the sound into pictures, and brought up a silent, four-minute segment of television on his computer screen. Six young women in bathing suits nodded their heads to music and high-kicked in synchronised fashion, the camera panning across them in an early television technique called 'hose-piping', used when there was only one camera. After digging in the BBC archives, McLean discovered that these were the Paramount Astoria Girls, appearing in the first-ever television revue, 'Looking In', on 21 April 1933.

McLean received another disc, rescued from a house clearance, in 1998. It had been recorded in east London by Marcus Games, an amateur film enthusiast and brother of Abram Games, the graphic designer later responsible for BBC Television's first animated ident, the 'Bat's wings' logo, in 1953. McLean once again weaved his computing magic. A low-resolution lady with glossy black hair and kiss curls appeared. It was the comedienne and dance band vocalist Betty Bolton, blowing kisses and exiting stage left. Although the higher quality of the image probably meant it was broadcast in 1934 or 1935, it could not be precisely dated: it was just one of the many forgotten nights of early television, a fragment of which, by a mixture of accident and technical perseverance, had reappeared on a computer screen. When McLean showed him the images, John Trenouth, a curator at the National Museum of Photography, Film and Television at Bradford, felt the hairs on the back of his neck bristle, and he realised 'how Howard Carter must have felt when the tomb of Tutankhamun was opened'.[26]

When these images had first been seen there were probably about 5,000 sets, including those made from DIY kits or cobbled together by amateur engineers, mostly in London and the Home Counties. Many at Broadcasting House thought this minority pursuit was taking resources away from radio. 'The BBC is most anxious to know the number of people who are actually seeing this television programme,' it announced in August 1933. 'Will those who are looking in send a post-card marked "Z" to Broadcasting House immediately. This information is of considerable importance.' The announcement worried investors, who feared that television might be finished if the response was negligible, and shares in Baird and other television manufacturers fell. The results of the postcard census were never made public, but a year later the *Daily Express* reported that 'the figures painfully surprised even the most pessimistically minded at Broadcasting House'.[27]

Television sustained itself not on its mildly disappointing present but on dreams of its future. The *Manchester Guardian* offered a prize of two guineas for the best suggestions for programmes. The entries revealed a continuing fascination with television's capacity to obliterate distance, to see distant events as they happened. One reader wanted to watch the Oberammergau Passion Play; another suggested High Mass at St Peter's. 'Perhaps I am a "televisionary",' wrote another, 'but I should like to see on the set of the future – the hotel where I am thinking of spending my holidays (all of it, not merely "a corner of the lounge") and the view (if any) from the bedroom.'[28]

The reverse side of this excitement that television might offer an intimate view of faraway things was the fear that it meant being spied upon. In January 1935, announcing the imminent arrival of a new high-definition television service, the Postmaster General, Sir Kingsley Wood, felt the need to assure people that it would not involve surreptitiously witnessing what was going on in other people's homes, as members of the public had feared in submissions to the Selsdon Committee on Broadcasting. 'I would like to reassure any nervous listeners,' he said in a BBC radio broadcast, 'that, wonderful as television may be, it cannot, fortunately, be used in this way.' For those unfamiliar with the science of radio waves, this was a common anxiety. One woman wrote to the BBC to complain of its effrontery in broadcasting to her on the wireless while she was in the bath. Anthony Burgess, speculating about the origins of George Orwell's telescreen, noted that, as late as 1948 when *1984* was written, some of the greener viewers believed that 'the TV set in the corner of the living-room was an eye, and it might really be looking at you ... I remember a lot of people were shy of undressing in front of it.'[29]

The Selsdon report used the words 'television-looker' and 'looker-in' but many found these words awkward and unlovely. The *Daily Express* offered five guineas for a word which, in the editor's opinion, best described the person watching a television broadcast. Thousands of readers wrote in with suggestions, usually 'tele-something' duplicated a hundredfold, but also radio-ogler, radioseer, ether-gazer, screen-reader, perceptor, visioner and opticauris. The winning entry was never announced. A *Daily Telegraph* reader, using the analogy of Bakerloo to describe the Baker Street–Waterloo line, suggested that the person who was both a looker and a listener could be a 'lookener' and the act itself 'lookening'. Only a tiny number of correspondents suggested 'viewer', a word that, even in the late 1940s, was still being placed in inverted commas.[30]

Alexandra Palace stands over 300 feet above sea level on the slopes of Muswell Hill, one of a gentle ridge of hills known as London's northern heights. In an otherwise low-lying city, it is an obvious place from where radio waves can radiate. Muswell Hill's transformation from countryside to suburb happened rapidly between the 1890s and the 1910s, creating a near-uniform architectural style: rows of red-brick villas with the odd sign of gentility like an ornamented gable or a stained glass window set in a leaded front door. Even before its colonisation in the 1980s by media professionals and other gentrifiers, Muswell Hill was quite well-heeled, the place where the wideboy Arthur Daley of the ITV comedy series *Minder* had 'a very respectable uncle'.

If you walk down these similar-looking streets today and look up, you will notice something that should really be obvious: the television aerials are all pointing the same way, as indeed they do on every street in Britain. In this case, they are all aimed at an elongated pyramid of latticed steel on the south-east tower of Alexandra Palace, like metal worshippers bowing before a giant metal god. The mast is at the unrenovated end of the building, with broken windows, 'anti-climb paint' and stern warnings against roller blading. In 1936 it was just as dilapidated: to get to the TV studios you had to walk through empty marble halls with unused slot machines, flea-bitten stuffed animals and peeling posters advertising tea dances from the building's heyday as the 'People's Palace' in the 1890s.

On 11 September 1935, after about 1,500 broadcasts, the BBC had closed its television station down, marooning several thousand televisors which were now useless. Baird and many lookers-in complained, but the corporation insisted that for a time it would just mean that it was offering a 'non-visual service'.[31] The experimental service had consisted of a blurry television picture of only thirty lines: rows of electrons fired from the back of the cathode ray tube and written and rewritten across the screen at the speed of light to make up a moving picture. Soon, in place of this crude image would come a new 'high fidelity' television picture made up of 405 lines, which was almost as good as a moving photograph.

Commuters on the London and North Eastern Railway line into King's Cross could see from their train windows one of Alexandra Palace's corner towers disappear, the hole being filled with seventeen tonnes of concrete and the new mast climbing rapidly each day to its final height of 215 feet. It resembled a giant piece of Meccano, that favourite interwar present for children of better-off families. Its summit was over 600 feet above sea level, 200 feet higher than St Paul's Cathedral and with a radiating radius of about twenty-five miles. Receiving vans toured all over the outer edges of London, testing the strength of the signals from the top of the mast to see how far they would reach.

Interwar radio listeners knew all about a band of ionised air in the upper atmosphere called the Heaviside layer, or the 'radio roof'. When Marconi first announced he would be sending a radio signal across the Atlantic, scientists were sceptical, believing that electromagnetic waves could not travel beyond 200 miles because they would meet that 100-mile high wall of water, caused by the earth's curvature, blocking the view from Britain to north America. But on 12 December 1901, Marconi stood on Signal Hill, Newfoundland and, as he had promised, picked up a Morse signal from Poldhu in Cornwall. A self-taught physicist, Oliver Heaviside, speculated in a 1902

Encyclopaedia Britannica article on telegraphy that a reflecting layer of ionised gases in the upper atmosphere may have bounced Marconi's radio waves back and helped them bend round the earth.

In the 1920s, another physicist, Professor E. V. Appleton of King's College London, demonstrated, with the help of the BBC's radio transmitter at Bournemouth, that this 'ionosphere' existed. Appleton also invited the early lookers-in to help him determine the properties of the Heaviside layer by writing to him with information about where they were receiving television images from and what the pictures were like.[32] But only ultra short radio waves could carry the amount of information in the new 405-line TV pictures and these would not be reflected by the ionosphere. They would travel in two directions from the television mast: vertically and horizontally. The vertical waves would shoot up, straight through the earth's atmosphere and into outer space. The horizontal waves would shoot outwards at the height of the transmitter, rather like a lighthouse beam trained on the horizon, and reach about as far as the eye could see from the mast.

London spreads out along the wide flood plain of the Thames valley, so high ground close to the centre of the city was in short supply. There were two possible sites for a mast, to the south and north: Crystal Palace on Sydenham Hill, where Baird already had a mast, and Alexandra Palace. Crystal Palace was the more prestigious address: viewable from eight counties, it was London's Eiffel Tower, and a homeowner's test of a good outlook was that 'you can see the Palace from here'. But the BBC chose its northern cousin because north Londoners, who were more prosperous and more likely to buy televisions, would get a better signal from it, and the coaches carrying performers and producers from Broadcasting House would take just twenty minutes to arrive. It turned out to be a wise choice. On the night of 30 November 1936, the staff of the fledgling television service watched aghast from the esplanade along Alexandra Palace's southern face as Crystal Palace burned to the ground along with the Baird television transmitter, the flames making a red glare in the sky that could be seen for miles around.

The move to Alexandra Palace coincided with the annual 'Radiolympia' show at the Olympia exhibition centre in Earls Court, held in early autumn at the start of the wireless season when people bought sets for the indoor months. A fraught message arrived at Alexandra Palace that hardly anyone was buying televisions, not unreasonably when nothing was being broadcast on them, and the radio industry was suffering from poor sales. So with just nine days' notice the television service was told to begin broadcasting from 26 August, to coincide with Radiolympia's opening day. Engineers started tests on 12 August and for the next fortnight a tiny number of viewers saw Leslie Mitchell, a pencil-moustachioed former actor already christened a 'Television Adonis' by the *Daily Mail*, talking off the top of his head to the camera. The new medium was simply filling time, a complaint that has echoed through the decades. But the television critic Kenneth Baily, watching Mitchell on one of the few commercial sets, reflected years later that 'the gagging act he did then, talking attractively about nothing in particular so that we kept the machine switched on, has never been surpassed on television'.[33]

At 11.45 a.m. on Wednesday 26 August 1936, BBC television broadcast the smooth sounds of Duke Ellington's 'Solitude' accompanied by a test card. At noon, Olympia's doors opened. Hundreds of people jostled to get inside the seatless, darkened viewing booths, black-draped boxes reminiscent of Victorian peep shows, or they perched on tiered seats in front of television sets in the main foyer like a theatre audience, to see the programme coming from ten miles away on the northern heights. The first broadcast, a variety show with a tuxedoed male voice trio called the Three Admirals and a pantomime horse called Pogo, began with Helen McKay singing a specially written song called 'Here's Looking at You'. Not all Radiolympians were enraptured. To keep the queues moving along, no one could watch for more than a minute and many saw little more than the back of other people's heads before being told to 'move along, please'. 'Is that all?', 'Better than I thought' and 'Good as the talkies; but rather small', said some of the first viewers.[34]

The next day's outside broadcast was more successful. Mitchell stood on the Alexandra Palace balcony and talked viewers through a panoramic view as the camera panned across the gently inclining tree-lined hill: 'On the horizon, the Lea Valley, and now we are passing over Hornsey and Finsbury Park, and I wonder if you can see the smoke that is just by the Harringay greyhound stadium? ... On the road below you will notice someone passing. There goes a car. Another one is just coming in ... This view we see every day, and I think you will agree there is not a finer view to be seen anywhere in London.'[35] Mitchell pointed out Hackney marshes, St Paul's Cathedral obscured by mist and children playing near the Alexandra Park racecourse. A neat trick designed to show that the television pictures were live, this broadcast conveyed something of the distance-obliterating miracle of the camera obscura, that primitive but enchanting form of television in which the outer world arrived on the white table of a darkened room through nothing more high-tech than mirrors, a periscope and light travelling through a pinhole.

Radiolympia was not the only place to watch television. At Waterloo Station, the Southern Railway turned a waiting room on platform 16 into a television theatre, with admission by train ticket only, and passengers, many of them off on holiday to the south coast, watched as they waited for their trains. On 4 September, a Douglas-Fokker airliner left Croydon and, after it had climbed to 4,000 feet, the curtains were drawn and a Baird television switched on. 'With hardly a flicker on the screen we saw and heard Charles Laughton in his new film, "Rembrandt", while high over Radiolympia we watched newsreel pictures of the Spanish Civil War,' wrote one passenger. 'Several thousand feet above Alexandra Palace the pictures became crystal clear, and every gesture of the actors was plainly visible.'[36]

The BBC television service officially began at 3 p.m. on 2 November 1936, when star of stage and screen musicals Adele Dixon sang a song called 'Television' which celebrated the 'mighty maze of mystic, magic rays' that would 'bring a new wonder to you'. Only about 400 sets were capable of tuning in. The new broadcasts were for an hour a day at 3 p.m. and 9 p.m., except Sundays. The first week of programmes included keeper David Seth-Smith bringing a party of animals from Regent's Park in 'Friends from the zoo', Montague Weekly presenting 'Inn signs through the ages' and animal impersonators from the pantomimes appearing in 'Animals all'.

On these first television sets, the screen, the fat end of the cathode ray tube, was at the top of the set facing the ceiling because the tube was so long it had be placed vertically in the wooden cabinet. As early cathode ray guns would often explode, another advantage of this arrangement was that, should this happen, the broken glass would shoot up rather than out into the living room. The television picture appeared on a mirror placed at an angle on the lid of the set, as though the magical moving images were hidden inside the box and could only be seen obliquely through this enchanted glass. The sound was vastly superior to radio, because it arrived on the same ultra short waves as the pictures, with more bandwidth than was needed. It was, said Douglas Birkinshaw, the delighted BBC engineer, 'like driving down a motorway one mile wide'.[37]

Some more critical voices, though, were starting to protest about the dullness of programmes showing champion exhibits from the National Cat Club Show or the transport minister lecturing on arterial roads. L. Marsland Gander, the *Daily Telegraph*'s newly appointed television critic, complained of drearily technical, lantern lectures on radio transmitter valves or the mobile Post Office. There was worse to come. 'I find that next Saturday a Mr J. T. Baily is to demonstrate on the television screen how to repair a broken window,' wrote Gander. 'Probably at some future time, when we have television all day long, it will be legitimate to cater for a minority of potential window repairers. Out of two hours, however, the allocation of 30 minutes to such a subject seems disproportionate. Incidentally, as television receivers are about £100 each, I think the average purchaser would be able to afford expert attention for his windows.'[38]

Gander did concede later that the first edition of *Picture Page* had been 'one of the outstanding events of a lifetime' which had 'filled me with an enthusiasm for a new artform that has never waned'. *Picture Page* had first been shown in October, as a test transmission, watched by a handful of people, including Gander. An enterprising manufacturer had brought a television to Fleet Street for the start of transmissions, but the only accommodation he could find was a seedy hotel bedroom. There the set was installed, looking incongruous against the faded floral wallpaper and an ancient washbasin. 'My colleagues and I gathered a little sceptically,' wrote Gander. 'We left converted.'

Picture Page featured well-known personalities and people in the news. It aimed to shift quickly, with the aid of dissolving shots, from interviewee to interviewee like someone flicking through a magazine. The Canadian actress Joan Miller, pretending to be a switchboard operator, introduced each of the guests with television's first catchphrase: 'You're through. You're looking at ...' In that first programme, Leslie Mitchell interviewed Ras Prince Monolulu, a racing tipster who wore a plumed headdress and claimed to have been born in Addis Ababa, the son of a Jewish chieftain (unlikely, since his real name was Peter McKay); John Snuggs, a performer who sang songs and tore paper into pretty shapes for theatre queues; and a Siamese cat called Preston Pertona. The star guest was Squadron-Leader F. R. D. Swain, a Farnborough test pilot who had just broken the world altitude record. Swain told Mitchell that, as he flew round in lazy circles, with a view of the English coastline from Land's End to the Wash, he had nearly suffocated and had to cut a window in his airtight helmet so he could breathe. In subsequent episodes, *Picture Page* featured the bagpipes player from Trafalgar Square, the London taxi driver who had taken a fare to John O'Groats and a silkworm that died of stage fright before it could be interviewed. Gander was so captivated that he watched every programme from the first to the fiftieth, before he went on holiday and broke his run.[39]

Early viewers seem to have shared Gander's tastes. In broadcasts around Christmas 1936, the owners of television sets were asked to 'let the BBC know of their existence' by sending their names and addresses to Broadcasting House on a postcard marked 'viewer' – one of the first official uses of this term. The BBC then wrote back to them asking for feedback. By the following June, they had received 118 letters. The least popular programmes were studio demonstrations of cooking, washing and ironing, 'which were condemned as of little interest to those who could afford television sets'. The most popular were plays, outside broadcasts and *Picture Page*, which was making Thursday 'stay at home night'.[40]

There were now over a hundred public viewing rooms dotted around London, including at a basement gallery at the Science Museum in South Kensington and EMI's Abbey Road studios. The General Electric Company also installed a set at a home for deaf and dumb people at Erith, south-east London. It was shown first to about thirty men who, as a fashion parade appeared on the screen, turned to each other and put their thumbs up. They followed intently a showing of zoo animals, a news bulletin and a short play, and applauded warmly at the end. 'For the great bulk of deaf people wireless has been quite useless,' said the home's superintendent. 'These experiments with television suggest that it can fill a great gap in their lives.'[41]

Many shops and hotels had also installed television. The *Radio Times* reported in March 1937 that in the television rooms of the big department stores 'there are still large crowds every day, though the numbers have dropped since the beginning of the year, when special arrangements had to be made to control the crowds'. Bernard Buckham in the *Daily Mirror* had heard about 'a poor couple who go to a London store every day and watch the programme through. It is certainly a cheap amusement.' In the summer of 1937, Michael Barry, the young artistic producer of the Croydon Repertory Theatre, saw television at Kennards department store on the high street, where the afternoon broadcast was shown in the sports section on the first floor. 'I stood behind a couple of dozen spectators crowded into a hessian booth and strained to watch, beyond their heads, midget dancers jiggling about on a small screen,' Barry wrote half a century later. 'It was, I thought, quite the silliest thing I had seen.'[42]

On the morning of 3 May 1937, a mobile television van pulled up beside the grass at Apsley Gate on Hyde Park Corner. The BBC cameraman pointed his equipment at the passing crowds, Monday's late-running commuters and sundry pedestrians. Alexandra Palace engineers stared at their sets. Through a slight blur, they saw the trees waving in the breeze and the Household Cavalry riding on Rotten Row. Passing cars came sharply into focus with even the registration numbers readable. Passers-by gazed confusedly into the camera. A young woman, oblivious to viewers, put on her lipstick. For two hours the engineers tested on a closed circuit. Then at 12.45 p.m. they decided to televise Hyde Park to whoever happened to be looking in, ringing up their wives in their suburban homes and telling them to turn on the set. Those who switched on saw a bright sunny day in the park. A man lit a cigar and smoked it and a little girl, in the middle of a riding lesson, sat awkwardly in the saddle. The act of distant looking seemed to transform this routine scene, showing viewers the unnoticed patterns and unstaged reality of daily life – the television camera as camera obscura again.

This strangely gripping programme was just a test for the coronation broadcast nine days later. When the Archbishop of Canterbury, Cosmo Lang, refused his request to allow cameras into Westminster Abbey, the BBC's director of television, Gerald Cock, found the one place in London along the procession where you could get a close-up without interruption: the central plinth of Apsley Gate. While the Post Office laid eight miles of television cable from Alexandra Palace, Cock went to Buckingham Palace and asked King George VI if he would smile into the camera when his carriage passed. The king agreed and wrote on a slip of paper that he kept inside the coach, 'Look right outside the window at Hyde Park Corner and smile.'[43]

The coronation crowds were fixated on how close they would get to the new king and queen and how much they would be able to see of them. The must-have item along the processional route was a periscope. When the king smiled directly at viewers, it offered them the proximity and sensation of real life that the crowds craved.

At a Southgate cinema, about a hundred people saw it on one small television, and stood up and cheered at the end. A similar crowd gathered round a set in a marquee at Ranelagh polo ground. Manufacturers' and retailers' estimates that over 50,000 people saw the procession 'astonished the most hopeful', although the BBC guessed more cautiously at 10,000. A small army of viewers scattered from Ipswich to Brighton had seen, said the corporation, 'a phenomenon which would have been hailed in any other age either as a miracle or as a piece of witchcraft ... Trains were an improvement upon stage coaches; mechanised flight, on ballooning; but television is an improvement on nothing. It is something new under the sun.'[44]

The most eagerly awaited programmes were outside broadcasts, particularly sport. The BBC was there on Monday 21 June 1937 for the first day at Wimbledon, although the link with Alexandra Palace was difficult because of the hilly terrain in between. To take advantage of the rising ground towards Wimbledon Common, the television signal was sent by cable across the car park to Barker's sports ground, 700 feet from Centre Court – an area now better known as Henman Hill, where fans gather to watch the fate of gallant British losers on a giant TV screen – and transmitted from an aerial on top of the turntable ladder of a London fire engine. Hornsey Central Hospital near Alexandra Palace was right in its way, but the hospital secretary agreed to suspend all diathermy activities (heating internal organs by electric current) while Wimbledon was on so as not to ruin the reception.

As viewers joined the tennis, Bunny Austin, the great almost-champion of Wimbledon and the last of the gentleman amateurs, was stuttering to a win against G. L. Rogers. The court was too big for the screen and the grass-stained ball could barely be distinguished from the grass, but critics stressed the positives. 'It has seldom been possible to watch the progress of the ball itself,' conceded one for-giving reviewer. 'But the strokes and the movements about the court have all been so clearly visible that the absence of the ball has hardly seemed to trouble the viewer after his eyes and his spectator's reac-tions have become accustomed in a minute or so to the strangeness of it all.'[45]

On 11 November 1937, the television cameras were at the Cen-otaph for a memorable two minutes' silence. Shortly after the last chime of Big Ben had died down, a man broke through the crowd and ran into the road, screaming 'All this hypocrisy!' and something else that sounded like 'Preparing for war!' Half a dozen policemen gave chase and, just yards from the prime minister, clambered on top of him and muffled his cries. The man turned out to be Stanley Storey, an ex-serviceman who had escaped from a mental asylum. The TV picture was in long shot so viewers just heard 'hypocrisy!' and saw the crowd swaying slightly, before it settled back into a vast, uniform mass, with just the background noise of distant traffic, birdsong and shuffling feet. This was why the BBC had lobbied hard in the 1920s to broadcast the silence on radio. It knew that simply shutting down the airwaves for two minutes would not have the same impact as this resonant near-silence. The effect, strangely, was magnified when you could see it. 'The television cameras make a naturally impressive scene even more impressive,' concluded the *Radio Times*. 'Watching the Silence, broken by the rustle of falling leaves in Whitehall, is an unforgettable experience.'[46]

Cyril Carr Dalmaine, viewing the silence in a room above Dorking High Street, had more technical concerns. He felt he was being offered a foretaste of what television would be like when the engineers had sorted out the problem of interference. 'As cars, buses, lorries outside switched off their engines and came to rest, so did the crackling fade from the sound reception and the spots from the viewing screen, rather as if some unseen smudge had been wiped off a palette,' he wrote. 'For those two minutes the picture came to us clean, clear and steady – like a photograph.'[47] Dalmaine was the real name of Jonah Barrington, the radio critic for the *Daily Express*, and both he and his newspaper were proselytisers for television. The *Express* had sold some of the first DIY television kits in the early 1930s and, at a time when the BBC was not listing an official reception map, issued its own unofficial ones: a radius around London with dark and light shading to indicate how likely it was you would get a good picture.

Like Gander, Barrington had high expectations of the medium, making it clear how unimpressed he was by the decision to televise the formal opening of the new lift at Alexandra Palace. In August 1937 he organised the *Daily Express* Television Exhibition and visitors came from as far as Penzance and Newcastle to see every make of television set. One woman, peering into one, said how wonderful it had seemed when she was young to hear someone's voice over a telephone: 'We never thought we'd have anything more marvellous than that, and now here am I, over seventy, seeing someone dancing eight miles away ...' A month later, Barrington organised a *Daily Express* exhibition touring the home counties with a television van showing the daily broadcasts, starting at the Grand Theatre, Woking. He inaugurated the exhibition live on television from Alexandra Palace, thus becoming, he claimed, 'the first man in the world to declare an exhibition open without bothering to be present'.[48]

The cameras were also there for Neville Chamberlain's arrival at Heston Airport after his meeting with Hitler at Berchtesgaden in September 1938. 'No one knew what had happened until, stepping from his aeroplane in front of the television cameras, he told them,' said *The Times*. 'This had a quality of history in the making that no other outside broadcast has equalled.'[49] The return from Munich later that month was also televised: this time the result was known and the mood celebratory. The broadcast, on a Friday afternoon, was not pre-announced so perhaps only a few hundred viewers saw the plane circle in the air, land and taxi up to the waiting group of cabinet ministers, and Chamberlain step out smiling. He aimed his famous, fluttering piece of paper at the newsreel cameramen and press photographers, but these viewers were the first to see it, and they could even make out traces of writing. The commentary, broadcast simultaneously on radio, was by a 25-year-old Richard Dimbleby, who had persuaded

BBC News to make him its first 'News Observer' and who was single-handedly creating a new sort of journalist: the on-the-spot observer with a microphone in his hand. 'It's a real triumph, this arrival,' Dimbleby said in a fresh, piping voice quite unlike its postwar incarnation. 'Oh now listen: a very tuneless version of "For he's a jolly good fellow" ... Those of you who are looking as well as listening to this will be able to see this ...'

Television could still not decide if it was a public spectacle or a domestic hobby. On 23 February 1939, Eric Boon fought Arthur Danahar to retain his British lightweight boxing title at the Harringay Arena, and the fight was shown on BBC television at three London cinemas, the first ever pay-per-view televised sporting event. So large was the crowd at the Monseigneur News Theatre in Leicester Square that about a hundred people swept aside the doormen and charged into the auditorium without paying the steep entry fee of one guinea. Police reinforcements arrived to halt the stampede, but the gatecrashers were allowed to remain. The Marble Arch Pavilion and the Tatler News Theatre in Charing Cross Road were also packed, with people standing along each wall and sitting in the aisles. Some were dressed in evening dress and ermine furs, others in cloth caps and mackintoshes.

The cinema-sized picture was far from perfect. A trainer's waving towel sent a band of whiteness rushing across the screen, and sometimes the pictures dissolved into irregular patterns, to the sound of whistles and catcalls. 'Boxers looked like ghosts,' wrote a reporter at the Marble Arch. 'You could see the ropes on the further side of the ring show through their bodies; you could see wicked punches that sailed straight through shadowy white figures. It was like moving spirit pictures. But if you went to see a fight, you forgot that.'[50]

The imperfections were indeed soon forgotten, as shouts and applause in the cinemas merged with the sounds from the arena. The audience could make out Danahar's textbook punch, the straight left delivered standing side on, while the smaller Boon stood flatfooted, ducking and weaving to get inside his opponent's longer reach. Both men floored each other several times until, in the fourteenth round, Danahar rose weakly and the referee declared Boon, his face splashed with blood and one eye completely closed, the winner. A nineteen- and twenty-year-old had pummelled each other into near oblivion, live on television. People in Boon's home town of Chatteris in Cambridgeshire had asked the police if they could watch the TV set in the station but they refused, in case it interfered with police work. But as soon as the referee stopped the fight, the local inspector sent up a firework to let people in the Fens know their man had won. Boon's mother watched at a friend's house in the town, turning her face away from the screen and wincing whenever her son was hit.

Many thought the Boon–Danahar broadcast was the future of television: large crowds congregating in cinemas and other public places to watch live sport and spectacle. But it was really Mrs Boon, watching in an ordinary living room, who foretold the future. As Alan Hunter wrote in the *Radio Times*, 'When on my home television set I see Jasmine Bligh announcing the programme, she seems to be speaking to me, not to thousands of others, as in a cinema. An aspect of intimacy, if you like. But one that can be utterly destroyed with even a small crowd in a demonstration room.'[51]

These home viewers were forging a strong, intimate relationship with the performers. The Alexandra Palace offices filled up daily with appreciative letters and cards. When the palace was shrouded in London fog, as happened often, and most dramatically on Christmas night 1937, viewers with cars rang to ask if they could drive the artistes back to their homes. When viewers called after a programme, the performers would speak to them on phones in the corridors outside the studio. The comedian Cyril Fletcher, who appeared regularly on pre-war television, got to know certain callers well. Just before Christmas 1938, Gerald Cock sat at his desk on camera and invited viewers to ring him up and ask questions. As they phoned from as far away as Birmingham and Margate, Cock feigned panic to his off-camera secretary, whispering out of the side of his mouth, 'Phew! I got over that fence.' Then to wind things up, just before a woman called to say that she thought television 'marvellous', the presenter of radio's *Children's Hour*, Uncle Mac, rang up to wish Cock a happy Christmas.[52]

In other ways, the audience seemed furtive and unreal, and Alexandra Palace residents had to find more creative ways to speculate about them. A young BBC producer, Royston Morley, kept a lookout, while driving his car, for television aerials on chimney tops, which he saw on average about every five minutes. On the palace esplanade, the performers looked out on to the redbrick avenues of Stroud Green, Finsbury Park and Hornsey, middle-class real estate and native soil of the television aerial. In the distance, they could make out the Kent and Surrey Downs, which blocked the TV signal's journey further south. Seventeen-year-old Dinah Sheridan, after performing in the play *Gallows Glorious*, stood on the palace steps looking at the shimmering lights of London and wondered 'how many of those houses had a TV set and had seen what we had just done. Probably less than a hundred.'[53]

An engineer wrote in *Wireless World* that unsentimental technicians like himself, who were 'steeled to derive no more interest or emotion from the most sublime sound than from a test oscillation', were now captivated by the television programmes. On the televising of the departure of the king and queen for Canada in May 1939, as they drove through waving crowds from Buckingham Palace to Waterloo Station, he noted that he had seen viewers cheering as if they were standing on the kerb while their majesties passed by, something that never happened in a cinema during the newsreels. Even the slow pace of television compared to the newsreels was an advantage, for you didn't feel 'battered and jerked around the high-spots of the week's action throughout the world in five breathless minutes like a thousand horse-power butterfly'. When an ordinary film was televised you immediately noticed the difference, for the commentator had that 'slightly breathless declamatory style, as if he is afraid of being thrown out before he has said all he wants to'. On television, speakers calmly addressed the individual viewer, and the sound of frying fat in a cookery demonstration was so convincing that 'one instinctively draws one's legs in to keep them out of range of grease spots'. Nor was the small screen a problem. If you were close enough it was the same size as a cinema screen viewed from the best seats, and 'a penny held at arm's length is in effect larger than the sun'.[54]

The domestic audience was middle-class, though not exclusively so: Bruce Forsyth's garage-mechanic father, for example, had bought a television for their house in the solidly working-class area of Edmonton in north London. The social makeup of most viewers probably accounted for the evening programme not starting until 9 p.m. The later-dining middle classes would finish eating about fifteen minutes beforehand, gather in the sitting room with coffee and cigarettes, and wait for the valves of the set to warm up and the picture to appear, with the same air of expectancy they might feel in the theatre. As a phenomenon yet to spread to the masses, television does not seem to have been an object of intellectual disdain. Virginia Woolf wrote to her nephew Julian Bell, teaching in China: 'Oh dear how I wish television were now installed and I could switch on and see you.'[55] As a loyal patron of Selfridge's, Woolf is likely to have seen television there. Her friend, Marcel Boulestin, an expat Frenchman who owned a Covent Garden restaurant which sought to wean the British away from stuffy haute cuisine, was the first television chef. Since all his dishes had to be prepared in fifteen minutes, one of his earliest broadcasts introduced British viewers to the kebab.

Other members of Woolf's social set certainly saw television. 'V. and I go round to the Beales' where there is a Television Set lent by a local radio-merchant,' wrote the National Labour MP and writer, Harold Nicolson, in his diary on 4 February 1939, after visiting a neighbouring farmer at Sissinghurst in Kent. 'We see a Mickey Mouse, a play and a Gaumont British film. I had always been told that the television could not be received above 25 miles from Alexandra Palace. But the reception was every bit as good as at Selfridge's. Compared with a film, it is a bleary, flickering, dim, unfocused, interruptible thing, the size of a quarto sheet of paper such as this on which I am typing. But as an invention it is tremendous and may alter the whole basis of democracy.'[56]

Nicolson's wife, Vita Sackville-West, busy creating her celebrated garden at Sissinghurst, might have been the BBC's first television gardener. The BBC had broadcast gardening talks on the radio from within a few months of its formation in 1922 and Sackville-West was a frequent speaker. She was considered for the role of radio gardener but the job went to an unknown county council horticultural adviser called Mr Middleton. In 1936, he also became the BBC's first television gardener, working in a purpose-built plot in Alexandra Park, with cable trailed across the road from the palace. He became such a well-known figure that the comic actor, Nelson Keys, impersonated him on television. Keys appeared in a mildewed hat and mangy coat, carrying a dead cat, and making lugubrious pronouncements like 'the thistles are doing nicely today' and 'add a little fish manure at the earliest opportunity'. The grassy slopes of the park had become an outdoor studio not just for gardening but for sheepdog trials, archery and golf. For one night-time broadcast, they reconstructed the Zeebrugge Raid of 1918 with model boats on the nearby lake.

The historian Ross McKibbin describes British television before the war as 'a cloud no bigger than a man's hand'. But to its contemporary viewers, it must have seemed more substantial than this. There were now some regular programmes, placemarks in the schedules. Sunday afternoons were for 'Television Surveys': outside broadcasts from the International Telephone Exchange at Faraday Buildings or from Watford railway junction to show how locomotives were overhauled and track was relaid. Once a month on Wednesdays the viewer went 'Down on the Farm' to see wheat rolling or lambing at Bull Cross Farm which, to keep out the curious hordes, was described as 'somewhere in the Home Counties'. 'Does sheep dipping make good television entertainment?', the *Listener*'s new television critic, Grace Wyndham Goldie, opened her review of this programme, concluding it with an affirmative.[57] Hit West End shows like *Magyar Melody*, *The*

Desert Song and *Me and My Girl* were shown live from the theatre, including shots of the crowds in the foyer and the stars in their dressing rooms. Other programmes drew on the sense of viewers as an ad hoc community. A common form of entertainment was the 'Bee', a participatory quiz show in which viewers were invited to spell difficult words or whistle 'Softly awakes my heart' from beginning to end.

The *Radio Times* presented television as a domestic entertainment but a social one, and urged viewers to hold television parties for their non-viewing friends. The magazine tried to draw on the growing sense of camaraderie among this group of pioneers. 'A week or two ago I was introduced to a neighbour of mine,' wrote the regular television columnist, 'the Scanner'. 'We talked sweet nothings until I said as a brother-viewer I was glad to see his roof was graced with a television aerial. A reaction of delight was immediate; it was like the meeting of two anglers.' After Edgar Charloe from Acton wrote to suggest founding a society of viewers, the Scanner reflected that 'there must be hundreds of viewers in that thickly populated suburb who feel the same way as he does'. The *Radio Times* liked to identify celebrities with televisions, such as the cartoonist David Low, the dance band leader Henry Hall and the comedian Will Hay. It awarded the title of oldest viewer to 91-year-old Mr E. C. Rolls of Walton-on-Thames, who had dim memories of the Crimean War and who, after seeing Noel Coward's *Hay Fever* on Christmas night 1938, was hooked.[58]

The magazine also unearthed a farmhand from Long Melford, Suffolk, called George Thomas Boar. After reading in the *Radio Times* that television was on its way, he had saved up £60, which was doubled by a small legacy, and in the autumn of 1937 had paid 120 guineas for a TV set, even though he lived fifty miles from Muswell Hill. Subject to a formal application, he allowed other villagers to come to his cottage and see the programmes for free. About a thousand people, including his farmer-boss, had come to watch in his two-room cottage, giving Long Melford easily the highest proportion of viewers in the country. After she had seen Boar's television, an 87-year-old woman shook her head and said, 'It cairn't be, it cairn't be.' Another farmhand sat through a programme composed of literary quotations and said, 'Those are the items we folks like.' Boar's face was 'alive with mingled pride and enthusiasm as he fondle[d] the television set with all the love which a stockman gives to a new-born calf or a leggy foal'. Television, he said, was the only way of 'taking part in the exciting life of London', which he had never seen. Had he lived three centuries ago, the magazine reflected, 'he would have been burned at the stake as a wizard or a sorcerer in good East Anglian style. But because he lives in the year 1939 he is looked upon for miles around as a fairy godfather who performs miracles.'[59]

The BBC was starting to flesh out the habits and rituals of this new tribe, the viewers, nearly 900 of whom were already writing regularly to Alexandra Palace about the programmes they had seen. In February and March 1939, the announcers Jasmine Bligh and Elizabeth Cowell asked viewers to apply to fill in a questionnaire, and over 4,000 – a huge proportion out of about 20,000 set owners – returned them. The survey revealed that viewers loved the announcers; they found extraneous noises of scene-shifting irritating; they thought continental films, operettas and ballets were boring; and they wanted a 'Children's Hour' as on the radio. They mostly disliked items being repeated, although some viewers welcomed this because television was so addictive: 'We look forward to a repeat of a programme we have already seen, so that we can go out for a walk now and again.'[60]

One June afternoon in 1939, seventy-five couples, chosen by ballot from the 700 who had applied, attended a 'television tea party' at Broadcasting House. Television's stars – Joan Miller, Jasmine Bligh, Elizabeth Cowell and Leslie Mitchell – wore 'stop me and ask one' identity buttons affixed to their coat lapels and handed out smoked salmon sandwiches, cakes and buns. Sitting in the raked, padded seats of the hall, the viewers plied Gerald Cock with questions. 'Why,' asked a man at the back, 'can't the evening's programme be given on the screen to save me looking it up in the *Radio Times*?' This was a matter for the engineers, replied Cock. 'Why is it that the television orchestra so often drowns the soloists?' Cramped studio space, came the answer. 'Why can't the morning demonstration film be changed?'

Because it cost £3,000 to make, Cock said. When he mentioned *Picture Page*, spontaneous applause filled the hall.[61]

'Of course *Picture Page* is our favourite,' said one woman to Grace Wyndham Goldie, attending for the *Listener*. 'And the plays. I do like the plays. Except the Insect Play. I didn't understand what that was all about. And I don't like the foreign films they put on sometimes. But the rest's splendid. It's all so friendly.' Goldie noted the enormous popularity of the announcers who also doubled up as interviewers and stunt people, having their palms read by chirologists or being rescued from burning buildings in fire displays. As the admiration for the announcers attested, television was already more informal than radio. Radio conversation at this time was often scripted, and Hilda Matheson, the BBC's director of talks, complained that many speakers read their scripts in a 'parsonical drone'. On television, by contrast, the announcers could not read from a script if they wanted to look at the viewer, and could not see much in the glare of the lights anyway, so they had to learn to be natural. Television's stars, reflected Goldie, would be 'the people who make direct contact with its small audiences. In other words, they will be the talkers not the actors, the Howard Marshalls not the Clark Gables.'[62]

With war approaching, Radiolympia in August 1939 was subdued. The main attraction was 'Television Avenue', a township of stands along which hundreds of different makes of set were arrayed. Mr Middleton tended a life-sized recreation of his Alexandra Palace garden and there was a huge model of the palace, sixty-five feet high, with miniature cameras and other equipment inside, like a giant doll's house. The radio trade predicted that 100,000 sets would be in homes by Christmas.[63]

Programmes remained light until the end: an alternative reality radiating from the northern heights. At Radiolympia on 1 September, with Germany having invaded Poland earlier that morning, Elizabeth

Cowell interviewed the Misses Reilly on 'all year round bathing' and Mr J. McIntyre on 'impressions of English life as seen by a West Indian', and Joe Loss and his band played 'If I had a talking picture of you'. As the evacuation of schoolchildren held up traffic out of London, a Disney cartoon, *Mickey's Gala Premiere*, was shown in full (and not, as legend has it, breaking up into static halfway through). Some test signals followed and, at around 12.35 p.m., closedown. The *Radio Times*, which went on sale that day, fleshed out the programmes for the coming week: a 'television fashion display', a programme about swans in literature, art and music which 'will be frankly high-brow, so don't switch on if your appreciation of bird life is limited to Donald Duck', and 'Interest Film: West of Inverness'. But a special issue of *Radio Times* issued three days later entitled 'Broadcasting Carries On!', made no mention of television at all.[64] The first casualty of war was the TV listings.

By October, as the phoney war dragged on, the BBC had received hundreds of letters asking for television to resume. 'Most of the letters say that, having got used to television, owners of now useless sound and vision receivers find that ordinary sound programmes are unsatisfying and not worth switching on to hear,' said a speaker at the AGM of Electrical and Musical Industries Ltd in December. 'With the present conditions prevailing in the London area, particularly at night, there is a real need for television.'[65] The BBC's stock reply was that television had been withdrawn for reasons of national security, the characteristic sound of the Alexandra Palace transmitter making it useful as a direction finding point for enemy aircraft. Most of the television engineers went to work developing radar, and those who remained to look after Alexandra Palace deployed its sound transmitter in what Winston Churchill named the 'battle of the beams', using it to jam the high-frequency radio waves which German bombers used to guide themselves on to targets. The only people watching television in Britain during the war were members of British intelligence, tuning in to German TV broadcasts drifting over from the top of the Eiffel Tower.

The *BBC Handbook* for 1940 plaintively recounted a brief, golden

hour it was not sure would return. 'To talk of the television programmes during those last eight months of the service is to stir wistful
memories,' wrote the BBC press officer, Ernest Thomson, as Britain
entered its darkest days of the war. 'We throw a glance nowadays
at the blank screens of our receivers and remember when they held
us like a spell. We recall the constantly changing scene: Royal processions, tennis at Wimbledon, comedies and thrillers in the studios,
the big fights at Harringay and Earl's Court, the living portraits of
"Picture Page" … and we ask with Keats, "Was it a vision, or a waking
dream?" … One day, we may hope that eager striving band of special-
ists will reassemble under their queer, futuristic mast in Alexandra
Park to resume the world's first high-definition television service. But
whether that happens soon or late, we had our glorious hour. Television was here – You Couldn't Shut Your Eyes to It.'[66]

3

A STRAIGHT PENCIL-
MARK UP THE SKY

A day in bed … Watched television with Joyce and Cole.
What a hideous and horrid invention.

Noel Coward, 4 January 1947[1]

On Saturday 6 October 1945, Nella Last, a housewife from Barrow-
in-Furness, decided to make the most of the last weekend before
the clocks went back for winter by making a shopping expedition
to Kendal. 'I saw my first television set but was not very thrilled,'
she confided to her diary, written for the social research organisation,
Mass Observation. 'The screen was so tiny any performers would
have looked like dolls.' Nella was looking through a shop window at
a dead screen. Broadcasts had not yet resumed after the end of the war
and, even if they had, the signal would not have reached the Lake District from Alexandra Palace. 'To most people with pre-war television
sets, and many who hoped to be viewers in the near future, the year
opened in delicious mystery,' wrote the *BBC Yearbook* of 1946, 'but
viewers-to-be were wondering what was really happening beneath
that spindly, bristling aerial-mast on London's northern heights.'[2]

It was not until 7 June 1946, a year after VE Day, that television
returned, just in time to broadcast the Victory Parade. At twenty-one
years old, Miss Beryl Romaril, of Grenoble Gardens, Palmers Green,

gained brief renown as the vision mixer at Alexandra Palace who was to turn the knob that faded up the first pictures for six years. The newspaper headline, 'Beryl to turn on television: 20,000 are waiting', probably overestimated the viewing figures. On that first night, the BBC showed a dramatic adaptation of a piece of French resistance underground fiction called *The Silence of the Sea* about an elderly man and his niece in occupied France forced to take in as a lodger a cultured German officer (Kenneth More), who talked about his desire for friendship between their two nations. After a trip to Paris he returned disillusioned with Nazism and left to fight on the Eastern Front, saying he was 'off to Hell'. 'It was a very touching and moving play,' remembered Peter Sallis, then a RADA student watching it on his parents' set in Leigh-on-Sea, 'and many years later when I was working with Kenny More, I told him I had seen it and he could hardly believe it. I think I was the only person, apart from close members of his family, who had ever seen *The Silence of the Sea*.'[3]

A slight exaggeration: Iain Logie Baird, television curator at the National Media Museum in Bradford, estimates that about 3,000 sets were lost to the Luftwaffe's bombs, and a few more refused to work after hibernating for so long, so there were perhaps about 15,000 working televisions. John Logie Baird, Iain's grandfather, had died of a coronary thrombosis on 14 June 1946, aged 58, a week after television resumed, an event that he had been excitedly anticipating. It was his company that had successfully shown the BBC pictures of the Victory Parade on big screens at the Savoy and Grosvenor House Hotels, but Baird was too ill to attend. He died at his rented home on Station Road in Bexhill-on-Sea, outside of the range of television. Even when television did reach the Sussex coast in the early 1950s, reception in Baird's old street was said to be terrible.[4] After its reopening, television received scant coverage in the thin, paper-rationed newspapers of the time, and its performers must often have felt, like Kenneth More, that they were speaking into a void. New television sets started to be made again in the autumn of 1946, but shortages of wood for the cabinets and glass for the cathode ray tubes severely limited production.

On 10 February 1947, in the middle of the harshest winter anyone could remember and an acute coal shortage, television was cancelled for over a month. 'I am assured on reliable authority,' wrote John Ware of Chelsea, one of the few aggrieved set owners, in a letter to *The Times*, 'that the total power consumption of a whole day's television transmission is approximately equal to that of one hour of any one of the sound broadcast transmissions.' But most of the country was far more worried about the rationing of the use of fires and stoves than a television service limited to a few hours a day and to the south-east of England. 'Last evening I and W went into the Sparks, next door, to wish them a Happy New Year and to look at their television picture of the Cinderella pantomime,' wrote an underwhelmed Herbert Brush, a retired electricity board inspector living in Sydenham with two female housemates, in his Mass Observation diary on New Year's Day 1948. 'My eyes are not good enough to see such a small picture well, but as, according to the announcer, it was the first time they have televised a theatre with its own light, perhaps I did not see the television under the best conditions.'[5]

The first intimation that television might be waking from its long period of torpor came with the London Olympics in the summer of 1948. Since most sporting events refused permission to film, until then television had been reduced to showing tug-of-war, Japanese swordplay, ping-pong and amateur football from Barnet. There were huge attendances for live sport since, with rationing still in place, rising disposable income tended to be spent on leisure. But the public's sporting tastes were domestic: league football, horse racing and county cricket. That summer's big event was Don Bradman's farewell tour of England in the Ashes. The Olympics, an international event that happened to be staged in Britain, was not anticipated with much relish.

Yet viewers soon found themselves caring about the fate of little-known athletes competing in unfamiliar events. The new Emitron cameras had a revolving lens turret with a close-up, medium-range and long shot, so they could follow runners all the way round the track. They were nearly as sensitive as the human eye, making outside broadcasts possible even in fading light, although the picture then tended to peel off from the corners like a sepia-tinted photograph. Viewers saw clear, velvety images of the giant Jamaican RAF war hero, 'Art' Wint, pounding the ground in grief after pulling a muscle and losing his team the 400 metres relay; the housewife and mother, Fanny Blankers-Koen, bringing victory for Holland in the 100 metres relay with her last stride; and the exhausted Belgian Étienne Gailly being heartbreakingly overtaken on the marathon's final lap. Even better pictures came from the Empire Pool, where swimmers were brought before the Emitrons still breathless and wet. The BBC's director general, William Haley, lukewarm about the new medium, was staying in a hotel in Devon and was astonished to overhear new arrivals from London talking animatedly about having seen the games on television in their homes.[6]

A programme called *Viewers' Vote* on Saturday evenings invited them to pass judgement on six selected programmes and send in a postcard. Of about a thousand postcards sent in each week, most rated all six programmes, suggesting a great deal of 'block viewing'. Viewers had stronger and more polarised reactions than radio listeners did to programmes, probably because it was harder for block viewers to tune out things they did not like. Ninety-one per cent of viewers watched the whole evening's broadcast from 8.30 p.m. to closedown at 10.15 p.m. Few radio programmes drew TV owners away from the set. The nearest things to a dilemma of choice were *Have a Go* with Wilfred Pickles on Wednesday nights and the comedy series *ITMA* on Thursday nights.[7]

The BBC's conclusions about this block viewing were worthy of the high-minded ideals of its first director general, John Reith. The problem with radio, concluded its researchers, was 'the difficulty of persuading listeners to keep their fingers from the tuning knob long enough for the programme to secure an entering wedge upon their attention'. Television, by contrast, might be able to 'enlist the interest of its public in new or unfamiliar fields'. When Mass Observation did a survey of prospective television owners in the spring of 1949, some thought that concentrated viewing in a semi-darkened room was better than absent-minded radio listening, while others worried that it required too total a commitment. 'There are so many things I can do in my leisure time while listening to and enjoying the wireless, for example, reading, carving and modelling, gardening,' said a 32-year-old school teacher. 'I am so afraid that television would prove so attractive that my spare time would be spent straining my eyes looking into a fixed distance screen.'[8]

Nella Last was not alone, then, among non-viewers in complaining that the nine-by-seven-inch screens were too small, a belief probably encouraged by the large Perspex magnifying glasses attached to some of them and the fact that people often saw them neck-craning among a jostling crowd on the pavement outside a radio shop. But this was not a complaint heard from television owners. 'This supposed shortcoming of television is voiced only by those who are not viewers,' John Swift assured potential set buyers in his book *Adventures in Vision*, 'and who base their assumptions on an inspection of a "dead", white screen in a shop window.' Like Nella Last, two-thirds of Britons had never even seen a television working. An image of the Alexandra Palace mast was now shown every night on the opening credits of *Television Newsreel*, its pulsing signals seeming to broadcast to the whole world to the tune of a confident wartime march, Charles Williams's 'Girls in Grey'. But the chalk hills of the Chilterns and the North Downs still formed a natural barrier against these signals, albeit a permeable one. The BBC's one known viewer in the Channel Islands reported pictures of 'excellent entertainment value'.[9]

Some postwar television personalities were already starting to emerge. Joan Gilbert, the presenter of the revived *Picture Page*, was an effervescent character prone to stumbling over her lines, laughing for no reason, and saying 'mmm' a lot while the interviewee was speaking as if she were preparing for the next question. She was, according to the theatre critic Harold Hobson, 'rather too boisterous for any but the biggest sets'.[10]

A tall, bespectacled, gas board official called Leslie Hardern, with a passing resemblance to the ascetic Chancellor of the Exchequer, Stafford Cripps, presented *Inventors' Club*, introducing back bedroom inventions sent in by viewers. The programme had been born in the economic crisis of September 1947, when Hardern went on holiday to the French Riviera in the last boatload of tourists to leave the country that year without needing government approval. Convinced that new products were needed for an export drive to rescue the country from economic oblivion, Hardern decided to use television to harness British engineering ingenuity. As soon as each programme ended, the BBC would receive enquiries from manufacturers. Mr H. M. Bickle from Ealing, who had invented a hand cream which could be used in place of soap and water by making dirt roll up into small balls and fall off, generated much interest – although it was his cardboard and metal container, 'the Bickle tube', that went into production. Mr Gill from Pudsey caused a similar stir with his washing machine that could also wash and dry dishes, peel potatoes and mix dough – but it remained in the prototype stage.[11]

Other entries to *Inventors' Club* – an 'ionette' to iron out face wrinkles, a blow-as-you-go foot warmer for those allergic to hot water bottles, an electric dog to scare off burglars, a plughole to make the bath water run away silently without gurgling, a gadget for whisking off bed-clothes – proved, as one critic said, 'that we are still the race from which sprang Lewis Carroll and Edward Lear'. The brainwaves were a barometer of postwar preoccupations: Hardern received a hundred different versions of a woolwinder submitted by arm-weary husbands of knitters, ninety-six cinder sifters for coal fires and several corporal punishment machines for caning schoolboys. He claimed to have had only one good idea from a woman, an iron with four little retractable legs that served as a stand. *Inventors' Club* suggested a growing sense of involvement in the medium among viewers, although there was no need to own a television to contribute, and many of its inventors had never seen it.[12]

Algernon Blackwood, then nearly eighty, was a favourite on *Saturday Night Story*. He appeared first in the Halloween broadcast on 1 November 1947, telling a tale, 'The Curate and the Stockbroker', in which the stockbroker disappeared. Alarmed viewers rang the switchboard when Blackwood, through the use of two identical chairs and a screen dissolve, was also made to disappear, while his echoing voice remained. Blackwood needed no script and refused to rehearse. He would take the Underground to Wood Green and walk the mile and a half up the hill to the studio, making up the story as he went, emerging out of the darkness and entering for a light dusting of makeup before appearing on camera with moments to spare. He had mastered the art of talking to the individual viewer, greeting them while seated in an armchair, before laying his book aside, taking off his glasses, brushing his eyelids and leaning forward to begin his tale. He told haunting stories based on his years of travel in frontier Canada, the Black Forest and the Danube marshes, and his long absorption in mysticism and magic. He always finished dead on time, though the sharp-eyed viewer might notice his gaze wandering towards the clock overhead.[13]

'Here's Terry-Thomas to help you sell more sets,' proclaimed an advertisement for Baird televisions in a trade magazine, exhorting retailers to use his face in cinemas to attract more viewers. In *How Do You View?*, Thomas played a cash-strapped, amiable bounder presenting the show from his bachelor pad. Even on black-and-white sets, his gold-banded Dunhill's cigarette holder and brocade waistcoat shone. A *Picture Post* article, 'The dandy comes back to W.1', argued that Thomas 'must be given much of the credit for the return of flowered waistcoats – he will lay you two to one that you cannot stand for three minutes outside the display window of the Piccadilly shop which supplies him with them, without hearing his name mentioned'. He was sent cufflinks, cravats and cummerbunds by viewers, and Thomas aimed the programme very directly at them. 'I think that if you have an audience in the studio you play to it,' he explained. 'The viewer at home becomes just an old auntie watching the show from the side of the stage, instead of being the person the show should be directed straight at.' At the start of each episode a tight close-up brought his full face on to the screen. 'How do you *view*? Are you frightfully *well*? You *are*? Oh, good *show*!', he would say. The camera went in even tighter on his gap-toothed grin, magically sweeping past the gap and dissolving into the next scene. Seven-year-old Sarah Miles, watching with her family in Essex, sometimes 'laughed so much that Mummy would scold me for peeing on the sofa cushions'.[14]

But most loved were the three main announcers: Sylvia Peters,

Mary Malcolm and McDonald Hobley, who was also known to viewers as the presenter of the Friday night variety show *Kaleido-scope*, with its popular segment, 'Puzzle Corner'. Viewers in a pre-announced town were invited to display a copy of the *Radio Times* in their front window and the live programme showed an outside broadcast van driving round the streets. 'It might be here, it might be anywhere,' Hobley would tantalise viewers, even though the contestant had already been collared by the production team.[15] The BBC's genial light entertainment producer, Ronnie Waldman, conducted the quiz by telephone, with the van parked outside the viewer's house, the technology being too primitive to film inside it.

Isolated clips of the announcers today, usually from the more formal occasions that have been preserved, suggest stultifyingly starched attire and pronunciation, although Lord Reith always claimed the BBC accent was an improvement on the overly refined Oxford accent ('theatah, the fahside and such like') and it aspired to be non-regional rather than class-specific. Contemporary viewers did not think the announcers aloof or formal, for breakdowns were common and their job was to fill in the time reassuringly. Once the interruption went on for so long that Malcolm advised everyone to make a cup of tea and she would call them back if anything happened. Her poodle, Fernandel, sat next to her on a bar stool, and would be told off for yawning while she announced the programmes. 'In good times and in bad times, through breakdowns, gramophone records and interludes, these people have stood by us with unwavering cheer,' wrote the television critic Caroline Lejeune. 'One has felt glad for their sakes when normal transmission was resumed; they are our familiar friends; may we never lose them.'[16]

In December 1949, *The Aeroplane* drew attention to a 'serious hazard' to aircraft some ten miles north of Birmingham along the Birmingham–Lichfield Road, on a lip of hills overhanging the Midland plain. 'We advise all pilots to put a red ring on their maps round Sutton Coldfield and keep clear of the area in low visibility,' the magazine warned.[17] The *Radio Times* twice carried a photo of this 750-foot-high hazard on its cover: first, in July when it wasn't yet finished, and then in December, when it was. This was a new feature in the landscape, more futuristic even than the mini-Eiffel Tower of Muswell Hill. It was poised like a giant pencil standing on its point, its tapering base resting on a ball-bearing smaller than a cricket ball, which nestled in a socket. Since rigid joints were vulnerable to metal fatigue and rust, this hinged bearing allowed the mast to move by up to two feet in high winds, supported by stays in the surrounding fields, as though it were a moored airship.

This mast, wrote the *Manchester Guardian*, 'does nothing to besmirch these pleasant wooded hills ... Soaring fantastically from a two-inch steel ball on which it is poised, its slender stay-ropes reaching across the fields like the strands of a giant web, it could hardly be regarded by the most ardent rural preserver with anything but admiration and awe'. Norman Collins was still more florid. 'It is a beautiful sight – that slender, gleaming mast ... it is the sort of thing that persuades me that, despite all they do to prove the contrary, engineers are artists at heart and, like other artists, have their lyrical moments, their supreme outbursts,' he wrote. 'You could stand there speechless and admiring for minutes on end, simply staring up at it as the clouds go cruising past and the aerial itself appears to be sailing off somewhere into Warwickshire.'[18]

As well as being the controller of BBC television, Collins was a writer and something of an amateur ethnographer, given to extrapolating the hidden life of his viewers from tiny visual clues. This side interest in domestic anthropology was evident in one of his first published pieces, written in 1929, when he was twenty-one, for the *News Chronicle*. In 'London from a Bus Stop', he observed the capital from the top of a double-decker bus late one afternoon, watching lights go on in the windows of rows of suburban houses, blinds being drawn and 'the tired city clerk push open the little gate of his small front garden and put his latchkey into his front-door'. In 1945 he had published a sprawling, bestselling novel called *London Belongs to Me*. 'If you start walking westwards in the early morning from somewhere down in Wapping or the Isle of Dogs,' he wrote in its preface, 'by evening you will still be on the march, still in the midst of shabby little houses – only somewhere over by Hammersmith by then.'[19] In the novel, Collins gradually reduces this immense, everyday sameness to readability through the intricate lives of his characters and their chance encounters with each other.

When he became controller of television in 1947, Collins retained this desire to imagine mass society and what was going on in those 'shabby little houses'. His office on the top floor of Alexandra Palace was like an eyrie, with a bay window out of which he could see the endless rows of redbrick north London artisans' villas arranged in parallel lines. He had a television in the office and when it was on, he would look out of his window and practise his 'stout Cortez act' by 'gazing with a wild surmise into the blue', wondering who else in this immense city might be watching too.[20]

Whenever he journeyed back to London on the train, Collins's spirits rose when he looked out of the window and saw the new pattern of H-shaped aerials peppering the skyline: 'Row upon row of small houses, where a year or so ago there was nothing to be seen but the usual huddle of cowls and chimney-pots, now carry these queer antennae on their rooftops as though every home were displaying some new brand of talisman.' His excitement, he wrote, stemmed from the fact that he felt he knew something about the life that went on in the homes beneath the aerials, and could almost spirit himself inside to look at the family sitting in front of the set, a sort of 'ghost across the suburbs' peering over 100,000 different shoulders at everything from Shakespeare plays to cookery demonstrations. On a trip to Sutton Coldfield just before the transmitter opened, Collins spotted a small cottage with a green gate and an aerial sticking out just above the eaves. He found himself touched by this 'simple act of faith' in anticipation of 'that magical moment on December 17 when the box in the corner is going to spring into life'.[21]

Collins was a populist who, before moving to television, had headed the new Light Programme on radio, launching well-loved programmes like *Dick Barton – Special Agent*, *Housewives' Choice* and

Have a Go! He was a great champion of the newer medium, soon
to resign in frustration at the low priority given to it by the BBC,
to become a key player in the development of ITV. A large part of
his job, he felt, was to persuade the people in the modest villas he
saw spread out before him to go to the radio dealers and put down a
deposit on a television set. In 1950, shortly after resigning his post,
he rebuked T. S. Eliot, who, after returning from the US where 'the
television habit' was now entrenched, had written to *The Times* to
express his apprehension. Collins's response was that seventeenth-
century Puritans had been anxious about the theatre-going habit, and
Victorians about the novel-reading habit. Eliot's fears were 'merely
anti-Caxtonism brought up to date'.[22]

The Sutton Coldfield mast opened just before Christmas 1949.
At 7.55 p.m. on Saturday 17 December, viewers waited in vain for
the tuning picture as McDonald Hobley said they were 'having a bit
of trouble', and an empty screen eventually dissolved to show Sylvia
Peters in Birmingham, apologetically welcoming the Midlands into
the TV family. There followed a variety revue from the King's Theatre,
Hammersmith, featuring Stanley Holloway and Jolly 'Dynamite' Jef-
ferson, and a game of ice hockey between Earls Court Rangers and
Nottingham Panthers from the Empress Hall, London. 'The interim
programme with music, showing the course of a river from source
to sea, was done with painted backcloths and seemed both slow and
dull,' said the *Manchester Guardian*. However, it conceded, 'a talk on
"Gates", warning the child about the dangers of leaving gates open in
the country, was attractively done'.[23]

Some thought the spread of television should not be a priority in
these austere times. The general secretary of the Post Office Engineering Union criticised the policy of 'TV cake for all' while there was a
shortage of telephones. It was absurd, he said, that a family within
seventy miles of Birmingham could sit in comfort and watch a cabaret
show in London but would have to search for a red telephone box to
call a doctor a couple of miles away. The telephone famine, he feared,
might not end for another twenty years.[24] He was overly optimistic: in
1972, 200,000 people were still on the waiting list for telephones.

But such dissenting voices were rare. The first Sutton Coldfield broadcast went far beyond its intended range. Pictures reached a busy main road in Moss Side in the south of Manchester, and the southern suburbs of Liverpool, although nearer the centre the traffic got in the way of reception. At Thorne in Yorkshire, eighty miles from the mast, an audience of 200 watched a single set in the town hall, with only slight interference from passing buses and a nearby fridge. Eric Foulkes, a radio engineer in Rhyl, reported that the pictures had made it all the way over the Clwydian hills and were only spoiled by flashes caused by car ignitions. At 7 a.m. the following morning, a Sunday, George Samways, a Cheadle Hulme radio dealer, was woken by a telephone call from a man who had seen television the previous night on a communal set and wanted his own set installed straightaway. By lunchtime, twenty more people had phoned with orders, too eager to wait until Samways's shop opened on Monday.[25]

The opening of a new transmitter tended to revive the habit of communal viewing. A Midlands viewer was watching the 1950 FA Cup Final at home when he was interrupted by two callers who asked if they could join him, and who said they belonged to a larger group that had split up and gone in search of television aerials. When a boxing match was televised from Birmingham, there were similar groups roaming the city's streets and willing to pay admission money, about two shillings and sixpence being the going rate, to enter houses with aerials.[26]

'Already some two millions are held nightly by our modern Ancient Mariner, spellbinding in its darkened corner,' wrote Fyfe Robertson in the *Picture Post* in February 1951. 'This newest bread-and-circus toy is irresistible. Though it will not replace tallow candles in the official index, it will join the pools in the unofficial cost of living.' Robertson conjectured hopefully that it would create 'a rounded understanding of common interests in the baffling world of human endeavour ... Television could most tellingly remind us that duodenal ulcers and young love and dandruff and the way we feel after a good meal are much the same everywhere.'[27] Robertson was wrong on one point. Five years later, televisions and replacement cathode ray tubes did replace tallow candles in the retail price index, together with other items no longer in everyday use, such as rabbits, turnips and distemper. In 1957, the rise of television was also decisive in the demise of that once best-selling photojournalism magazine, *Picture Post*, and Robertson had to find alternative employment as a reporter on BBC television's *Tonight*.

Working out where the new television masts were to go was much more complicated than simply picking the highest hills in the most populated areas. Unlike light, which travels only in straight lines, electromagnetic waves behave in strange and stubborn ways, bending round obstacles or bumps in the landscape, passing through trees, buildings and even hills, and reaching further than normal during electrical storms or other freak conditions in the upper atmosphere. Areas immediately below the transmitter can also suffer from signal 'passover', when the line-of-sight radio waves fail to percolate downwards quickly enough from the high ground. Even the subsoil can affect reception: granite, for instance, forms a blanket under the earth that traps the radio waves. The first sign of television's arrival in an area was, therefore, the sight of captive balloons, with TV aerials attached, suddenly appearing on likely hilltops and escarpment edges, while a BBC van travelled round the area seeing how far the test signals could reach.

This is how a union flag and a BBC flag came to be flying above a soaring new mast at Holme Moss in the Pennines, 1,700 feet above sea level on the border between Derbyshire and Yorkshire. It was a lonely spot where only sheep, their fleeces grimy from the industrial breezes coming over from Manchester, grazed obliviously. 'The giant stays which hold it, tethered to their concrete bases, stride away between the banks of the black moss for all the world like one of Wells's Martian machines arrested in mid-career,' wrote the *Manchester Guardian*. 'The mast itself from a little distance looks as fragile and filigree and ten times more dramatic than the Skylon.'[28]

The Skylon was the starkly modern, cigar-shaped metal folly erected on London's South Bank for the Festival of Britain earlier that year. Like the new breed of tethered TV mast, it had a steel lattice-work frame supported on cables, so that it seemed to float above the ground – the joke being that, like the UK economy, it had no visible means of support. Posters and mugs of the Skylon became collectors' items and it was used to promote the biro, the new pen it allegedly resembled. Holme Moss, which similarly seemed to float above the earth and was also spectacular when lit up at night with warning lights, generated a similar excitement.

The arrival of television in the north of England was an important moment in the symbolic forging of a postwar national identity. In an era before motorways and shuttle flights, southerners still regarded the north as another country, and carried over from the 1930s an idea of the region as one of slums, smokestacks and dole queues. Many north-erners, while baulking at these stereotypes, felt distant from London or 'that Lunnon'. Leonard Mosley in the *Daily Express* contrasted the coming of television to Luton and Blackburn. For Luton, which was only an hour by train from London and which shared the early release of new films with the West End, television was 'a pleasant dollop of cream on top of an already rich entertainment cake'; for Blackburn, where Charlie Chaplin's silent film *City Lights* was still showing twenty years after it was made, and an evening trip to Manchester was a rare and middle-class treat, its coming was momentous. For the north, television would be 'a revolution in the routine of a million lives'. Among those northerners who could already get television, Mosley had met pub regulars earnestly discussing the merits of Jimmy Jewel and Ben Warriss's comedy shtick on *Turn it Up*, and miners who loved the ballet dancers. 'Regular whippets, some of these kids,' he overheard one say.

Mosley, a Lancashire expat living in London, then began to under-mine his own argument by being offended on the north's behalf. He had detected with rising irritation the insult to the north in nearly every newspaper reference to the opening of Holme Moss, particularly the southerner who talked of 'the inevitable increase in cheap entertain-ment, the debasing of cultural values' which this new audience would demand. Mosley predicted instead a howl of protest from the north when it saw what the south had been putting up with: 'TV debased by the north? This home of the Hallé Orchestra, of the Liverpool Rep., of Manchester Public Library, of Wilfred Pickles, black puddings, Eccles cakes? The north will drag TV's standards up from the mud.'[29]

But there was no such howl of protest on Holme Moss's opening night, as Alexandra Palace offered an extended taster of its regular features for new viewers. A genial, bearded chef, Philip Harben, known for his striped butcher's apron, one-handed way of breaking an egg and habit of talking to his Prestige saucepans, made a three-minute omelette. Annette Mills sat at a grand piano and introduced the string puppet Muffin the Mule, who danced on the piano top and whispered in her ear, against a white background so you couldn't see his strings (much). The comic actor Eric Barker, presenter of the sketch show *The Eric Barker Half-Hour*, warned northern viewers not to adjust their sets during the still frequent technical hitches.

The following January, 'Professor' Jimmy Edwards, the radio comedian, warned students at his installation as Rector of Aberdeen University that an 'even greater menace [than radio] is lurking across the border. Preparing to insinuate its way into your lives is the tangible terror of television ... Already the first Kirk O'Shotts have been fired.' Kirk O'Shotts was the site of the new transmitter, a piece of barren north Lanarkshire moorland near an old Protestant Kirk and the former coalmining town of Shotts and just a few hundred yards from the main Edinburgh–Glasgow road. John Watson, the mast rigger, had to climb it once a week in an insulating flying suit to chip off great hundredweight clumps of ice and dislodge 'streamers', congealed wet fog clouds formed by strong winds. At the top of the mast he could see as far north as Stirling, the gateway to the Highlands, and, on a clear day, could make out one of the spans of the Forth Bridge. At night he saw the villages between Glasgow and Edinburgh, which would soon be welcoming television, 'stretching in a kind of fairy-light chain from East to West'.[30]

Television arrived in Scotland at a delicate time in the history of the union, when the Scottish Covenant, a petition to create a devolved parliament, had been signed by around 2 million Scots. Scottish MPs constantly reminded their English counterparts that John Logie Baird had been a Dunbartonshire man and that if Scots continued to be deprived of one of their great inventions, they would lose faith in the Act of Union. Jean Mann, the Labour MP for Coatbridge and Airdrie, argued that television might induce Scots to stay in the mining districts and Highland villages, as well as solving 'the problem of juvenile delinquency and matrimonial disturbances – why wives leave home and why husbands leave home'.[31] Scots also complained about the increase by a third of the tax on television sets imposed in the 1951 budget, which would mean an extra £20 on the cheapest sets when television finally arrived.

But Professor Edwards was not the only observer looking coolly at the new mast. The BBC's director in Scotland, Melville Dinwiddie, a former church minister who originated what became the religious 'thought for the day' on the Home Service, warned Scotland's prospective viewers in the *Radio Times* that 'discrimination is essential so that not every evening is spent in a darkened room, the chores of the house and other occupations neglected. We can get too much even of a good thing.' On Friday 14 March, the day of television's official arrival, the *Glasgow Herald* judged it generally good value for the £2 licence: 'While some of it may not be of high quality, there is the consolation of the odd and the unexpected – the period films which appear on occasional afternoons and, recently, the well-thought-out substitute for a programme on NATO, a film about liver fluke in sheep. With all that, the television owner cannot possibly regret his purchase.'[32]

That evening, just before 7.30 p.m., the TV signal began its epic journey on an underground cable from Alexandra Palace to Holme Moss. From there it was beamed across a series of seven unattended hilltop masts, each about thirty miles apart, all the way to Scotland – rather as beacon fires had once been used on the Scottish borders to warn of English raiders. The penultimate link in the chain was a shining saucer-like reflector high up on the ramparts of Edinburgh Castle, which bounced the radio waves to Kirk O'Shotts.

James Stuart, the secretary of state for Scotland, opened the new service, sitting at a desk in what looked like a school hall, with tartan and the lion rampant on the curtain behind him. Even the young, said Stuart, had to regard television as remarkable. To him it seemed 'not only uncanny but – were it not proved possible – impossible'. But he also worried it could interfere with school homework and might in politics 'give to the telegenic orator an undue advantage over a less flamboyant, but no less thoughtful, rival'. Charles Warr, Dean of the Thistle, spoke a prayer of dedication followed by ten minutes of country dancing. 'Speeches dreadful,' wrote Cecil McGivern, controller of television, in a memo. 'This sort of television dullness is most depressing.' But Scottish viewers did not seem to find it dull. Outside Parkhead Public Hall, a crowd of people were let in 300 at a time to watch the single television set at half-hourly intervals. An audience of 200 in the Couper Institute, Cathcart would only move out and let the next audience in when the television sets were switched off.[33]

'I desperately wanted a television set,' recalled Richard Whiteley, aged eight in 1952, the son of a textile mill owner living in the west Yorkshire village of Baildon. 'I used to go round to Anthony Naylor's after school and watch his. His father was a surgeon in Bradford and therefore rather richer than us ... They had a TV with a purple screen and a magnifying glass.'[34] Eighty per cent of the population was now within range of a TV signal, but at £70 upwards, a television remained a big expense. On Tuesdays, the boys Whiteley and Naylor joined almost everyone else in sight of a set and watched *Billy Bunter*. The adventures of the Fat Owl of the Remove at Greyfriars School had sprung half a century earlier from the now defunct children's comic *Magnet*, and had been transferred to television by his creator Frank Richards, now in his late seventies.

Each episode was screened twice, at 5.25 p.m. for children and 8 p.m. for adults. It revived an archaic Edwardian language for the TV age: 'I say, you fellows', 'look here, you rotters!', 'leggo, you beasts!' While he was out in public, people would playfully kick Gerald Campion, the 29-year-old father of two who played Bunter, in the seat of his pants, just as Bunter's classmates did to him. An eternal cadger of money, forever waiting on a postal order that never arrived, Bunter was a fitting antihero for a nation still short of capital and resources after the war. Some even read political symbolism into Bunter's usually thwarted schemes to liberate sticky buns from the tuck shop. The Bradford MP Maurice Webb, in a debate on the crisis in food supplies in May 1952, protested that at the last election the minister of food had encouraged 'the building up of his name as some sort of synonym of plenty, on the assumption that we are a nation of Billy Bunters and that the Conservative Party would provide some sort of lavishly stocked tuckshop when they got back to power'.[35]

On Saturday evenings at 8 p.m., Whiteley's parents went round to the Naylors to watch *Café Continental*, an English mirage of 'Gay Paree' broadcast from the BBC's Lime Grove studios in Shepherd's Bush. It was a forty-five-minute Gallic fantasy of escape from the seemingly unending burden of postwar austerity, although the champagne buckets on the studio tables were actually filled with bottles of ginger ale. As each show began, viewers found themselves in a moving cab, with taxi and Parisian street noises supplied by BBC library sound effects, stopping in front of the café. A liveried commissionaire opened the cab door (a plywood cutout on castor wheels) and ushered them through the doors, the camera pausing to glance at the billboard on the right of the entrance with the names of the stars on that evening's bill. The bearded maître d'hôtel (and real-life West End restaurateur), Père Auguste, beckoned viewers in, announcing in a guttural French accent: 'Ah, bonsoir, m'sieurs, 'dames! Your table is reserved, as always. Entrez and amusez-vous bien.' Inside were actors playing hat check girls, barmen and waiters scurrying round with napkins and trays, together with about a hundred invited viewers, the ones at the front all required to wear evening dress.

Many show business managers had an unofficial television ban on their artists, not wanting their acts, perfected over many years, to be seen by millions and used up in one night. The producer Henry Caldwell realised he could conquer this problem by employing European artists such as singers, mime artists, conjurers and balloon sculptors. The acts had to be musical or visual because few of the performers could speak English, making it an ideally televisual show. The luminous Hélène Cordet ('Et maintenant we breeng you ...'), who had been spotted performing cabaret in London's Pigalle restaurant, was compère. Although viewers often complained that they could not understand her because of her accent and her habit of looking away from the microphone when she announced the acts, men, in particular, forgave her these faults. 'You should be put in the background of every programme,' one wrote to her, 'so that, if it is a dreadful bore, we can always look at you.'[36]

Richard Whiteley, while being driven across Baildon Moor one Saturday lunchtime, was so excited to see a bottle-green BBC outside-broadcast vehicle, a links van picking up the television signal and beaming it to Holme Moss, that he got his father to stop the car so they could meet the duty engineer. The engineers at these remote transmitting sites were the public's main contact with the BBC and they were mildly heroic local figures, emissaries of the medium of the future. Like many schoolboys of this era, Whiteley was fascinated by television technology and spent the whole of the 1953 coronation broadcast trying to second guess the director's camera positions and spot TV equipment in shot.[37]

For a brief period the television mast was part of the industrial sublime, that awkward British genre which has emerged at various historical moments to get excited about railway bridges or electricity pylons. These high-guyed steel lattice masts, the tallest of all human-made structures, were like modern-day cathedral spires, their sight and even their names evoking provincial pride and signalling the arrival of modernity. The *Radio Times*, a leading patron of modern graphic art, put a series of television masts on its covers, usually drawn by one of its favourite artists, Cecil W. Bacon: concentric circles of radio waves pulsing out like ripples on water from the top of the mast, and houses with aerials on top, waiting expectantly to receive the signal. Drawing in delicate pen or scraper-board in a way that resembled wood engraving, Bacon made these new structures seem both excitingly modern and familiarly British.[38]

The transmitter was also a symbol of regional pride, even when the promiscuous reach of the television signal did not always map neatly on to cultural identities. With the opening of the new Wenvoe transmitter in the Vale of Glamorgan in August 1952, the people of south Wales learned that they were expected to share their mast with north and east Devonians, and the West Country was only marginally less dismayed than Wales at this dent to regional self-esteem. The first Welsh language programme, in March 1953, was a portrait of the famous quarryman turned autodidact and bibliophile, Bob Owen of Croesor. It excited many complaints from the English viewers who had to watch it as well, despite it being only twenty minutes long and in a slot normally filled by the test card. 'I hope the English will cry with pain,' wrote the *Western Mail*'s broadcasting correspondent. 'The louder they cry, the sooner Wales will have its own television service.' Another urgent patriotic requirement was to find a settled Welsh word for television, *Radiolygiad* (radio eye), *Radlunio* (radio pictures), and *telefisiwm* all being used without enthusiasm. A competition was launched and in May 1953 the chief judge T. H. Parry-Williams, professor of Welsh at Aberystwyth, announced the winner, *Teledu* – even though, as someone pointed out, this was also the name of the Malayan stink badger.[39]

The life of engineers in the more isolated transmitter sites like Holme Moss and Kirk O'Shotts was a peculiar and solitary one, resembling the hardy masculine culture of an Antarctic base camp. To cope with the extreme cold, the walls of the transmitter building were built double and the roof covered with a thick layer of vermiculite to protect against clumps of ice falling from the mast. At Holme Moss, which was often snowbound in winter as heavy drifts formed on the flanks of the hill, the crew had iron rations and emergency living quarters. When the road was cut off, a local farmer walked across the snowy moors with bread, milk and eggs. During the long breaks in transmission in those early days, the mostly male members of staff amused themselves by playing cricket on the forecourt in the summer and sledging downhill in the winter. They would also play 'drosser rolling', a lethal-sounding game which involved liberating loose rocks from dry stone walls and rolling them down towards the reservoir 1,000 feet below.[40]

In the demonstration film shown each weekday morning for the benefit of engineers and sales assistants trying to sell televisions in radio shops, a long section dealt with the construction of Holme Moss to the music of an organ voluntary from Westminster Abbey, McDonald Hobley's voiceover explaining that the mast builders had to cope with bitter winds from the Russian Urals and that the underground cable bringing the TV signal north from London had to zigzag through Macclesfield's silk mills. The same demo film could be seen hundreds of times each year, the words 'Holme Moss' being thus very familiar to viewers, not just those from the north, who also saw it on their apology caption when television broke down. Holme Moss was such a common placemark in the mental topography of 1950s Britain that it was probably inevitable it would be climbed by Manchester University students in a rag week stunt and crowned with a university pennant, just as the Skylon had once been climbed by a Birkbeck College student. 'Every age,' explained Hobley in the demo film, 'has left its landmarks on the country – the stone monolith, the cathedral spire, the Martello tower, the Victorian railway station, the television mast ... drawn, like a straight pencil-mark up the sky ...'

On 1 June 1953, an eccentrically attired individual known only as 'the Doctor' landed his flying police box in Muswell Hill on the day before the coronation of Elizabeth II. Puzzled by a concentration of television aerials on the same ordinary working-class street (Florizel Street, which the televisually literate would know as the original name for *Coronation Street*), the Doctor and his partner, Rose, discovered that a radio trader, Magpie, was selling them television sets for the absurdly low price of £5. They swiftly uncovered a plot whereby these television sets were turning viewers into faceless zombies by sending electrical rays through the set and sucking out their souls, while the police hid the victims so as not to spoil the upcoming festivities. An alien being called the Wire had turned itself into electrical form,

and now, disguised as a female announcer speaking in strangulated received pronunciation on Magpie's television sets, was introducing dull panel shows in black and white. On coronation day, the Wire planned to complete its regeneration by imbibing the souls of the millions of Britons watching TV. Just in time, the Doctor climbed to the top of the Alexandra Palace mast while its electrical waves crackled across north London's rooftops, turned the receiver back into a transmitter and reduced the Wire to a white dot.

This was not, of course, a moment in the history of television but a 2006 episode of *Doctor Who* called *The Idiot's Lantern*. But it does usefully summarise the vulgate view, that television in 1953 was primitive and lifeless, that only a tiny cohort of the middle classes had seen it and that it was ripe for Cinderella-like transformation by the coronation. 'Like many others of the postwar generation, my first memory belongs to the young Queen: in my recollection her coronation in June 1953 heralded the arrival of a television in the corner of the living room and consequently the start of the dissipation of my juvenile sense of reality,' wrote the broadcaster Nick Clarke in 2003, in his book *Shadow of a Nation*. Surveying half a century of TV since then, Clarke saw this new Elizabethan age as one of growing cynicism, tawdriness and discontent. Television, he wrote, 'was the butterfly that emerged from its chrysalis' in the 1950s and 'grew into a ravening beast'. Its culminating nadir was reality TV, 'one of the great misnomers of the age', which proved only that Britain was suffering from 'the dry-rot of unreality'.[41]

But this idea of the coronation as a watershed for both television and the nation is unconvincing. By then, television in Britain was nearly thirty years old, had accumulated thousands of broadcasting hours and been seen by millions. One reason for this widespread belief that 1953 was television's year zero is the sparse evidence of moving images before then. The coronation marked the start of the wide use of telerecording, a crude method of making a copy of a programme as it went out live by pointing a 16mm film camera at the screen – which had the side effect of giving us a poor sense of what it was like for viewers to watch at the time, for it is like looking at the world through a Vaseline-smeared lens. Hardly any pre-1953 television survives, consigning once unforgettable characters like Joan Gilbert and Algernon Blackwood to the prehistoric era, a half-memory getting ever fainter as each year the number of viewers who saw them declines.

Nor does it seem right, as historian D. R. Thorpe suggests, that 'it was actually the television coverage of King George VI's funeral, watched in countless shared "front rooms", that sparked off the mass purchasing of sets in time for 2 June 1953'. The king's funeral procession was certainly seen by the largest television audience yet, about 4.5 million people. Kirk O'Shotts was even opened for a single day on 15 February, a month before its official opening, to broadcast it, although, since the BBC only announced this the day before, it is unlikely that many Scots saw it. The funeral was also an event made for televising. The black-veiled new queen, the lilies on the coffin quivering in the breeze, the birds flying above Windsor Castle's Round Tower as the flag was lowered, all showed up in beautiful chiaroscuro. 'Almost it seemed too intimate a picture for public diffusion,' wrote Reginald Pound in the *Listener*. 'One's impulse was to step back from the screen, to have no part in this magnificent trespass.' But the coming of mass television was a continuum, not something sparked by one event. The number of new television licences rose from 400,000 in 1950, to 700,000 in 1951 and 1952, to 1,100,000 in 1953, suggesting that the sales hike for the coronation was part of a steady, inexorable rise.[42]

A Coronation Commission, chaired by Prince Philip, had ruled that the Westminster Abbey ceremony would not be televised, the sole concession being to allow cameras west of the organ screen so the processions could be seen. The phrase 'west of the organ screen' was repeated ad infinitum over the course of 1952. For some it came to symbolise the anachronism of a pre-war caste system which offered a privileged view to the favoured few. 'Beyond the precincts of Westminster, from the shores of Cornwall to the grey waters of the Clyde, from the warm sunlight of the Weald of Kent to the green-blue loveliness of the Lakes,' wrote the *Daily Mirror*'s Cassandra, 'at least fifteen million of Her Majesty's subjects will be abruptly shuttered off by what appears to be a monumental piece of mis-judgement.' For others, the organ screen defended precious tradition from the pernicious instincts of mass voyeurism. In this camp was the Archbishop of Canterbury, Geoffrey Fisher, who, preparing to sail home from the US in September 1952, told reporters, 'The world would have been a happier place if television had never been discovered.'[43]

The undisclosed reason for the Commission's decision was the Queen's reluctance to be televised. There were no cameras in the Abbey at her wedding in 1947, she refused to let her Christmas broadcast be filmed and she had asked the BBC not to let cameras settle on her face during Horse Guards Parade or Trooping the Colour. A number of grey eminences, notably Lord Swinton, a veteran in Churchill's cabinet, succeeded in persuading her, and in October, the Commission decided that cameras would be allowed beyond the screen, as long as there were 'no close-ups'. There was a rumour that the Queen's grandmother, Queen Mary, had been decisive in allowing television into the Abbey because she would be too ill to attend in person. But the rumour was untrue – and irrelevant because, three months before the coronation was broadcast on television, she died.[44]

The news that the coronation would be fully televised increased the pressure to make television truly national. Worried about a resurgent Germany and the onset of the Cold War, in 1951 the government had diverted money into rearmament and indefinitely postponed the building of more transmitters. In the north-east, miners' lodges passed resolutions against the region's continuing televisual deprivation, and Whitley Bay council lobbied the government on behalf of the 3 million people cut off by the Pennines from the Holme Moss signal. In October 1952, the same month that the Coronation Commission reversed its decision, the Postmaster General announced that transmitters at Pontop Pike, a moorland peak in County Durham, and Glencairn Hill, in the Belfast hills overlooking the city, would be built after all, so that people in these areas could see the coronation. Opening on the same day, 1 May 1953, these one-kilowatt masts were makeshift, austerity affairs housed in old pre-war outside-broadcast vans, with none of the soaring grandeur of Sutton Coldfield or Holme Moss. On each hilltop, a skeleton staff of eight engineers lived in a rudimentary wooden hut with an Elsan chemical toilet.

The Belfast signal had to be routed through Kirk O'Shotts, across seventy miles of Scottish hills and thirty miles of sea, and by the time it was scattered over the rooftops of the six counties to about 900 TV aerials, the results were mixed. Belfast and the flat country surrounding the city got a passable reception, but beyond it there were only fading pictures and the sound arriving in whispers. In this poorest part of the kingdom there was little clamour for television, but Ulster Unionists welcomed it as a sign that Northern Ireland was fully part of the UK, while Irish Nationalists were deeply suspicious not only of the coronation but of the anglicising influence of BBC television. Thomas Henderson, MP for the Shankill, said that 'all creeds and classes not only in Northern Ireland but throughout the great British Commonwealth of Nations' were looking forward to the coronation 'with pleasure and joy'. The existence of a Royal Ulster Constabulary armed guard, stationed at the transmitter, suggested otherwise.[45]

Many who had rented or bought televisions especially for the coronation had them installed in time for the FA Cup Final, the first football game to reach a mass TV audience, and the first to be postponed until the end of the football league so that people watching it on television would not affect attendance at other games. One BBC executive commented that the main worry in the north-east was 'not whether the transmitter will be radiating in time for the coronation, but whether it will be working in time for them to see the Cup Final'.[46] The twenty-year-old John Moynihan, later a football writer, was invited to an FA Cup Final tea party at a mansion block in St John's Wood to watch on a set owned by his friend's father, a Jewish antique dealer. The roar that greeted the teams, he wrote, 'resounded out of every crack of Mr H's set' and 'the ball made a tump thumping sound in the television like firm punching in a boxing ring'.

The game was dull but with a thrilling ending: Blackpool, 1–3 down to Bolton with twenty-two minutes left, managed to win 4–3 with two goals set up by the 38-year-old wizard of dribble, Stanley Matthews, whom most of the 10 million viewers were seeing for the first time, and who turned most neutrals into Blackpool fans. As he started to run the game, Moynihan wrote, 'the pitch even on that small set seemed to push Matthews towards us and out into the room so that tiny, weaving figure was now the prince of the earth'. Blackpool's winning goal in the dying moments saw the living room come to life as 'men seized cushions and hugged them to their bellies ... The room was electric, the television screen swarming with Blackpool players hugging and embracing and we were hugging and embracing.'[47] It was already clear that televised football could rouse the most passive viewer in a way that a royal event never could. The mass viewing of the 'Matthews final' was a watershed in the acceptance of the FA Cup Final as the key English national sporting ritual. Comparing it with the Lord's Test on the same day, where England's batsmen had struggled, the great cricket writer Neville Cardus wondered if the 'drama and heroism' of the final was indicative of football replacing cricket as the 'game of the people'.[48]

In the days leading up to the coronation, viewers adjusted their sets while picking up the build-up programmes. On *About the Home*, the television chef Marguerite Patten told them how to pre-prepare melon cocktails and salmon mousse to eat in front of the television. Two Metropolitan police officers gave advice to viewers on preventing house burglars on coronation day, and how to behave along the coronation route. On coronation eve, cameras on the Mall showed the already continuous line of pavement occupants and occasional tree dwellers preparing to spend the night in the rain. The BBC's Barrie Edgar talked to some of them, including a Swiss mountain guide and a family who had sailed all the way from Australia in a ketch. It was perhaps the first attempt at manufacturing atmosphere through a new genre, the vox pop, which Nick Clarke would later call 'one of the most artificial kinds of broadcasting ever devised'.[49]

On Tuesday 2 June, BBC television opened earlier than ever, at 9.15 a.m., with the test card, to allow people to tweak their aerials. A million and a half people were gathering in public places, such as town hall ballrooms, hospitals and parish churches, which had all been granted a special collective licence to watch television. In London's Royal Festival Hall, 3,000 holders of tickets, which had sold out within fifty-four minutes of going on sale in April, arrived at 10 a.m. and collected a packed lunch at the doors. The same number filled the Odeon at Leicester Square. Butlin's holiday campers in resorts like Filey, Skegness and Clacton watched on big screens. In clubs along the Mall like the Reform and White's, members watched in darkened rooms where they could also look through the windows at the curtained grandstands to see the procession in real life. A reporter present in one of these clubs wrote that 'the experience seemed to break down some stubborn middle-class prejudices against television'.[50]

Some 20.4 million people watched at least half an hour of the service, nearly double the radio audience, with almost as many watching the processions. Since there were only 2.7 million television sets, that meant an average of seven and a half people to a set, excluding children, who were not counted in the stats. A Mass Observation researcher on the London Underground noticed how every family party was 'carrying bags with food or bottles. And those with just bottles grinned at each other in an understanding sort of way. They were obviously all people going to TV parties.' Bradford in the early morning, according to another Mass Observer, was 'full of people crossing the city, with baskets of provisions and thermos flasks ... half Bradford seemed to be off early to a television party with the other half'. Viewing parties had their own etiquette. Best clothes were the norm, with children sporting coronation favours and carrying their own cushions, and guests arriving with a small gift. The *Daily Herald*'s doctor advised that the set should be on the floor, resting on books, for 'the best way to strain your eyes and get a first-class headache is by looking upwards'.[51] Living rooms across Britain soon gave off a heady mixed scent of flowers, furniture polish and sweat.

We do not know how many viewers followed the pious instructions of newspapers that they add their own 'Amens' to the prayers and stand and repeat the cry 'Vivat Regina!' along with the Abbey congregation. Mass Observation's investigators discovered that a reverent silence was certainly not being observed in front of all TV sets. Among the working classes, who tended to be neither strong royalists nor resentful republicans, comments were jocular. 'Look at the Queen. She's like a plum pudding by now, they've put so many dresses on her,' said a young woman in an ice-cream parlour in a poor area of London where television and free ice cream for children were provided. 'I bet they've doped him with bromide,' said the hostess in a house in Finsbury Drive, Bradford, when the camera rested on Prince Charles in the gallery, with his hair neatly plastered down.[52]

Among the VIP-only audience at the Gaumont cinema, Manchester, there was the odd burst of applause for the Queen and Winston Churchill, combined with much shuffling, chatting and fidgeting. Nineteen-year-old Alan Bennett, on leave from his national service, watched at a friend's house. 'As so often with the central rituals of English life, I was in two minds about it,' he said later. 'Yes the pageantry was moving, the music thrilling, but I was a soldier. I knew there was no pageantry without a great deal of bulling.' Bennett could already do an impression of Geoffrey Fisher who, despite his fears about television, seemed to be enjoying himself at the ceremony with his resonant recitations, and whom Bennett thought emblematic of that yet unnamed thing, the Establishment: 'Not a whiff of doubt ... that mixture of hypocrisy and self-assurance that will always get you to the top in English public life.'[53]

Mass Observation asked children to keep diaries before and after the coronation. Almost all watched the TV, often at aunties' or grandparents' houses, many making journeys of fifty or sixty miles in cars and on public transport to do so. Some were confused by what they saw – one thought the Queen was being crowned by Winston Churchill – and others were disappointed that it was not in colour, perhaps because they had heard so much beforehand about the Queen's golden coach and her red velvet train. There were some non-viewers. 'I hope that someone will at least be kind enough to let me have a short look at their Television Set,' wrote eleven-year-old Peter Johnson, deject-edly. 'Our next door neighbour has a Television Set but all I have seen of it is the aerial.'[54]

Many adults seemed unimpressed with the padding surrounding the ceremony. One Mass Observer pronounced himself 'bored by the crowd reportage and lame bits of interviewing, and the three night-mare New Zealanders who the commentator seemed unable to get rid of'. Four other Mass Observers said they found the procession 'boring'; another fell asleep during it. After the event, 109 viewers were asked what they thought was the day's most inspiring moment. The crowning came second with eleven votes, seven behind that day's news of the conquest of Everest, a moment unrecorded by television.[55]

Over 20 million viewers still left many people unaccounted for. 'I did not fancy accepting any of the numerous invitations to TV as I regard it as a very inferior cinema and I felt the conversation would be inane,' wrote one Mass Observation diarist. While this television agnostic actually ended up watching briefly at a friend's house, another went walking on Dartmoor, 'determined to avoid at all costs any news and activity connected with the Coronation'. Another arranged an anti-coronation party at which 'republican songs were sung, the Queen symbolically executed and various anti-royalist parlour games played'. A student who tried to avoid the coronation by cycling through Sussex country lanes kept being reminded of it by the deserted villages, with bursts of noise coming from houses with television aerials and the curtains drawn. Joan Bakewell did not bother to watch with her fellow students on a TV set newly acquired by Newnham College, Cambridge, and she noted later that she had made no reference to the coronation in her diary for that day: 'So much for all that fanciful talk about new Elizabethans.'[56]

Among those who watched it, though, there were some converts among the quasi-republicans. At 6 p.m. in Finsbury Drive, Bradford, the Mass Observation investigator dispatched someone to buy a bottle of Dry Fly sherry, and they all toasted the Queen, with remarks along the lines of: 'Who could have thought that we would all have turned such Royalists?' There was high praise for the BBC and the medium of television itself. Huw Wheldon, then BBC Television's Publicity Officer, gave out audience reaction figures: ninety-eight per cent said they had enjoyed the broadcast 'very much'. When a *Daily Express* reporter wondered what the recalcitrant had objected to, Wheldon replied, 'If Our Lord came back to earth two per cent of the people would complain, "There He goes again, always walking on the water".'[57] Many praised Richard Dimbleby's softly sonorous commentary, so expertly woven in between the Archbishop's words and the blasts of trumpets that it was as though he were conducting the ceremony himself.

Viewers also commended the BBC on the quality of the pictures, for the newer television sets no longer had those curved screens like cod's eyes which warped the image when viewed at an angle. TV cameras now had derivative equalisers which eliminated distortion, and there were none of the blank screens and juddering images which used to occur when switching from one camera to another. The new zoom lenses allowed cameras to move in smoothly and, as Queen Elizabeth walked down the aisle, her face grew bigger in the frame as the ill-defined rule about close-ups was disregarded. The popular historian and eager monarchist Arthur Bryant reflected that television was best when the actors were unconscious of it, thus avoiding 'that note of forced insincerity which, as in early Victorian photographic groups, is its besetting fault as an artistic medium'. By these lights the Queen was a TV natural, with 'the same unchallengeable ascendancy over the eye and mind of the watcher that Charlie Chaplin had on the cinema screen'.[58]

At 5.20 p.m., after the Queen's last appearance on the Buckingham Palace balcony, twenty-six per cent of the adult population carried on watching the children's programmes and about the same number stayed for the rest of the evening until, at 11.30 p.m., Richard Dimbleby delivered an unannounced, impromptu sermon, summing up the day from an empty, silent Westminster Abbey – 'an epilogue sublime, touching and human as had been the great day itself', according to the *Television Annual for 1954*.[59]

Many viewers must still have been watching this late because traffic was slack until midnight, when a rush of people returned home from their television parties and the last trams and buses were full. For the first time in British history, television had emptied streets and becalmed the nation. Thousands of viewers sent congratulations to the BBC or the *Radio Times*. 'Praise may seem paltry and congratulations colourless but we must try to express our overwhelming gratitude,' wrote Donald Davey of Uppermoor Pudsey. 'To all who brought us such joy we can but say thank you, and again, thank you.' In many parts of the provinces and regions, though, the feeling that the coronation was a London affair persisted until the day itself, 'and even this was not entirely broken down by the chance to participate offered by the television'.[60]

People who rented sets just for the coronation usually held on to them, and the normal summer slump in television sales failed to materialise. By autumn, manufacturers were able to lower production costs and reduce prices. The TV screens at the Earls Court radio show in August had increased in average size from twelve to seventeen inches: no longer would anyone complain about the picture being too small. When the Christmas trade in 1953 broke all records for furniture and electrical goods, retailers speculated that this was due to 'the stay-at-home propensities induced by television' and 'the television party ... fostering a new pride in the home'.[61]

The post-coronation television boom coincided happily with the end of rationing. The easing of restrictions on hire purchase in July 1954 was probably more important than the coronation in turning television into a mass medium, for people could now walk into a shop and buy a £60 TV for £6 down, or sometimes no deposit at all, with the repayments spread over as long as the shopkeeper would allow. For those who could still not afford a set on the 'never never', pubs now had televisions. A glossy new publication, *TV Mirror*, featured a 200-year-old inn in south London which advertised 'Good Beer and

Television Nightly' and photographed a woman wearing field glasses so she could see the screen more clearly.[62]

The rural writer and conservationist John Moore, living on the rustic borders of Gloucestershire and Worcestershire, noted that three out of five cottages in his nearest village, Bredon, now had an aerial on the roof. He had overheard farmers and labourers talking about Margot Fonteyn and Shakespeare, after switching on for the boxing and variety shows and finding these programmes by accident. 'Whereas the countryman always regarded sound radio with a faint awe, he accepts television as a commonplace,' reflected Moore after watching the coronation in his local, the Fox and Hound. 'Standing there in the bar – and yet standing, it seemed, within a few feet of the altar in Westminster Abbey – we accepted that sheer magic of the business without turning a hair.' Watching the majestic occasion in this ordinary setting, though, Moore felt 'doubtful and afraid … it took a lot of foam-flecked horses, and a lot of bonfires, too, to bring to us the first tidings of Waterloo … The countryman is a country-man no longer. The TV camera has given him one of the dubious gifts which the Devil gave to Faust: the privilege of "looking in" at whatever he wanted to see. It didn't do much good to poor Faust.'[63]

The televising of the coronation heightened the sense of injustice in those towns and villages that still did not have television. Unlucky places like Southampton, Aberdeen and Plymouth had missed out because of the awkward shape of the island, and its fractal coast-line, which the TV signal strained to reach. Brighton had managed to acquire a signal, just in time, from a temporary mast mounted in an old wartime trailer, hastily resprayed BBC green to conceal the military camouflage, high up on the South Downs at Truleigh Hill on the site of an old radar station. There was much muttering among its coastal cousins about how exactly the well-connected 'London by the Sea' had managed to acquire pictures while they remained televisionless.

Another area of contention was Cornwall, which generated the first major opposition to the building of a television mast. The BBC insisted that Hessary Tor, a 1,650-foot summit overlooking Prince-town and Dartmoor Prison in the middle of Dartmoor National Park, was the only available site from which television could be transmitted over the peaks and troughs of Devon's moorland to Cornwall. At the public inquiry, the inventor of radar, Robert Watson-Watt, said that the shape of Dartmoor made it 'a holidaymaker's paradise but a television engineer's purgatory'. The Dartmoor Preservation Association contended that the mast's alien presence would be 'a perpetual reminder of that modern "civilisation" which most people come to a national park to forget' and that it would not even guarantee a reception for the peninsula's western extremities, so towns like Truro, St Ives and Penzance would be 'bereft of this latest benefit to humanity'. Although the Hessary Tor mast was not completed until 1955, Mrs Sylvia Sayer, the DPA's chairman, complained that the BBC was cashing in on 'Coronation TV hysteria', a clamour raised 'by those who would quite willingly sacrifice Her Majesty's personal feelings to make a TV holiday'.[64]

Questions in parliament from MPs about the absence of television in their constituencies became more insistent. A rumour spread among Welsh television owners that Wenvoe was not transmitting on full power, but had been in the days before the coronation to trick the Welsh into buying sets. 'We cannot ask any friends or children in to view because of poor reception,' complained Mrs Aimee Havard from Abergwili, 'and we have felt so mean over Christmas, but I could not risk disappointing the children.'[65] Viewers in the long, narrow south Wales valleys found the hills disagreeable to viewing. In mining communities, terraced rows were often built along the valley sides in a hand-and-fingers pattern, and the TV signal found these houses especially hard to reach.

On the Isle of Man, whose uncertain status as a crown dependency nurtured a strong patriotism among its citizens, the council was unwilling to pay for a booster mast for the coronation and also forbade council tenants from putting aerials on their roofs, even evicting one tenant, Norman Clarke, who erected one in his garden. After an enterprising radio dealer had built an unofficial transmitter on Douglas Head, just in time for the island's loyal subjects to watch on 2 June, the Home Office demanded that this unauthorised mast be shut down after the coronation, while in return moving the island to the top of the waiting list. But siting a transmitter on this island of hills bisected by a central valley was difficult. After several failed attempts, the BBC engineers rented a room in a farmhouse on Carnane, the hill overlooking Douglas, and poked a mast out of it. Television officially arrived on the island in time for *Television's Christmas Party*, with Norman Wisdom, Max Bygraves and the Beverley Sisters. Reception was terrible, particularly in the south of the island, where the new mast was worse than the pirate mast. 'Perhaps, again, we should be patient and give the BBC engineers a chance,' the *Isle of Man Examiner* said, 'but their apology to the dealers and potential viewers in the South is poor compensation to both when sums up to a hundred guineas have changed hands for a useless piece of machinery.'[66] Six years earlier, television had been barely missed when it was cancelled for weeks. Now those who could not receive it felt cheated of citizenship.

In other ways, though, little had changed. Viewers may have outnumbered listeners for the coronation, but British radio was enjoying a golden period. The number of sound only licences remained double that of TV licences, and the *Radio Times* still printed the TV schedules, as an addendum, at the back. The most popular radio shows, like *The Archers* and *Mrs Dale's Diary*, inspired intense loyalty and the anarchic creativity of *The Goon Show*, which relied on painting surreal pictures in the listener's mind, had no televisual rival.

In Scotland and Northern Ireland, where incomes were lower than average and the coverage of the transmitter erratic, television would not eclipse radio until well into the 1960s. While television was mostly relayed from London, the Home Service still had a strong regional component. The Scottish Home Service had already moved its popular programmes into the early evening as part of its 'high tea' strategy, devised after the war to fend off the new Light Programme. The routine in most working-class Scottish homes was to have a main meal at lunchtime and a light evening meal called high tea at around

6.30 p.m., with the radio on in the background broadcasting Scottish dance music, comedy or the hugely popular soap opera about a working-class Glaswegian family, *The McFlannels*. By 7 p.m. the family was settled in front of the fire for the rest of the evening, and many quite highbrow programmes, broadcast later on, got huge listenerships.[67] This strategy had worked against the Light Programme and now, since evening television did not start until around 7.30 p.m., it had great success against TV.

The McCooeys, a radio soap about a Belfast working-class family that ran until 1957, was the most popular programme ever broadcast in Northern Ireland, in any medium, its catchphrases – 'You're a comeejan', 'shloup with vegabittles' – repeated throughout the province. Here there might be one television set per street or neighbourhood. After they won the League in 1954, Wolverhampton Wanderers played a series of televised friendlies with sides like Moscow Spartak and Moscow Dynamo. At his home in Belfast, eight-year-old George Best would boot a ball repeatedly against the wall outside the house of a neighbour, Mr Harrison, about ten minutes before kick-off to persuade him to let him in to watch his TV set, the only one in the vicinity. Wolves' ground, Molineux, was the first to install the floodlighting that made it possible to televise night games, and, Best wrote later, 'it was the floodlights which made them magical for me, made football into theatre'.[68] For the rest of the decade, television in Northern Ireland tended to be watched communally and remained an occasional indulgence reserved for special occasions like football matches.

Ten-year-old Philip Norman, living in Ryde on the Isle of Wight, also inhabited this world where radio and older entertainments still prevailed, although later, in his memoir *Babycham Night*, he probably overestimated television's primitiveness. At the time of the coronation, he claimed, 'only a few thousand people in the whole country owned television sets' and 'unless you lived within a couple of miles of the BBC's London transmitter, reception tended to be poor'. Soon after the coronation, Philip's parents acquired a television and he would lie on the Chesterfield sofa with the curtains drawn and watch 'all of what little was on – Test cricket, Russian ballet ... I knew every note of the long drawn-out overture played as a sound track to the test card before transmission began.' Beside him in the gloom sat Mrs Kennie, the Scottish home help deputed to keep him company, clicking her knitting needles and judging every programme 'verra gude'. But on the Isle of Wight, at least until the Rowridge transmitter opened in November 1954, 'the picture would collapse sideways into horizontal black and grey stripes, or flick downward in individual squares like frames of film'.[69]

One place in Ryde, jutting half a mile out to sea and back towards England, got better reception. Philip's father, who ran the Seagull Ballroom on the pier, domesticated their room there with two easy chairs, a one-bar electric fire and a Cossor television, and here they watched the American comedy shows the BBC had begun showing, like *Amos'n'Andy* and *The Burns and Allen Show*. Even here, though, the dit-das of Morse code messages from passing ships kept breaking up the picture.[70] In the hard-to-reach inlets of the British coast, those struggling to get a reception must have felt they were being offered a tantalisingly patchy glimpse of the future.

If it did not have as radical an effect on the nation's viewing habits as is often supposed, the coronation does seem to have had a profound impact on the monarchy's attitudes to television. The Queen, newly returned from a tour of the Commonwealth on 15 May 1954, even delayed appearing on the Buckingham Palace balcony until she had finished watching Gracie Fields in the BBC's *Welcome Home Ball*. When ITV arrived in London in September 1955, she and Prince Philip made sure the Buckingham Palace sets were converted ready for when they returned from Balmoral. All the Queen's residences were exempt from TV licensing laws; by 1960 there were fifty sets in Buckingham Palace alone.[71] By the late 1960s the Queen was reported to be a fan of *Dad's Army*, *Morecambe and Wise* and the wrestling on *World of Sport* – as was Prince Philip, who especially admired

Johnny Kwango's signature move, the flying headbutt. In Richard Cawston's film *The Royal Family*, shown by the BBC and ITV on two separate nights in one of the televisual events of 1969, viewers saw the Queen washing up, feeding carrots to her Trooping the Colour horse, announcing 'the salad is ready' at a Balmoral barbecue, with Princess Anne on the sausages and Prince Philip on the steaks, and watching television with her family. The royals had inadvertently invented a new genre: the 'fly-on-the-wall' documentary.

A week after *The Royal Family*, all three channels showed the investiture of the Prince of Wales. The coronation had been an event filmed by television, with much agonising over what could be shown; the investiture was a televised event, conceived so that everything could be seen from all angles by TV cameras without the cameras being visible. Lord Snowdon's stage set at Caernarfon Castle – carefully antiquated coats of arms made of expanded polystyrene, and a central dais designed like an Agincourt tent with a see-through canopy, 'just like Henry V would have done it, if he'd had Perspex'[72] – was mock medievalism made for colour TV. Caernarfon residents had been given free paint to do up their house fronts in architect-approved colours – pink, green and cream – to look good on television.

Unlike the coronation, the investiture was watched by most viewers in their own homes, although the few who owned colour sets did invite neighbours in to watch on BBC2. The estimate that Caernarfon would have its population swollen to 250,000 proved to be wildly optimistic. Police outnumbered spectators on the processional route and the misnamed crowd control barriers restrained only scattered groups of people. Like a party host trying to convince guests that everything was going well, the BBC commentator, Richard Baker, pointed out that 'everyone is inside, watching television, where they can get a more comprehensive view of what is going on'. The events of 2 June 1953 may not have turned the nation instantly into a community of viewers, but within half a generation most people were sitting indoors in front of the TV.

4

THE PALE FLICKER OF THE LIME GROVE LIGHT

I peer into my magic mirror like a fourteen-stone cigar-smoking Lady of Shalott ... I have already passed uncounted hours half-hypnotised by the jiggling and noisy images ... [Television] does not seem to bring the outside world closer to me but pushes it further away ... I feel I am taking a series of peeps, perhaps from the darkened smoke room of a giant spaceship, at another planet, with whose noisy affairs I am not involved at all.

J. B. Priestley[1]

In July 1951, Gilbert Harding began chairing a new TV quiz show, *What's My Line?*, in which panellists had to guess what members of the public did for a living. It did not go well. He mistook a male nurse for a panel beater and kept interrupting him to say his answers were wrong. When the nurse revealed his mistake, Harding told viewers, 'This is the last time I ever appear on television.' But he reappeared as a panellist on the show a few weeks later and seemed no happier, telling one equivocal contestant, 'I'm tired of looking at you.' A viewer complained: 'I felt like walking out of my own drawing room.'[2] There was talk of scrapping the programme, not because Harding was rude but because it was as dreary as he had feared it might be.

Gradually, though, viewers were drawn into the panel's attempts to identify jelly baby varnishers and pepper pot perforators. By the end of the year it was the most popular show on television. *What's My Line?*, the *Glasgow Herald* assured its readers before the opening of Kirk O'Shotts, 'is good fun, and when the challenger happens to be a saggar maker's bottom knocker, can be hilarious'. One panellist, Lady Isobel Barnett, was sent paintings and needlework portraits of her face, modelled from the TV screen by viewers. Newspapers ran on their front pages the story that another panellist, Barbara Kelly, had dropped an earring under her chair. But Harding was the main attraction and he inspired that odd mixture of veneration, resentment and illusory intimacy that we now associate with celebrity, a phenomenon wrongly thought modern. 'Right, I've seen Gilbert Harding now,' said one man loudly as he passed him in the street. 'You can take him out and shoot him.'[3]

Often he appeared drunk, for which occasions the BBC coined the phrase, 'Mr Harding was overcome by the heat from the studio lights.' But he really was troubled by the hot arc lights, and would often remove his jacket on screen. In December 1952, he appeared in the middle of the Great Smog, the worst of London's pea soupers. Showing the panache for penitence that endeared him to viewers, he telephoned the Press Association later that evening stating that his behaviour was caused by 'asthma aided by fog – I may have over-fortified myself against it … viewers were not wrong in thinking I was a bit tiddly'.[4] Well-wishers sent in cough mixtures and bronchial cures. But a few weeks later, with no London smog to exonerate him, he upset people again by being rude to the ventriloquist's dummy, Archie Andrews.

Many watched the programme hoping Harding would be rude. A friend told him he imagined *What's My Line?* as a bullfight, with Harding as the bull, the challengers as the picadors and the host Eamonn Andrews, awarding points against him, as the matador. While demurring, Harding conceded that he did detect 'the elemental odours of the bull ring – and of the bear pit – in what is supposed to be a mild Sunday evening's amusement'.[5] Hilde Himmelweit, a social psychologist and director of a four-year Nuffield Foundation research project on children and television, argued that TV offered 'the appeal of infringed conventions' in a way that was safely enjoyable because it was vicarious and contained elements of roleplay and pretence. She found that children, perhaps unfamiliar with this wish-fulfilling aspect of the medium, were left uneasy and anxious by Harding. Joan, herself 'a rather aggressive child', said, 'He's just horrible. I don't like him. Everybody claps when he comes on, but I think he's absolutely disgusting. He's absolutely born to disgust me. I hate him.'[6]

The rising levels of rudeness were a familiar postwar anxiety. Since the late 1940s, commentators had been noting the increasing incivility of the working classes, particularly ex-servicemen who seemed reluctant to return to pre-war standards of deference. The writer J. L. Hodson called it 'a mild revolt against society'. As Ross McKibbin has argued of this period, the middle classes valued apolitical qualities such as niceness, humour and 'not making a scene', which they used implicitly to contrast themselves with the bolshy working classes.[7] Although he had the look of a reactionary old colonel, it was clear which side Harding was on: he disliked genteel obfuscation and had a column in the *People* campaigning forcefully on behalf of victims of rapacious landlords, bad service or poor food.

'My favourite TV star is Gilbert Harding,' wrote Mrs R. B. Dring from Spalding, Lincolnshire in a letter to *TV Mirror*. 'Why? Because he is all the things I am not. I am a mouse. I eat badly cooked food in an hotel without a word of complaint … Oh! To demand good food for my good money! To tear off a strip to someone who annoys me. To say "shut up" to people whose idle chatter bores me. To refuse a cracked cup and to be grumpy when I feel grumpy.' Harding's rudeness spoke to a vague impatience that postwar life had not lived up to the wartime promise of a better, fairer society to come. The Oxford historian A. J. P. Taylor, himself a combative performer soon to be nicknamed the 'sulky Don' after an appearance on the TV discussion programme *In the News*, defended Harding in a *Daily Herald* column titled 'Let's be rude!' 'I have no sympathy with those amateur schoolmarms who sit over their television sets, waiting for something that offends them,' he wrote. Harding was 'a symbol of protest against the soft good-taste that surrounds us at every turn', and what people called rudeness was really 'pulling down the curtains of pretence that keep out the noises of the world'.[8]

But Harding's ill temper had another source closer to home: his discomfort with television as a medium. A Cambridge graduate with abortive careers as a teacher, barrister and *Times* journalist behind him, he was frustrated, among other things, by what he felt to be the waste of his talents in his new career as a 'tele-phoney'. In his *People* column, he pronounced himself mortified at being pointed out on a Tube train while T. S. Eliot was ignored, no doubt happily so, in the same carriage. 'Do you think that I planned and plotted, or lost a wink of sleep, scheming to spend a considerable part of my life trying to identify hog-slappers, cheese-winders' clerks, or theatre fireman's night companions?' he asked. He had better things to be doing, and so, he implied, did his viewers. This attitude was quite common. After becoming famous for appearing on *What's My Line?*, the actor Robert Morley fretted that it was 'all too easy, the values are all wrong'. The writer and journalist Marghanita Laski also suffered guilt pangs when, after being on the panel, she was sent butter and apples through the post and offered nylons under the counter, all 'for a parlour game I wouldn't even have played at home'.[9] Both relented, Laski returning to the screen as *Panorama*'s book reviewer and Morley going on briefly to host *Sunday Night at the London Palladium*.

Harding's solution to the trivial inconsequence of *What's My Line?* was more eccentric: he over-invested it with seriousness and meaning. He disliked the way that women preened themselves before coming on the show, so they all looked alike and he could not tell the black pudding stringers from the knitting needle knobbers; and he resented the diploma that challengers were given to say they had beaten the panel, because he thought it encouraged oblique and evasive replies to his questions. The public fascination with *What's My Line?* bemused him and he hoped one day he 'might be able to watch the programme, and try to find out for myself what it is that makes it so popular'.[10] He could not, of course, watch himself, because almost all television at the time was broadcast live, a fact which perhaps displeased him as much as its phoniness. He reserved his greatest praise for those whose achievements had a more enduring memorial than the fast and fleeting fame of the new media age. His Christmas radio broadcast in 1953, in which he quoted Macaulay's description of the Puritans ('Their palaces were houses not made with hands: their diadems crowns of glory which should never fade away') moved many listeners to tears. He seemed uniquely unsuited to an evanescent medium which simply died on the evening air.

'Why, at this stage of progress,' asked Harding in January 1954, 'should we need to have these seemingly interminable intervals of 8–10 minutes, watching the tide coming in, or two palm trees waving to us from the beach?'[11] These were the BBC interludes, a stock of ambient films put into service when there was an underrun or one of the still recurrent technical breakdowns. Their purpose was to rationalise and anonymise the stop-start interruptions that had bedevilled the viewing experience since the war. At first, announcers would bustle into camera position and announce an emergency musical interval accompanied by a caption reading 'Please do not adjust your set'. Then there was a gramophone record of whichever announcer was on duty ('We apologise for the fault …') with the needle always poised at the right point so it could be deployed as needed. The interludes, introduced in February 1952 with a film of vespers music at St Benedict's School, Ealing, automated this process still further. Apart from the Jamaican beach mentioned by Harding, and a few films of Scottish lochs and rivers, they were mostly versions of southern English pastoral. A team of horse-drawn ploughs gradually worked their way across a field in Tillingham, Essex. A windmill's sails slowly turned over some harvested wheat in Pakenham, Suffolk. A boat made a leisurely trip down the Thames near Maidenhead.

The interlude most notorious for its hypnoidal qualities was the potter's wheel, in which a potter's hands worked away perpetually at a ball of clay that seemed at times to be tantalisingly metamorphosing into a bowl, or a high-sided pot, but was never, ever finished. The interludes were meant to be storyless and circular like this, because they could be pulled at any time and the viewers returned to the programme. Their accompaniment was the kind of light music, with its origins in seaside and palm court orchestras – short divertimenti, with swooshing harps, trilling flutes and cascading violins – that was the BBC's background noise well into the rock'n'roll era. As much as the potter's wheel itself, this music, by composers like Charles Williams, Haydn Wood and Leslie Bridgewater, evokes television's ambience in the Edwardian summer before ITV. 'The BBC had things all its own way and in the early years of the fifties it reflected life in Britain accurately enough: well mannered, class-ridden, deferential and exceedingly dull,' writes the broadcaster John Humphrys in his autobiography, précising this established view. 'Heaven help us, but we really did sit for what seemed like hours between programmes watching a pair of hands moulding a chunk of wet clay.'[12]

Harding's writings as television critic for *Picture Post* offer some corroboration of this retrospective judgement on his own era. He especially disliked the raft of shows, spawned by the success of *What's My Line?*, in which dinner-jacketed men and evening-gowned women played parlour games with challengers, guessing which famous relatives they had or why they had been in the news. 'Static, sedate, sedentary and verbose,' Harding judged them. 'The people we are expected to sit and listen and look at would hardly be called attractive, even by their mothers.' At a public Brains Trust held in Liverpool, Harding heard several in the audience say they had either returned or sold their TV sets because there was nothing on them worth watching. One elderly lady, no longer able to walk, had banished her set from her room except for *What's My Line?*.[13]

But Harding was torn about television. He could find it suffocatingly formal, as for instance while watching the imperious Douglas Craig presenting *Opera for Everybody*, when he felt as though he ought to raise his hand and ask to leave the room. But he could also find it overly familiar, complaining of the ugly, cloying habit of using Christian names, which he thought 'almost as bad as the "Good evenings" in *What's My Line?*'. At a time when many work colleagues still addressed each other as Mr and Mrs, this was a frequent complaint. A newspaper leader criticised 'this quite unnecessary air of intimacy on the part of people who may have never set eyes on each other before'. Evelyn Waugh refused all requests for television interviews because of 'the bandying about of Christian names and so forth, of the kind which deeply shocks me in some of the performances I have sometimes begun to hear'.[14] These people worried not about the boring interludes, but, as people have always done, about television propelling its viewers too quickly into an unfamiliar future.

Television, in this supposedly soporific era before the arrival of ITV, was probably not as dull as it is remembered. The BBC was, for instance, beginning to create fresh forms of television comedy suitable for both northerners and southerners, who had such different tastes in the pre-television era that variety producers ran separate shows for different ends of the country. 'Before television,' the comedian Reg Varney recalled, 'if you went up north and they suspected you were a cockney they did *not* want to know.' The comedian most successfully bridging this divide was Southampton's Benny Hill. In 1951, after being slow handclapped at the Sunderland Empire – which had a daunting reputation among southern comedians, because the audience, many of whom were from the shipyards, would throw washers at acts they didn't like – he came off stage and was sick in the dressing-room sink. A few weeks later, Hill had a triumphant debut on television. His habit of underplaying, which was swallowed up on the big stages, was ideal for the small screen. In 1953 he rented his first TV and watched it constantly at home in Kilburn, absorbing every detail.[15] He began to fashion a definitively televisual comedy, doing impressions of Philip Harben and a famous take-off of *What's My*

Line? in which he impersonated all the panellists, including Harding, using rapid camera cutaways.

The *Charlie Chester Show* brought the American-style 'giveaway' quiz to British television before ITV did, although the modest prizes – such as nylon tights, a razor blade or a packet of crisps – reflected a residual asceticism. Another well-loved programme was *Ask Pickles*, in which Wilfred Pickles and his wife Mabel made viewers' dreams come true by, for instance, allowing them to meet a tame kangaroo or play a Stradivarius. *Ask Pickles* viewers were clearly fascinated by television, for the most common request was to be able to see how a programme was made. George Aubertin of Compton Potters' Arts Guild, a William Morris-inspired artists' collective in Surrey, appeared on the show as the owner of the hands in the potter's wheel interlude. Aubertin explained anticlimactically that he wasn't making anything in particular, just doodling away as he had been asked to do.[16]

Children especially loved *Ask Pickles*, although according to the Nuffield television inquiry, these 'comprised mainly duller children from secondary modern schools', and 'being duller they were also the most gullible and the most cliché-ridden'. The universal favourite with all children, irrespective of their dullness, was *Fabian of the Yard*, based on the real-life exploits of Detective Inspector Robert Fabian, played by Bruce Seton, who would scream round the London streets in a Humber Hawk squad car solving grisly murders, a year before PC Dixon began plodding round Dock Green. Even Gilbert Harding praised the inventiveness of children's television. 'I miss Mr Turnip so much,' he confessed to *Picture Post* readers after the bad-tempered string puppet from the Saturday afternoon show *Whirligig* was retired. 'Some of the B.B.C.'s programmes for children are absolutely enchanting,' Lord Hailsham told parliament. '*Andy Pandy*, for instance, at four o'clock in the afternoon.' At Manchester University, its official historians note, women students could be found knitting while watching *Andy Pandy* in their union lounge.[17]

Just as they secretly liked watching Harding explode, viewers seemed to welcome a mild subversiveness elsewhere. The most popular character in The Grove Family, an otherwise pedestrian soap opera about a north London builder and his family interspersed with Archers-style homilies about how to buy a television licence or secure your windows against burglars, was the cantankerous ninety-year-old northerner Grandma Grove, a grown-up child whose catch-phrases were 'I'm faint from lack of nourishment' and 'I want me tea'. The Daily Mail's Peter Black saw the actress who played her, Nancy Roberts, waiting on a bench at London Airport for a plane, 'surrounded by curious and reverent fans'.[18]

On Thursday nights, a snatch of a Bach violin sonata and a box spinning on an electric Lazy Susan announced the start of Animal, Vegetable, Mineral? A panel of archaeologists, or sometimes art historians or anthropologists, tried to identify objects donated by a museum, with the chairman, Glyn Daniel of St John's College, Oxford, awarding points to either the panel or the museum. It had started in 1952 but only became a national craze, watched by over 5 million viewers, towards the end of 1953, when, according to Picture Post, the 89-year-old Egyptologist Dr Margaret Murray 'brought the house down when she successfully identified a nineteenth-century mid-European wicker bed-bug trap'. Remembered now for its Reith-ian earnestness, the programme actually had a fine sense of show-manship. A young production assistant, David Attenborough, visited the museums and developed a knack for selecting objects with narra-tive potential: a moustache-lifter made by the Hairy Ainu of Japan, a horse's knucklebones used as Roman dice, a crocheted mid-Victorian fly settle. The rakish archaeologist Mortimer Wheeler was the star. He would twiddle his moustache, pretend to be baffled and then iden-tify the object with a flourish, often claiming he was there when it was dug up. 'It is no good picking up something and saying "this is a Samoan cake mould" – viewers want to see how you arrived at your decision,' he said.[19]

Buried Treasure, in which Wheeler and Daniel explored ancient sites like Pompeii and Orkney's Skara Brae, got even higher viewing figures than Animal, Vegetable, Mineral? with a similarly winning mix of didacticism and diversion. Its first episode, in June 1954, 'The Peat

Bog Murder Mystery', about the discovery of the strangled Tollund Man by Danish peat cutters, ensured its immediate popularity. The programme began with Tollund Man's head revolving on a turntable to reveal a remarkably preserved, serene face. Back in the Lime Grove studios, the announcer Noëlle Middleton served Wheeler and Daniel a reconstruction, based on Tollund Man's stomach contents, of his last meal: a greyish, oily porridge made mainly of barley and linseed. After Wheeler concluded that Tollund Man 'probably committed suicide to escape his wife's cooking', an offended Dane wrote in insisting his ancestors would never have tolerated such food. This was probably Wheeler playing to the gallery again because, according to the producer Paul Johnstone, 'the actual taste, though unexciting, was quite reasonable ... The mash that many farm-horses are fed on is not very different.'[20]

Librarians reported that shelves on which archaeology books had sat neglected for years were suddenly empty, and museums noted an upsurge of interest in their collections. 'Especially for those of us who were in our fifth and sixth forms at the time, this was really the Golden Age of archaeology on television,' wrote the television producer Paul Jordan in 1981. 'It is not too much to say that these programmes created the classes of '59, '60 and '61 that have gone on to include some of our leading academic archaeologists and excavators.' Glyn Daniel was less certain of the value of television, being 'on the whole disappointed with its educative impact on the general public' and worried that it might have given an impetus to 'bullshit archaeology', the 'ley-hunters and the pyramidiots' who emerged with the 1960s counterculture and who found 'the signs of the zodiac in the quiet hedgerows of the English countryside'.[21]

David Attenborough went on, at the end of 1954, to present *Zoo Quest*, a programme with a similarly shrewd eye for what would entertain viewers. The mission to capture animals in west Africa for London zoo provided a strong narrative line, while studio scenes showed the captured animal in the kind of close-ups they were unable to get on location with the film and lenses then available. To persuade people to keep watching, Attenborough gave the series an objective, a rare animal to pursue: *picarthates gymnocephalus*, the bald-headed rock crow. He doubted this creature would be alluring enough, but when his cameraman Charles Lagus was driving him down Regent Street in an open-top sports car and a bus driver leaned out of his cab and asked him, in a neat piece of tmesis, if he was ever going to catch 'that *Picafartees gymno-bloody-cephalus*', he knew it had lodged itself in the public mind. The most memorable episode of *Zoo Quest* came at the end of the third series, in 1956, when Attenborough managed to trap a Komodo dragon, an antediluvian ten-foot lizard that many viewers had thought was mythical. 'We regard Attenborough as the finest type of young Englishman – unpretentious, humorous, resourceful and humane with his animals,' said a fitter and turner on the BBC's viewer panel. 'A grand boy! How well he tells his story too.'[22]

Another quasi-educative programme popular with viewers was *Television Dancing Club*, which began each week with Victor Silvester's ballroom orchestra playing the signature tune, 'You're dancing on my heart'. On this show, amateur dancers competed with each other, their efforts judged by postal vote, with about 8,000 viewers sending in postcards each week to Lime Grove, London W12. 'Don't just pick the best lookers,' Silvester cautioned viewers, '– the prettiest girl and the best looking man, but give your vote to the couple that you think show the best style, footwork, rhythm and movement.'

Over the fixed smiles of the dancers came the voice of the announcer Patti Morgan: 'Now, Doris's dress has gathered lace in the underskirt, and shot ribbon round the neck … Doris's father is a taxi-driver, and you would never guess that he spent the last week of his holidays helping her to sew on the sequins …' Since the late 1920s, Silvester had championed the modern English Style, with its strict tempo and firm policing of steps. This dance band culture was now under threat from an Americanised culture of star vocalists, dance crazes and hit records marketed through jukeboxes and radio disc jockeys. Still unsure about pop music, though, BBC television helped to prolong the era of the dance bands, giving airtime to band leaders like Geraldo, Ted Heath and Billy Cotton long after the rise of rock'n'roll. '*TV Dancing Club* has helped to bring back grace, elegance, beauty and style to dancing in this country,' wrote Douglas Brent in May 1954. It was the answer to 'a new horror that is seeping into the ballrooms of Britain, an ugly, dreary, lifeless way of dancing known as The Creep … Teenagers in exaggerated Edwardian clothes (The Teddie Boys and Girls) gyrate stiffly in monotonous procession.'[23]

Television Dancing Club included a short dancing lesson with Silvester and his partner Peggy Spencer explaining how to do the Turning Cross, the Side Hover or the Lock Step. Ballroom dancing was still beating broadcasting as the second largest entertainment industry after the cinema, and every local palais had a learner night. So we can assume that at least some viewers were carefully following Silvester's and Spencer's feet, although the size and picture quality of their TV screens must have made it difficult. Betty Maxwell and her husband Robert, a publisher and businessman, peered at their tiny television and tried to learn the steps. 'We would clear the furniture in the drawing room to one side and have such a lot of fun, trying to follow the instructions to the tunes of Silvester's orchestra,' Betty wrote later. 'We would inevitably collapse in laughter, and after most sessions would end up making love on the carpet.'[24]

Rather than boredom, the emotion most likely to be generated by the television set at this time was fear. On 14 December 1954, the *Daily Express* headline read, 'Wife dies as she watches.' Beryl Kathleen Mirfin, a forty-year-old mother of two, watching 'the TV horror play' on Sunday at home in Herne Bay, with her husband and two friends, had collapsed and died of a heart attack. When the doctor arrived, he asked, 'Was she watching the TV play?' The story was not quite as alarmist as the headline. Mrs Mirfin had died only about half an hour in, and the shocking scenes of Peter Cushing as Winston Smith lying in a makeshift coffin while receiving electric shocks did not come until the final half hour. 'My wife enjoyed TV,' said her estate agent husband. 'I don't think the play itself caused her collapse. She was mending a glove during the play and talking of making a trip to London today. She was not a nervous type of woman.'[25]

Even if it did not kill Mrs Mirfin, the adaptation of George Orwell's novel, *1984*, did upset many viewers. 'If the play "Nineteen Eighty Four" is intellectual, thank God I have no brains,' wrote S. Challacombe from Torquay to the BBC. 'You have endeavoured to open the gates of Hell to millions of people only just recovering from two diabolical wars and who are painfully seeking a tranquil mind with which to inspire the coming generation,' wrote another viewer. A number of letters complained about *1984* following *What's My Line?*; even more complained about it being shown on a Sunday.[26]

Sixteen-year-old John Sutherland's Colchester home did not have a TV set but, intrigued by the playground gossip about *1984*, he booked a place with a better-off school friend for the repeat performance, which went ahead the following Thursday despite demands in parliament that it be cancelled. Sutherland thought the Big Brother on the posters in the TV film had 'a disconcerting resemblance to Gilbert Harding, the moustachioed grump on the *What's My Line?* panel'.[27] Apart from the moustache the resemblance was slight, but the connection made sense, for Harding's face in 1954 was almost as ubiquitous as Big Brother's in 1984.

'Is the Minister aware,' the MP for Central Norfolk asked in parliament, 'that owing to the almost entire absence of television reception in East Anglia, many people there do not even know what Mr. Gilbert Harding looks like?' But this surely wasn't true. Harding's face appeared all the time in newspaper advertisements selling everything from Kraft Salad Cream to Basildon Bond writing paper. While working in a Lambeth branch of Boots the Chemist, Christine Homan noticed that his endorsement of Macleans Double-Action Indigestion Tablets started a trend for customers requesting named brands: instead of 'something for indigestion', they wanted 'those Gilbert Harding Tablets'. Roger Storey, later employed as Harding's secretary, would see his face, dominated by his heavy-rimmed glasses, in a poster for his 'Man o' the *People*' column opposite the railway station at Penge where he lived. 'It was a scraper-board drawing, about twenty times larger than life, showing him in his most ferocious, glowering mood,' Storey wrote later. 'Seeing it every morning as I started for the office almost made me flinch.'[28]

In the 1953 film *Consider the Oracle*, Harding, playing an augur who lived at the bottom of a well, was instantly identifiable by his resonant voice, heard often on the radio as well as on TV. This voice was so familiar it was broadcast by loud speaker at the Serpentine Lido in Hyde Park, reminding people to use the litter baskets. In 1954, Harding was Britain's semi-benevolent Big Brother – a phrase that the TV play, rather than Orwell's book, interleaved into the national imagination. Five days after the first broadcast, a Nottingham jury acquitted Eric Lee, who had drunk six pints of beer and driven on the wrong side of the road, after his counsel suggested to a police officer that he went to grab Lee 'like Big Brother'.[29]

The terror inspired by *1984* was not unusual. Sitting in darkened rooms in front of the low-definition picture and echoey sound of a 1950s television set, children were especially fearful. *The Quatermass Experiment*, a series about an astronaut returning to earth infected with the spores of an alien life-form, was shown quite early on Saturday evening, at 8.15 p.m., in the summer of 1953 and watched by many children. Pam Ayres, then aged six and watching on a newly bought set in Stanford in the Vale, Berkshire, found it 'bleakly terrifying'. She did not know whether to 'watch it and be mortified, or remove myself to another part of the unheated house and there, frozen and alone with my imaginings, quake anyway'. The Nuffield television inquiry discovered one boy who, for three weeks after watching *Quatermass*, had turned his bed round the other way.[30]

An adaptation of *Jane Eyre* and a dramatisation of the life of Edgar Allen Poe also aroused a nameless dread in children. One mother noted that her ten-year-old daughter and six-year-old son were frightened to go to bed and would shout 'Jane Eyre' loudly in their bedrooms to scare each other. 'It showed you the coffin,' said an eleven-year-old boy of the Poe programme. 'It showed you – *you* were supposed to be inside the coffin and there was a glass top to the coffin and you could see them turning the earth on top of it and he kept on shouting "No! No! It's not safe! I'm alive!" And they take it away and you kept on seeing the earth being poured in. (pause) Horrible.' The most startling result of the *1984* broadcast was that thousands of people seemed incapable of turning off the television even if they were petrified, rather as though it were a two-way telescreen in Oceania. 'Mother said, "They hadn't ought to be allowed to put this sort of thing on the telly," but she made no effort to leave the room or switch it off,' recalled Jean Baggott, then aged seventeen, watching in the Black Country. That Thursday, they sat down together, 'frightened witless', to watch the repeat.[31]

Some people saw this as an argument for a commercial channel, so at least people could turn over to 'the other side', but it is hard to find much evidence of great dissatisfaction with the BBC at this time. The viewer Harding discovered in Liverpool, boycotting the television except for *What's My Line?*, seems atypical. The readers' letters from the *TV Mirror*, admittedly a self-selecting sample, suggested that TV was enriching their lives, introducing them to archaeology, opera or well-known public figures, widening their range of interests. 'My husband is now taking an interest in ballet, and I in boxing,' wrote one contented viewer. 'My wife and I are invalids and aged 75,' wrote another, R. S. Craven of Vicarage Road, Alton, Hants. 'We have our television set in the bedroom. Our last meal is taken at 4.30 in the afternoon and then we get into bed. We listen to the radio until TV is due to come in in the evening.' A Radio Rediffusion survey of people who had returned its rented TV sets found some dissatisfaction with the BBC, particularly among the working class: 'I just couldn't keep on paying, especially for the awful programmes that were shown on it.'[32] But this was a skewed sample of people who had returned televisions, when far more people were renting or buying them.

Meanwhile the number of licence owners had risen steadily to over 4 million, and the Postmaster General estimated that there were now

170,000 owners of unlicensed sets. The temptation to evade payment became stronger on 1 June 1954, when a combined TV and radio licence increased from £2 to £3, while the radio-only licence remained at £1. These 'TV pirates', who were getting the programmes free while others subsidised them, were newspaper folk devils. The new TV 'detection van' was a familiar and feared sight by late summer, with eleven in service. It followed the same principle used during the war to sound out secret radios operated by German spies. Equipped with three loop aerials on its roof, tuned to the magnetic field in a working TV, it could pinpoint a set in an actual room, so even people who lived in blocks of flats were not safe, although many thought they were, and others believed that removing their outside aerials would help them evade discovery. Queues formed at post office licence counters wherever the van was spotted. A piece of folk legend, the dummy aerial erected by non-TV owners to impress the neighbours, turned out to be true. The detection van engineers sometimes asked about these aerials, and the embarrassed householder would hurry off to buy a licence they did not need.[33]

On 22 September 1955, London viewers tuned in, many with a mild sense of guilt at being disloyal to the BBC, to 'independent television'. Posters on the Underground had warned viewers they would need to adjust their aerials, and every TV installation man in London was busy converting sets to receive 'Channel 9'. Just after 7 p.m., the familiar tones of Leslie Mitchell, who had inaugurated BBC Television nineteen years earlier, announced over elevated shots of the capital that 'a new public service is about to be launched over the rooftops of old London ... a new Elizabethan enterprise ... is about to pass into the exacting domain of public life'. Over on the newly named BBC television service, Mortimer Wheeler was saying to Professor Thomas Bodkin on *Animal, Vegetable, Mineral?*: 'Come, come Tom: it doesn't matter what you say. Nobody is watching us tonight.'

After ITV's sedate opening, the shows were certainly fresher and faster-paced than on the BBC. The ITN newsreaders weaved in phrases like 'you'll remember my saying on Tuesday ...' and 'If you play chess you may be interested to know ...' On shows like *Gun Law*, *The Adventures of Colonel March* or *The Scarlet Pimpernel*, American-style pregnant orchestral throbbing enlivened the action. More 'ordinary people' appeared on screen, eating bowls of jelly with chopsticks or agonising about whether to open boxes that might contain a star prize or a tie pin. New linkmen, like Michael Miles and Hughie Green, winked and gurned at viewers while manhandling guests and saying things like 'I want you to turn round so you can see all our nice friends at home.' The fight for ITV had been a bitter one – Lord Reith compared its arrival with earlier invasions of smallpox and the bubonic plague – and for the BBC monopolists, Hughie Green's cyclamate charm summed up the vulgarity of sponsored television. His populism, though, was heartfelt. 'People do not want three hours of fucking *King Lear* in verse when they get out of a ten-hour day in the fucking coal pits,' he said privately, 'and fuck anybody who tries to tell them that they do.'[34]

The advertising jingles were designed to stick in the memory like adult nursery rhymes. The jingle king was the composer Johnny Johnston, 'the thirty-second Mozart': *Keep going well, keep going Shell. One Thousand and One cleans a big, big carpet. Sleep sweeter, Bournvita. Rael-Brook Toplin, the shirts you don't iron. Beanz meanz Heinz.* In November the *Sunday Dispatch* published the results of a readers' poll of favourite commercials: the runaway winner was a cartoon bearskinned soldier refusing to answer his sergeant major until he had finished a mildly minty, buttery lozenge. Unusually for a jingle, this one ('Murray mints, Murray mints, too good to hurry mints') had the right rhythm to enter the skipping repertoire. The anthropologists of children's street games, Iona and Peter Opie, found it still being used as a skipping song among Edinburgh schoolchildren as late as 1975, long after it had ceased to be on television.[35]

The commercial breaks portrayed a society not quite yet entering the age of consumer plenty, with many residues from the era of thrift and austerity: advertisements for starch (before the rise of shirt collar stiffeners in the 1960s), home perms (killed off by the decline of the shampoo and set), and laxatives and liver salts (when 'inner cleanliness' was prized). The ads ushered in an unfamiliar world of applied science and market research, from white-coated men testing washing power to blind taste tests proving 'you can't tell Stork from butter' (adapted by parents of mumbling children to 'you can't tell talk from mutter'). Viewers learned that margarine was pronounced with a soft 'g', armpits should be called 'underarm', and there was an important difference between 'fast relief' and 'express relief' of headaches. Toilet paper became softer and thicker, Andrex having raised such expectations. By 1961, there was nearly twice as much toothpaste used as in 1954.[36]

A more subtle transformation wrought by the arrival of ITV was in the nature of the televisual day. Just before the new channel launched, the Postmaster General increased the maximum permitted weekly hours of broadcasting from thirty-five to fifty per channel. ITV used these hours to greatly expand daytime television. Mary Hill, editor of the new *Morning Magazine*, directed it at young mothers who, she felt, would be busy in the afternoon with the two o'clock feed and fetching over-fives from school, but who might, after tidying and dusting, have a mid-morning breather with their babies having been settled down to sleep. 'If you are one of those who can't sit still there are lots of odd jobs that can be done while viewing – from ironing or polishing brass or silver to peeling the apples for lunch,' she told *TV Times* readers.[37]

ITV's extended hours dealt a glancing blow for the apathetic majority who wanted the most draconian Sabbath restrictions to be lifted against the well-organised minority who did not. In 1953 a bill to permit more Sunday amusements had been defeated after strong lobbying from the churches and the Lord's Day Observance Society. But the Postmaster General now ruled that television on Sundays could start from 2 p.m., although no children's programmes would be allowed until 4.30 p.m. to protect Sunday School, and 6 p.m. to 7.30 p.m. would remain blank to protect Evensong. The Sabbath honed out of the new ITV schedules was a continental one, a Sunday morning left clear for churchgoing and an afternoon made up of the sequinned costumes and shiny candelabras of Liberace, the singing cowboy Roy Rogers and his horse Trigger, and then, at 5.30 p.m., one of the biggest draws of the week, *The Adventures of Robin Hood*. Iona and Peter Opie found this new schedule swiftly integrated into children's lore. In October 1956, travelling to Alton, Hampshire on a school bus, they heard children sing a new song to the theme tune of *Robin Hood*: 'Liberace, Liberace, riding through the glen, Liberace, Liberace, with his band of men …' By 1957, the singing cowboy had been added to a skipping song used by eleven-year-old girls in Swansea: 'Hi, Roy Rogers! How about a date? Meet me at the corner at half past eight …'[38]

ITV also introduced tighter, better defined schedules. Many BBC shows only appeared fortnightly, and overruns were common since, with just one channel, viewers tended to watch whatever came along and there was no pressing need for punctuality. But this was changing slowly even before ITV: BBC audience research suggested weekly series had more impact, and the corporation began a 'get tough' policy on sticking to time sheets. In December 1954, the comedian Max Wall was faded out when Saturday night's *Variety Parade* overran, to make way, to viewers' dismay, for a talk by the Welsh novelist Jack Jones. Two months later, 200 viewers complained when a Brazilian mime artist was cut off in mid-flow after *Café Continental* went over time.

Many of the ITV moguls and producers, like Lew Grade and Val Parnell, had a background in variety where the running order was sacrosanct. If acts went over time in variety theatres, they risked not being booked again, and so they would often time themselves with a cigarette; when it burned down to the stub, they knew they had to get off. ITV went straight to the American pattern of weekly shows in the same slot each week, with meticulous timing because commercial breaks had to be met. Faced with its slick rival, the BBC began to use its interludes only in emergencies. 'I think the policy of giving the public "time off" to make a cup of tea or other activities is over,' said one BBC executive just before the arrival of ITV. 'I do not think we can afford to let go of our audience for a moment.'[39]

'There is something spectral about the television public,' a *Times* leader put it a fortnight before ITV began. 'It does not shuffle forward in sturdy queues or suddenly flood the street outside a theatre, but is glimpsed in desolate forests or delicate traceries of aerials and alarming, faceless statistics.'[40] But the arrival of ITV made the nation's viewers an object of serious social-scientific study for the first time. The BBC had only started collecting viewing figures systematically in 1952. Women researchers, the 'clipboard queens' who were such a feature of daily life in the 1950s, would interview about 2,500 people in the street each day about their previous night's viewing. But the BBC's head of audience research, Robert Silvey, was a highminded man, a Quaker, who hated the idea of publishing 'top twenty' ratings lists and thought the BBC should be trying to attract non-viewers to the set rather than competing with ITV.

This suspicion of ratings charts was quite common: when the Top Twenty programme began on Radio Luxembourg in 1948, it was not a countdown of the bestselling records, but of the most popular sheet music. Bestseller lists for books, routine in the US since the 1890s, did not properly arrive in Britain until the *Sunday Times* began printing them, contentiously, in 1974. ITV, needing solid data for its advertisers, could not afford to be so squeamish. So it contracted TAM (Television Audience Measurement) which took a representative sample of several thousand homes and connected an electromechanical 'Tammeter' to each TV set. By working out which wavelength the television was tuned into, this could tell advertisers what programmes people were watching. As TAM's publicity put it, 'Time Buying's like Trawling. The Chap Who Knows Fish, NETS 'EM.'[41]

Every week a little booklet from TAM arrived on the desks of commercial television programme planners, with BBC and ITV ratings graphs printed side by side. They showed mass decampments from one channel to the other, a stark piece of propaganda for market populism. *Double Your Money* pulled in the millions, then the Hallé Orchestra or *Foreign Press Club* got rid of them. You could also track mass exoduses as viewers left part way through a programme. On 10 October 1955 the BBC put on a lavish production of *La Traviata*. TAM's figures revealed that viewers showed willing by tuning in to watch (perhaps because, initially, there was only the Hallé Orchestra on the other side), then started fidgeting a few minutes in until, by the end, almost the entire audience had evaporated. The most spectacular migrations were to be found during party political broadcasts. When the prime minister Anthony Eden appeared on the BBC, four out of five viewers turned over to ITV's *People Are Funny*. From March 1956, the BBC and ITV were required to air such broadcasts simultaneously.[42]

Many people, unfamiliar with or suspicious of scientific sampling, felt these ratings had a bizarre and misleading precision. The expanding industries of market research and data analysis attracted particular unease on the left, the critic Richard Hoggart attacking the desire to 'elevate the counting of heads into a substitute for judgement'. This new cult of number crunching seemed to reduce people to mere statistical agglomerations, and to have little interest in what they really thought and felt. The Labour newspaper *Tribune* accused programme planners of relying on figures issuing from the 'TAM Fairyland', of catching 'Galluping consumption' and being 'Chart drunk'.[43]

Whichever way the ratings were calculated, the new channel was popular. At first it was only available to those within range of its single transmitter, on Beulah Hill, Croydon. By October 1955, though, 2 million people were listening to it on cable radio relayed by the Rediffusion Group, which was often available in council flats. *Sunday Night at the London Palladium* got the biggest radio audience, though much of it, from the Tiller Girls lifting their legs at the start, to the stars waving on the revolving stage at the end, was surely meant to be seen. Many knew about the programmes without having seen them. Comedians on BBC television and radio mimicked the transatlantic vowels of Hughie Green and the side-of-the-mouth speech of Sergeant Joe Friday in *Dragnet* ('just the facts, ma'am'). Members of Burton-on-Trent Archery Club equipped their arrows with whistles because they made this noise in flight on *Robin Hood*. By the end of 1957, seventy-two per cent of viewers with access to ITV watched it more than they did the BBC.[44]

The concept of 'primetime' emerged, partly because ITV could fulfil its public service obligations by putting its more serious shows outside those peak hours. ITV had plenty of highbrow material – fortnightly Hallé concerts, conversations with Edith Sitwell, Jacob Bronowski discussing science, A. J. P. Taylor delivering extempore history lectures – but this tended to be shown outside primetime. Even in graveyard slots, though, these shows were often very popular. Kenneth Clark's ATV series, *Art and Artists* and *Five Revolutionary Painters*, made a greater impact among ordinary viewers than his later, more lauded *Civilisation*. Despite his patrician manner, Clark had mastered the difficult art of looking through the camera to the viewer at home – learned by example, he said, when he saw Arthur Askey, on the opening night of Granada TV, go right up to the lens and shake his fist at it in mock anger. A friend of Clark's told him that in a Covent Garden pub 'he found two of the market porters discussing Caravaggio; he thought he was suffering from an hallucination. The railway porters at Charing Cross used to sit up with their children long after bedtime to listen to talks on Michelangelo.'[45]

Britain, wrote the *Daily Mirror*, was suffering from 'Telemania', a collective madness for which it listed a number of symptoms. When ITV broke down on Sunday 22 January 1956, delaying *Sunday Night at the London Palladium* for nearly an hour, thirty-one per cent of viewers had carried on watching the dead screen. The BBC bachelor announcer Peter Haigh, with his carefully trimmed moustache and beautifully modulated voice, had received over 10,000 letters from women that year and dozens of marriage proposals. 'I adore all your loving, charming ways you have for me, Peter,' Edna from Derby wrote. 'I absolutely idolise your wonderful personality ... Life could be very lonely without you. Peter, please be mine for ever ...' Numerous ailments were blamed on television, from thrombosis to asthenia ('television legs'). In the *British Medical Journal*, a consultant noted several cases of 'television angina' at London's St Mary's Hospital. Westerns, he discovered, were the most likely to produce heart pangs in viewers, though they had little effect on the Welsh, who were more likely to be affected by sad programmes. All viewers found commercials 'entirely painless'.[46]

In a series of *Sunday Times* articles, the freelance anthropologist Geoffrey Gorer explored the effects of 'televiewing', based on interviews with English people between school and retirement age in November 1957. On a typical Sunday evening, Gorer noted, two out of five of them were watching TV, so 'with the possible exception of listening to broadcast news bulletins during the gravest periods of the war, it seems probable that never in recorded history have so many English people been so concentrated in a single occupation'. Gorer was particularly concerned that television was corroding the tradition of nonconformist self-discipline among the working class. Nearly half of working-class viewers were 'addictive', watching for four hours a night, 'all sense of proportion lost in their gross indulgence; their family life, if not wrecked ... at least emptied of nearly all its richness and warmth'. Housewives were especially prone to addiction. The ATV medical soap opera *Emergency – Ward 10* created compulsive symptoms in its mostly female audience, with mothers and teenage daughters eagerly working together to clear away dinner plates in time to watch it, and husbands corralled into washing up on Tuesdays and Fridays.

Gorer compared these findings with those he published in his book *Exploring English Character* in 1955. Then, a significant proportion of his interviewees saw inactivity as 'sloth'; now they called it 'relaxing' and considered it good for them. Rather conveniently ignoring the fact that television was widespread by 1955, Gorer concluded that 'this quite profound change in the way English men and women view their own inactivity is very closely connected with the spread of television'. In private notes written after watching television for ten nights in October 1957, Gorer betrayed some of his preconceptions. Television, he felt, was 'a key-hole, a hole in the wall, gratifying or scopophilic, voyeuristic, spying, what have you, desires ... with all the feelings of superiority, gratified curiosity, brothel visiting'.[47]

If you read beyond his impulsive conclusions, Gorer's findings were less shocking. Three men out of four and three women out of five made no special arrangements to view programmes. Only about a quarter of viewers regularly discussed television with their intimates; it served more as a comfortably neutral conversational topic for comparative strangers, like the unseasonableness of the weather. Gorer also classified a sixth of Britons as television 'abstainers', people who were far more numerous among the middle-aged, elderly and prosperous. They worried that television would come to rule their lives, 'as though they considered the TV set an uncanny object, almost with a will of its own, in some ways analogous to the "influencing machine" which is so regular a feature in the delusions of many mad people'. The children's author Enid Blyton wrote to Gorer twice after reading his articles, worried about television's trance-like effect on her young readers. But she herself loved Peter Scott's nature programmes and the TV plays too much to stop watching: 'I shall never be an abstainer, though I do feel, after reading your article, that, for the sake of the sanity and well-being of the world eventually, there MUST be at least a quota of these.'[48]

A small quota did exist. Lord Beveridge, the wartime architect of the welfare state, told the House of Lords in January 1957 that he and his wife had seen BBC television while convalescing for ten days on the south coast. It seemed mostly, he felt, to consist of 'hideous shouting by hideous people ... Our conclusion, from our week of strenuous watching in the Bournemouth Hotel, is that we have both decided that we would not have television, even if it were offered us as a gift.' 'A TV set will enter Manchester Grammar School over my dead body,' said its High Master, Eric James. The poet John Betjeman had no television at The Mead, his house in Wantage, which was typical in his upper-middle-class social set. 'Not to have a "telly",' Betjeman's biographer notes, 'was as much the done thing as to drive a Land Rover.' When Betjeman appeared on the 'idiot box', he asked his church friends Bart and Jessie Sharley – a primary school teacher and former secretary untroubled by class anxieties about the medium – if he could come to their house and watch it.[49]

The self-educated working class was often similarly hostile to television. Conducting research among working-class families in Huddersfield, the sociologists Brian Jackson and Dennis Marsden found a Mr and Mrs Abbott, who had no educational qualifications and had never been further than Blackpool, but who were voracious collectors of travel books and maps: 'We get this map out of the Holy Land on a Sunday night and settle down to it. Others can have their TV. We don't want that row!' Jackson and Marsden found other working-class autodidacts in the town with a similar attitude: 'Television, we don't want that. Give me a book. Them chaps can't put that picture that you can see when you read them books on to them screens, can they? No chap can. It's here [tapping his head].'[50]

The Labour Party, still wedded to John Maynard Keynes's vision of an automated future in which the biggest problem would be how to fill the expanding hours of leisure, argued that governments needed to provide more cultural and sporting facilities and wider access to the countryside, to compete with the passive charms of television. In his influential The Future of Socialism, the Labour MP Anthony Crosland called for more open-air cafés, pleasure gardens, local theatres and later closing hours for pubs. Many on the left worried that television watching would reduce working men's participation in public life, particularly at union meetings. Apathy had always worried the Labour Party most, because it had most difficulty getting its vote out in elections. It complained in vain to ITV about its schedule for general election night in October 1959, believing that Clint Eastwood in *Rawhide* at 7 p.m. followed by the quiz show *Dotto* at 8 p.m. would deter people from the polling booths.[51] (Since the election was a Tory landslide, this tempting night in is unlikely to have made much difference to the result.) The Labour leader Harold Wilson had more success in 1964, persuading the BBC to shift *Steptoe and Son* an hour later to 9 p.m., when the polls closed.

Dennis Potter, a coalminer's son just graduated from Oxford, articulated these fears about working-class apathy and impoverished cultural literacy in the telemaniac age in his books *The Glittering Coffin* (1960) and *The Changing Forest* (1962). Potter noted how, as TV sets had invaded his native Forest of Dean, the working men's clubs emptied, the rugby team struggled to make up the numbers and chapel membership fell. The television, the most beautiful object that had ever entered a miner's house, had turned the mostly unused 'best' room, the front parlour, into a proper living space and 'a minor revolution was finally consummated when supper was eaten in the room to the pale flicker of the Lime Grove light'. On the BBC radio programme *The Brains Trust* in April 1960, Potter forecast gloomily that the twenty-first century would be dominated by 'twenty-one-inch television screens in every room and the constant throbbing of commerce'.[52]

Television was at the heart of other anxieties about social change. The boom discipline of sociology was beginning to map the lost community of the slum terraces that were knocked down in the great postwar clearances, and to worry about the modern dormitory suburbs and housing estates where boredom and neurosis ('new town blues') germinated, particularly among young wives. In *Family and Kinship*

in East London, Michael Young and Peter Willmott contrasted the dense social networks of the Bethnal Green streets, where nearly every turning had a street party for the 1953 coronation, with the London County Council's housing estate in Dagenham, where neighbours glanced at each other through the net curtains and watched television. In Dagenham, 'the magic screen in its place of honour in the parlour' had privatised life and fragmented community. In one home, where a two-month-old baby was stationed in its pram in front of the set, 'the scene had the air of a strange ritual. The father said proudly: "The tellie keeps the family together. None of us ever have to go out now."'[53]

Willmott and Young probably overestimated the vibrancy of traditional working-class street life, mining huge symbolism from a sporadic phenomenon, the coronation street party, when they might instead have focused on the coronation as a moment that consolidated the rise of television. Most coronation street parties were actually moved to the Saturday before, or late afternoon on the day itself, to avoid clashing with watching the event on TV.[54] The inner-directed television households that Willmott and Young found in Dagenham were simply an acceleration of a trend occurring just a few years later in Bethnal Green.

Television certainly did inflict some collateral damage on other social habits. Cinemas began seriously to decline in the late 1950s as their mainly working-class audiences acquired TVs on a large scale. Between 1945 and 1959, over a hundred variety theatres shut down and those few that survived were dominated by nude revues or topliners made famous by television. John Osborne's play *The Entertainer* (1957) makes only passing reference to the new medium ('Now who do you think would want a television in a pub? Blaring away, you can't hear yourself think'), but his failed music hall act, Archie Rice, who performs with a nude revue, is clearly its casualty. At the beginning of the 1960 film version, a family walks past the hoardings outside the theatre where he is performing, saying 'I've not seen him on the television' and 'he's never been on TV'. Between 1953 and 1956 the number of provincial repertory companies halved, to around fifty-five, as they failed to compete with plays on television. 'Once the audience had been introduced to solid-looking walls, furniture that they didn't know by heart, and a butler who looked like a butler and not a heavily made-up eighteen-year-old,' wrote the former repertory actor, Timothy West, 'the end was clearly not far off.'[55]

It was also harder now to lure audiences to the West End from the suburbs. The 'Aunt Ednas', as Terence Rattigan called the middle-class theatre audiences who wanted well-made, conventional plays with strong curtain lines, could find such middlebrow entertainment on television. The drama critic Philip Hope-Wallace concluded that theatre managers should 'cease trying to appeal to the lowest common factor in amorphous groups of coach-trippers, narrowing the score rather to the hard core of metropolitan theatregoers'. The decline in reputation of playwrights like Rattigan and Noel Coward has usually been seen as an inevitable cultural revolution, a clearing away of pre-war dead wood, but the success of new writers like Osborne and Harold Pinter surely owed something to changes in the theatre dictated by television. By 1960 only about three per cent of the population was prepared to go to the theatre, and the industry was coming to be dominated by the West End and subsidised, civic theatres, catering for an educated minority ushered in by the postwar expansion of universities, and presenting a serious and improving face in order to get Arts Council and other funding. In an era when single dramas were popular commissions, these serious playwrights also found an audience on television. Pinter once worked out that it would take a thirty-year run of *The Caretaker* at the Duchess Theatre to get the same audience (6.3 million) as his Armchair Theatre play, *A Night Out*, shown on ITV in May 1960.[56]

Rather than television simply wiping out other social habits, though, enthusiasms flowed in other directions. Many defunct cinemas were converted into bingo halls and there was a brief craze for ten-pin bowling. In the course of the 1950s, annual borrowings at public libraries rose from around 300 million to over 400 million. And one hobby flourished with the arrival of television: knitting. A familiar sound in living rooms was the clicking of needles followed by the sudden, unconscious pause when something interesting came on screen. The cultural historian Claire Langhamer argues that knitting was popular among women at this time because it contained a residue of the work ethic, and so time spent watching TV while knitting was not 'wasted' because it was being used twice over. 'I have little races with myself,' said a 77-year-old woman. 'I say, "Can you finish that pattern before the nine o'clock news?"' The swing in the late 1950s away from heavy, chunky yarns to lighter, quick-knit types was probably television-led. A Walsall woman searched in vain in three towns before being told, 'There is no call for Fair Isle patterns, people cannot concentrate on them and watch television.'[57]

Geoffrey Gorer found two-thirds of his women viewers either knitted or did needlework when they watched, 'addicts' preferring the former and selective viewers the latter. 'The more they watch the more they knit,' he noted. 'Today's tricoteuses are not alarming creatures.' In February 1959, after the women's section of the British Legion banned knitting at its meetings on the grounds that it destroyed concentration, *Panorama* brought a group of women to Lime Grove (accompanied by BBC television's resident knitting expert, James Norbury) to knit through an episode, and then questioned them about how much of the programme they had absorbed (a lot, as it happened). According to Gorer, gardening was the one activity from which even the most addictive viewers could not be distracted. For all the panic about telemania, television seemed to have found its place, not necessarily killing off old habits but slotting itself between and around them. The literary critic William Empson wrote to Gorer to say that, while he found his research 'rather terrifying ... the race of man is not destroyed so easily; it seems clear that, in the end, if they have time, they will manage to acquire a "tolerance" for their new poison'.[58]

For the future *Monty Python* member Terry Jones, television began in the 1950s as 'something that happened down the road at my friend John Campion's house'. Terry and John would rush home from school to watch the cowboy series *Hopalong Cassidy*. Every Saturday morning they watched the same BBC demonstration film, with the same haunting bit of early film footage of a man attempting to fly from the Eiffel Tower and falling to his death, 'into oblivion and history at the same time ... This was the bit we ghouls all waited for with horror and fascination.' When the Joneses finally kept up with the Campions and bought a set of their own, though, Terry soon tired of it and migrated to the bedroom to write poetry, tempted downstairs only to watch Michael Bentine's *It's a Square World*. 'Television was never really my thing,' he recalled. 'In those days the image was only 425 lines [*sic*] and a rather murky purple colour.'[59]

This was normal behaviour among members of that newish tribe, the teenagers, who preferred shows aimed clearly and cultishly at them, such as *77 Sunset Strip*, with its character Edd 'Kookie' Byrnes, unlicensed detective and adolescent role model. Constantly tending his ducktail haircut, he added jive talk to the British vocabulary, calling everybody 'Dad', an idea a 'bulb' and praiseworthy things 'real nervous'. ABC Television published a glossary of Kookish ('a pile of jive gone square') to aid viewers. Teenagers also watched on the rare occasions that television offered glimpses of their musical heroes. When Buddy Holly appeared on *Sunday Night at the London Palladium* in March 1958, his 'nationwide guitar-class', including John Lennon and Paul McCartney in Liverpool, was watching intently. But, according to Holly's biographer, Philip Norman, the lesson they had hoped for failed to materialise: 'One could hardly see Buddy's guitar, let alone what his fingers might be doing on its fretboard.'[60]

Six-Five Special, the BBC's first attempt at a popular music show, kept about a quarter of teenagers at home on Saturday evening, although the historian Peter Hennessy notes that, because its opening titles showed an A4 Pacific steam locomotive pulling the Edinburgh–Aberdeen express over the Forth Bridge, it also appealed to the large number of boys, like himself, who were trainspotters.[61] Although presented by Pete Murray doing an impression of youthspeak ('Time to jive on the old six-five'), the show took pride in the wide age range it attracted, from children to pensioners. The BBC's other pop show, *Juke Box Jury*, was another case study in generational compromise, as the older showbusiness stars on it would make snide comments about records, ventriloquising the views of parents. As television co-opted rock'n'roll into the light entertainment mainstream, teenagers migrated to their bedrooms and to Radio Luxembourg, which, after ITV had stolen its family audience, was now playing pop music late into the night, for those listening covertly under the bedclothes with their transistors.

The arrival of television in an area was marked by a new skyline, a critical mass of aerials, like Chinese ideograms, along thousands of miles of rooftops. The best blackbird and thrush song was now heard from aerials, and in coastal towns, herring gulls sat on them and caused them to sag, knocking them out of line with the transmitter. The collared dove was so renowned for using the aerial as an opportune perch that Germans renamed it the *Fernsehtaube* or 'television dove'. The ornithologist Jeremy Mynott wonders if the rapid expansion of collared doves in northern Europe after the late 1950s was due to 'the endless horizon of TV aerials they could see stretching over affluent Western Europe'.[62]

The abundance of aerials became part of a general fear that Britain was being uglified by 'subtopia', an all-purpose word coined by the critic Ian Nairn for postwar clutter from advertising hoardings to concrete streetlamps. A cinema newsreel, 'Down with aerials!', condemned the 'hideous disfigurement' of 'the ugly crop of television aerials, like demented hatstands' in Chesterfield. A letter to *The Times* lamented the blight of aerials spreading across the Cotswolds, where even thatchers had learned to leave a convenient gap in the straw for the aerial to stick out of, and 'these Heath Robinson-like objects ... utterly ruin the varied and picturesque roof-lines'. Television abstainers looked askance at the aerial. 'We used to say that the people who dropped their aitches put them up above their houses,' remembered the playwright Peter Nichols about the H-aerials which would soon be mentally edited out of view and vanish into the everyday landscape along with roof tiles and chimney pots.[63]

Just like electricity pylons and arterial roads before the war, the TV aerial suggested the spread of cultural sameness across the land, the dilution of local diversity and tradition. 'As the bends on the roads are removed and the television signal spreads, doom is on hand for even these places; it's all becoming *Whicker's World*,' wrote Malcolm Bradbury in his 'poor man's guide to the affluent society', written after returning to Britain from a year studying in America in 1958–9. 'The crudest of modern desires, desire for membership of the present, was displaying itself … The past I had come back to was already in hiding, confined to the places where the television signal had not yet reached.'[64]

Partly to allay these fears that the new mass media was destroying local identities, ITV had been divided into regional companies, their franchises stipulating that they produce some local material. One of the most enthusiastic advocates of this idea was Sidney Bernstein, the charismatic new chairman of Granada TV, who was described by the journalist Harold Evans as 'a smooth silver-haired talker of creative vitality, who looked like a cross between a Roman emperor and a beaten-up boxer', and who claimed he had been persuaded to bid for its northern franchise by looking at two maps, one showing the distribution of population in England, the other the pattern of rainfall. He repeated this claim over the years like a creation myth, by which time even he may have forgotten that his deputy, Denis Forman, had dreamt it up as a conceit. Bernstein was a brilliant propagandist for his company and its region. 'The North is a closely knit, indigenous, industrial society,' he told the London School of Economics in 1959, 'a homogeneous cultural group with a good record for music, theatre, literature and newspapers … Compare this with London and its suburbs: full of displaced persons.'[65]

The vast Granada region, covering 13 million potential viewers from north Wales to Lincolnshire, could just about be correlated with that emotive but indefinable entity, 'the north'. Northerners travelling south were surprised to see the name 'Granada' attached to TV rental shops, cinemas and motorway cafés, so habituated were they by the famous channel ident – 'From the North: Granada Presents', with an upward-moving arrow – to associating it with their region. Granada drew on a tradition of proud provincialism associated with the *Manchester Guardian* (which, ironically, was about to drop its adjective and relocate to London) as well as anticipating the northern new wave headed by writers and filmmakers like David Storey, Tony Richardson and Shelagh Delaney. Granada was at the vanguard of a new idea of the north that emerged in the early 1960s, after more than a decade of Tory rule, promising a new vigour and vitality in place of a stale, southern Establishment.

Granada's serious programmes, like *What the Papers Say*, its groundbreaking, in-depth reporting of the 1958 Rochdale by-election and its 1959 'Marathon', in which all the parliamentary candidates in the north delivered an election address, drew on the idea of the region as a citadel of autodidacticism and civic responsibility. When the 1962 Pilkington Report accused ITV *tout court* of vulgarity and commercialism, a wounded Bernstein proudly cited Granada's non-stop coverage of the TUC and party conferences, 'some of which have had the lowest ratings with the public ever known'.[66]

To describe this northern kingdom, united by its ability to receive his company's programmes, Bernstein coined the inspired term 'Granadaland'. Oddly, the name probably resonated more because it had no connection with its region, for Bernstein had chosen the name Granada for his cinemas in the 1930s to evoke the exoticism and romance of Spain. Many viewers at first pronounced it to rhyme with 'Canada'. 'Land', meanwhile, had originated as a suffix in America to describe the communities created out of wireless listening ('you folks out there in radioland'). Bernstein declared the half-serious ambitions of marking Granadaland's borders with customs posts on major roads and of moving a member of the royal family to Harrogate. With Denis Forman he devised 'an up-to-date version of Cobbett's concept of London as the Great Wen, a cesspool of sin, corruption and idleness'.[67]

This was mostly PR. Granada still filmed many of its shows

from the Chelsea Palace on London's King's Road, from where it broadcast a networked variety show with the incongruous opening announcement, 'From the north, Granada presents: *Chelsea at Nine*', made even more incongruous when it sometimes went out at 8.30 p.m. Much of Granada's quota of local programmes was filled with cheap outside broadcasts filmed by its distinctive pale blue Travelling Eye cameras: sand-yacht races at Southport, traffic on the Barton Bridge, dairy farmers making Cheshire cheese, a visit to a glass factory, Manchester after midnight. 'Today these OBs would seem grotesquely primitive,' conceded Denis Forman later, 'and even then they were exceedingly boring, but ... the experience of showing the North to the North in a workaday manner was something new and astonishing.' On his return to Bolton in 1960, after conducting a Mass Observation survey of the town in the late 1930s, Tom Harrisson noted that the town was fortunate to be in this ITV region, for 'Granada is deeply interested, in a conscious and intelligent way, in the Manchester area complex, in which Bolton somewhat unwillingly lies'. Harrisson noted approvingly that, when he had offered him 'a privately conducted tour of the inner workings of Bolton', Bernstein had jumped at the chance.[68]

Coronation Street, which began in December 1960, was partly commissioned to increase Granada's northern content. But Bernstein worried that it sent out an outdated image of the region. 'When I get driven in from the airport I can see many houses that are much nicer than those on your street,' he told the producer, Harry Elton. 'Is this the image of Granadaland that we want to project to the rest of the country?' But northern viewers recognised immediately its authentic core. Richard Whiteley, now a sixth-form boarder at Giggleswick School in north Yorkshire, was doing his evening prep in the study when his young English teacher, Russell Harty, came in. He had one of the early portable television sets – the fourteen-inch Murphy, with its distinctive purple handle – in his rooms. 'I've just seen this wonderful thing on TV,' Harty said. 'It's about a street in Manchester and there's a woman with a hairnet in it.'[69]

The debut broadcast of Scottish Television, on 31 August 1957, a variety show called *This is Scotland*, evoked a nation only marginally less invented than Granadaland. After the Jacobite song 'The Hundred Pipers' and Kenneth McKellar singing 'Scotland the Brave', a kilt-wearing James Robertson Justice, a Scottish Nationalist who claimed improbably to have been born under a distillery on the Isle of Skye, laid it on thick in an accent rather more Celtic than the one he used for the *Doctor* films: 'Good evening, this is Scotland, the land of sunshine and clouds, the land proud and ancient as history itself, yet young, strong and vital as the flowers that bejewel our northern summer ...' 'The whole thing culminated as might have been prophesied with a pipe band marching down the plywood hills,' reported the *Glasgow Herald*. 'For what it was, a glorious inevitability, it was well enough done.' STV's Highland mythology reached about 190,000 lowland televisions, the reception outside Glasgow and Edinburgh being mostly dreadful. This was not, as some engineers claimed, because of the pine-forested hills of Argyllshire (although conifers, in leaf all year round, do affect reception), but because the new ITV mast on Black Hill, near Kirk O'Shotts, had a duff aerial design. St Andrews received faint pictures; Ayr had blank screens; Perth got sound only.

Wales was even less fortunate, for it had to share its regional company, Television Wales and West, with the West Country. Like the Wenvoe transmitter, the ITV mast at St Hilary was near the Severn Estuary and you couldn't send a signal north of there without also sending it south. In any case, TWW needed the advertising revenue that its flank of English viewers would bring to make a profit. For fear of alienating people in the West Country and in industrialised, Anglophone south Wales, its Welsh language programmes were shown late at night. Many Welsh nationalists thus saw ITV as a further incursion of Anglo-American culture into the homeland.

The private, domesticated act of watching television also seemed to threaten indigenous Welsh traditions of live, communal entertainment, like the *Eisteddfodau*, the evenings of music and poetry known as *nosweithiau llawen* ('happy nights') and the *noson lawen*, informal gatherings in people's homes similar to the Scottish *ceilidh*. In 1961,

Blodau'r Ffair, the journal of the Welsh League of Youth, published 'This enlightened age', a poem by the Carmarthenshire poet David Henry Culpitt: 'The Devil's forks can now be seen / On the corner of the chimneys of Hendre Fawr ... And pretty girls with naked legs / Fill the space where the wise Psalmist used to be.' The same issue had a cartoon showing a doctor diagnosing a patient: 'Lack of sleep, I'm afraid – watching too many Welsh programmes.'[70]

The smaller ITV regional stations relied on still more makeshift identities. Tyne Tees Television, starting in January 1959, covered an area with a strong sense of its own apartness but little unity. The 'north-east' was a recent and nebulous term, first used widely in the interwar years in connection with the Jarrow march and efforts to revive the region's economy. But Tyneside, Wearside and Teesside all had different newspapers, with no equivalent of, say, the *Yorkshire Post* or the *Western Mail* to unite the region. The new channel had provisionally been called 'North East Television' but its owner, George Black, was worried that its acronym could be extrapolated to 'Nettie', Geordie slang for toilet. For similar reasons, the name Tyne, Wear and Tees Television was also vetoed.[71] The new company soothed the wounded feelings of Wearsiders by commissioning a start-up theme called the 'Three Rivers Fantasy'.

Anglia Television, broadcasting across the flatlands from the Wash to the Thames Estuary, had an agricultural feel. Dick Joice, a tenant farmer dressed in cavalry twills and brogues, who did not own a television until he started appearing on it, was the face of the channel. As well as presenting *Farming Diary*, a programme interspersed with commercials for fertiliser and new types of sugar beet, he was the anchorman for *About Anglia*, the first regional news programme with its own weather forecast, keenly watched by the region's many farmers and fishermen. In one memorable edition in January 1963, in the middle of the coldest winter of the century, Joice presented the programme from Wroxham Broad in Norfolk, sitting at a desk perched on the frozen water while reporters skated round him under the arc lights.[72]

Southern Television's catchment area ran along the south coast from the New Forest to the agricultural prairies of Kent. Its chalk streams were some of the best fishing waters in the country, and the programme controller, Roy Rich, wanted a series about the region's speciality, fly fishing, then a rich man's sport and thus attractive to advertisers. So began, in 1959, Jack Hargreaves's *Gone Fishing*, which mutated the following year into a much-cherished series about the countryside, *Out of Town*. Its format barely changed in twenty-one years. Viewers discovered Hargreaves in a set made to look like a shed, dressed in tweeds, gumboots and a fly-festooned cap. Sitting at a trestle bench and smoking a briar pipe, he would simply start talking, without introduction, about an old country skill like cider making or onion stringing, before leading into a film about fishing for roach or cutting the Winchester water meadows.

Hargreaves avoided that glassy, eyeball-swivelling, autocue stare at the viewer, for he had intuited, like Kenneth Clark, that the most successful television presenting is really a form of soliloquy. He had no script, believing that stumbling over words and repeating himself was more natural, and he did not always look at the camera because he felt that people in conversation often looked away from each other. 'I'm not talking to two million people 20 miles away,' he mused. 'I'm talking to three people exactly 14 feet distant. That's the average size of any TV audience, and the distance they sit from their set.'[73] His sentences had a comforting, epigrammatic quality. *The countryside would fall apart without baler twine. There's nothing more dopey than a dopey cod. Freezers have taken the fun out of beans.* In the Southern region, *Out of Town* regularly beat *Coronation Street* in the ratings.

Another local programme, *In Kite's Country*, presented by a former army major called Oliver Kite, was also regularly in Southern Television's Top Ten. Like Hargreaves, Kite was a 'spieler', simply ad-libbing in his slow rich voice over film of him catching grayling while blindfold or with a paper bag over his head. He received about 350 letters a week from viewers, a huge number for a programme never shown outside the region. One man, who wrote to say how sorry he was that he would no longer be able to watch *In Kite's Country* now that he was leaving the area, was found to be awaiting release from Parkhurst.[74]

The most artificial ITV region was Border Television, broadcasting from September 1961 to a population of about half a million, outnumbered four to one by sheep, and awkwardly straddling two countries, from Walter Scott's fairy-haunted lowlands to the Cumbrian lakes. Its most popular programme was *Cock of the Border*, a weekly knockout competition in which rival quizzers, piano players and darts throwers from places like Workington, Stranraer or Kelso competed against each other – a canny way of bringing together a region made up of small, dispersed towns.

But the most difficult balancing act of all was the responsibility of Ulster Television. Its declared aim was to build bridges across the divided community, a commercial imperative anyway since it needed to reach as many viewers as possible. But straightaway its late-night religious spot, *End the Day*, created a row between Catholics, Protestants and Presbyterians about the allocation of slots. Ulster TV's approach to the emerging Troubles was simply to ignore them. The channel director Brum Henderson wanted it to provide 'television for the Shankill and Falls Roads', the working-class, Protestant and Catholic areas of west Belfast, rather than for the BBC viewers along the Malone and Antrim Roads, the affluent suburbs of the north and south.

With only about 50,000 televisions in the whole of Northern Ireland, UTV had modest advertising revenue and little money for its own programmes. Its local flavour came from shoestring but very popular early evening shows such as *The Romper Room* with 'Miss Adrienne', in which a group of invited local children listened to stories and played games, and *Tea Time with Tommy*, in which a former salesman from London's Mile End Road read out viewer requests and banged out tunes on his piano. Ulster TV's slide promotion ads, a still picture with a voiceover being a bargain at £1 per second, also added to its regional feel. 'It would make a big difference to our appeal,' thought Henderson, 'if Ulster Television was not only promoting Surf and Pepsodent, but also car dealerships on the Newtownards Road and animal feed producers in Cookstown.'[75]

Despite their improvised, amateurish feel, the regional stations inspired great loyalty from viewers. Although often seen through a sea of static, Scottish Television was soon trouncing the BBC in the ratings, a combination of its populist network programmes and its symbolic break with Londonism. On Friday nights, it broadcast a piece of cathode ray tartanry called *Jig Time*, an evening of reels and figure dances in 'the old barn', which began with the doors opening and the presenter inviting the viewers in to 'sit on the straw'. Its popularity led the BBC to respond with the *White Heather Club*, an even more sanitised *ceilidh* where the men wore kilts with sensible shirts and ties, Andy Stewart compèred and Jimmy Shand's accordion led the band. Delivering the McTaggart lecture at the Edinburgh International Television Festival in August 2007, Jeremy Paxman cited it as definitive proof that television never had a golden age.

The most popular local programmes were the ramshackle lunchtime variety shows shown in most regions. STV's *The One O'Clock Gang* was hosted by an Italian-born Glaswegian, Larry Marshall, whose lowlands fame was such that when he visited Lanark one Saturday afternoon, the streets were closed and mounted police deployed to disperse the crowds. Advertisers loved the rather similar *One O'Clock Show* on Tyne Tees because most women in this region did not work and many north-east men and children came home for lunch. Over 150,000 viewers, the biggest lunchtime audience in the country, watched the comedian Jack 'Wacky Jacky' Haig (later known to the nation as Monsieur LeClerc in the French resistance sitcom *'Allo 'Allo!*) and George Romaine, a former electrician at Shildon Wagon

Works, billed as 'Shildon's Singing Son'. Instead of the *TV Times*, Tyne Tees had its own ITV listings publication, *The Viewer*, which was soon the biggest selling magazine in the north-east with 300,000 readers, not all of whom had televisions.[76]

Tyne Tees had promised to be the most regional of the ITV stations but the oral nature of much of the area's popular culture, from dialect humour to song, did not easily translate to television. Bobby Thompson, the local comedian who had been such a hit on regional BBC radio as 'the Little Waster', looked uncomfortable on TV and his show was quietly dropped. Radio shows broadcast on the regional Home Service like *Wot Cheor, Geordie!* and *Voice of the People*, which used the new portable tape recorders to conduct vox pops with locals, attained record listening figures well into the 1960s.[77]

In all regions, the main attraction of ITV for viewers was the national, networked programmes, which often caused some confusion over where they originated. Viewers turned up at the Tyne Tees studios on Newcastle's City Road wanting to meet Hughie Green from *Double Your Money* or Michael Miles from *Take Your Pick*, and a woman arrived with her two grandsons hoping to see the horses from *Wagon Train*. The regions made the networked programmes their own. Ulster Television was the first region to buy *Coronation Street* from Granada, Brum Henderson intuiting that viewers in the cobbled terraced streets of Belfast would feel at home with such a setting.[78]

But these new ITV fiefdoms, defined by nothing more concrete than market convenience and the reach of the TV signal, had confused identities and leaky borders. Tyne Tees stretched beyond the north-east into the North Riding of Yorkshire and up to the Scottish lowlands, and was even reported to have been seen in Esbjerg, Denmark. A viewer in Monster in South Holland photographed his television to prove that he could pick up Anglia TV. Bloodless military campaigns were fought in fringe areas, trying to get viewers to swivel their aerials. Anglia was notorious for its imperialist raids on rival enclaves. From its 1,000-foot Mendlesham mast, then the tallest structure in Europe, it soon extended deep into Lincolnshire and Bedfordshire. After it built its new transmitters at Sandy Heath and

Belmont in 1965, its catchment area reached from Buckinghamshire in the south to Yorkshire in the north. Anglia's best known face, Dick Joice, fronted the campaign to persuade viewers to turn their aerials. He spent three months visiting every fringe town and village of any size to 'beat the Anglia drum', enjoying particular success along the eastern coast where they preferred Anglia's agricultural programmes to the urbanite offerings of Tyne Tees and ATV.[79]

The TV signal is no respecter of human-made borders; the only ruler it obeys is the landscape. The engineers could try tilting the beam of the transmitter a little to produce what they called 'asymmetrical radiation', but the signal mostly went where it wanted to go, alighting on whichever aerials happened to be pointing in its direction. In Northern Ireland this was a serious political problem. Ulster TV, from its transmitter at Black Mountain above Belfast, reached half the population south of the border, where there were about 90,000 sets in a country that officially had no television. Northern Irish viewers would often complain about their southern neighbours, the 'lookers-in over the wall', watching their programmes for free. A feature of the skyline in Irish towns was the multitude of especially tall aerials erected to pick up the distant signals of British transmitters. A chartered Aer Lingus plane full of these aerials had left Cardiff Airport for Dublin a few days before the coronation in 1953. When Jeremy Lewis left England to study at Trinity College Dublin in the autumn of 1961, the first thing he noticed coming in to the city on the train were 'the outsize television aerials on top of all the houses, bending in the direction of Wales like arms stretched out in supplication'.[80]

If it had acknowledged the existence of these viewers, Ulster Television would have been able to charge higher advertising rates. But Telifis Éireann was due to begin broadcasting and the signal from its new mast on Truskmore Mountain in Sligo was going to reach into Fermanagh, Tyrone and Derry, many Republicans viewing television as a weapon in the struggle for unification. Wishing to remain aloof from this struggle, the ITA asked TAM to stop short at the border on their maps showing the coverage of Ulster TV. Officially, no southern Irish viewer watched ITV. The Post Office would not even allow

Northern Irish cable companies, of which there were many because television reception in the region was so poor, to pipe Telifis Éireann into homes.[81]

British TV had also gained a foothold on the French mainland along the north-western coastal strip of Brittany and Normandy, as far south as Rennes. Tall thirteen-element television aerials began appearing on the stone-grey houses, pointed towards the BBC link transmitter on Torteval, on the south-west tip of Guernsey. Television had been slower to make an impact in France than in Britain and in 1959 there were still just a million sets, with many middle-class families only admitting to having TV 'pour les gosses' [for the kids]. But installing a specially adapted set for the BBC programmes was a status symbol among the coastal bourgeoisie and there were enough French viewers for the English programmes to be listed in the regional newspaper *Ouest France*.

A Monsieur Bourdet had bought a TV set as early as 1946 to pick up the BBC, and got good pictures for the coronation. By 1955 his set was so well known that it featured in *Ouest France* with the headline: 'Hundreds Pack Cherbourg Back Street Watching English Television Through Window.' When Channel Television started broadcasting ITV in 1962, *Coronation Street* became so popular in north-west France that, in a hotel at Carteret in Normandy, the proprietor changed the mealtimes so guests could watch it. There was even some (illegal) French advertising on Channel TV and in the coastal town of Dinard they founded 'a Cercle des Amis de Channel'. The TV signal made the most unlikely, intrepid journeys. In October 1956, an NBC official picked up a BBC broadcast in New York and immediately telephoned the corporation and said, 'I'm looking at a lady stirring pudding.' It was Marguerite Patten making bread.[82]

While the TV signal stretched beyond Britain's borders, some parts of the country remained out of reach. The bringing of a signal to these sparsely populated areas was technically difficult and expensive, and certainly not justified by the small amount of increased licence fee money it would bring. But one of the BBC's responses to the start of ITV was to exploit the fact that the commercial channel had erratic coverage across the nation. The director of BBC Television, George Barnes, declared in the *Radio Times* that the corporation aimed to be national in both range and character: 'Television must reach into every home that wants it, and events must be televisable wherever they occur.'[83]

The last big group to be deprived of television were the million or so Scots thinly spread through the Highlands and Islands. Here even electricity was an innovation. In the early 1950s the North of Scotland Hydro-Electric Board had begun a massive project for heading new dams and diverting rivers. This brought electricity lines on steel pylons to the remotest crofters, who could finally dispense with their tilly lamps and peat-burning hearths. Television aerials now sprung up hopefully in improbable places. In August 1957 the BBC opened a new transmitter at Rosemarkie in the Black Isle on the west coast, which reached another 100,000 people and made television available to ninety-three per cent of Scots. Men began walking about remote areas of the Highlands with portable TV sets, searching for a signal like prospectors looking for mineral wealth. But isolated villages were often too scattered to justify the cost of a booster mast and the Highland peaks and inlets might have been designed by a disapproving Presbyterian god to get in the way of graven images.

Jo Grimond, the Liberal leader and MP for Orkney and Shetland, often warned the House of Commons that the absence of a decent television reception in his constituency would lead to an exodus from the islands. The first televisions had arrived on Orkney in October 1955 when a new transmitter opened at Meldrum in Aberdeenshire, 250 miles away. A fourteen-inch set cost over fifty guineas, at a time when the average Orkney farm wage was less than £10 a week, and many parts of the islands did not yet have electricity; but some of the islanders who did have it were prepared to take a chance on getting a reception. 'We rubbed our eyes the other morning, for only a few fields away on a prominent chimney we saw an absolute outsize among television aerials. We thought that this must be the first one in Orkney, but we are credibly informed that there are now three in the town,' wrote Ernest Marwick, a Kirkwall bookshop assistant, in the *Orkney Herald*. 'Reception on Wednesday was first-class and we watched entranced even that incredible opening programme, a discussion on thumb-sucking. We felt then that there was more than an element of truth in the old man's comment, "Soon there'll no' be a sock mended in the country."' Orkney was well outside Meldrum's theoretical range but the lack of trees on the islands, and the flat terrain, aided reception. 'Later in the week when the screen yielded nothing but a fluorescent blizzard,' Marwick cautioned, 'we felt that after all television to Orkney is indeed in the thumb-sucking stage.'[84]

Some doubting Thomases at the Pier Head in Stromness, where old men gathered to gossip and set the world to rights, thought that Orkney's supposed 'viewers' were telling fibs. The owner of the local radio shop was moved to put photographs of TV sets in action in his window. 'There is a stir of wonder at the Pier Head these days because a new phenomenon of this mighty scientific age has reached Stromness,' reported another *Herald* columnist. 'After water-closets, telephones and concrete streets has come Television, and it has conquered nearly all hearts ... Those from the Pier Head who managed to insinuate themselves into the houses where TV was installed saw wonders surpassing all they had ever imagined ... But perhaps the word "saw" had better be qualified. Sometimes, in the midst of his mirth Wilfred Pickles disintegrated. Sometimes the lovely ladies reading the news were pelted with violent all-obliterating hail-storms. Sometimes, especially when a car passed, the footballers were swept clean from the screen in a flash of white light ...'[85]

These words were written by a 34-year-old poet, George Mackay Brown, who was always wary of new technology. Although he rarely left Orkney, he had by chance seen the first day of television in the lowlands. As a mature student at Newbattle Abbey College in Midlothian, Brown had taken a day trip to Dalkeith with a friend one spring morning in March 1952. Walking up the high street, they noticed a small crowd standing in the lobby of a radio dealer's. Brown made his way to the front and saw a screen on which a doctor was explaining rheumatism to a woman patient. '"Man, man," said an old man at my elbow, "It's wonderful, is it no? Soon they'll be able to see into your very mind,"' Brown told his *Herald* readers. 'It was a horrible thought.'

All that week, Brown saw radio dealers' vans running along the streets of Dalkeith bringing television to miners' houses. The next Saturday evening he went to Newbattle's local pub, the Justinlees tavern, and was astonished to see his local MP, Jo Grimond, in a roundtable discussion on TV. As a heavy drinker, Brown was especially interested in television's effect on pubs and their bar receipts. Some miners, he noted, drank only a pint in front of the TV, hypnotised 'by the flickering articulate shadows', while others drank twice as fast. He and his friends did not dare ask for a set to be installed in college 'for we knew instinctively how those ancient austere walls would have disapproved'. In his often ill-tempered, jeremiadic column in the *Herald*, Brown worried about what this 'startling box of tricks' would do to the islands when it arrived.[86]

While his local MP hoped that television might keep at home those young people who would otherwise leave, Brown feared that television would give them a taste for the cities, and cut islanders off from their common traditions, particularly the storytelling culture carried over by the Norsemen a thousand years before. His friend, Ernest Marwick, agreed that Orkney's rich tradition of improvised entertainment and house-to-house visiting was imperilled. He worried that children's imaginations would become 'entirely identified with flickering, over-heated vacuities'.[87]

Orcadians gave short shrift to these Cassandras. Unlike other remote parts of Scotland, two brakes on the relentless progress of television were largely absent: the strictest forms of Presbyterianism had not taken hold, and most islanders did not speak Gaelic as they did in the Western Isles. Brown had been present at the official ceremonial switching on of electricity in Stromness in 1947 and he always feared that, having leapfrogged the industrial revolution and come late to the modern age, Orcadians would be greedy for new gadgetry. He was right. They swiftly embraced television, especially during the winter when it was dark for all but six hours, although the reception was crackly and sometimes interrupted by interference from Russian TV.

Then, in January 1959, came the opening of Orkney's own TV mast on the site of a former radar station at Netherbutton. Hundreds of second-hand sets from the south were unloaded daily by plane at Grimsetter airfield as Orcadians prepared themselves excitedly for clear pictures. One farmer told the *Herald* that before television, the cold nights used to keep visitors away and his wife would end up talking so much he was forced to pretend he was asleep. Now they had brought pails and a grinding stone into the living room so they could prepare food for their hens and calves while watching TV. As elsewhere, television in Orkney did not obliterate other activities – borrowings from the county library reaching record levels in 1959[88] – but it surely hastened the death, two years later, of the hundred-year-old *Orkney Herald*.

The relentless advance of the TV signal meant that Gilbert Harding, from his stuccoed terraced house near the Brighton seafront, could now get three channels: the BBC from Crystal Palace, Southern Television from the Isle of Wight and Anglia from Mendlesham. His housekeeper, Joan Smith, would change the stations for him frequently. For a man who professed antipathy to the medium, he watched a lot of it. Most evenings he would sit, drink and watch TV, wearing only a dressing gown and pyjamas while his colleagues wore dinner jackets on screen. He especially liked westerns and quiz shows and, having a low opinion of modern schooling, became exasperated when a contestant couldn't answer simple questions: 'I knew that when I was ten!'[89]

Brian Masters, a friend of Harding's, said that he would carry on one-way discussions with people on the television and would 'get quite violent about it' – on one occasion arguing intensely with the *Tonight* presenter Cliff Michelmore on screen and then phoning him up to continue the argument for real. Harding would cook meals for himself and his housekeeper, starting to prepare these before the evening's viewing began and then sitting himself down in a chair in the hallway so that he could watch the BBC on the living-room set and ITV on the dining-room set, slipping back to the kitchen during a boring bit or an ad break. Often the food was not ready to eat until television had closed down for the night.[90]

By now Harding had been displaced as the most recognisable face on television by a man he likened to 'obsequious granite': the BBC's ever-present anchorman, Richard Dimbleby. His voice's gentle ascension and declension was heard on all important state occasions, issuing from somewhere above The Mall or Horse Guards Parade, or the soundproofed commentators' box high up in the triforium at Westminster Abbey. From here he produced an unremitting rivulet of words, with never an 'er' or 'erm' to separate them, the result of being well prepared, speaking slowly and making pauses seem pregnant with intention and meaning. On general election nights, he kept up a non-stop salvo of comment, combining Reithian authority with boyish enjoyment. And he was watched by one in four adults every Monday night on *Panorama*, 'the weekly window on the world'. When this programme's reporter James Mossman did a piece on the City, warning small investors of the risks of high share prices by showing them a picture of a high window ('all the better to throw yourself out of, my dear'), and the next day stock market shares tumbled after a wave of selling orders, the newspapers described it as 'Dimbleby's dip'.[91]

Like Harding, Dimbleby was a devoted viewer. While he rationed his children's viewing and worried about it damaging family life, at home in his Sussex farmhouse he watched *Phil Silvers*, *Perry Mason* and the *Black and White Minstrel Show* without fail, explaining feebly that doing so was a professional duty. According to his son Jonathan, when he watched current affairs programmes 'he kept up a barrage of critical comment like a football manager barracking the opposing team ... "Who's that nincompoop masquerading as an interviewer?", "Get camera one in close, for God's sake" ...' Dimbleby had his own critics, particularly of his panegyric, neo-Gothic style of commentary on royal occasions, with that King James Bible feel for rhythm and cadence, exemplified by his famous sentence in 1953: 'The moment of the Queen's crowning is come.' Even before the coronation, the *Sunday Express* filled a page with letters for and against him, the againsts calling him a 'cat-been-at-the cream' and a 'banana-oil exuding character'.[92]

Mostly, though, Dimbleby was trusted and treasured. A flawless filibusterer, he was made for the unpredictability of live television, and his fifty-five minutes of shameless padding when Princess Margaret was late reaching the Royal Yacht *Britannia* after her wedding in May 1960 showed a master at work. He refused to use the new-fangled 'teleprompter', regarding it as a device that would cut him off from his viewers. Instead he relied on notes scribbled on his left hand or shirt cuff, effortlessly stretching or contracting his links to order and fingering his spectacles or touching his ear to cue up the film. His fleshy face and ripened voice, the way he put his hands in his suit jacket pockets to conceal his girth, his rolling chuckle, his gentle sparring with the *Panorama* camera crew – all had a calming effect. The *Daily Sketch* called him 'an institution of the television age, a comfortable, rotund embodiment of security and promise, the Town Crier of the Telly whose very appearance seems to bring assurance that it's 8.25 and all's well'.[93]

While Dimbleby assumed the role of national town crier, Harding was no longer as gripping a personality as he once was. 'Only hunger will drive me to take part in panel games again,' he had pledged, rashly and wrongly, in 1955. Harding's rudeness on *What's My Line?* tailed off slightly, partly because he had cut down on drinking as his health deteriorated. When he appeared on *Face to Face* on 18 September 1960, his fame was only the equal of his interviewer, who had also risen rapidly to prominence in a medium he mistrusted. John Freeman did not normally watch TV but he had recently been in hospital and, immobile and unable to read, had been a captive audience. 'I emerged from the long vigil driven half mad with irrational frustration and resentment directed, perhaps unreasonably, at some of the nation's best-loved figures,' he wrote in the *New Statesman* that May. 'I cannot help feeling depressed and alarmed by the utter triviality of nine-tenths of the flood of pictures which are so earnestly and expensively hurled at us.'

On *Face to Face*, Freeman's face was unseen. Kingsley Martin, his editor at the *New Statesman*, called him 'the only man who made himself famous by showing the public his backside',[94] although, with the camera pointing over his shoulder, he actually showed them just the back of his head. When people recognised Freeman on London buses, an experience he hated, it was his voice they registered.

The *Face to Face* interview with Harding is remembered for one moment – a famous few seconds to which, when the programme's producer, Hugh Burnett, died in December 2011, all his obituaries referred. As Harding slumped slightly in his chair, breathing heavily, the camera homed in on his sad, pouchy face, sweating as usual under the arc lights. Burnett was constantly urging his cameramen to go in tighter, believing, as the ancient Greeks did, that the face was the mirror of the soul, that 'the twitch of a muscle in the corner of a mouth gives no room for compromise or manoeuvre'. Freeman then asked Harding if he had ever been in the presence of a dead person. Harding's face panicked, rather like that infinitesimal flicker of doubt that revealed a facecrime in *1984*, and he choked out, 'Yes. Only once', while his shaking hands flicked at his cigarette lighter. Harding's mother, to whom he was very close and who had once said of television that 'it seems such a silly thing to make him famous', had died a few weeks earlier.[95]

Monday's newspapers accused Freeman of humiliating Harding. Viewers complained about him 'sweating under a police interrogation' and 'positively frying under the lamps', and criticised the merciless close-ups. 'I would not be surprised to see the lights go up and find an S.S. man with rubber hose standing in the corner,' said one viewer. 'A little less menacing, please.' Another described Freeman as 'professionally impertinent' and said it had been 'like watching a doctor probe a wound'.[96]

Thus was the folk memory of the Harding interview swiftly entrenched, with Harding as the repressed Englishman who, like a character in a Rattigan play, had feeling finally wheedled out of him. But there was no need for wheedling; Harding had been painfully direct right from the start of the interview, admitting he was profoundly unhappy because 'there's not much point asking people whether they're coal heavers from Wigan or chimney sweepers from Stoke on Trent'. He had long been a fan of *Face to Face*. After watching the first episode, an interview with the Nuremberg judge Lord Birkett, he rushed to Lime Grove from his West End flat to offer his congratulations. Nor was his own appearance on the programme a live ambush as many thought. The BBC had acquired its first Ampex video recorder two years earlier and this episode of *Face to Face* was pre-recorded, because Harding was appearing live earlier that evening on *What's My Line?* Indeed, the interview had been trailed on the cover of that week's *Radio Times* with some of its key lines printed inside next to the TV listing.[97] Harding had seen and approved the programme beforehand.

Freeman did not make Harding cry, as the folk memory insists he did – unless you define weeping, as some scientists do, as anything from a lump in the throat upwards. Nor, even if he had cried, would he have been the first person to do so on television. Tears were fairly common on *Ask Pickles*, which one critic described as 'embarrassing in its encouragement of public cuddling as a national characteristic', and the 'glycerine grief' of *This is Your Life* was a regular source of press opprobrium. On 17 February 1958, the actress Anna Neagle had cried on *This is Your Life* – after being shown a clip of Jack Buchanan, a close friend who had died the previous year – and the panicked director kept the scene in long shot, while Eamonn Andrews awkwardly patted Neagle's head. The next week's newspapers called the show a 'revolting emetic', a 'stomach-heaving pie', a 'subtly disgusting programme' and 'the cruel keyhole'.[98]

But people were less shocked by Harding's 'tears' than by his announcing straightforwardly that he 'should be very glad to be dead'. The *Daily Express* made no mention of him crying but printed a screen capture with the headline: 'The very moment he said it.' Suicide was about to be decriminalised in the 1961 Suicide Act, but strong religious and moral objections to it remained. 'If a man wants to be dead he has every right to say so, shouting it from the grave tops,' wrote the journalist Merrick Winn, defending him. 'I question only Mr Harding's knowledge of human psychology. No man, sane, can ever want to be dead, however much he thinks he does ... So long may he live.'[99]

Eight weeks later, Harding was crossing the pavement opposite Broadcasting House after recording a radio programme, when he collapsed. 'Only his chauffeur was with him,' said *The Times*, seemingly eager to turn Harding's death into an allegory about the ultimate loneliness of fame. In fact he had fallen into the arms of Christopher Saltmarshe, a BBC producer and old friend from Cambridge, and a group of home-wending office workers milled around as his driver rushed to get his oxygen cylinder from the car. Alice Capan, a charwoman entering Portland Place, also spotted him. 'Oh look! It's Gilbert Harding!' she said to her two workmates, just as Harding, holding an inhaler, fell to the floor.[100]

Despite the suddenness, for only the previous Sunday he had appeared live on *What's My Line?*, Harding's death was not a great shock. He had long seemed mortal. Throughout the 1950s, newspaper readers were familiar with the same story appearing in euphemistic form: 'The BBC announced last night that Mr Gilbert Harding, on advice from his doctors, has "sorrowfully been compelled to cancel his immediate engagements for sound and television broadcasting" ... Mr Gilbert Harding has been ordered by his doctor to remain in bed for an indefinite period ...' Many of the Harding obituaries anticipated that his memory would fade as quickly as a television set ticked away its heat.

'I fear that Yorick will survive only as a legend,' wrote his friend, the novelist Compton Mackenzie, while the TV cook Fanny Cradock called him 'a twentieth-century Johnson who lacked a Boswell'.[101]

The waters did seem to close quickly over Harding's fame. Newspapers published an appeal for contributions from friends and admirers for a book on him, but four months later they had received fewer than forty letters. He seemed to belong to the era of transient live television that was now coming to an end. As Brian Masters pointed out, part of the viewers' excitement at *What's My Line?* had been that they thought they were seeing a real person in the raw, unmediated by direction or autocue.[102] A superb impromptu speaker with a natural feel for the musicality of a sentence, his words had come alive on air but had no afterlife. He had published few words of note other than dictated newspaper and magazine columns and two mostly ghost-written memoirs.

The death of Richard Dimbleby resonated far more with viewers. After his son, David, revealed in November 1965 that his father had cancer, 7,000 people wrote to him in hospital, including several who feared they might have cancer themselves and had now been emboldened to face their doctors. A Berkshire road worker wrote to say, 'Hope you get better soon, Mr Dimbleby – see you down my road one of these days.' When he died on 22 December, one of the letters received by his family said, 'It is with tears in my eyes that I learn tonight of Richard Dimbleby's death. It is as though a part of England itself had gone.'[103]

By then Harding was mostly forgotten. Madame Tussaud's, which had once displayed his effigy with the caption 'The Most Famous Man in Britain', had melted it down. The Brighton Wax Museum also melted down their Gilbert Harding in 1963; according to his biographer, although this sounds rather too neat, it was recycled to make a model of Christine Keeler. But as it turned out, Harding's contemporaries were too pessimistic about his name being writ on water. While the minor authors or Oxbridge dons to whose number he might have belonged survive only as library catalogue entries or unnoticed portraits in college halls, his memory endures, though only a few snatches of his face and voice remain. As someone whose fame was limited quite precisely to the 1950s, his photograph was used in the 1990s in an experiment to assess the long-term face and name recognition of Alzheimer's patients.[104]

In 1961, the MP for Salford East, Frank Allaun, revealed that shortly before he died, Harding, in one of those random acts of kindness that made his grouchiness more affecting, had paid for eight televisions for housebound elderly people in his constituency. After ensuring the televisions were installed, Allaun had received effusive thank-you letters: 'I usually go to bed at 9 o'clock because I am alone, but last night I stayed up until 12 o'clock.' 'This is to tell you I will not have another lonely winter ... I cannot thank you enough for the wonderful present I have received.' 'What great happiness and pleasure it will bring me in my lonely hours ... I am delighted.'[105] Allaun was speaking in a House of Commons debate about whether to allow TV licence waivers for pensioners – a concession finally granted by the Chancellor of the Exchequer, Gordon Brown, although only for those over seventy-five, thirty-nine years later.

A television set was now within most people's means. A new sight in the urban landscape was the unwanted telly left on the local tip or on a roadside skip, as affluent viewers upgraded to bigger and sleeker models. At the end of 1960 a long-agreed change on the cathode ray tube production lines made the standard television set nineteen inches wide. 'This was the most expensive two inches in the industry's history,' wrote the *Economist*, 'for the only way to dispose of nearly one and a half million sets with seventeen-inch screens was by virtually giving them away.' In August 1961, a boy in Luton bought two seventeen-inch televisions for a shilling and a penny the pair.[106] Older sets were reconditioned as 'shilling in the slot' televisions with a meter attached, an expensive way of watching TV that appealed to poor people because it did not require a deposit or leave them in debt.

Television had been feared as a dazzling, enticing medium liable to produce 'telemania'. But more detailed research suggested, as Geoffrey Gorer put it, that it acted as 'a mechanical tranquilliser', inducing only a light hypnosis. Gorer's interviewees said they bought televisions for relaxation, 'to alleviate loneliness or immobility' or as 'a device for having their grandchildren around them'. Even children failed to be spellbound. According to the Nuffield study, viewing soon became 'a habit on which the child fell back when nothing more interesting was available'. Iona and Peter Opie concluded that television had only a 'superficial effect' on street rhymes, chants and games, and that it was 'remarkable how little the new arts have affected child lore'.[107]

Tom Harrisson, while in Bolton, noted disapprovingly the habit of what he called 'negative viewing', simply having the television on, comparable to the housewife's pre-war habit of 'keeping the radio on all day'. But he still felt that people overestimated television's influence. Its greatest impact among 'culturally unsophisticated' Lancashire people was in 'presenting something which they have been doubtful, suspicious about, as if it was a *fait accompli*, an ordinary accepted part of respectable thinking and opinion, controversial or otherwise. The moment a thing has got on to TV, it exists in another level of reality.' The best example of this, he felt, had been the growth in prestige of the painter L. S. Lowry after he appeared on TV. Conversely, a television programme on art galleries in Lancashire 'might almost incidentally shatter Bolton's complacency about its dreadful collection'.[108]

For Frank Allaun, TV was a cheap way for his poorer constituents to press their faces up against the glass, like Victorian urchins, and experience remotely the new world of consumer affluence. He told the Commons that the opening and closing credit shots of *Coronation Street* were filmed in his constituency: in Archie Street, in the congested district of Ordsall alongside the Manchester Ship Canal. There were Coronation Streets in every town in the north, he said, in a far worse state than the one on television, with houses without hot water, inside toilets or damp courses. But many had TVs – now an everyday luxury, a way for the poorest in the country to arrive in the modern era on the cheap and view its new abundance from the edges. The BBC producer Tom Sloan had a similar insight one wet Sunday in 1961, after driving up to Liverpool to do an outside broadcast. 'For the first time in my life, I saw the industrial north of England, the rows of terraced houses, fronting on to the cobbled roads, glistening in the rain,' he said. 'The sheer ghastliness of it all was overpowering, but on the roof of every house, there was a television aerial. Antennae reaching for escape to another world. And, heaven knows, why not?'[109]

5

THE INVISIBLE FOCUS
OF A MILLION EYES

*There was life before Coronation Street, but it didn't add up
to much.*

Russell Harty[1]

One Monday evening in May 1961, a calamitous power cut plunged
a whole swathe of south-east England into darkness. The lights went
out all over London, Surrey, Kent and Sussex, in the biggest failure the
National Grid had yet known. For two and a half hours, chaos reigned.
Cars piled up at intersections when traffic lights stopped working,
trains stopped when the signals stalled, Scotland Yard was flooded
with calls from misbehaving burglar alarms, planes at Gatwick were
grounded as the runways blacked out, and at a blind people's rally in
Kent, the blind had to guide the sighted out of the building. When
the surge of current returned around midnight, two television sets in
Southend Road, Beckenham exploded and burst into flames. The Electricity Board blamed the short circuit on a huge increase of demand in
Wimbledon at 9.27 p.m., just after the end credits had rolled on that
week's episode of ITV's western series *Wagon Train*.

Wagon Train was one of the most popular shows on TV, and
that evening the BBC was showing *Time Remembered*, a play by
the absurdist French dramatist Jean Anouilh, thus siphoning even

fewer viewers away from ITV than usual. Westerns like *Wagon Train*, *Laramie*, *Maverick*, *Bonanza* and *Rawhide* were some of the most popular programmes on TV, probably because they were definitively televisual. Even young children could work out what was happening when, either through youthful incomprehension or the bad acoustics of their TV sets, the dialogue went over their heads. Heroes were always clean-shaven, villains always moustachioed and scarred. Those shot from behind would always throw back their shoulders and jerk up their heads; a shot from the front always occasioned an instant clasp of the stomach. 'Virtually every day,' recalled Griff Rhys Jones, seven years old in 1961, 'we sat in front of the black-and-white television in the brown, shiny Bakelite box with an armoury of "Lone-Star" cap-revolvers and Winchester repeater rifles close by on the sofa, in order to shoot down the "baddies".'[2] Gunfire crackle from the TV rang out incessantly in Britain's living rooms, especially since the guns were always so badly aimed, hundreds of shots being fired before anyone was even hit.

Broadcasters had long been aware of the power they held to synchronise human behaviour in remarkable ways. As early as 1935 Lord Reith noted that engineers could gauge the popularity of radio programmes by the drop in water consumption and the sudden peak load when they ended. In the mid 1950s they began to notice a similar effect in television, when *Children's Hour* – especially when a cultish, anarchic glove puppet called Sooty, his ears darkened with soot to show up on black-and-white TV, was on – seriously depleted electricity supplies, because it started at 5 p.m. and overlapped with the working day. The Electricity Board estimated that, if the BBC would only shift the programme half an hour forward, it would save the equivalent of a full power station on peak demand.[3]

The ending of popular shows placed a particular strain on the National Grid, because the electricity used in running TVs was small compared to the much greater amounts needed to operate lights, electric kettles and water pumps for flushing toilets. No longer did people open the fridge door or make a pot of tea as a matter of individual whim; television immobilised them all for set periods before springing them into life when a programme ended. Surges in demand of half a million kilowatts, the output of a large power station, could occur at the end of certain shows, threatening the knife-edge balance of the country's electricity supply. Thus, after the catastrophic impact of *Wagon Train* on Wimbledon, was a new yardstick created for assessing the popularity of TV programmes.

To avert a similar disaster in future, the Electricity Board began employing statisticians to track the popularity of television programmes and to trace demand curves across each evening. These half a dozen men, the 'demand forecasters', would sit in the new national control room in Park Street, London, leafing through copies of the *Radio Times* and *TV Times*. One of their jobs was to map the 'TV pickup', the peak moment at which millions of people stopped watching television. It was a phenomenon felt most strongly in Britain, with its relatively few commercial breaks and large number of tea drinkers boiling electric kettles – unlike, for example, the Japanese, who used gas stoves.

In the control room the forecasters would monitor demand, relying on a mixture of intuition and experience, and instruct Britain's power stations to increase or reduce production accordingly. By the mid 1960s, computers had been introduced, enabling the impact of factors such as peak-hour viewing, mealtimes and seasonal changes to be accurately assessed. The computers would then issue instructions and, seconds later, vast turbines would rumble into life like waking monsters, just to maintain the state of electricity in the grid at the magical frequency of fifty cycles a second. For television was now a basic amenity, like electric light or tap water, that people expected to have at the flick of a switch. In seven British homes out of ten, a bluish-grey flicker radiated through the front windows each night.

Engineers had been trying for years to get television's high frequency radio waves to travel over longer distances and somehow override the curvature of the earth. In the late 1940s, they floated the idea of carrying TV transmitters high up in the air on tethered airships, barrage balloons, or aeroplanes travelling in lazy circles 30,000 feet above the earth, sending out signals that would blanket the earth's surface like giant, upended ice-cream cones. Another more audacious plan was to bounce radio waves off the surface of the moon. In May 1959, in an experiment sponsored by the television manufacturer Pye, the radio telescope at Jodrell Bank in Cheshire sent morse code messages to the Cambridge Air Force Base in Massachusetts by this method. But the reception was poor and the signals could not be sent once the moon had set. The start of the space age intervened and on 10 July 1962, the Telstar satellite set off round the earth on an egg-shaped orbit, during which it would be visible on both sides of the Atlantic for just one hour. Several million viewers stayed up after midnight to watch a special broadcast from Goonhilly Downs on Cornwall's Lizard peninsula, not far from where Marconi had first sent his radio waves across the Atlantic.

Goonhilly, a sparse heathland at Britain's most southerly point, could almost have been designed for satellite broadcasts by a benevolent god familiar with the nature of the radio wave. During the war it had been home to RAF Drytree, which provided radar cover for Britain's Western Approaches, as it offered a sweeping view from horizon to horizon – which now allowed Telstar to be tracked easily as it raced across the sky in low orbit. It was away from industrial interference and radio noise: 'electronically quiet', in engineer speak. And on the Lizard peninsula, an old sea bed lifted 400 feet above the waves, the Precambrian rock is made up mainly of serpentine, on which little grows except *Erica Vagans*, a heathland plant unique in its tolerance of magnesium in stony soil. There are thus few trees or bushes to block the path of the TV signal. Serpentine is also hard enough to bear the thousand-tonne weight of the giant satellite dish built to pick up Telstar's signal.

Drawn by a sense of history in the making, crowds of Lizard locals and holidaymakers had pitched their tents and started camp fires near the floodlit dish, jamming their cars along the narrow lanes leading on to the moors. At 12.45 a.m. viewers on both BBC and ITV heard the voice of the Post Office engineer, John Bray, stationed at Goonhilly, saying that the huge dish had begun tracking, searching the skies along the predicted orbit for Telstar's signal. Bray had long been excited by television's ability to communicate over long distances. In the late 1920s, as a teenage engineering apprentice in Portsmouth's naval dockyards, he had built his own version of Baird's spinning disc receiver to pick up the thirty-line images from the BBC's mast on Selfridge's roof over sixty miles away, and a decade before Telstar, he had secured his footnote in television history by inventing the TV detector van. Bray had spent eighteen months overseeing the building of Goonhilly Earth Station. Although Telstar's most profitable line would be taking international phone calls, he knew it was satellite television that would excite the public. But as the public watched, Goonhilly's TV screens were picking up only static. The steerable dish searched the skies in vain for a signal that was as weak as that which would be received from a one-bar electric fire on the moon.

Then, at around 1 a.m., viewers saw a TV flicker tantalisingly into life, and a fuzzy image move manically up the screen as an engineer tried to tune it in. 'That's a man's face …,' spluttered the BBC's commentator Raymond Baxter. 'That's the picture … there it is. It's a man … there is the first live television picture across the Atlantic with rather less than four minutes of available time left.' Over on ITV, Ian Trethowan floundered in similar fashion: 'Something is … there's a picture there … there is something different *there*. It looks like a face. It *is* a face. This is almost certainly, this is the first television picture to come across the Atlantic. It's a face. Madly fiddling with it or trying to, trying to hold it, just like you would at home. But this is … this is a face. It's bouncing around but you can see absolutely clearly this is a man, sitting behind a desk.' The face settled for a few seconds before vanishing. An aerospace firm placed an advertisement in several newspapers, showing the screen capture: 'Do not adjust your set: THIS IS ONE OF THE GREATEST TV PICTURES EVER! … the Hawker Siddeley Group is proud to have supplied much of the tracking equipment.'[4] It was indeed a blurred image of a besuited, bespectacled man sitting behind a desk: Fred Kappel, chairman of Telstar's funder, AT&T.

Somehow the precariousness of the satellite connection, the faint, wobbly image of a head appearing out of nowhere being interrupted by capering wavy lines, added to the sense of enchantment. For those with a living-room aerial, adjusting it was a long, nightly ritual, and viewers were well used to twiddling the vertical hold button on their sets just as the Goonhilly engineer had done to tune in Fred Kappel. Reception was still a hit or miss affair. Everything from faulty electric blankets to hairdryers caused interference. A feature of the urban landscape at this time was the construction cranes assembling highrise buildings, which produced ghost images on TV sets. Prince Philip, attending the congress of the International Union of Architects in London, complained to representatives of a building firm that their new eighteen-storey building in Victoria Street was interfering with his viewing of the Test Match.[5] Metal gasometers also stopped the TV signal getting through, although less so in the evenings, when their iron tanks sank back down as they released gas to homes.

Even televisions close to a transmitter were prone to getting pictures in negative form, known to engineers as the 'Penge Pub Effect' because it was first identified in a public house near the new Crystal Palace mast soon after it opened in 1956. Now that most of the country had television, poor reception had replaced no reception as a common grievance. Early one Sunday morning in April 1961, Reginald Bevins, Postmaster General and MP for Toxteth, was asleep in his house in Queens Drive, Liverpool when he was awakened by a loud banging on the front door. His teenage son, sent to answer it, was confronted by a hundred television viewers from Peterborough who had driven 200 miles in a nine-van convoy to protest to him about the poor reception they were getting for ITV. They had brought a petition with nearly 20,000 signatures.[6]

Telstar had its own power system and onboard computer to retransmit the signal it received. This little space postman, not much bigger than a beach ball, seemed almost human and rather vulnerable, a tiny dot in the emptiness of space. At the Earls Court Radio

Show, a working model of Telstar revolved above a miniature Lizard peninsula bathed 'in a wondrous green twilight like something out of a Chesterton story, as if the Flying Inn were just on the other side of Goonhilly,' as one visitor put it. The Scottish poet, Edwin Morgan, wrote a playful concrete poem, 'Unscrambling the waves at Goonhilly', in the form of a Telstar transmission which relays the names of real and imaginary aquatic creatures – dogfish, sardine, sardock, telfish – before identifying the magical, similarly seven-lettered name of the satellite itself.[7] Two weeks after the launch of Telstar, more than half the population of Britain watched a live link-up between Europe and America which began with a short segment of a baseball game between the Chicago Cubs and the Philadelphia Phillies, and ended with Eamonn Andrews balancing upon the rocks of the Lizard and a London bus passing over a floodlit bridge on the shimmering Thames.

On the night of 10 July, the record producer Joe Meek had been watching television alone in his flat-cum-recording studio above a leather goods shop at 304 Holloway Road, London. Now a twenty-four-hour off licence next door to the Titanic Café, it has a small round plaque nailed to its first floor wall, next to a satellite dish, which says: 'The Telstar Man Lived, Worked and Died Here.' Meek had long been fascinated by the capacity of radio waves to send magic rays invisibly through space. In 1948, at the age of nineteen, he had completed his national service as a mechanic at radar installations in the West Country, putting in long, lonely shifts in one-room buildings perched on isolated hills, directing his gaze and imagination skywards. When still in his teens he had built a nine-inch television set, the first in his home town of Newent on the edge of the Forest of Dean, although, since there was still no nearby TV mast, all it gave out was white noise.

In 1950 he went to work at an electrical shop in Newent, repairing

TV sets, a steady job in those days when sets were unreliable. He built another TV for his parents, ready for the first transmissions from Wenvoe in 1952. 'It was a little 12″ screen,' his brother Eric remembered. 'And it used to come on about half past seven at night, and we'd all get in there in the dark, draw all the curtains, switch it on and sit there till the Epilogue at about 12 o'clock. And when we put the lights on, the house was full – chock-a-block, full of people! They just used to sneak through the door and nobody said a word.'[8] Meek came to London and serviced TVs in a radio shop on Edgware Road, before moving into record producing. He became increasingly unstable, dabbling in the occult and conducting séances to contact the spirit of Buddy Holly. Something of a late Victorian, he had made an imaginative association between the ability of humans to commune with each other through electrical wires and radio waves and the slightly older practice of telepathy.

Past midnight on 10 July, Meek sat on his sofa, enthralled by the television picture of Fred Kappel at his desk. After reluctantly going to bed, he lay there imagining Telstar orbiting several thousand miles above the earth. A tune gradually came into his head – something evocative of the speed of this little satellite and the vast distances it was covering – and he ran straight to his studio to hum it on to a tape.[9] Later that week, he recorded his instrumental, 'Telstar', with the Tornados. The deathless tune, played on a clavioline, conveyed the sense of a countdown, blast-off and ascent into the skies, followed by a plateauing guitar break evoking orbit. Meek passed the tape through compressors and echo chambers to make the sound echoey and uncanny. By the beginning of October the single had reached number one, where it stayed for four weeks. Its rinky-dink catchiness and ethereal strangeness seemed a fitting soundtrack for this new age of television. A rumour spread that the background noises on the track came from recording Telstar's launch and its aural signal in space. In fact, the rocket launch sound at the start was Meek's toilet flushing played in reverse, and the sound evoking radio waves was a pencil scraping against an ashtray.

In her Christmas TV broadcast, the Queen used Telstar as a

metaphor for a world changing almost too rapidly. 'This tiny satellite has become the invisible focus of a million eyes,' she said, striking an oddly melancholic note. 'Yet some people are uncertain which star to follow, or if any star is worth following at all. What is it all for, they ask, if you can bounce ... a television picture through the skies and across the world, yet still find lonely people living in the same street? The wise men of old followed a star: modern man has built one.'

Marshall McLuhan, the modish cultural theorist on both sides of the Atlantic in the 1960s, argued that, with the arrival of electronic media, we were seeing a revival of tribal humanity, a return to the archaic world of orality in contrast to the privatised, abstracted world of print, which he called, in the title of a book published in the year of Telstar, *The Gutenberg Galaxy*. A Catholic convert, he wrote quasi-religiously of the new global media creating 'a general cosmic consciousness' and a 'unified sensorium'.[10] McLuhan often appeared on television, his intellectual style – synoptic, scatty, epigrammatic – being well suited to it. He seemed the perfect prophet for the space age, which briefly revived that earlier delight in television's ability to annihilate physical distance and watch remote events in real time.

But the space-age glamour of satellite television was fleeting. Telstar's successors did not career round the earth in a low oval orbit, from where their beeping progress could be eagerly tracked. They were parked in a geostationary orbital garage called the Clarke Belt, named after the sci-fi writer and visionary Arthur C. Clarke. In an article in *Wireless World* in 1945, Clarke had first located this region, 23,300 miles above the equator, where satellites could circle the spinning earth in exactly twenty-four hours and so remain stationary above it. Here, unlike Telstar, the satellites would be mostly forgotten. As President Lyndon B. Johnson addressed Europe live at 7 p.m. on 7 May 1965 via Early Bird, the first satellite to be placed in such an orbit, Michael Miles carried on regardless on ITV's *Take Your Pick* as he had done for a decade, offering contestants money for the key to a box which might contain a star prize or some bread and dripping ('I'll give you four pounds for that, five, six, seven – look, there might be a boiled egg in that box ...') while the studio audience shouted advice ('Open the box!', 'Take the money!'). On *Tonight* on BBC1, they showed a brief clip of LBJ before moving on to a film about the Land of the Midnight Sun. Another Tornados' single, 'Early Bird', also written and produced by Joe Meek, failed to trouble the pop charts.

A special Early Bird simulcast from New York was another damp squib. 'The nearest approach to live visual novelty that I saw was the corpse of an elderly baseball fan being carried out of the vast Astrodome at Houston,' wrote one TV critic. The same was true of *Our World*, a mammoth satellite link-up in June 1967 in which nineteen different nations presented segments, remembered now only for the Beatles singing 'All You Need is Love'. 'As we switched from pictures of cars streaming back into Paris on a summer evening to the enthralling spectacle of an iron and steel works in Linz,' wrote Michael Billington in *The Times*, 'I was reminded of the melancholy truism that modern man has at his disposal fantastic power of communication and very little to say.'[11]

Even when Telstar launched, sceptical voices pointed out that American television was already here, and that seeing it instantly might not advance the cause of civilisation. Richard Dimbleby, hosting the Telstar broadcast, wryly observed that satellite TV would mean 'instant *Laramie*'. And Telstar began its life in space just as, back on earth, the Pilkington Committee on Broadcasting was criticising the 'vapid and puerile' programmes on American-style commercial TV. It identified triviality as 'a natural vice of television' and (quoting the Christian socialist historian R. H. Tawney) as 'more dangerous to the soul than wickedness'. The committee examined the offerings of the six TV stations in New York on a winter evening, and found, to its chagrin, a choice of six westerns between 7.30 p.m. and 9 p.m.[12]

The committee's most influential member was a 43-year-old English lecturer at the University of Leicester. Richard Hoggart had been appointed to the committee on the strength of his widely read *The Uses of Literacy* (1957), about the impact of mass media on the vernacular culture of the working class. This book ignored the now dominant mass medium of the time, apart from some brief generalised references to the dangers of reducing people to 'a condition of obediently receptive passivity, their eyes glued to television sets'. The simple reason for the omission was that the Hoggarts had no television, only buying one in late 1957. Soon after, Hoggart became a public figure and his son Simon remembered 'the neighbours cramming into our living room to see him appear on some earnest early Sunday evening inquiry into education'.[13]

On his appointment to the Pilkington Committee in 1960, Hoggart's wife, Mary, unguardedly told the *Sunday Times* that he liked *Hancock* and documentaries when he had 'nothing better to do', but that 'a whole fortnight might go by without him turning on the set'. But Hoggart was coming to believe that television had an unrivalled ability to guide popular attitudes. 'Spend a week regularly watching television on either or both channels,' he wrote in a 1960 essay, a kind of addendum to his book entitled 'The Uses of Television', 'and you almost feel the cakes of custom being cracked open.' Hoggart began to watch more television and, standing in as the *Observer* TV critic in the summer of 1962, was generous in his praise of *Steptoe and Son* and Benny Hill, 'a fugal comedian in both the musical and the psychiatric senses'.[14]

It was not until late on Saturday 25 November 1962, though, that Hoggart became convinced that 'the box in the corner could offer, was prepared to offer, a funny and slightly subversive angle on our lives'. At 10.45 p.m., the first edition of *That Was the Week That Was* went out – scheduled then because, according to the BBC's assistant controller Donald Baverstock, viewers on a Saturday night were the furthest distance from the working week and at their most relaxed, private and prepared for irreverence. Malcolm Bradbury, a young English lecturer at the University of Birmingham, similarly recalled the 'enormous euphoria' the programme inspired among his contemporaries, 'as if the great British log jam was being broken at last'.[15]

TW3, as it came to be called, relished the fact that lots of people were complaining about it. One of its weekly features was a score-card of who had phoned in to complain or congratulate them about the previous programme, the latter number invariably being the greater. The team summed up what the presenter David Frost called 'the ludicrousness of the incipient Grundyism'[16] – Mrs Grundy being the personification of priggishness in Thomas Morton's 1798 play *Speed the Plough* – with a sketch in the final programme of the first series in which Millicent Martin and Roy Kinnear played a suburban couple watching *TW3* at home. 'It was satire wasn't it?' said Kinnear. 'Mucky jokes. Obscenity – it's all the go nowadays.'

And yet when the *Daily Telegraph* criticised the programme in a leader, its letters page suggested that readers mostly dissented. 'Let us be thankful,' wrote one, 'that, at last, there is at least one television programme offering adult and stimulating entertainment.' *TW3*'s viewers – a near exact cross-section of the population, geographi-cally and demographically – were overwhelmingly positive about it. A 92-year-old couple wrote to say it had transformed their lives, and teenagers, television's ficklest audience, were regular viewers. Schoolteachers reported that pupils had begun reading newspapers; the headmistress of a girls' school instructed her sixth form to stay up to watch it. After the TV technicians' union leader George Elvin made a bewildering statement on the programme, Frost immediately invited any children watching to précis his words. By Monday he had received thousands of replies, which surprised him with their 'hipness and intelligence'.[17]

Richard Hoggart hoped that television might help to create an intelligent common culture that would enrich the lives of those who did not have access to the usual routes to intellectual and cultural capital – a sort of free education by stealth and serendipity. Television, he felt, could 'offer sudden flashes of insight in pictures or words: epiphanies, which we do not forget'. He later recalled watching Jacqueline du Pré performing Elgar's Cello Concerto on television – most likely Christopher Nupen's BBC *Omnibus* film broadcast in 1967, which included a complete performance of the concerto – as the cameras moved in close on her swaying, rapt style of playing, with those familiar crescendo jumps in her seat, all done without looking at a score. It was, thought Hoggart, 'an extraordinary instance of totally absorbed creativity by an artist … Without television one could simply not see this happening at all, and that is a great gift.' So it is clear why he was so energised by *TW3*'s appeal to all classes and ages. Its success, he said, proved that 'people are more intelligent and discriminating than they are allowed to be by those who simply exploit the sentimental and glamorous side of their tastes with big commercial variety shows'.[18]

When *TW3* returned to the nation's television screens amid much anticipation in the autumn of 1963, though, its first few programmes were disappointing. As its producer Ned Sherrin put it, quoting Cole Porter, the public's love affair with the show had been 'too hot not to cool down'. If television did offer the possibility of an intelligent common culture, the audience for it seemed capricious and liable at any moment to be tempted away by what was on the other side. For a new craze had taken over late on Saturday nights: ITV's adventure series *The Avengers*, with the kind of preposterous plotting and pop sensibility which that autumn seemed to contrast so freshly with *TW3*'s satirical earnestness. It was the favourite TV programme among Eton College boys, which probably had less to do with its old Etonian star, Patrick Macnee, than with his co-star Honor Blackman, playing an anthropology PhD and judo expert called Cathy Gale, who threw men through plate glass windows while dressed in black leather utility suits and thigh boots.[19]

Just as *TW3* was losing its edge, someone emerged who would certainly have been seen by its team as a reincarnation of Mrs Grundy. Norah Buckland, the wife of the rector of Longton, Staffordshire, hearing complaints from her husband's parishioners about television, had hired a set and was troubled by what she saw. She shared her fears with her friend, Mary Whitehouse, an art teacher from Claverley near Wolverhampton. On 5 May 1964, Buckland and Whitehouse launched a 'Clean Up TV' campaign at Birmingham Town Hall. 'We recognise that the period between 6 and 9.15 is a period for family viewing,' Whitehouse told the 2,000-strong audience, consisting mostly of churchgoing housewives like herself. 'Well, I think we're being palmed off, because last Thursday evening, we sat as a family and we saw a programme that started at 6.35. And it was the dirtiest programme that I have seen for a very long time.'

Whitehouse did not name it, but according to the listings it was the first episode of *Between the Lines*, a satirical Scottish comedy show billed as 'a series of light-hearted enquiries into matters of no importance' with Fulton Mackay, later more famous as the warder in the sitcom *Porridge*, as its linkman. '*Between the Lines* is "an enquiry in depth",' went the *Radio Times* billing. 'And there is no limit to the depth to which we may sink during the next six weeks. For the subject of our first report we have chosen "The Tender Trap". Or, in a word (an unfortunate word): marriage! Among future subjects are "Jock, The Vanishing Aboriginal" and "The English. Are They British?"' Whitehouse disliked this new kind of irreverent comedy – one critic called *Between the Lines* '*TW3* in kilts' – almost as much as she disliked the *Wednesday Play*, which she felt indirectly censored vast areas of normal, suburban life. 'We are told that the dramatists are portraying real life,' she said to her Birmingham audience, 'but why concentrate on the kitchen sink when there are so many pleasant sitting rooms?'[20]

'Clean Up TV' was not just about cleaning up TV, but about which versions of reality should emanate from the television screen. One of Whitehouse's favourite programmes was *Dixon of Dock Green*, a Saturday teatime ritual in the form of a weekly, secular parable. At the start of each episode, PC Dixon appeared in front of the local police station, saying 'Good evenin' all', to viewers and announcing the scripture for the day, the criminal case study with a moral message that was to follow. At the end of the story he addressed a brief homily to the camera based on what viewers had just seen, before wishing them 'Goodnight, all'.

Richard Hoggart dismissed *Dixon of Dock Green* as a form of 'half-art' with little relation to police procedure. He noted that one Lancashire force had switched from wearing caps to helmets simply as a public relations exercise because, after PC Dixon, helmets were associated with the reassuring traditional bobby. Hoggart preferred *Z Cars*, a case-hardened series about a police force in a northern new town which had turned the flawed Chief Inspector Charlie Barlow (Stratford Johns) into one of the best-known characters on television, and upset many police officers who felt it brought the force into disrepute. Lincolnshire's chief constable, John Barnett, one of nineteen chief constables who signed Whitehouse's Clean Up TV petition, insisted that *Dixon of Dock Green* was more accurate, and went on to propose civil disobedience against the BBC's proposed licence fee increase.[21]

It is hard to know exactly how widespread Whitehouse's concerns were, because the BBC had a non-disclosure policy about complaints, and news of them filtered out erratically, such as on *TW3*. When the BBC2 arts show *Late Night Line-Up* revealed that the corporation had been 'flooded with protests' after the backstreet abortion drama, *Up the Junction*, was broadcast in November 1965, its producers were admonished for ignoring a rule that 'no reference should be made to numbers or the tone of calls of protest received' because of 'a determination not to allow the lunatic fringes, who, as the Duty Log shows, are so often the majority of the callers, to dominate the front pages'. For the BBC's director general Hugh Carleton Greene, the killer fact about Clean Up TV was that, at the Birmingham meeting, literature from the right-wing Christian group Moral Rearmament was available. The BBC's attitude to complainants combined a determination not to give in to interest groups with a professional confidence verging on aloofness. 'Viewers – at least the peculiar kind who write letters – see only what they want to see,' concluded Kenneth Robinson, an early presenter of the BBC feedback series, *Points of View*, which began in 1961. Taking all the letters home to read was, he wrote, 'an unbelievable weekly wallow in viewers' bigotry, prejudice and illiteracy'.[22]

The BBC did divulge that its drama about homelessness, *Cathy Come Home*, shown in December 1966, prompted 'dozens of telephone calls and letters', which seems a small figure for what is now regarded as a consciousness-changing television event. Whitehouse said later that the play had led to the launching of the charity, Shelter, making it a piece of propaganda which was contrary to the BBC charter. But Shelter was already in existence, and shrewdly placed an advert in newspapers the day after the repeat in January 1967: 'Did you see Cathy last night?' It had just been announced that St Pancras Station's buildings were to be saved from demolition, after a public campaign led by John Betjeman. After the *Cathy Come Home* repeat, many viewers rang the BBC and wrote to newspapers, suggesting that St Pancras's empty hotel rooms and offices should be used as a hostel for the homeless. But the angriest viewers of *Cathy Come Home* were the council housing officials who felt their profession had been besmirched by it. When it was repeated, the Local Government Information Office asked the 2 million council employees in England and Wales to watch it and check for factual inaccuracies.[23]

By 1965, Clean Up TV, now with a membership of 7,000, had become the National Viewers' and Listeners' Association and was calling for a National Viewers' Council, without which, it said, the licence fee was 'taxation without representation'. It stood for a nascently Thatcherite sense of lower middle-class grievance in what was not yet called 'middle England', a land occupied by the decent provincials ignored by the cliquish, metropolitan professionals. Whitehouse saw herself as an envoy of the silent, suburban millions watching stony-faced at home while the London-based programme makers amused each other, and their rowdy studio audiences yelped sycophantically at their jokes. She called them the 'intellectual freebooters of the South' and an 'in-grown intellectual coterie', and in a letter to the *Financial Times* asked: 'Is it not time that common sense was allowed to blow away the hot air generated by the power-houses of the "intellectuals"?'[24] Her support, which did tend to be strongest in Wales, Scotland and the northern English provinces, seems to have been substantial without ever constituting a majority of viewers. A petition to clean up TV, delivered to the House of Commons on 3 June 1965, contained 366,355 signatures.

But what of the millions who did not sign? In a BBC paper, the corporation's director of television Kenneth Adam tried to build up an 'identikit' of the average viewer, a rarely spotted animal who spent about two and half hours a day in front of the TV. Occasionally he enjoyed a memorable event like the Telstar broadcast, wrote Adam, but mostly he liked familiar shows with which he resented interference, and indeed was outraged far more by overruns and rescheduling than sex or violence. He disliked arguments about religion, but 'enjoyed the vague well being which good hymn singing brought him'. He was quick to spot errors of fact in quizzes or anachronisms in dramas, which for Adam suggested a deep-rooted desire for participation which television was not satisfying. A significant minority of viewers, he claimed, were 'addicts'. They wrote 'somewhat illiterately' to complain that TV finished too early, and made up the several hundred thousand people who, during a recent TV strike, had sat watching the test card.[25]

Adam soon found some painful corroboration for his portrait of the typical viewer as habit-loving and boredom-fleeing. When BBC2 started in April 1964, he announced that the new channel called on the viewer 'occasionally to stretch himself a little further' and 'to push back the horizon a little'. But when faced with the new schedules – highlights of the first week including *Materials for the Engineer*, an evening with the Russian comic Arkady Raikin ('Mr Khrushchev's favourite funny man') and a youth theatre production of *Julius Caesar* from the Ashcroft Theatre, Croydon – viewers seemed unwilling to have their horizons pushed back. By June, fewer than a fifth of those who had seen BBC2 intended to become regular viewers and nearly half thought its programmes worse than those on ITV and BBC1. Among BBC2 viewers there were twice as many men as women – probably, said the polling company, 'due only to male intellectual curiosity'.[26]

While public arguments raged about cutting-edge drama or satirical shows, most people carried on watching programmes like *The*

Man from UNCLE or *Dr Finlay's Casebook*. Richard Hoggart's new Centre for Contemporary Cultural Studies at the University of Birmingham announced itself as more interested in this broad mass of popular shows than the occasional piece of bad language on TV. In his inaugural professorial lecture, Hoggart worried about the tendency for charming compères and saccharine serials to make life seem easy, so that anyone finding it hard felt like an exile in front of the television set. *This is Your Life*, for instance, represented 'hopes, uncertainties, aspirations, the search for identity in a moving society ... the wish for community and the recognition – far down – of an inescapable loneliness'.[27]

According to Barry Miles, a member of the 1960s underground who, in April 1967, helped organise a happening called the '14-Hour Technicolor Dream' at the now deserted Alexandra Palace, 'the sixties began in black and white and ended in colour'. Britain in the first half of the decade still clung to austerity greys and browns and much of the mediated world – newspapers and much photography and cinema – was in black and white. The Beatles were a monochrome band, all grey suits and half-shadowed photographs, before they burst into primary hues in the films *Help!* and *Yellow Submarine* and on Sergeant Pepper's gatefold cover. Richard Avedon's psychedelic, tone-reversed posters of the Beatles ornamented countless bedsit walls and started a trend for colour solarisation on albums and posters. Psychedelic culture's embracing of colour was a way of conveying synaesthesia, the sense that sounds could be seen as bursts of colour when under the influence of LSD.

The arrival of colour television at around the same time as this more general embracing of colour was no coincidence. As early as 1961, when colour TV was clearly on its way, the *Sunday Times* owner, Roy Thomson, argued that 'newspapers must reply to colour with colour', and the following year his newspaper created the first colour supplement.[28] The same was true of film: no one, it was thought, would go to see a black-and-white film in the cinema with colour TV at home. Publishers started using more colour on book covers and the full-colour paperback was born, especially in a new generation of children's books like Brian Wildsmith's *ABC* (1962) and Maurice Sendak's *Where the Wild Things Are* (1963). But the colour that entered the television set was of a more subtly reshaped reality than the day-glo colours and kaleidoscopic whirls of the counterculture. On 21 April 1967, about fifty BBC executives sat in front of huge colour sets in half a dozen houses watching *Late Night Line-Up*. 'It was a revelation, a vision of the noumenon,' wrote Anthony Burgess, appearing on the programme with Jonathan Miller and Angus Wilson. They all kept getting up to look at the monitor screen to see each other in colour.[29]

On black-and-white television, certain hues had to be avoided to keep the picture stable, including checked or striped clothing and, oddly, black and white. (The 'white' coats worn by the doctors in *Emergency – Ward 10* were yellow and the BBC's male announcers would wear beige shirts under their dinner jackets.) Now, in colour, the *Late Night Line-Up* presenter Joan Bakewell was encouraged to wear simple, not too bright colours; black and white showed up particularly well. 'I shall be surprised if there is not a strong move to pastel shades in clothes for both men and women by 1969,' Kenneth Adam predicted confidently (and wrongly) about colour TV's effect on fashion.[30] The engineers experimented tentatively with *Late Night Line-Up* over the next few nights, at one point bravely placing a bowl of fruit on a coffee table.

The arrival of colour television had been long delayed because of the failure to agree internationally which colour system to use. When Europe finally agreed on a standard, the 625-line BBC2 was the only British station with the technology to go colour immediately. David Attenborough, the BBC2 controller, wanted the kudos of making his channel the first colour one in Europe. It was believed that the Russians intended to introduce a colour service in time for the fiftieth anniversary of the Bolshevik revolution in October 1967, and the

French were also thought to be planning a start at the end of the year in time for the Winter Olympics in Grenoble.[31] But Attenborough did not want to repeat the mistake of the American TV networks, which had started colour gradually and so treated the few hours of colour each week as a spectacular advertisement for it, making programmes of self-defeating complexity which most viewers, watching in monochrome, found disappointing.

Colour would thus arrive in two phases: a 'colour launching period' of about four hours a week, which would whet the public's appetite and allow the retail trade to begin selling colour sets, and a full-scale, official unveiling of colour TV in December. Zero hour for the launching period was Saturday 1 July 1967, with a live transmission from Wimbledon: an obvious choice because it was easy to film with just three colour cameras. At 2 p.m., BBC2 switched from monochrome shots of Henley regatta and the colour camera panned in on the presenter Peter West, artfully flanked by flowerpots and a green umbrella. The Radio and Television Retailers' Association guessed that there were no more than 5,000 colour sets in Britain; the manufacturers' body put the number in the hundreds.[32] The industry had been thrown by Attenborough's decision to steal a march on the Europeans and there weren't enough sets to sell to those who could afford them – who were not many, since they cost £300, a third of the price of a new Ford Zephyr. Colour viewing parties swelled the numbers slightly, and a few TV critics were allowed to watch in colour at BBC Television Centre, in the hope that they would reveal this miraculous vision to the unconverted. Even so, the first day of colour TV was probably viewed by about 10,000 people, 5,000 fewer than were watching in real colour on Centre Court.

America's NTSC system for colour television, known contemptuously to British engineers as 'Never Twice the Same Colour', was a natural heir to the hyperrealistic, highly saturated hues of Technicolor film. As Jonathan Miller told a New York audience for whom he had arranged a private showing of his BBC monochrome production of *Alice in Wonderland*, their colour TV was 'all gangrene and custard'. Attenborough insisted that Britain's colour TV would be more 'natural' than monochrome, a more accurate representation of what the eye perceived. This was the continuation of an argument running all the way through western art between metaphysical and realistic notions of colour. In the former tradition, colour was a quality to be celebrated in itself, from the opulent religious art of the middle ages to the intense colour contrasts of the abstract expressionists. In the latter, painters like Leonardo and Rembrandt used restrained colours and chiaroscuro to bring the viewer closer to reality. Attenborough, in aesthetics as well as by profession, was a naturalist, convinced that the 'honeymoon of delight' on first seeing bright colours on a television set would wear off and the real gain would be that it would add information, give a sense of perspective and be more restful on the eye.[33]

Those who saw the first match in colour, in which another of Britain's Wimbledon nearly men, Roger Taylor, beat the South African Cliff Drysdale, were impressed by its naturalism, with the flesh tints, the hardest thing to get right, nothing like the luminescent skin tones of MGM musicals. Colour imposed a new drama on the game, with the players' faces darkening theatrically as clouds crossed the sun. The keen tennis fan noted the varied colour of the Centre Court turf and could see where the grass was sappy and a player might slip, and where it was brown and the ball might bounce awry. One detail inspired much comment: the bottles of orange and lime barley water by the umpire's chair. A little like the LSD trippers in the summer of love happening elsewhere, the first colour TV watchers found themselves reintroduced to the world, from the greenness of grass to the orangeness of orange juice.

In the launching period, it was the trivial detail that mesmerised: the cherry-red shirt of the Virginian, the chestnut-brown eyes of Joan Bakewell, the swirling clothes of the flower-bedizened Haight-Ashbury hippies on *Whicker's World*. There were also a lot of dull trade test colour films repeated over and over again, including 'Prospect for Plastics', an industrial film documentary about the influence of plastics on our lives, and 'Overhaul', a guided tour of London Transport's Aldenham bus overhaul works, before the full colour service began at last on Saturday 2 December 1967. The big draw of the first weekend's schedules, moved from BBC1 especially for the occasion, was *The Black and White Minstrel Show.*

A small number of dissenters preferred the austere contrasts of black and white to what they saw as the bogus glamour of colour. Ken Loach said he would rather have made his 1967 film *Poor Cow* in monochrome, and John Boorman, who was moving away from making television documentaries into filmmaking, considered himself lucky to have been 'trafficking in a contiguous monochrome world … a familiar reality transposed into a parallel universe … Reality is what we live, film is metaphor.' Others worried that colour would disenchant the world. The BBC's head of light entertainment, Tom Sloan, pointed out that colour TV was much less kind to skin than monochrome, mercilessly revealing brewer's bloom, bloodshot eyes and stained teeth. The comedian Dick Emery had a complete set of plastic crowns made for his new BBC2 colour show.[34]

Most critics, however, welcomed colour for its re-education of their vision. An emetic yellow tanktop worn by a right-wing Rhodesian in an interview 'commented on the poor taste that goes with moneyed racism as well as a yard of closely argued print would have done,' wrote Peter Black. Nicholas Garnham felt that BBC2's new colour series on the life of Christ beautifully conveyed the Biblical symbolism of water as a lifegiving force, through the glaring white of the Dead Sea's foreshore salt and the emerald green Jordan surrounded by parched ochre. William Hardcastle, watching the US open golf championship, suddenly saw the whole point of colour TV when the camera caught 'the full plump face of Nicklaus, furiously contemplating a putt, between the brightly trousered legs of a caddy'.[35]

The BBC Natural History Unit's *The Major*, a tender study of a year in the life of a village green oak tree destined to be felled, had already been shot in colour in 1963, ready to become one of BBC2's most repeated shows after the arrival of colour TV. Relying only on the understated revelations afforded by high-fidelity colour, it delicately interweaved images of local life, from Morris dancing to cricket matches, with footage of the wood ants and blue jays that made the oak their home. Ron Eastman's *The Private Life of a Kingfisher*, with its stunning underwater shot of a kingfisher on the River Test in Hampshire diving to catch a fish, was also repeated many times.

Earlier 405-line black and white was not high definition enough to show a fishing line clearly, so fishing programmes tended to involve a presenter waggling a bendy stick unproductively in the air; but BBC2's new *Anglers' Corner*, with Bernard Venables, conveyed beautifully in 625-line colour the choreography of rod and line against the changing light of a day on the water. Percy Thrower, meanwhile, had been presenting *Gardening Club*, a studio programme with glassless greenhouses and soil bussed in each week, in black and white since 1954. In colour a studio garden looked unconvincing, so BBC2's new *Gardeners' World* was filmed at Magnolias, Thrower's own garden in Shrewsbury. Colour TV thus inadvertently created a more intimate relationship between gardening presenters and viewers. Thirty or forty cars were often parked by Magnolias, as people came to look at the garden, armed with binoculars. When Thrower held charity open days, thousands came, parking coaches and cars in nearby fields.[36] These tourist trips to see someone's fairly ordinary back garden would never have happened without colour TV. It introduced viewers to the parochial natural world they thought they already knew, from gardens to river banks, and made them see it afresh.

Only about 20,000 of Britain's 15 million sets – one home in every 750 – were yet in colour. The Postmaster General's decision to let BBC2 go it alone, and for colour TV to begin, in his words, as 'a rich man's toy', meant that few viewers were willing to pay for colour just for the minority channel. Only England had the television transmitters set up for colour, and in some parts of the country there was still no television at all. In the remote crofts of the Scottish Highlands and Islands, they complained of 'television starvation'. Local dealers often took it upon themselves to bring television to the farthest flung outposts before the official transmitters arrived. Television had arrived unofficially on the Isle of Lewis in 1959, six years before a mast officially arrived in the Outer Hebrides on Wester Ross, when a Stornoway TV dealer bought an old radio mast for £25 and brought the first TV, illegally, to about 1,000 homes.[37]

In 1964 an electrician discovered a weak signal on the top of Mallaigvaig, a hill behind the port of Mallaig on the mainland opposite Skye. He installed a portable, battery-powered set on the hilltop and the town's residents climbed up in darkness to watch the evening programmes. A local firm tried unsuccessfully to install piped television from there to the town. The proprietor, David McMinn, said: 'We have had persistent letters to MPs but we have been getting nowhere … The demand … well everybody's frantic for it. Take the winter up in this west coast. There is nothing by way of entertainment in these places.' As for the Isle of Skye itself, its relay transmitter kept being delayed. The islanders' anger came to a head in September 1963 when, according to the *Stornoway Gazette*, many Skyemen had to travel as far as Fort Augustus or Inverness to see the Rangers v. Real Madrid European Cup tie on television.[38] The mast on Skriaig in Skye finally opened in March 1966, just in time for the World Cup for which Scotland had failed to qualify.

'Is this not the land of the bens and glens and the heroes?' asked the chairman of the Broadcasting Council for Scotland, Sir David Milne, quoting an old Scottish song. 'But it is the bens, and there are so many of them and so much of them, which get in the way of the viewing and listening of the heroes, and the heroes' wives and families.' The most ambitious project to bring television to the Highlands was the 'Great Glen Chain', a ribbon of transmitter links running from Rosemarkie on the Moray Firth to Oban on the west coast, along the loch-filled geological fault that bisects Scotland. Finished in 1963, it brought television to remote outposts on the western seaboard like Ballaculish, Kinlochleven and Ardgour. The Scottish secretary Michael Noble said that not since the time of General Wade, the eighteenth-century army officer who built roads and bridges as a way of controlling the Scots, had the Highlands been made so open to the influence of the south. He did not underrate 'the dangers to Gaelic culture inherent in what the transmitters would bring'. By the mid 1960s, ninety-seven per cent of Scots had TV reception.[39]

In the Western Isles and parts of the Highlands, the Free and Free Presbyterian Churches of Scotland, formed in the mid-nineteenth century, still held a puritan grip on cultural life. Their kirks were unadorned, Presbyterians believing that the word of the Bible was all, and best heard without visual diversions, so they were naturally ill-disposed to television. In the summer there was a communion season, an elongated Sabbath from Thursday to Monday with church services twice a day. Sermons focused on the dangers of the congregation 'backsliding', through Sabbath breaches like drinking, driving and watching TV. 'A flood of lurid salacious matter emanates into our homes via a means which to date has resented and resisted all attempt at control and stricture,' stated the 1966 annual report on Religion and Morals issued by the Synod of Glenelg in Lochalsh. 'The Sabbath, for some unknown reason, seems to be the day when this medium excels in its foul moral oozings.'[40]

But there was also a great appetite for television in isolated regions, particularly in the far north. The Highlands and Islands Film Guild, fighting a rearguard action against depopulation, had begun a touring cinema in 1946, showing films in the hamlets and villages of the crofting counties. Villagers in remote areas eagerly awaited the arrival of the Guild and the showing of the films would often be followed by a *ceilidh*. But the spread of television from the early 1960s onwards affected attendances drastically, especially among the over-thirties. On the edges of the nation, the march of technological progress was accelerated: Shetland, which had only seen its first film in 1950, had television thirteen years later. Struggling to attract audiences, the Guild folded in 1970.

On the Isle of Harris, the new Hattersley looms, installed in crofters' homes to make tweed, could be operated while watching television, because they did not require the weaver to change bobbins, they stopped automatically if a thread broke, and cards could be inserted to make patterns. In crofting communities, knitting was another common source of extra income, and another trade practised easily while watching television, although a (male) writer in the Dundee-based *People's Journal* worried that TV would distract the womenfolk from this important cottage industry.[41]

The wave of English hippies who came to the Western Isles in the late 1960s in search of a simpler life found themselves at odds with the islanders' embrace of modernity. When the folk singer Vashti Bunyan arrived with her boyfriend Robert Lewis on the Hebridean island of Berneray in 1969, having spent a year and a half driving all the way from London in a horse-drawn cart, they found newly minted rows of electricity and telegraph poles and television installed in the crofters' cottages. Their ambition to live a bucolic life was met with puzzlement and suspicion by the natives of Berneray, who were not prepared to turn their backs on modernity when it had barely arrived. 'Remote areas are obsessed with communications,' wrote the Oxford anthropologist Edwin Ardener. 'The world always beckons – the Johnsonian road to England, or the coast, or wherever it is, is an attraction to the young, for it leads from your very door to everywhere … The assiduity with which television is watched in remote areas has a particular quality. A programme on the Mafia is squirrelled away as part of the endless phantasmagoria of life that begins at Oban or Kelvinside.'[42]

Many in the Hebrides welcomed the late arrival of English TV as a way of breaking down the 'brimstone curtain' imposed by the Free Church. The poet Iain Crichton Smith, brought up in Upper Bayble, a tiny Gaelic-speaking village on the Isle of Lewis, was ambivalent about TV because he was a fierce defender of Gaelic while lamenting the power of the Free Church, which he thought insular and philistine. He also resented tourists and exiled Hebrideans romanticising the islanders as noble savages. These were the kind of people, he thought, who, when they saw television sets in Hebridean houses, regretted their presence as if the natives had somehow let them down: 'How could the islanders have betrayed him so profoundly, so cheated him of his dream?'[43]

Television was also getting more ambitious at depicting these remote areas of Britain to the rest of the country. Over a July weekend in 1967, six climbers scaled Orkney's Old Man of Hoy live on BBC1, in the most technically complex outside broadcast yet attempted. Even before the broadcast could begin, sixteen tonnes of equipment had to be ferried from the Firth of Clyde into Rackwick Bay in army assault craft and dragged on sledges over a peat bog to the cliff edge by a Scots Guards platoon. The impact the ensuing broadcast had on viewers is more surprising because televised climbing was inherently methodical and laborious and had been tried several times before with little impact. The BBC had first experimented in 1963 with a live programme from Snowdon, but the action was so misted up by rain and the climbers so hard to pick out that one reviewer commented that it was 'several hours of watching dirty cotton wool twitching in a draught'. Dougal Haston, one of the Old Man of Hoy team, could never understand why viewers wanted to watch such slow, repetitive moments, and wondered if, subconsciously, they were hoping someone would fall off.[44]

The BBC executive Chris Brasher, who was the commentator for the Hoy climb, was a compelling, driven character – already well-known as the pacemaker for Roger Bannister's four-minute mile in 1954 and as an Olympic gold medallist in 1956 – and he managed to get the climb commissioned in the face of doubters in the corporation. He insisted that it should not be just Saturday afternoon padding on *Grandstand* as the previous climbs had been, but a big event broadcast live to give it 'a touch of the Colosseum'. It was also as stage-managed as it could be, with bolts and pitons pre-fixed partway up so the climbers could make a smoother ascent when they were live, but with the equipment artfully concealed. Viewers never saw the climbing cameramen or the sherpas carrying equipment.[45]

The climbers turned out to have a pleasingly rough-hewn eloquence, describing the crumbling sandstone on which they were trying to gain purchase as 'cracking biscuits', 'hard sugar' or 'like climbing over gigantic dinner plates breaking under your feet', and reacting dryly to the fulmar petrels spraying vomit right into their faces. 'If anything goes wrong,' one of them said, 'the only medical equipment we'll need is a spade.' There was an intriguing contrast between the earnest, monosyllabic hard men, like Dougal Haston and Pete Crew, and the new breed of climbing personalities whom Tom Patey called the 'Telstars' – like Patey himself, who in one vertiginous moment swung out fifteen feet from the cliff on the rope, just for a laugh.[46]

The real Telstar, however, was the photogenic sea stack itself: 450 feet of Orcadian sandstone almost exactly level, as Brasher kept pointing out, with London's new Post Office Tower, bringing the mingled terror and pleasure of the Kantian sublime to BBC1. A sailor wrote to the *Radio Times* to say that he had sailed past the Old Man on many occasions, but it took this broadcast to reveal to him the immensity of the cliff faces. It looked spectacular on the Saturday night, floodlit with the arc lights against the swirling Atlantic waves, while the climbers bivouacked on a ledge. 'I suspect that the Old Man of Hoy broadcast will never be superseded as the perfect live broadcast,' wrote another of the climbers, Chris Bonington. 'It had every ingredient – a perfect, very obvious summit, a scale which was also perfect, since the climbers clinging to the tower were dwarfed by its size, yet were not totally lost in its immensity.' Fifteen million people saw them reach the summit late on Sunday afternoon. One viewer said that the pictures were so clear they gave him vertigo.[47]

The broadcast ended with an abseil down to the bottom by Bonington, a dramatic single plunge because of the overhang at the top of the stack, his frame silhouetted against the sky. 'Once upon a time, you had to go all the way to Everest to earn public acclaim,' reflected Patey with typical self-deprecation. 'Now, you need only appear on television hanging upside down from the end of a rope. In more ancient times, the same sort of enthusiasm was aroused by public hangings.' By creating an event that could not easily be outdone, though, the BBC ensured that climbing would not become a fixture in the schedules. The first colour TV climb, of the Anglesey cliffs on 30 August 1970, was an anticlimax, not helped by being on what was traditionally the worst viewing weekend of the year, the August bank holiday, for which the BBC's head of drama, Sydney Newman, always used to save what he called 'the real dogs' among its output of plays.[48]

As so often in the history of television watching, the climbing of the Old Man of Hoy had resonated with viewers through a strange chemistry that was unique and unrepeatable.

'The conceit of this long-haired brigade is appalling,' complained one Brighton viewer. 'The Beatles have become an embarrassment to Britain,' agreed Dorothy Roberts in Great Yarmouth. 'Even my fifteen-year-old son admits they are tripe now.' On Boxing Day 1967, around 14 million people had watched, or at least started to watch, *Magical Mystery Tour*, billed anodynely in the listings as a 'coach trip by the Beatles around the West Country'. Given its plum place in the Christmas schedules, at 8.35 p.m. just after a Petula Clark special, they could not have anticipated what they saw, a faux new wave film based on self-indulgent improvisations. The phone calls began before the programme ended, dismissing it as 'rubbish' and 'piffle', or simply asking, 'What was it all about?' 'They must have made it up as they went along,' said a pensioner from Chelsea, perceptively. 'They needn't have bothered for me.'[49]

The reaction to *Magical Mystery Tour* supported Kenneth Adam's findings about British viewers, in the sense that its audience seemed most irritated not by the brief striptease scene or the reference to naughty girls and knickers in the song 'I Am A Walrus' to which Mary Whitehouse had objected, but by the wilfully boring and obscure. 'We tried to present something different for the viewers, but according to the newspapers it did not come off,' said Paul McCartney, graciously, on David Frost's chat show on 27 December. 'Was it really as bad as all that? Some people must have liked it, surely.' A few did – like Garth and Carol Tucker from London W4, who wrote to the *Listener* to say how pleased they were that TV, normally an insipid medium, had shown some bite. They placed the film 'within the anarchist/surrealistic tradition that stretches back to Vigo and early Buñuel'.[50]

The Tuckers would have been dismayed at some further evidence that television and its viewers were addicted to linear narrative and suspicious of the avant-garde. The most ambitious serialisation the BBC had ever undertaken, *The Forsyte Saga*, had started to be shown on Saturday nights on BBC2 from January 1967, which at the time was only available to 8 million viewers. Many people on Britain's fringes could still not get the new channel; others did not want or could not afford the new 625-line set necessary to receive it. 'My own small gesture will be to cancel the regular order for the *Radio Times*,' wrote a disenfranchised Galsworthy fan, Sigrid Morden, from Montacute Road, Catford. But the saga did succeed in attracting a new audience to BBC2, viewing figures growing at a rate of 200,000 a week and eventually reaching 6 million, as well as dramatically hiking the sales of Galsworthy's novels. Malcolm Muggeridge deplored the new trend, which he was sure Galsworthy would have hated, of putting colour photographs of the actors from the series on the covers of the Penguin paperbacks.[51]

But it was only in September 1968, when the series began a re-run on BBC1 on Sunday nights, that its popularity reached critical mass, particularly among those viewers who felt alienated from the radical bohemianism of the decade. 'We are tired of having a guilty conscience if we are luckier than our neighbours, and of trying to take the burdens of Vietnam and Biafra on our shoulders,' wrote Mrs A. Boydell, fastening on the saga as a still point in a turbulent world. 'Above all, we are sick of the sight and sound of scruffy teenagers and students and kitchen sink drama!' An antiques dealer interviewed for BBC1's *Talkback*, gesturing to a series of art deco statues which he could not have given away a year earlier but which were now worth about £30 each, thought the saga had been 'tremendously effective in conjuring up the terrible disease of nostalgia'.[52]

There was a further stark reminder that not every TV viewer felt at home amid the liberal currents of the time: when Soames Forsyte raped his wife Irene after she had appeared to be unfaithful to him, *Late Night Line-Up* canvassed the opinion of Oxford Street shoppers and discovered that fifty-four per cent supported Soames. But perhaps this figure is slightly less shocking when one considers that Soames had by then become an intricate, many-sided character, whose very unlovability earned him sympathy from viewers because he seemed aware of it yet powerless to change. Alan Hewitt, a civil servant, reflected shrewdly that Soames 'believed in the sanctity of contract; he was an obsessional type of character, which is why he was drawn to the law, which always has an intellectual answer ... He's got no flair for human relationships at all, I would say, wouldn't you?'[53]

The most repeated fact about *The Forsyte Saga* is that it forced vicars to abandon Evensong. This fear about the decline of Sunday churchgoing had been voiced since television emerged as a mass medium. A survey conducted among Methodist ministers in 1952 suggested that, while most Sunday services ended before the evening's television began, congregations were increasingly unenthusiastic about after-service activities if these prevented them getting home in time to watch it. One minister complained that television was turning worshippers into clock-watchers and if he dared to go overtime in the Sunday evening service there was a mass flit during the final hymn. 'It's no use hiding the fact that *Sunday Night at the London Palladium* is more popular than going to church on a cold winter's night,' said a Woking vicar after the start of ITV, explaining why he had moved Evensong half an hour back. By the mid 1960s, many other vicars had shifted Evensong to an earlier time so their parishioners could be home in time to watch the Sunday night film.[54]

Churchgoing had been declining since the end of the Victorian era, and Evensong had long been especially endangered because it was intended for two dwindling groups, farmworkers and servants (which was why the upper and middle classes had their main meal early on Sunday afternoon, so that their servants could attend). The dramatic fall in religious observance from the late 1950s onwards, both in adult churchgoing and children's attendance at Sunday School, was often blamed on television – not an argument heard so much in America, where the medium was even more entrenched but where about half the population still attended church regularly. Mary Whitehouse's campaign to clean up TV was underpinned by her belief that Britain was a Christian country and should have its values reflected on its televisions, combined with a fear that churchgoing was giving way to television viewing.

There was supposed to be no television on Sundays between 6 p.m. and 7.30 p.m. to encourage church attendance, but a blind eye was turned so long as the programmes shown were religious. White-house had no objection to the congregational, non-denominational hymn singing of *Songs of Praise*, introduced pragmatically by the BBC in 1961 to make use of outside broadcast units lying idle after filming football games on Saturday afternoons. But she was dis-mayed at the BBC's acknowledgement in this slot of the existence of humanists and the kind of radical, questioning theology promoted by Mervyn Stockwood, Bishop of Southwark, and his suffragan John Robinson, Bishop of Woolwich. One of the BBC's 'God Slot' programmes helped to inspire the Clean Up TV campaign: *Meeting Point*, so-called because it sought 'to bring together those who believe that man is a spiritual being and those who believe no such thing'. Its episode on 8 March 1964, about which Whitehouse heard second-hand from her pupils, had a panel of experts debating the morality of premarital sex. *Meeting Point* was, she wrote, 'a classic example of the way in which the BBC, with its penchant for "South Bank" religion, was allowing itself to be used as a launching platform for the "new morality"'.[55]

The threat to Evensong posed by *The Forsyte Saga* was part of these wider battles. Not even the Forsytes, in fact, could kill it off for good. Many vicars simply changed the time of the service, as they had done before for other programmes. *The Times* ran a correspondence from clergymen, some arguing that the BBC should alter the sched-ules 'to satisfy those who wish to follow their devotions to both God and the Forsytes', and others insisting that 'the important thing is that people should worship God, not that they should worship Him at 6.30 p.m.'. The decline of Evensong had a special undercurrent of pathos because it was a liturgically lyrical ritual with a plangent, evocative name and valedictory associations with twilight and night-fall. 'The familiar Sunday evening ritual in parish churches, with a few gathering to sing the evening hymns, and to hear again the prayer to Lighten Our Darkness – that was now over,' wrote A. N. Wilson about the 'defining moment' of *The Forsyte Saga*.[56]

The Sunday night period drama, from *The Forsyte Saga* to *Downton Abbey*, which the historian Simon Schama would later accuse of 'servicing the instincts of cultural necrophilia', came to acquire that same sense of valediction, a raking over of the dying embers of the weekend, as Evensong. Sunday evening, as a Sabbatarian hangover from churchgoing and pub opening hours, was the night when people were most likely to stay in, and they wanted to watch something calming and cheering before work and school in the morning. In a column in the *Church Times*, Ronald Blythe blamed the demise of Evensong on 'the best television of the week, plus, I used to suspect, some connivance by the clergy to rid themselves of this service'.[57]

As for that mythical era, 'the 1960s', most people lived it vicariously through the TV screen. In July 1969, Bernard Davies, a tutor at Chorley College of Education, watched *Top of the Pops* in a shabby, unpainted docklands youth club by the Leeds–Liverpool canal. 'On the screen, swaying bodies, gay and fashionable clothes, space-age décor, music to match,' he wrote. 'The weekly ritual confirmation of youth's popular image. Freedom, wealth, confidence, unconventionality – all unmistakeably symbolised.' Meanwhile, all around him, he saw 'a microcosm of Lancashire's imprisoned youth', sitting in shapeless sweaters and jeans, their faces drawn and undernourished. In these places which the affluent society had not reached, the revolution was watched on television.[58]

Ronald Blythe's 1969 book, *Akenfield*, suggested that the counterculture had also bypassed the English village but that television was changing it in slower and subtler ways. Blythe had spent several months riding round the Suffolk village of Charsfield and its environs on a Raleigh bike, talking to three generations of villagers and transcribing their oral histories. These interviews included familiar laments about viewers hiding away in their houses: the local branch secretary of the National Union of Agricultural Workers worried that television kept men away from union meetings, and the Women's Institute president noted that the attractions of television were making it difficult to attract new members, and that when they had a quiz the teams could always identify commercials (which she could not, being unfamiliar with ITV).

But television was having more positive effects among the more taciturn gravediggers and farmworkers, 'breaking down their silences' and getting them 'accustomed to the idea of dialogue'. Farm-minders who had never left the parish boundaries saw the wider world opened up to them nightly on television. Derek Warren, a 29-year-old ploughman, had not been to a pub for six years, preferring to watch television with his wife, enjoying travel programmes about 'the tribes of people faraway'. 'The big beer-drinking days are gone,' Francis Lambert, a 25-year-old forge worker, agreed. 'They drank because there wasn't any television. Their houses were so boring, they were glad to get to the pub.' Lambert liked TV drama, and was always on the lookout for scenes allowing him to indulge his professional interest. 'You may not have noticed, but telly plays are full of wonderful ornamental ironwork,' he told Blythe. 'There was this programme the other day about the fiftieth anniversary of the Russian Revolution which showed a pair of gates. Marvellous, they were.'[59]

Although living only just outside London, the author J. G. Ballard was another viewer watching the set detached from the zeitgeist. In 1964 he had been widowed when his wife died suddenly of pneumonia while on a family holiday in Spain, and he was left bringing up three young children on his own in a semi-detached house in the west London suburb of Shepperton. Watching television was a habit that could fit easily into his disjointed routines as an author and single parent, a short story or book chapter being dashed off 'in the time between ironing a school tie, serving up the sausage and mash, and watching *Blue Peter*'.[60]

Arriving in postwar England from Shanghai as a teenager, Ballard found the country decrepit and backward-looking. He watched TV with his parents for the first time in Manchester around 1951, when the screen seemed to be 'about the size of a light bulb'. In his first published short story, 'Escapement' (1956), the central character discovers to his horror that he is living out his life in the same, endless fifteen-minute time loop, in which various dull programmes repeat themselves on his television, including a panel game, modelled on *Animal, Vegetable, Mineral?*, in which three professors and a chorus girl try to guess the origins of a Roman pot while the question master, 'a suave-voiced Oxford don', makes feeble puns.[61] Ballard welcomed the fresh air of ITV just as he embraced what he saw as other belated arrivals of Americanised modernity like motorway flyovers and airports.

Ballard's youngest child, Bea, noted that her father was unusual in that, unlike her friends' parents, he did not ration his children's television watching, and in the school holidays the Ballards became aficionados of daytime soaps and magazine shows, before all gathering round the television in the evening, after homework, to watch *Dad's Army* or *Steptoe and Son*. Ballard thought Steve McGarrett in *Hawaii Five-O* ('Book 'em, Danno, murder one!') was the epitome of cool, partly because he drove a 1968 Mercury Park Lane Brougham, and he had always admired the kind of powerful, streamlined American cars he first saw in Shanghai, while himself only ever driving mid-range family saloons.[62]

As often with Ballard, this bathetic life in front of the television was at odds with the apocalyptic tone of his fiction, which tended to take an acknowledged condition of modern life, such as the television-watching habit, and extrapolate it into a cultural pathology. In his 1972 short story, 'The Greatest Television Show on Earth', Ballard described a near future in which the world's population, its appetite whetted by live broadcasts from Vietnam, sits supine in front of the television as it travels back in time to show the Battle of Waterloo or John F. Kennedy's assassination, complete with real deaths. Ballard's own life in front of the set was more prosaic. 'The 1960s,' he wrote later, 'were an exciting decade that I watched on television.'[63]

Given his laissez-faire and catholic approach to television viewing, and his professional interest in sci-fi, it seems likely that Ballard would have stayed up with his children late into the night for the televisual event of the decade's end, the moon landing. Viewers had already watched a full-scale dress rehearsal of this event just before Christmas 1968, when the crew of Apollo 8, the first humans to escape earth's gravity, presented twenty-minute broadcasts at about 1.30 p.m. British time. The first, on 22 December, showed the astronaut Neil Anders clowning around with a toothbrush, turning weightlessness into a party game, and, also for the first time in history, a glimpse of the earth from interplanetary space, as James Lovell pointed his cigar-box sized camera out of the cabin window. Sadly the telephoto lens failed to work, turning the earth into a tiny blob of light, resembling a distant bicycle headlight on a dark road.

The next day, though, viewers could clearly see the earth from 175,000 miles away. Britain was in the shaded area, shrouded in cloud. Raymond Williams, watching in his cottage at Hardwick, a village just outside Cambridge, considered it 'a new way of seeing' and compared it to the revolving earth that had been BBC1's channel ident since 1963. He saw 'the north and west in ragged shadow; the bright Caribbean; the atlas shapes of the Americas … I glanced from its memory to the spinning globe of BBC-1 presentation: light, untextured, slightly oiled. It was necessary to remember that both were television.'[64]

Earlier that year the editor of the *Listener*, Karl Miller, had invited Williams, a Cambridge English don, to write a monthly television column. Williams was a relative newcomer to the medium, having bought his first set only in 1964, but he soon made up for lost time. An old friend, David Holbrook, who would call up at the family cottage to find Williams watching something unlikely like a gymkhana, said, 'I had the impression he watched for *hours* … he'd leave the set on while we tried to talk, and it just flowed over him.' Williams was a prominent figure in the New Left, making the occasional foray to London to speak and protest about Vietnam. When at home, however, this private man, who often felt tired in the evenings, spent much of his time watching television.

With a background in adult education, Williams had long seen the value of TV and radio as 'jet-propelled missionaries',[65] and in 1963 he had taken part in Anglia TV's 'Dawn University', shown at quarter past seven each morning – a forerunner of the Open University that began eight years later. Like Richard Hoggart, he hoped that television might form part of what he called 'the long revolution' towards an educated, participatory, democratic culture in its blurring of the distinction between high and low culture, a division infected by the class system that had afflicted British society since at least the seventeenth century. Like Hoggart, he found television often fell short of these expectations.

Writing for the *Listener* gave Williams's television viewing a raison d'être and a routine. He would buy the *Radio Times* and *TV Times* on Friday, highlight things to watch the next week and then write about them the following Sunday morning. There was little he would not watch and have an opinion about, from the *Horse of the Year Show* to *Sportsnight with Coleman*. A rare exception was the investiture of Prince Charles in July 1969, which, as a Welsh nationalist and republican, he boycotted. Staying in Wales at the time, he claimed that he forgot about it until the shops at Abergavenny began to close early, and was then too busy building a dry stone wall.[66]

Williams aimed to write as a normal viewer, watching television programmes blend into each other rather than, as most television reviewers did, seeing them as discrete entities like plays or films. For he could see that television's defining quality was its surreal and jarring combinations, compounded in the case of the Apollo 8 broadcasts by the fact that the spacecraft reached the moon on Christmas Eve, and festive specials like *Christmas Night with the Stars* and *Doddy for Christmas* were interrupted by ticker-tape summaries, moving across the bottom of the screen, informing viewers that the astronauts were now in orbit or were having a sleep. Patrick Moore, commenting on the Apollo mission for BBC television, complained of one especially egregious intrusion. On Christmas Eve, as he was commenting on the 'critical burn', a perilous moment in the mission when the astronauts had to fire the lunar module's rocket to lock them into a closed path round the moon, the BBC interrupted him to go to the children's programme *Jackanory*.[67]

No one was really sure how to turn these events into television: the contrast between the domesticity of the medium and the enormity of the achievement was too great. On 20 July 1969, the night of the moon landing, ITV started early at 6 p.m. with *Man on the Moon*, a variety and chat show with a revolving panel of guests, hosted by David Frost. 'Hello and good evening on the night of the great adventure,' Frost welcomed viewers. 'The end of an incredible voyage and the beginning of what may be a whole new world for all of us. Because tonight man lands on the moon and steps into the age of Flash Gordon ...' There were some odd tonal shifts as Frost segued from interviewing the astronomer Sir Bernard Lovell and the historian A. J. P. Taylor to introducing Cilla Black singing or Eric Sykes doing a sketch about a Mancunian bullfighter.

Outside broadcasts, from a London discotheque and a big screen in Trafalgar Square, gauged the public mood. A phone-in, an idea Frost had imported from New York, inspired a Mr Roberts of Eastbourne to call and ask if moondust could help him grow bigger pumpkins. BBC1, meanwhile, ran its normal programmes until 8.45 p.m., just half an hour before the touchdown, being reluctant to cut into *Dr Finlay's Casebook* and *The Black and White Minstrel Show*. The BBC's viewer panel judged BBC1's moon-night *Omnibus* special, 'So What If It's Just Green Cheese?', featuring Pink Floyd, the Dudley Moore trio and actors reading poetry, to be 'a last minute shambles ... a scrappy and boring "hotch-potch" that did scant justice to so historic an occasion'.[68]

This is probably why 14.5 million viewers watched ITV's coverage of the touchdown compared with 12 million on the BBC, the first time ITV's ratings had overtaken the BBC's for a major news event. During the descent, ITV showed live pictures of the moon as seen from the top of ITN's Kingsway HQ, along with a static shot of the team at Mission Control, with pre-prepared captions. At 9.18 p.m., the words 'The Eagle has landed' appeared on screen a couple of seconds before Neil Armstrong said them. The majority of viewers were back with

James Burke and Patrick Moore on the BBC for the moonwalk and Britain's first ever all-night TV broadcast – a hastily prepared one, since it had been supposed that the astronauts would sleep until commencing their moonwalk at around 6 a.m. GMT. Many children, and some adults, came down early next morning, switched on the television and found that they had missed it all.

Those who had heard about the schedule change in time saw, just before 4 a.m., Armstrong's left boot leaving a blurred piece of ladder and stepping gingerly on to the moon. For Christopher Hitchens, a 21-year-old student at Balliol College, Oxford and member of the International Socialists, the moonwalk summed up his ambivalent feelings about America. 'I remember distinctly looking up from the quad on what was quite a moon-flooded night, and thinking about it. They made it! ... Who could forbear to cheer?' he wrote later. 'Still, the experience was poisoned for me by having to watch Richard Nixon smirking as he babbled to the lunar-nauts by some closed-circuit link. Was even the silvery orb to be tainted by the base, earthbound reality of imperialism?' Most British televisions were still 405-line black-and-white sets, giving off a smoky, lunar glare that added to the unearthliness of the images which, for sleep-deprived Britons, must have had the quality of a dream. At his home in Gospel Oak, north London, Michael Palin finally went to bed at 5 a.m., 'with the image in my mind of men in spacesuits doing kangaroo hops and long, loping walks on the moon, in front of a strange spidery object, just like the images in my mind after reading Dan Dare in the old *Eagle* comics'.[69]

'The frequent silences more moving than sound ... the strange transparent ballet as the astronauts became "moon happy" ...,' wrote Joan Broadbent from Alcester to the *Radio Times*. 'It was all exciting, of great interest, and wonderful.' But the rock photographer Ray Stevenson, watching the moonwalk with his friend David Bowie and Bowie's girlfriend, Angela Barnett, found it disappointing. 'It was dull, black and white fuzzy footage of people walking slowly,' he said. Bowie had just released a song called 'Space Oddity' and told *IT* magazine that he wanted it to be 'the first anthem of the Moon, play it as they hoist the flag, and all that', while also describing it as an antidote to 'space fever'.[70]

Bowie claimed the song was inspired by Stanley Kubrick's film *2001: A Space Odyssey*, which he saw three times when it was released in 1968, but the music critic Peter Doggett points out that it may also have been triggered by the BBC sci-fi drama *Beach Head*, broadcast on BBC2 in colour on 28 January 1969, just as Bowie was writing it. This was about a disillusioned space pilot, Commandant Tom Decker, who has a breakdown while push-buttoning his way through his thirty-seventh mission to an alien planet. The song, which has Major Tom looking back at earth from his tin-can space capsule and reflecting on its vulnerability, also suggests that Bowie saw the Apollo 8 broadcasts. Watching the moonwalk, he was amazed to see that the BBC had complied with his wishes and used 'Space Oddity' as background music. 'I couldn't believe they were doing that,' he said. 'Did they know what the song was about?'[71]

In order to make the expensive experiment of colour TV a success, it had to become domesticated and routine. Viewers were urged not to put the saturation up too high on their colour sets, to go for the muted, restful tones in the middle rather than the dazzling colours at the top of the dial. 'There are those who seem to feel that a streak of gold across the forehead of an actor, just under the line of his hair or wig, is a pleasing effect,' wrote the musicologist Henry Raynor. 'The accurate tuning of a colour set is an art which some people seem to be quite happy to leave unlearnt, as though colour, like beauty, is in the eye of the beholder.'[72]

BBC1 and ITV agreed on a single date for the launching of a full colour service: Saturday 15 November 1969. That month, travellers at London Euston were treated to a 'Colour Comes to Town' exhibition which had been touring the country since starting at Croydon two years earlier – in order to show off colour TV and dispel some of the myths about it, including the nasty rumour that its radiation made men sterile. Programmes premiering in colour that weekend included *Dixon of Dock Green*, *The Harry Secombe Show* and *Match of the Day* – and Sunday's Royal Variety performance, which showed comedian Ronnie Corbett nursing a black eye, more visible in colour, after walking into a door. The hundreds of viewers who rang the BBC and ITV to complain that their sets were still showing black-and-white pictures were gently informed that they needed to buy colour TVs.[73]

One of the highlights of that first colour weekend was the opening episode of a five minute stop-frame animation series conceived especially for colour, and inspired by its co-creator Oliver Postgate's viewing of the moon expeditions. It told of a race of pink, mousey creatures with long noses, Clangers, who lived on a moon-like planet and spoke in an echoey, whistling, nonsense language. Clangers were so named because they hid under clanging metal lids to avoid the junk left floating around their orbit by the earth's space programmes, and the first episode included a shot of a lonely earth from space that must surely have been inspired by the Apollo 8 broadcasts. Meant for children but broadcast late on Sunday afternoons just before the news, it soon acquired a loyal adult following. Postgate picked up a hitchhiking university student who recognised him solely from his euphonious voice, and another group of students wrote asking for his recipe for the Clangers' signature dish, blue string pudding. The *New Scientist* praised the programme's 'gentle chaffing' of 'the whole sober apparatus of science that spends countless millions to enable selected Americans to murmur monumental platitudes over the vasty reaches of space'.[74]

The second moon landing on 23 November, the first in colour, was an anticlimax. The coloured moon in orbit turned out to be a light shade of concrete. 'If I wanted to look at something I thought was the same colour I'd go and look at my driveway,' the Apollo 12 astronaut, Pete Conrad, told viewers, deflatingly. On the moon itself the colour camera broke, and the moonwalk reverted to monochrome. 'As marathon television, moon-landings have already lost their edge,' concluded the jazz musician and critic George Melly. 'This seems odd, even somehow disgraceful, but I think it's true for most people. A troupe of acrobats, accompanied by a drum roll, finish their act by doing their most difficult feat but, unless they fail, they only do it once. This mission, dramatically, was identical with the first.'

In July 1969, BBC1 had begun showing a new series, *Star Trek*, with an unfortunately timed second episode: in 'The Naked Time', screened the day before Apollo 11 landed on the moon, the Starship Enterprise tried to evacuate a team of scientists from a planet which was about to break up, only to find they had all mysteriously died. Compared to *Star Trek*, the moon missions were untelevisual, and sci-fi's scientific accuracy about outer space made them more a corroboration than a revelation. Between blast-off and splash-down there was not much to see apart from the short daily updates from the astronauts, and not much to listen to except the flat intercom sounds of mission control. Melly reflected on this from the perspective of his peer group, perhaps the last generation, he speculated, to be excited about the technology of television. It was hard, he decided, 'to flog one's sense of wonder hour after hour', especially when the moon's surface looked like 'a hard-sell commercial for Maltesers'.[75] If you had seen one moon landing, you had seen them all.

Marshall McLuhan's argument that the electronic age would recreate an archaic world of communal orality fell down when it came to television, an inescapably visual medium. He skirted round this problem by arguing that TV was still essentially an oral phenomenon because it offered such a poor quality image – which may have been true of the flickering images posted by Telstar, and the shadowy messages sent from the moon, but wasn't true of Cilla Black in 625-line colour. 'We see colour with the cone of our eye, black-and-white with the edges,' said McLuhan. 'Colour is more in demand in a primitive society. So are spiced dishes. I predict a return of hot sauces to American cuisine.' But most viewers, at least in Britain, welcomed colour television not for its spicing up of reality but for its revelation of the ordinary. 'Instead of making you feel that it is a modern marvel, one feels it is just what we deserve,' wrote the TV critic Stanley Reynolds of this new invention, which he saw as a natural progression rather than a paradigm shift.[76]

For its first festive season in full colour, BBC1 adopted a new, light blue globe ident including the words 'BBC1 colour', a gentle hint to the ninety-nine per cent of viewers watching in black and white to buy a colour set. And the end of the year saw a new ritual: the Christmas double issue of the *Radio Times* and the *TV Times*, with their separate covers clearly illustrating the cultural differences between the BBC and ITV and their idea of their viewers: the former, a tasteful montage of ribbons, wintry scenes and wassailers, and the latter, Des O'Connor in a Santa hat. Flicking through these bumper issues, you could see the Christmas schedules padded out with Morecambe and Wise, *Aladdin* with Bernie Winters, *Singin' in the Rain* and *The Engelbert Humperdinck Show*.

Television had gone all the way to the moon and discovered its viewers preferred instant *Laramie*. 'Back in the roomful of furniture and family, we sit watching Petula Clark singing "Holy Night",' wrote the playwright Peter Nichols, spending Christmas Day crammed into the tiny living room of his in-laws' semi-detached house in Bristol with extended family. 'Val Doonican crooning a lullaby to Wendy Craig, the Young Generation dancing the life of Jesus. The children are shouted at every time they block an adult's view. They want to play with the toys they've been given, not grasping that the important part, the giving, is over for another year and they should sit like grateful mutes and let us watch our favourite stars.'[77]

6

THE DANCE OF
IRRELEVANT SHADOWS

Millions might watch television, but on the other hand, last night's television was even deader than yesterday's newspaper because you couldn't even wrap fish and chips in it.

John Osborne[1]

Late one Sunday night in October 1969, a bearded castaway clambered out of the sea, collapsed on to a deserted beach and, to the strains of Sousa's Liberty Bell march and a surreal cartoon flattened abruptly by a giant foot borrowed from Bronzino's painting, *Venus and Cupid*, introduced a new comedy series on BBC1. The first show included a sketch about a joke so funny it caused people to die laughing. If the scattergun, bemused laughter of the studio audience was any indication, there was no danger of this happening in Britain's living rooms. But for those who found it fresh and funny, *Monty Python's Flying Circus* offered an exhilarating sense of discovery. 'The most gratifying feature of the show's success,' Michael Palin (the bearded castaway) confided to his diary, 'is the way in which it has created a new viewing habit, the Sunday night late-show. A lot of people have said how they rush home to see it – in Bart's Hospital the large television room is packed – almost as if they are members of a club.'[2]

The BBC's seemingly lukewarm support for the series encouraged this *esprit de corps*. Placed in the slot usually occupied by religious programmes, it was taken off for two weeks after the first episode and then its time-slot kept being shifted. The second series, starting in September 1970, went out at 10.10 p.m. on Mondays, when the regions could opt out and show local programmes, so only London and northern England saw it, at least until the repeats. *Monty Python* was made by six young men who had obviously been watching television since the early 1950s, and was aimed at a televisually literate audience familiar with its genres and conventions. At least one of the Pythons must have seen the Old Man of Hoy broadcasts, for their sketch about climbing the north face of the Uxbridge Road was clearly based on Chris Brasher's excitable commentary in 1967, and in another episode Eric Idle announced that 'Lulu will be tackling the Old Man of Hoy'.

As it was nudged round the schedules, the Pythons played on the confusion by delaying the opening credits or adding a hanging joke after the end credits. They subverted the whole continuity grammar of television, from BBC1's rotating globe to awkward transitional phrases like 'And now for something completely different', coined by *Blue Peter*'s founding presenter, Christopher Trace. The Pythons saw that, because television feared silence and awkwardness, it ended up normalising the abnormal: an anchorman could spout nonsense as long as he carried on talking with po-faced reasonableness. With its strange segues, *Monty Python* mimicked the tendency for TV shows to meld together with the confabulated fluency of a dream. George Harrison, going through the Beatles' painful break-up, thought it 'the only "real" thing on the BBC'. 'I remember watching the very first Monty Python show that ever came on, on BBC2 [*sic*],' he told *Melody Maker*. 'Derek Taylor [the Beatles press officer] and I were so thrilled by seeing this wacky show that we sent them a telegram saying "Love the show, keep doing it." ... I couldn't understand how normal television could continue after that.'[3]

But normal television did continue. Nearly 24 million viewers watched the Miss World contest, held in the Albert Hall in November 1970. The compère, Bob Hope, was introducing the event when twenty-five women burst on to the stage mooing like cows, blasting whistles and squirting water pistols filled with ink. Thus were ITV viewers introduced to a new movement, Women's Liberation, of which most of them had never heard.

Women's Lib followed the pattern of much post-1968 radical protest: it aimed to disrupt public spectacles and jolt the audience out of their roles as docile consumers. The Miss World contest, watched by half the country with a casual, unthinking sexism, was an obvious target. 'The spectacle is vulnerable,' reflected two of the instigators, Laura Mulvey and Margarita Jiminez, in *Shrew*, the London Women's Liberation Workshop journal. 'However intricately planned it is, a handful of people can disrupt it and cause chaos ... The spectacle isn't prepared for anything other than passive spectators.'[4] This group of women realised, rather like the Pythons, that television naturalised the absurd, and they aimed to draw attention to this fact by rendering the event even odder than it already was.

After a minute of pandemonium, however, the women were dragged away and Miss World carried on. As usual, the contestants all walked to the camera with one hand resting on their hips, shoulders swinging, maintaining their grinning rictuses throughout, and they all longed to travel on the *QE2* or meet Prince Charles – an unflinching observation of the solemn, anaphrodisiac ritual later satirised by the Pythons in their 'Summarise Proust Competition'. Miss World remained one of the highest rated TV shows for the next decade, although it is unlikely viewers took it as seriously as its organisers. 'I think it's very funny,' said Germaine Greer, author of *The Female Eunuch*, which was published a month before Miss World 1970, 'and certainly every time I've ever watched it, there's been more malicious comment in the room, more fun made of the whole business, than people sitting open-mouthed at what they imagined was a real contest of female pulchritude.'[5]

Popular memory likes to package decades into unified entities with a particular character. This kind of decadology sees the 1970s as an era of sequinned, tinselly entertainments, such as Miss World, and of political and economic crises: Britain as 'Weimar without the sex', in Christopher Hitchens's phrase, with kitsch television rather than decadent cabaret being the wilful distraction from the world outside the living room.[6] But while Britain faced serious problems, such as rising unemployment, spiralling inflation and a falling pound, these were not experienced with the same intensity throughout the decade. Most 1970s television reflected the normal resilience and continuity of ordinary life rather than any desire to escape from harsh realities. Nor was Miss World especially typical of the rest of television; in the expanding schedules, there were just as many programmes with the cleverness and complexity of *Monty Python*.

It is part of the mythology of *Monty Python* that it was unappreciated at the time, which makes it seem less of its own era than an avant-garde foretaste of the future. But perhaps this is also too simple. The BBC's Annual Report for 1969 said that *Monty Python* had 'got away to an encouraging start' and that the pet shop skit about a dead parrot was a candidate for 'best-new-sketch of the year'. A highlight of 1970, said the report for the following year, was Monty Python's 'Ministry of Funny Walks [*sic*]'.[7]

One unassailable fact about this period in British cultural life is that lots of television was being watched. In October 1970 a commission on tourism in the Isle of Man reported that the favourite holiday pastime was watching TV, and recommended that the Manx government establish television theatres for holidaymakers from the mainland. Anthony Sampson noted that Britons had the most TV sets in Europe and spent the most time watching them (about eighteen hours a week, more than double that of Belgians, Swedes or Italians). 'A broad picture unfolds,' he wrote, 'of the British living a withdrawn and inarticulate life, rather like Harold Pinter's people, mowing lawns and painting walls, pampering pets, listening to music, knitting and watching television.'[8]

Television's ubiquity was striking because in other ways Britain lagged behind its European partners in indicators of affluence. In 1971, ten per cent of homes still had no indoor lavatory or bath, thirty-one per cent had no fridge and sixty-two per cent had no telephone; but only nine per cent had no TV. 'One of the things that worries me, which you can't very well say if you are a Director of Programmes,' said David Attenborough in a television interview in December 1972, on resigning from this post at the BBC to return to programme making, 'is that people watch television too much. The average man spends more time watching TV than any other activity except his work and sleeping.'[9]

A familiar sight on screen at this time, however, was a caption apologising for the interruption in programmes. In an era that is sometimes unfairly remembered as one of perpetual strikes and stoppages, TV technicians were rightly notorious for their militancy. In the summer of 1970 there was a walkout at Granada, which left those in the north-west without ITV and the rest of Britain without *Coronation Street*. Granada's strike music, excerpts from light classics like 'Fingal's Cave' and 'Claire de Lune' played over its apology caption on a two-hour loop, became so popular that the company printed lists of the music to send to interested viewers.[10] At the end of that year there was an ITV 'colour strike', with technicians demanding more money for working with the new colour equipment. The whole channel reverted to monochrome for three months. Another periodic event was the 'work to rule' at power stations, which meant either blackouts or voltage reductions, when lights became dimmer, electric fires duller and television pictures smaller – an eerie evocation, for those with long memories, of the earliest days of postwar television when viewers were huddled round a tiny screen in the cold and dark. For many families, their most vivid encounter with the escalating political and economic crisis was via the television set.

In July 1971 the Chancellor of the Exchequer, Anthony Barber, had launched his 'dash for growth', a mini-budget that reduced purchase tax and relaxed hire purchase controls. This created a sudden surge in demand for colour TVs in the UK, with just over 2 million sets being produced in the peak year of 1973 – one of the bright spots in the monochrome economic gloom. This totemically modern object in the centre of the living room, the colour TV, looked curiously retrograde, for people paying £300 or a higher rental charge wanted a prestige piece of furniture in return. Unlike the short-lived astronaut-themed sets of 1970, with their rounded white bodies like space helmets, most colour sets concealed their electronics in a genteel granny look with splayed, tapered legs, sliding tambour screens, teak louvred speakers and satin-finished consoles.

But Barber's dash for growth simply accelerated the decline of the British television industry, for domestic firms were unable to meet the demand for new sets. In what became almost as classic a manifestation of national economic decline as British Leyland, cheap Japanese imports flooded the market and proved to be much more reliable than British colour sets, which frequently overheated and were known in the trade as 'curtain burners'. Colour television deliveries reached their peak in autumn 1973, with demand stoked by the impending wedding between Princess Anne and Mark Phillips. In the lead-up to the event, though, Britain's economy seemed on the verge of collapse, with a huge trade deficit and the Bank of England hiking its lending rates to prevent a run on the pound. With an acute energy shortage caused by the refusal of coal miners and electrical engineers to work overtime, the government proclaimed a state of emergency.

Despite fears that it might be blacked out, the televising of the royal wedding went ahead. The journalist Auberon Waugh reflected that 'the nation is as united as any nation can be – in a gigantic effort to be entertained ... We are citizens of the world's first satirical Ruritania.' The writer and architectural historian James Lees-Milne meant not to watch at his club, Brooks's, until he saw members gathering round the television set brought downstairs into the bar: 'Curiosity impelled me to look ... The beauty of the bridegroom's uniform and the back of his well-shaped head with glossy chestnut hair riveted me for an hour.'[11]

This was a brief respite. In December the OPEC oil crisis combined with the miners' dispute to bring the national crisis to a head. On Thursday 13 December, after an episode of *Some Mothers Do 'Ave 'Em,* the prime minister Edward Heath gave a special broadcast in which he warned that the country was facing 'a very grave emergency' and 'a harder Christmas than we have known since the war'. He announced a three-day week to save energy, starting from January.

One austerity measure, though, was to start the following Monday: television would end by 10.30 p.m.

On the first night of the curfew, ITV dropped an unfortunately timed documentary about what miners did during their holidays, and BBC1 cancelled the Burt Lancaster film *The Swimmer*. ITV and BBC agreed to stagger the switch-off by a few minutes because the Electricity Board feared a catastrophic power surge as viewers boiled the nation's kettles at closedown. As BBC1 played the national anthem and, a few minutes later, ITV's *News At Ten* wound up its lighthearted 'and finally' item, the Electricity Board engineers in the national control room in London nervously watched the lights and dials on large, illuminated, overhead boards to monitor the load on the National Grid. To their relief they saw that instead of a 'TV pickup', the normal increase that came after the ending of popular TV programmes, there was a 1500 megawatt drop in demand.

Overall, though, the curfew is unlikely to have saved much energy. The government, after much chivvying, released figures that it saved only 600 tonnes of coal a day, less than 0.25 per cent of total production, and there was no way of knowing how much of this was simply displaced into other energy-consuming activities. Since TV sets take up little electricity, there was a case for encouraging families to huddle together in one room to watch television rather than disperse to separate rooms to do their individual electrically powered things. BBC and ITV both argued that they would save more electricity by coming off in the daytime, but Heath said he did not want to cancel schools programmes.

Many Labour MPs saw it as an exercise in psychological warfare, an attempt to turn the middle classes against the miners. Some even saw it as revenge on the TV-watching classes by a man who, on arriving at number 10, had cancelled Harold Wilson's television rental and installed a grand piano. 'The 10.30 curfew on television is an impertinence, an intrusion, an absurdity, an ungracious act,' wrote the columnist Keith Waterhouse. 'Only one who spends his evenings playing the bloody organ, instead of watching a trashy old movie like any normal human being, would have thought of it.'[12]

After a four-day Christmas reprieve the curfew resumed into the new year. Contrary to popular belief, a concern that it would lead to a rise in the birth rate nine months later was unfounded. TV commercials for free contraceptives, featuring a cartoon of a stork with the caption, 'Make sure your baby is a wanted one', appeared just before close-down. BBC Radio Leicester, which closed down in the early evening, came back on air from 10.30 to midnight with a show called 'Tranny by Gaslight'. The fledgling form of the phone-in, the cheapest form of radio, now came into its own, with callers complaining bitterly about losing *Sportsnight* or the late film. On BBC Radio London, Robbie Vincent's 'crisis phone-in' proved so popular that it long outlived the crisis.

The phrase 'Big Brother' recurred regularly in letters to newspapers about the curfew, and most saw it simply as another annoyance to add to all the other privations. Peter Hughes of Epping wrote: 'When for many of us it is a daily battle to get to and from our work; when for some the security of our jobs is threatened; when we are confronted by looming, disconcerting instabilities in our society; when those with cars are urged to stay at home for their recreation; when a bewildered public feels itself beleaguered between the panzers of union militancy and the Maginot line of government obduracy; when the lonely and the old especially feel battered by events, is it not just one more act of petty-minded victimisation to deprive so many of a major source of pleasure and relaxation? That makes this curfew spiteful.'[13]

Others admitted that their anger was partly synthetic, and that they were quite enjoying the reassertion of human contact, from board games to pillow talk. On 7 February, Heath called a general election and lifted the curfew, not because the fuel crisis was over but because he felt that full coverage had to be given to the election. This, as the Nuffield study of that election pointed out, had the instantaneous psychological effect of diminishing the crisis atmosphere on which the prime minister was hoping to capitalise.[14] The restoration of late-night television announced the return of normal life.

Northern Ireland's viewers, suffering the bombing campaigns and summary violence of the Troubles, particularly welcomed the sense of normality created by television. Belfast city centre had become a ghost town outside opening hours, as people retreated to their homes under unofficial curfew. Many bars, restaurants and cinemas went out of business and those theatres and entertainment venues that remained open could not attract stars from elsewhere. Primetime television took the place of these entertainments. The BBC, which had long treated the province as a 'half region', now expanded its Northern Ireland service, giving it the same status as BBC Scotland and Wales and funding more local programmes.[15] Northern Irish viewers, the slowest in the nation to take up television when it arrived in the 1950s, now embraced it as a salve and balm for the region's troubled public life.

The most popular show in the province was *Saturday Night*, first broadcast on 14 October 1972 from the tiny Studio 8 in BBC Belfast, as an 'opt-out' after *Match of the Day*. (Viewers in the rest of Britain would probably have needed subtitles and explanatory notes to make sense of it.) That year was the most violent of the conflict, before or since – the year of Bloody Sunday and Bloody Friday, the start of direct rule from London and the spreading of IRA violence to the 'mainland'. *Saturday Night* starred the comedian James Young, known as Our Jimmie, whose recordings of his one-man theatre shows were the biggest-selling albums ever on both sides of the Irish border. But in May 1971, Belfast's Group Theatre, the venue where he performed his shows, had closed as the Troubles led to a slump in business, leaving the way open for his long-overdue television stardom.

Much of *Saturday Night* was filmed in one of the little terraced side streets off Belfast's Dublin Road: the 'wee street' inhabited by comic characters like Derek the camp window cleaner (first heard in the radio soap *The McCooeys*), Orange Lil, a Protestant woman bedecked in Union Jack facepaint, and Ballymena Sarah, who refused to have Sunday papers in her house, all played by Young himself. It was a street in which Catholics and Protestants anachronistically inhabited the same row of terraced houses, for in this period there were huge population movements as families dispersed, often after intimidation, to live among people of their own religion. Young often put on a slight southern Irish accent when playing a Catholic, to avoid hitting too close to home.[16]

He had a soft spot for mawkish monologues, one of which was called 'Such a little time' and ended, 'For we're here such a little time and there's just no time to hate.' Each show ended with him saying, to long applause: 'It's a great wee country. Do us a favour, will yis – stop yer fightin'.' At the end of 1972, the BBC's Broadcasting House in Belfast received hundreds of letters and Christmas cards, thanking them for cheering them up with *Saturday Night*. 'When the story of that period is written,' recalled Pat Loughrey when he was controller of BBC Northern Ireland in the 1990s, 'I believe James Young will be seen as a major figure. I for one will never forget his weekly entreaty "Will you stop fighting". He was a very shrewd judge of this place and of all our hidden prejudices.' When Young died suddenly of a heart attack, aged 56, in July 1974, he was mourned across the divided community. The funeral procession ran all the way from his home in Ballyhalbert, a small village on the east coast of the Ards peninsula where he lived, through different parts of Belfast. On the Newtownards Road in Protestant east Belfast, housewives gathered in small groups, men stood outside pubs and workers downed tools. Along May Street in the Catholic Markets area, locals blessed themselves as the coffin went by, many of them weeping.[17]

The belief that laughter could help to sew up the torn social fabric was not an attitude confined to Northern Ireland. The primetime schedules were full of sitcoms and light entertainment aimed at the whole family, for in 1975 only six per cent of homes had more than one television set. All comedy was performed in front of a studio audience, a Greek chorus inside the television set intending to prod the viewers at home into laughter. All television comedy producers at this time were, consciously or not, disciples of Henri Bergson, who believed that 'laughter appears to stand in need of an echo … laughter always implies a kind of secret freemasonry … How often has it been said that the fuller the theatre, the more uncontrolled the laughter of the audience!' Philip Jones, head of light entertainment at Thames Television, had a theory that farces no longer worked on film because actors could not time laughs without an audience. Nineteen thirties screwball comedies had been shown to preview audiences and then sent back to the editing suite so the laughter-making moments could be spaced apart. They did not seem as funny as they once did, Jones felt, because 'we are subconsciously missing the urf-urf-urf at the local Odeon'.[18]

Jones, like James Young, also believed that laughter was inherently inclusive and conciliatory, and that difficult social issues might somehow by smoothed over by sitcom conventions. *Love Thy Neighbour*, the Thames TV comedy series about the conflict between a black and a white family living next door to each other, would, he told the *Daily Express*, 'help take some of the heat out of race relations'. Tania Rose of the Race Relations Board disagreed, saying she hadn't met a black person who wasn't 'offended to hell by it'. A primary headmaster in Fife reported that children in his school had made a black worker's life a misery, 'calling him names like "coon" and "sambo", having picked them up from the programme *Love Thy Neighbour*'.[19]

A common complaint from viewers was that the audience in the studio was overreacting and finding everything far too hilarious. The BBC and ITV companies had vast operations doling out free tickets to works outings, schools and pensioners' clubs who came up in coachloads to watch shows being recorded, and creating studio laughter was a fine art. The comedian Ronnie Barker was convinced that fat people laughed more readily because their fleshy bottoms did not feel so uncomfortable on the hard seats. Ken Dodd believed in limbering up his studio audience with one-liners to 'get the chuckle-muscles working'. Producers like David Croft, co-creator of *Dad's Army*, were masters at creating the right ambience: hiding the tubular steel rostra seating with curtains so the audience were cosied up and the sound was warmer, balancing the microphones above the audience's heads like an orchestra and winding up the fader at exactly the right moment to create a rush of reassuring laughter. Croft moved each recording along quickly, tolerating minor slip-ups by the actors so the audience would not get bored and would not have to feign laughter at endless retakes.[20]

Any autosuggestive living-room laughter that these techniques generated quickly rose and died behind the walls of millions of private houses, leaving little evidence that it ever existed. We do know that on one Monday evening in March 1975, a fifty-year-old bricklayer from King's Lynn laughed so heartily at an episode of *The Goodies* about Lancashire's answer to Kung Fu, the school of Ecky Thump, that he slumped on the settee and died of a heart attack. The journalist Brian Viner remembers his adoptive father laughing so hard at the first episode of *Fawlty Towers* in September 1975 that he fell off his Parker Knoll armchair. As with *Monty Python*, though, some needed to learn to find it funny. Michael Palin laughed a little at his friend John Cleese during that first episode, while his house guests remained silent. But the last episode in the series, in which Basil Fawlty offended some German hotel guests by repeatedly mentioning the war, had Palin 'laughing as long and as loud as anything since *Hancock and the Vikings*'.[21]

This orthodoxy that viewers needed a studio audience to nudge them into laughing created a certain sort of comedy. Script editors would tick a script for the laughs and actors tended to clown, to go for the guffaw rather than a throwaway or wry effect. Like characters in Ben Jonson comedies, those in *Dad's Army* had a distinctive humour, reverberating through their catchphrases: 'We're all doomed.' 'Don't Panic!' 'Do you think that's awfully wise, sir?' 'Stupid boy.' Croft reinforced this reassuringly one-note quality with his distinctive end credit sequences, which had the words 'you have been watching' and the actors performing a curtain call, a little vignette of their characters over studio applause.

Few now remembered how contentious *Dad's Army* had been before its first broadcast in 1968, when there was a disastrous showing of a pilot episode to an invited audience, the evidence for which Croft hid at the bottom of his in-tray, and several on the BBC's viewer panel expressed unease at its mockery of the Home Guard. When it was broadcast, however, only one ex-Home Guard soldier wrote to express mild offence. After a few weeks, former Home Guard members were writing in with reminiscences and ideas for episodes, drawings of home-made weapons and offers of fatigues and buttonhole badges.[22]

The programme's tone, a masterful juggling act of ridicule and tenderness, had quickly turned away wrath.

Croft's other sitcom from this era, *It Ain't Half Hot, Mum*, depicting the exploits of a Royal Artillery Concert Party based in Deolali, India, in the war, was more problematic. With the studio a mock-up of a parade ground with charpoys and mosquito nets, and a sand pit and conifer wood near King's Lynn standing in for the North-West Frontier, it recreated the Raj just as Asian immigration was becoming a focus of attention. The tightening of controls in the 1971 Immigration Act had led to an increase in migration as wives and children, fearing further restrictions, came to reunite their families. Racial violence intensified, with paint and fire bombs thrown at immigrants' houses.

Croft's co-author Jimmy Perry said later that they had written the series 'to explain why we had so many Asians living in the UK and how we became a multiracial society; it was the effect of the aftermath of Empire. But when people started to dismiss the show as racist it filled me with despair ... The strange thing is that British Asians loved it – and still do – they call it "our programme".' It does seem that, at a time when the National Front was growing in popularity and 'paki bashing' by gangs of skinhead youths was at its height, many Asians found *It Ain't Half Hot, Mum* reassuring. Shelina Zahra Janmohamed, whose east African-Asian parents had emigrated from Tanzania during the Zanzibar Revolution of 1964, recalled her family being 'swept away by the rarity and simplicity of the portrayals, happy to see ourselves on television at all. At least the characters representing us in comedies appeared human and humorous, not barbaric, oppressed or rebellious.'[23]

Meera Syal, a teenager living in Essington near Wolverhampton, associated the programme with the fun-poking culture of the Punjab, from where her family had emigrated. She still felt uneasy about one character: the obsequious native bearer, Rangi Ram, played by a blacked-up English actor, Michael Bates. But Syal's parents liked Bates because, having served as an officer in Burma, he sometimes spoke in Urdu and Punjabi on the programme, as did Babar Bhatti as the punkah wallah Rumzan, and it gave them a feeling of insider knowledge. According to a reporter for *The Times* who interviewed Asian families in Southall, sometimes known as 'little Punjab', in the summer of 1976, they often found little else on British TV that they liked. Southall had three cinemas, showing a diet of Indian films, and they were all thriving when, in the age of colour television, most others in the country seemed to be in terminal decline.[24]

The government's General Household Survey, published in April 1976, showed the extent to which TV now dominated people's waking lives. Ninety per cent of Britons watched television as their main leisure pursuit: women for an average of twenty hours a week, men for seventeen. In 1976 more than a million households switched to colour licences, which for the first time outnumbered monochrome ones. As colour TV crossed from luxury item to near-universal symbol of affluence in the middle of a recession, a press campaign about welfare 'scroungers', launched by the National Association for Freedom and supported by right-wing Tory MPs such as Iain Sproat, focused on how they were wasting their handouts on colour TVs. Urban myths flourished: immigrants were buying colour TVs with Social Security furniture vouchers because the sets had stands and doors that allowed them to be classed as furniture; those on supplementary benefit got grants for colour TVs as 'essential' household items.[25]

Since the start of the decade, a new phrase had entered the estate agents' vocabulary of mod cons: 'Col/TV rec'd', announcing the arrival of the colour transmitter in an area. But on Britain's extreme edges, its arrival was overdue and often technically difficult. The colour TV signal for the Channel Islands had to travel all the way from Stockland Hill in Devon to Alderney, and had more water to cross than any other signal in the British Isles, making it vulnerable to what engineers call 'scattering' from the surface of the water. The signal, when it arrived, was weak and liable to interference from French TV transmitters. But a new, manoeuvrable aerial christened SABRE (Steerable Adaptive

Broadcast Reception Equipment) was able to amplify the signal from Stockland Hill and nullify interference from any French transmitters using the same channel. Channel Islanders had colour images by July 1976, just in time for the Montreal Olympics.

Four days later, colour TV reached the Outer Hebrides. A signal a foot wide, containing the colour programmes on all three main channels, left the Rosemarkie transmitter on the east coast and, in a giant game of virtual pinball, was deflected around mountain ranges by booster transmitters until it arrived at a new mast at Eitshal, towering over a peat bog on the Isle of Lewis. Colour came to Shetland when an unmanned transmitter opened on the bird sanctuary of Fair Isle late afternoon on Christmas Eve 1976, just in time for the *Jim'll Fix It Christmas Special* and a film called *Million Dollar Duck*. Apart from a few isolated pockets like the Isle of Barra, which could still only get BBC1 in grainy black and white, colour TV now covered the kingdom.

On Orkney, which had beaten its North Sea neighbour to colour by eight months, the poet George Mackay Brown recorded the excitement among his fellow islanders about the building of the colour TV transmitter on the high moors in the centre of the mainland. Over the last few years he had been chronicling the spread of television on Orkney with resentment merging into resignation. By the mid 1960s, BBC television had become fully part of island life and the giant communal bonfires that used to celebrate ancient festivals like Beltane and Lammas had mostly been replaced by the lacklustre flicker of thousands of cathode ray tubes. 'TV personalities like Cliff Michelmore, Inspector Barlow and Fanny Cradock are spoken about more familiarly by islanders now than are the people who live in outlying farms,' Brown complained. 'The shadows on a screen have become more real than their flesh-and-blood neighbours.'[26]

Brown lived with his elderly mother, Mhairi, in a council house on the Stromness seafront. In the evenings she watched TV, and he had to try to blank out the noise from *Dr Who*, *Top of the Pops* and *The Monkees* with the sound turned up high. For Brown, who believed that the perfect poem was 'a cold pure round of silence', it was the booming sound of the television set he objected to more than the pictures – that and the tedious pub talk it spawned about last night's programmes. 'The story-teller is being pushed out by the frightful bore who will give you opinions about Vietnam and the colour problem and heart transplants,' he wrote, 'not really his own opinions at all but some prejudiced odds and ends that have stuck in his mind from a discussion witnessed on *Panorama* the night before.'[27]

For Brown, the obsession with new technology on the islands was a form of displaced religious idolatry. 'Progress is a goddess who, up to now, has looked after her children well. The sky is scored with television aerials,' he wrote in 1969 in *An Orkney Tapestry*. 'The notion of progress is a cancer that makes an elemental community look better, and induces a false euphoria, while it drains the life out of it remorselessly.' Brown dated this zeal for progress back to the arrival of newspapers on the islands in the 1820s, which turned language from 'a sacred mystery' into 'the stilted elegances of a newspaper column'.[28]

In this long view, however, lay the seeds of an eventual accommodation with television. Mary Whitehouse, without Brown's deep historical sense, thought television a new and explosively dangerous phenomenon. For Brown, antagonistic to modernity in general and regarding the Reformation and the industrial revolution as terrible wrong turnings, television carried no special weight. Slowly he found himself prepared to give 'half a genuflection in the direction of the goddess Progress' that his fellow Orcadians had so eagerly embraced. After his mother's death in 1967, he moved a few hundred yards to another council flat where, despite still not possessing a fridge or a phone, he had installed a rented black-and-white television set. 'How easy it is, in the evening after the day's work,' he conceded, 'to sit back in the armchair and let the facile images flood through the mind.'[29]

In 1971 Brown began a weekly column for the *Orcadian*. Since writing for the *Orkney Herald* in the 1950s, his tone had softened, and he now regaled his readers with the trivia of his everyday life. He lamented the fact that he no longer walked up Brinkie's Brae, the hill overlooking the town, as the lure of TV became too great, and that his television watching, and that of his fellow Stromnessians, had killed off the local cinema which had brought the townfolk together twice a week. In May 1973, the debut production of John McGrath's touring radical theatre company, 7:84, came to Stromness. *The Cheviot, the Stag and the Black, Black Oil* was a powerful piece of theatre about how the Highland Scots had been disinherited to make way for more profitable sheep, stags and North Sea oil. Brown, though, did not go to see it. Guiltily, he stayed in to watch *Cider with Rosie* on BBC1. But he did later catch the performance in Orkney's main town, Kirkwall, after which he admonished his fellow Orcadians, more gently now than he used to do in the *Herald*, for their addictive TV watching and unconcern about the world beyond their living rooms.[30]

Brown felt that, despite the howl of rage from one end of the country to another, the TV curfew in the winter of 1973–4 had been one of the best things to come out of the economic crisis. Instead of being 'lulled to sleep by the nightly anodyne – the benediction of that old one-eye in the corner of the living room' with its 'dance of irrelevant shadows', it had been a relief to yank the plug out of the wall and write a letter, talk or 'simply drink your ale and dream'. The return of television with the general election campaign had been a rude awakening. So important did politicians think themselves, he felt, that the fuel shortage was forgotten in favour of piped TV with 'the three superstars, and their satraps, posturing and mouthing'. This, he thought, only added to the general feeling of apathy and disillusionment.[31]

But Brown's broadsides against television were becoming faint-hearted: a mark of respect, in part, to his dead mother, a lover of the lowbrow with a vast, non-judgemental capacity for enjoyment. His argument was with progress, not with the tastes of ordinary Orcadians, with which he had always tried to connect. He disliked what he saw as a tendency to obscurity and angst in modern art and literature and realised that television could sometimes offer what he wanted to produce: an accessible and ecumenical folk art. Now, once 'that mysterious potent mast' on Keelylang Hill was up and running, he reminded Orcadians in the spring of 1976, they would have three channels instead of just BBC1. He could watch the nature programmes on BBC2 and, on Grampian Television, that unfamiliar cultural form, the commercial, with its 'melting rapture of voice and image'. And for the first time, it would all be in colour, although Brown himself clung mulishly to monochrome. 'We old-fashioned ones are living in a drab workaday world – greyly we spend our evenings,' he noted with a residue of proud asceticism.[32]

In its issue for 23 October 1976, the *Radio Times* revived its 1930s tradition of a fireside issue heralding the start of the autumn schedules. The artist Peter Brookes's cover for this issue, 'Home for the evening', showed autumn leaves cascading down on to an armchair with a jug of Ovaltine and a copy of the *Radio Times* on a side table, its subheading suggesting that the turning back of the clocks meant 'an extra hour's darkness for viewing'. If you flicked through the pages of this issue, the first day of the TV listings was, as usual, a Saturday night. Thanks to the scheduling skills of its head of light entertainment, Bill Cotton, and the controller of BBC1, Bryan Cowgill, the BBC was winning the ratings battle on this key night of the week (although slightly less key for ITV, because Sunday closing meant that advertisers were keener on the Friday and Sunday slots) and for the first time ever most people were watching in colour. The BBC1 schedule for that Saturday night, 23 October, has entered popular memory as a classic seven hours of popular, quality entertainment: the golden age condensed into a single evening's television.

The BBC's ascendancy began at 4.50 in the afternoon, when about a million viewers turned over from the ITV wrestling especially to watch the 'full classified football results' on *Grandstand*, ninety minutes of footballing melodrama turned into a simple, soothing litany of numbers and names delivered in alphabetical order. Len Martin's reading of the results had the quality of a rite, bringing calm to the late afternoon, disturbed only by the scraping of pencils against pools coupons. His urbane BBC voice, carrying the merest trace of its antipodean origins, pre-announced the results through cadence and intonation, so viewers could tell whether the first-named team had won, lost or drawn without looking up from their coupons.

At 5.30 p.m., after the news and *Tom and Jerry*, came *The Basil Brush Show*, hosted by a glove puppet fox with a gap-toothed grin, taste in natty suits and plum-cake accent inspired by Terry-Thomas. Like much of that evening's entertainment, the show addressed viewers through the dual register of pantomime: Basil's staccato laugh and self-admiring response to his own jokes ('Boom boom!') appealed to children, while his topical jokes and subversive comments about British Rail or 'Mary Lighthouse' kept adults interested. 'Basil is a great creation and I recommend his raucous tomfoolery to the producers of *Masterpiece Theatre*,' wrote the playwright Tom Stoppard in the *Radio Times*. For the poet and critic D. J. Enright he was 'a cuddly innocent and a hard-boiled sophisticate: a fantasist who can suddenly turn coolly rational ... Basil Brush belongs to that small band of anthropomorphised animals, headed by Toad of Toad Hall, who operate successfully in both worlds.'[33]

At 6 p.m., the whirling, electronic theme tune and time-tunnel graphics announced the arrival of *Doctor Who*. The BBC's head of drama Sydney Newman had created this programme thirteen years earlier to stem the haemorrhaging of fathers from the TV screen on late Saturday afternoon in the hiatus between the end of *Grandstand* and the start of *Juke Box Jury*, and the need to attract adults as well as children had lain behind the decision to make the Doctor a mature man rather than a juvenile lead. The mid 1970s was *Doctor Who*'s most popular period, with a new producer, Philip Hinchcliffe, who moved the series into Gothic, grown-up areas, and a new doctor played by Tom Baker who, after a teething period in which viewers were unsure about his displacement of the well-loved Jon Pertwee, had settled into the role as a jelly-baby-eating, cerebral eccentric with a floppy hat and long stripey scarf.

Like *The Basil Brush Show*, *Doctor Who*'s audience was diverse. While more than half its viewers were over fifteen, Mary Whitehouse also blamed it for an epidemic of nightmares and bedwetting among under-sevens. One of the historical clichés about children's reactions to this programme may have originated with Baker himself, who told a group of schoolchildren that *Doctor Who* frightened him so much he watched it from behind the sofa. Many young viewers, though, delighted in its scariness. After one 1976 episode, 'The Seeds of Doom', they wrote in. 'I liked the episode very much. I think it was one of the most scariest ones of all,' said one. Another commended the producers on their ingenious methods for killing off characters, such as 'when Scorbie was pulled under the water when the plant came up and when Chase was killed in the compost machine'.[34] That Saturday night saw the end of a chilling four-part story, *The Hand of Fear*, about a fossilised hand attempting to bring its previous owner back to life at a nuclear power station. It also saw the poignant departure of Sarah Jane, the most loved of the Doctor's female companions. Distracted by a summons to Gallifrey from the Time Lords, the Doctor shooed her out of the TARDIS in what he confidently (but wrongly) told her was Hillview Road, south Croydon.

At 6.25 p.m., as living room lights came on across the country, came *The Generation Game*, presented by Bruce Forsyth, celebrating its 100th edition. It was unusual for the evening's star attraction to be on so early in the schedule, but Bill Cotton felt that weekend viewers were especially likely to stick with one channel, being won or lost by the success of the early 'build'. Forsyth's job was to hook in viewers to BBC1 and keep them there, just as he had done when working as the second-spot comic on variety bills. 'Every Saturday, to the mortification of Independent Television, in the fireside months from September to January, about 18 million people, fresh from football matches, sweeping leaves, or moody contemplation of betting slips, watch this man and his young wife go through a routine of whose every small thematic variation an idiot could be a connoisseur,' wrote the critic Richard North.[35] 'Ladies, gentlemen and children,' Forsyth began (the show often being the last thing younger children were allowed to watch, washed and in their pyjamas), 'Nice to see you; to see you nice.'

The Generation Game felt fresh because, although studio recorded, it had the atmosphere of a stage show. Forsyth asked for the first rows of seating to be lit, so he could see the audience's faces, and he moved the show along quickly as though it were live, to build up momentum. He had learned early on the value of the audience in creating an ambience when he had first appeared on television, aged eleven, in August 1939. The studio set at Radiolympia was designed to look like a lounge in someone's home. 'There was no audience seated in front of me in rows of wooden chairs – and, somehow, I had to create my own atmosphere,' Forsyth recalled with a wince. 'The moment passed ignominiously.'[36] On *The Generation Game* he was like a human Basil Brush, all fake snarls and eyes raised to heaven as he mocked the contestants' attempts to throw pots or stretch dough. He claimed to have learned this skill in wartime concert parties, studying faces in order to pick the right person to ridicule. The prizes at the end of the show passed on a conveyor belt, a panoply of 1970s consumerism: canteen and cutlery sets, teasmaids, his'n'hers bathrobes, matching vinyl luggage, cuddly toys.

At 7.25 p.m., about 12.5 million people carried on watching for *The Duchess of Duke Street*, a new period drama in the mould of ITV's *Upstairs Downstairs* which benefited from being sympathetically sandwiched between *The Generation Game* and, at 8.15 p.m., *The Two Ronnies*. This slickly professional show, now drawing in nearly 20 million viewers, had not changed its formula in half a decade. In between the comic sketches, there was Ronnie Corbett narrating a long shaggy-dog story from an armchair; a filmed comedy series, in this case a Spike Milligan-penned romp called 'The Phantom Raspberry Blower of Old London Town'; and a musical pastiche finale, all of it bookended by Corbett and Barker sitting at desks reading fake news items ('And in a packed programme tonight … and it's goodnight from me …').

At 9 p.m. came *Starsky and Hutch*. With a pulsating musical score pushing the action on, the crime-fighting duo screeched and wailed through the streets of LA in their red Ford Torino with the go-faster stripes, crashing through piles of cardboard boxes as they went, before jumping over walls and fire escapes and apprehending felons by handcuffing them on the bonnets of cars. One measure of *Starsky and Hutch*'s British appeal was the way it had turned a previously drab item, the cardigan – the chunky-belted type with Aztec patterns worn by Starsky – into an image of urban cool and the most popular item both in knitting patterns in women's magazines and at British Home Stores.[37]

After the news, at 10.20 p.m., the famous Barry Stoller theme tune heralded the start of *Match of the Day*, which could still bring in 13 million viewers late on Saturday night, often catching pub-goers who had left just before closing time. At the end, its donnish presenter, Jimmy Hill, reminded viewers to put their clocks back, and then at 11.20 p.m., 10 million viewers stayed up to see Glenda Jackson and Desmond Morris being interviewed on *Parkinson*, which brought the glamour of late-night American talk shows to British television. At twenty past midnight, Michael Parkinson signed off and ended this classic Saturday night, the armchair nation united on BBC1.

Of course, history is rarely so neat. A consensus can be suffocating for those who feel excluded from it, and underneath the communitarian noises of primetime television there lay buried tensions. These tensions emerged a few weeks later, on 1 December, when an unknown punk band, the Sex Pistols, appeared on Thames TV's live teatime magazine programme, *Today*, to promote their first single, 'Anarchy in the UK'. The presenter Bill Grundy, unsympathetic to punk and a little over-refreshed, invited the band to 'say something outrageous' and one member, Steve Jones, obliged with 'you dirty bastard' and 'what a fucking rotter'. After this unedifying exchange, Thames broadcast a full apology on screen twice later that day and quickly suspended Grundy. Next day's tabloid newspapers seemed especially exercised about the time of the swearing: at 6.25 p.m., in the middle of 'family viewing', just before *Opportunity Knocks*. A lorry driver, who was so enraged that his eight-year-old son had seen it that he kicked in the screen of his new £380 TV set, was widely quoted. 'I was so angry and disgusted with this filth that I took a swing with my boot,' he said.[38]

The imagining of the Sex Pistols' TV appearance as a seminal moment in recent British cultural history is partly retrospective. *Today* was only shown in the London area, and the tabloids played their allotted role in helping a band seeking notoriety to become notorious. Some younger viewers, though, did seem to welcome the Sex Pistols for cutting through the blandness of family TV. 'It was like someone had jumped into the television from the real world and shouted out to me to wake up and start living,' wrote Jonathan Ross, then aged sixteen and living in Leytonstone. 'It made those of us who had seen these naughty kids show no respect for an authority that we all secretly knew was lousy and hypocritical feel like fabulous, dangerous rebels.' Aged twenty-two, Declan McManus, who had just signed for Stiff Records for £150 as Elvis Costello, was similarly energised. Waiting for a train on Whitton station the next day on the way to his job as a data entry clerk in London, he saw 'all the commuters were reading the papers when the Pistols made headlines ... It was as if it was the most awful thing that ever happened ... it was a great morning – just to hear people's blood pressure going up and down over it.'[39]

Young people had been progressively distancing themselves from primetime television since the mid 1950s, when the emergence of TV as the main domestic entertainment meant the decline of radio as a family form and its pursuit of the young listener. The mid 1970s represented perhaps the peak of their alienation from television. As the music critic Simon Frith points out, television added little to popular music: most people's TV sets had poor sound quality and the sound was now relatively worse compared with the improved definition of the hi-fi and FM radio. Much of the music on 1970s television was anti-rock, a sort of counter-revolution against the 1960s. The musical diet of *Opportunity Knocks* consisted largely of youth brass bands, citizens' choirs singing 'Bobby Shafto', crimplene-clad pianists and boy sopranos in kilts. *Top of the Pops* required its acts to lip-synch, an affront to rock's growing insistence on liveness and authenticity. It was a light entertainment show, with scantily clad dancing girls, garishly dressed DJs and glitter balls, a visual cornucopia that probably accounted for the initially surprising fact that it was the favourite programme among deaf children.[40]

As the only programme on television with chart music, it was still watched avidly by teenagers, many of whom would wait impatiently each Thursday evening for *Tomorrow's World* to end, with a cassette recorder and microphone poised near the television's speaker. *Top of the Pops* was a lodestone of the generational tensions that were an inevitable feature of one-television households, as something unfolding unexpectedly on screen could uncover an issue that ordinarily remained unspoken, delighting teenagers and shocking parents who had mostly grown up before rock'n'roll.

One such charged moment had come in July 1972, when David Bowie performed 'Starman' on *Top of the Pops* dressed in a multicoloured lycra catsuit, languidly putting his arm round guitarist Mick Ronson and looking at him seductively. Many key figures in popular music from the late 1970s onwards – Pete Shelley of the Buzzcocks, Ian McCulloch of Echo and the Bunnymen, Dave Gahan of Depeche Mode, Marc Almond of Soft Cell – have cited this broadcast as a watershed in their musical and sexual education. For a fourteen-year-old Chislehurst schoolgirl called Susan Ballion, later Siouxsie Sioux, it meant three minutes of miraculous flight from her surroundings, for she watched it while ill in hospital with ulcerative colitis in a room where 'people were coughing their guts up or walking around with blood hanging from a cradle on a support'.[41]

Forty years later, the journalist Dylan Jones wrote a book, *When Ziggy Played Guitar*, entirely about these three-and-a-half minutes of television which, he wrote, 'caus[ed] havoc in millions of sitting rooms all over Britain … It was thrilling, slightly dangerous, transformative. For me, and for those like me, it felt that the future had finally arrived.' But then, shocked to discover that he must have seen it, as a twelve-year-old, on a black-and-white set when he remembered watching it in colour, he wondered if he was 'a victim of False Memory Syndrome, and this was my mutable past, a patchwork of dates, times, and pictures, images that rattle past like a scratched DVD'.[42] Not for the first time, a moment of television had merged with the mythologising memory of it.

Another memorable, consensus-shaking event occurred in

December 1975, when John Hurt played Quentin Crisp in the ITV drama *The Naked Civil Servant*. Fourteen-year-old George O'Dowd 'watched it open-mouthed ... Everyone thought he was "disgusting". I thought he was brave and stylish, I wanted to meet him.' 'Quentin' became a taunt at his school, Eltham Green Comprehensive in south London, but O'Dowd, already chased by skinheads for being effeminate, saw in Hurt's impersonation of Crisp the seeds of his own later reincarnation as Boy George. Another teenager, Martin Degville from Walsall, rushed back home to watch it. 'After about fifteen minutes of this thing being on,' he recalled, 'my father's face was starting to go red, and he started faffing, and then turned it off. So I turned it back on. And he's going, "You can't watch this, these people!" ... My father got so incensed he actually kicked the TV. He's a very straight guy, fought in the Second World War and everything, so to him this kind of thing was very disgusting.'[43]

Degville, later lead singer of Sigue Sigue Sputnik, was as intrigued as O'Dowd by Crisp's aesthetic. The New Romantic look adopted by many of these teenage television watchers when they reached adulthood in the late 1970s, of dyed, lacquered hair, rouge and painted fingernails, owed something to Quentin Crisp as well as to Bowie. But the emerging gay liberation movement was disapproving of Crisp's fatalistic, asexual acceptance of his camp otherness. '[Quentin Crisp] has set the "gay" world back twenty years,' wrote an anonymous letter-writer to *Gay News* after watching *The Naked Civil Servant*. 'There is no need to slap us and the hets in the face with "high camp" ... Quentin, keep it to yourself. No need to write books about it, have it on the box. Who wants to know?'[44]

Undeclared, comic homosexuals were a staple of the TV screen, another symptom of the generation gap. Dick Emery had originated many of his TV characters, including the lisping, pink-trousered Clarence with his catchphrase, 'Hallo honky tonk', during his time in RAF gang shows in Normandy, where cross-dressed entertainers were a necessity and a camp subculture, with its own lingo and mannerisms, thrived. Emery conceded that 'most comedians recognise that by becoming a little precious they can raise an instant laugh', a useful ploy 'when you're faced with an unresponsive audience staring blankly at you across their plates of steak and chips. Why the suggestion of homosexuality should be funny is imponderable – perhaps our laughter is defence, a reaction against hidden fears about our innermost tendencies.'[45]

Younger gay activists thought that camp held back the cause of equality. 'They do not come much lower than Larry Grayson,' wrote *Gay News* of the effeminate comic whose catchphrases were 'shut that door', 'what a gay day' and 'look at the muck in 'ere'. 'He will become a "superstar" while he confuses and distresses our young teenage brothers.' Another gay rights campaigner thought Mr Humphries, the fey sales assistant played by John Inman in the department store sitcom *Are You Being Served?*, was 'like a nail in the coffin of what we were trying to achieve'. In 1977, when *TV Times* readers voted Inman television personality of the year, gay rights protestors picketed his show at the Brighton Dome.[46]

No one in the 1970s thought television was passing through an Elysian age, but then no one ever does when they are passing through one. Even before the Annan Committee on Broadcasting described the BBC's attitude to complaints as 'not only cavalier, but aggressive and arrogant', there was a growing sense within the corporation that it needed to be more responsive to its viewers. 'If a churchy gloom suddenly darkens the BBC Club, somebody somewhere is bound to be talking about access,' wrote Jonathan Raban in the *Radio Times*. 'How does one stop television from turning into a bland, glittering monster, owned by vast corporations and manned by the trained professionals, who are the only people equipped to understand how the damn thing works?'[47]

Sensing the political mood even before Annan reported in 1977, the BBC published leaflets titled 'It's your BBC' or 'It's one BBC – and it's yours', explaining how viewers could contact them, and it held the first of a series of a public meetings in Truro in 1976. These tended to be polite affairs. At a meeting at the Octagon, an eighteenth-century chapel in Bath, in October of that year, the audience was drawn mostly from representatives of local societies, like the Walcot Townswomen's Guild and the Loyal Order of the Moose, and 'concluded with the clergyman thanking the BBC for taking so much trouble, offering an assurance that the corporation is deeply loved'.[48]

A lesser known subtext of this era is that it was one of energetic experiments in access television. Alongside the lavish light entertainment of primetime, a parallel make-do-and-mend universe of local TV had formed. Community television had begun in the early 1970s as an offshoot of the cable TV network which had grown up in areas where reception was poor or the transmitters did not yet reach. Now the spread of transmitters meant that the cable companies were worried that they could no longer promise clearer pictures in most areas, and they needed to find new markets. So in 1972 the government allowed them to start a small number of community TV channels with programmes made by local people.

Greenwich Cablevision, which should really have been called Plumstead Cablevision because it operated from a shop next to a greengrocer's on Plumstead High Street, had a Saturday night variety show called *Greenwich Meantime* which offered an early career break for the comedy duo Hale and Pace, and a weekly *Special Report* on subjects such as 'Behind the scenes of the Entertainments Department of Greenwich Council'. Community television benefited from the fact that some areas still had poor reception. The people of Plumstead had a dreadful TV picture from the Crystal Palace transmitter which, on its way east, bumped into the immovable object of Shooters Hill, one of the highest points in London. Greenwich Cablevision solved this problem by picking up its signal from a mast on top of one of the borough's new high-rise blocks and piping it to thousands of homes. Reception in Sheffield was almost as bad: the city nestles in a natural amphitheatre with much of it built on the hillsides, and it has over 2 million trees, a particular problem for television signals in the summer when they are in leaf. The fact that tenants in Sheffield's

20,000 council homes were forbidden to erect roof aerials was a further boost for the new channel, Sheffield Cablevision, which broadcast dominoes and darts from Sheffield pubs and *Hullabaloo*, an anarchic Saturday morning children's programme inspired by ATV's *Tiswas*.

Since they were not allowed advertising, the community TV channels were perennially poverty-stricken. Swindon Viewpoint, whose programmes included *This is Swindon* and *Report Swindon*, was the last to stop broadcasting in 1976, even EMI's bequeathing the station's equipment for £1 having failed to save it. But community TV had one last hurrah: Milton Keynes Channel 40, which went on air in December 1976. Milton Keynes, built on a sloping hill with a valley to the north and east, and with thousands of London plane trees planted along the main boulevards, also got bad TV reception, and the Milton Keynes planners approved of cable television because they, as in Sheffield, preferred not to have unsightly TV aerials ruining the skyline.

A child of the Labour government, Channel 40 was generously funded by the Milton Keynes Development Corporation, and intended to foster a sense of community in a new town full of displaced families. Groups could borrow facilities to make their own programmes and it was piped in to all new houses for free, for four hours per week. In the almost primetime hours between 6 p.m. and 7.30 p.m., it pulled in sixteen per cent of the available audience.[49] It ended in 1979, not because it made an ill-advised April Fool's joke about the new city being razed to the ground, but because the new Tory government was hostile to the no-strings, direct grants on which it depended.

The local aspect of community television made it watchable: there was novelty in seeing your own high street, the local school's Christmas play, or neighbours talking about lacemaking or model trains. In Milton Keynes, organisers of protests about a nursery school closure and library cuts managed to reverse the decisions after making programmes about them. But most people wanted to watch television, not make it. The tiny number of volunteers were mainly techno-literate single men, with a seasonal rush of students and schoolchildren in the summer months. By contrast, the access programmes on the main channels – BBC2's *Open Door*, HTV and Tyne Tees all offered studio facilities and airtime to members of the public to make their own programmes – were oversubscribed. But, the Annan committee found, viewers were rather less enthusiastic about watching local pressure groups campaigning against urban motorways or arguing for cuts in the rates.[50]

Another crack in the image of the unified armchair nation was that regional television was flourishing. The Annan committee saw the ITV–BBC duopoly as a metropolitan élite imposing its tastes on the rest of the population and stifling the voices of the regions. From today's perspective, this judgement seems harsh. The ITV regions had always been strange, makeshift entities, defined mainly by the reach of the transmitters, and fighting for viewers with the fickleness and ferocity of Balkan states. The regions were also at the mercy of the ITV franchise rounds: in the last big one of these in 1968, Granada-land had been cut to half its size, reduced to a rump west of the Pennines. The Granada chairman Sidney Bernstein's half-serious threat to appeal to the United Nations fell on deaf ears.

The arrival of colour TV in the late 1960s also created problems for the regions because more transmitters were required and, until a transmitter was built, no one knew for sure how far its signal – what engineers called its 'fall-out' – would reach. When Yorkshire TV built a colour transmitter at Bilsdale on the North Yorkshire Moors in 1969, Tyne Tees discovered to its dismay that the signal could reach as far as Newcastle, and the two companies were forced to merge under a holding company.[51] A similar problem occurred when the signals from Anglia's new colour transmitter at Belmont strayed into Yorkshire; Anglia ended up renting out the mast and many Norfolk viewers suddenly found themselves watching Yorkshire Television.

And yet, just as with the 'historic' English counties which are really nothing more than pragmatic divisions of fairly recent vintage, ITV viewers became oddly attached to their regional companies. Each had their start-up themes for the beginning of the day's television, jaunty marches like Border's 'Keltic Kavalcade' or Southern Television's 'Southern Rhapsody', composed by Richard Addinsell (better known for the Warsaw Concerto), accompanying a montage of regional scenes. Each had their short idents to introduce the programmes they had made, usually with bold brass and vibraphone fanfares similar to those used by Hollywood studios at the start of films. London Weekend Television's ident was three coloured stripes forming to depict the course of the River Thames through the capital which, at least according to its designer Terry Griffiths, resembled the initials 'L' and 'W'. Colloquially known as the 'stripey toothpaste', for London viewers it announced the arrival of the weekend. Thames TV's London skyline mirrored in the river may have been associated more mundanely with the working week, but it was still the most famous ident on the network, an emblem of metropolitan self-assurance.

Non-Anglia viewers mainly saw its revolving silver knight before the syndicated and hugely popular quiz show *Sale of the Century*, when the snatch of Handel's Water Music, arranged by Sir Malcolm Sargent, ended with the perhaps anticlimactic affirmation, 'And now, from Norwich, it's the quiz of the week.' ('Thanks to this opening line, a lot of people thought I lived in Norwich,' said the show's host, Nicholas Parsons.)[52] Granadaland, with its 'G-arrow' ident, now symbolised the north-west – stretching from Liverpool Bay to the mountains of Snowdonia and the Lake District, and from the Pennine ridge to the Black Country chimneys – just as eloquently as it once had the north, although Liverpudlians always resented the fact that its centre of gravity was unmistakably Mancunian. Westward TV's galleon, a model of Sir Francis Drake's *Golden Hind*, and Grampian's eight notes from 'Scotland the Brave', were the defiant motifs of minnow stations wresting airtime from the big ITV companies.

The nation mainly got to know Southern Television's star-like ident ('the station that serves the south') through Jack Hargreaves's *Out of Town*, which by the 1970s was being shown throughout the country. It now aimed at being as evocative as it was informative, giving urban viewers what the former Southern Television controller

Roy Rich called 'a dream of the green fields beyond'. Beyond the Southern region they saw *Out of Town* episodes out of synch and long after they were made, happily watching fish being caught in the middle of winter or lambing in August. Noting that Hampshire, where he lived, emptied in the morning as people travelled to London for work, Hargreaves realised that many of his viewers no longer had any real contact with rural life. 'I've got to hook every sort of viewer, particularly the ones who have never held a fishing rod,' he said. 'You can't do that just by showing them a lot of floats and telling them how to breed champion maggots.'[53]

Most of Hargreaves's viewers were unaware that he was a Southern Television executive and former magazine editor who felt just as at home in the Savile Club as on the River Test. The Clydeside trade union leader, Jimmy Reid, watching in Glasgow, thought *Out of Town* 'a gem of a programme' and 'the answer to those TV moguls who plead poverty as an excuse for diminishing standards'. Another fan, George Harrison, now living in semi-rural seclusion near Henley-on-Thames, had the idea, while watching one episode on restoring old leather books, of publishing his autobiography/lyric book, *I Me Mine*, as a hand-bound limited edition.[54]

Farming programmes were a familiar feature of the regional schedules for Sunday lunchtime, often with little concession to what was called the 'over the shoulder' lay audience. Despite this, viewing figures for Tyne Tees' *Farming Outlook* suggested that at least two-thirds of its viewers were non-farmers, unfazed by in-depth items about crop rotation and tied cottages. The show was mini-networked to Yorkshire TV, Border, STV and Grampian, and the presenter Peter Williams found himself being hailed by lorry drivers as far north as Aberdeen. At a time when 15,000 men were leaving farming each year for the factories and docks where, even during a recession, they could earn in a week what a farm paid in a month, these programmes also alerted urban viewers to the realities of agrarian capitalism. 'These agricultural programmes do yeoman service,' said the Annan Report, 'explain[ing] the importance of agriculture and forestry to our largely urban community who consume agricultural products without understanding much about the toil and hazards of production.'[55]

Regional opt-outs were common. The Tyne Tees show, *What Fettle?* (Geordie for 'How're you doing?'), was one of the north-east's most popular programmes, with entire villages being bussed into the studio to watch folk music, ballads and comedy themed around the region's great interests, such as coal, fishing or football. When the impressionist Mike Yarwood began mimicking Russell Harty on his BBC show, the studio audience laughed; but those in the landmass between London and the Scottish Highlands must have been baffled, for Harty's LWT chat show was transmitted in the London area only, and then, for obscure reasons, by Grampian. At a reception in the Town Hall of his hometown in 1975, the Mayor said to Harty, 'You may be a big cheese in London, but you're bugger-all in Blackburn.'[56]

The campaign for a Welsh language television channel, spearheaded by the small but vocal Welsh Language Society, was also reaching a climax. At the national *Eisteddfodau*, speakers often pointed out television's baleful influence in not only presenting an almost unbroken diet of English but also in cutting down the amount of talking, which could have been in Welsh. Welsh language protestors, many of them students or lecturers at Welsh universities, began climbing up television transmitters and trying to disrupt programmes. At 9.05 p.m. on 4 March 1977, protestors invaded the buildings at the Winter Hill transmitter on the West Pennine Moors and managed briefly to switch off the ITV series *Raffles* across the Granada region. 'I tried to explain that radio and TV signals are no respecters of geographical or political boundaries,' wrote the duty officer, 'and I tried to point out to them that inhabitants of N. Wales did not have to tune their sets to the Granada channel if they did not wish to receive it. But all this fell on deaf ears.'[57]

Advocates of a separate Welsh channel professed concern for the non-Welsh-speaking majority who had to put up with Welsh programmes like the BBC's Carmarthenshire-set soap opera, *Pobol y Cwm*. This had long been a complaint of Wales's non-Welsh speaking majority. In 1964, more than 5,000 viewers in Aberystwyth signed a petition protesting about the launch of a new BBC television service for Wales, fearing they might lose their favourite programmes, like *Z Cars* and *Steptoe and Son*, for Welsh language ones. According to a Radnorshire parish council in a 1973 submission to the Committee on Broadcasting Coverage, these Welsh programmes made most Welshmen 'aliens at their own firesides'. Wales had become 'a television electrician's paradise', with non-Welsh speakers paying to have their aerials retuned and turned towards English transmitters.[58]

The writer Gwyn Thomas, the unofficial poet laureate of the English-speaking southern valleys and an eloquent regular on chat shows like *Parkinson*, dismissed Welsh as 'elitist gobbledygook'. Even some Welsh language loyalists did not want a separate channel. Jac L. Williams, Professor of Education at Aberystwyth, wrote many letters to newspapers from 1973 until his death in 1977, arguing that it would exile Welsh speakers to a broadcasting ghetto on an obscure wavelength. By the end of the 1970s, a 'Ban Welsh Telly' group had acquired 30,000 members in monoglot Avon and Somerset. The movement was strongest in Weston-super-Mare, where 'Ban Welsh Telly' stickers adorned the rear window of every other car. Even today, the town's residents attribute antipathy to the Welsh to the days when they had to watch Welsh-language television. When, in September 1978, HTV, the Welsh ITV station, dubbed the western film *Shane* into Welsh, the 'Ban Welsh Telly' group complained to the newly formed Commission for Racial Equality. Both Welsh and non-Welsh speakers seemed equally disapproving of Wyoming cowboys conversing in Cymraeg, and it was sufficiently imprinted in the nation's memory that, twenty-three years later, the MP for Ceridigion, Simon Thomas, told parliament: 'That experiment has gone down in Welsh history and will never be tried again.'[59]

On the evening of 25 December 1977, 28.5 million people arranged themselves in front of a television, between 8.55 p.m. and 10.05 p.m., to watch *The Morecambe and Wise Christmas Show*. This moment has entered British folklore as the culmination of television's potential to bring the extended national family together. For the historian Ben Pimlott, updating his late father's social history, *The Englishman's Christmas*, in 1978, this viewing figure suggested that Morecambe and Wise had taken over from the Queen's Christmas broadcast as the essential element of the secular festival, especially 'for those who digest their mid-day Christmas dinner in an armchair' – and this despite the fact that it was the least festive show in the schedules, with barely a slither of tinsel or a Santa hat in sight. In Jonathan Coe's 1970s-set novel *The Rotters' Club*, the sixteen-year-old protagonist watches the show with his parents and experiences an epiphanic moment, 'a sense that the entire nation was being briefly, fugitively drawn together in the divine act of laughter'.[60] The moment of unanimity ended with a certain narrative neatness when, in January 1978, Morecambe and Wise defected shockingly to ITV, after which their careers, by common consent, went into sharp decline.

Morecambe and Wise were certainly loved, but not uncritically or universally so. It was in fact a recurring motif among TV critics throughout the 1970s that Morecambe and Wise's Christmas show was not as funny as last year's. 'Ernie and I have always prided ourselves on seeing the red light before anyone else,' Morecambe said in 1973, predicting that the show would not survive much longer. 'We think there is a saturation point at which people can take so much of a good thing.'[61] In 1974, after their new series slipped down the ratings, they took a break and were off screen for over a year.

Television's weakness as a medium is that it relies a lot on repetition, prolonging a successful formula long after its potential is exhausted. And Morecambe and Wise, who had learned their trade in the variety halls where resuscitating old gags was the norm, believed in letting the audience eternally in on the joke. They depended so much on the reassuring reiteration of stock phrases and comic business that it is hard to pin down the invisible moment when this may have tipped over into staleness. The Radio 1 DJ John Peel found them 'extravagantly unfunny' and thought 'their best work in several years was the current television commercial for Texaco'. Watched today, the 1977 show does not seem like a classic. It started with a lame skit on 'Starkers and Krutch' and finished not with the triumphant 'There is nothing like a dame' number from *South Pacific* that everyone remembers, but with Elton John playing piano in an empty studio while Eric and Ernie, dressed in drag as cleaners, looked on. 'I thought the ending didn't quite come off,' the comedian Les Dawson said. Many felt Morecambe had been funnier ad libbing with Dickie Davies on ITV's *World of Sport* on Christmas Eve.[62]

ITV's Christmas programmes in 1977 were so unappetising that when the schedules were announced a few weeks earlier, several advertising agencies officially complained. On Christmas Day, ITV showed *Sale of the Century*, *Stars on Christmas Day* and, at 9 p.m. when Morecambe and Wise were on, a re-run of the film *Young Winston*. To have detained half the nation for an hour and ten minutes with this on the other side was no great achievement. In any case, ratings at this time were disputed, the difference between BBC and ITV claims often being huge. The famous figure of 28.5 million viewers came from the BBC's own audience research, based on telephone interviews and viewing diaries. ITV's figures, which sampled homes using electronic measuring devices attached to TV sets, suggest that the 1977 Christmas special was only the eleventh most-watched programme of the decade with 21.3 million viewers, behind less fondly remembered shows like a 1977 episode of *This is Your Life* and a 1971 edition of *The Benny Hill Show*. According to ITV, even the 1977 *Mike Yarwood Christmas Special*, which preceded Morecambe and Wise on BBC1, got more viewers (21.4 million), so that, far from uniting the nation in laughter, Morecambe and Wise made 100,000 people switch over or turn off the TV.[63]

But the national affection for Morecambe and Wise was real enough. They may never have been as good as they used to be, but they were always popular and, albeit fitfully, funny. After moving to the BBC in 1968 and acquiring a new writer, Eddie Braben, they had become distinct characters: an idiot disguised as an intellectual (Ernie) and a subversive disguised as an idiot (Eric). It was Braben's idea to have them sitting up together in a double bed, Ernie working on 'the play what I wrote' while Eric read *The Dandy* and smoked a pipe. The television playwright John Mortimer called it 'an English marriage, missing out the sex as many English marriages do'.[64]

They evolved a unique way of engaging with viewers, melding theatricality with intimacy. Clinging to their variety background, they worked on a raised platform that looked like a proscenium stage with tabs and wings, and at some point in each show they clowned in front of a plush red curtain. While this staginess gave the show a sense of occasion, their producer John Ammonds also got them to look at specific cameras, with Morecambe watching carefully for the camera light to come on so that he could treat its lens as a mirror, adjusting his tie, flashing his smile and wiggling his spectacles at viewers. John McGrath, a former *Z Cars* writer who had given up TV to try to create a genuinely proletarian theatre, and whose touring show George Mackay Brown had seen on Orkney, respected Morecambe and Wise as creators of a real folk art with the same direct engagement with its audience and the same democratic variety – of songs, playlets, sketches and stand-up comedy – as the Welsh *noson lawen* and the Scottish *ceilidh*.[65]

While Morecambe and Wise were performing their Christmas shows for the BBC, television had yet to acquire a reliable collective memory. Archiving was erratic. Even when shows began to be video-recorded in the late 1950s, the tapes were as expensive as a small car and so engineers routinely wiped and reused them. Peter Cook pleaded in vain for his 1960s comedy series, *Not Only ... But Also*, to be preserved, even offering to pay for the tapes and the storage costs. Despite this, the BBC taped over the series, an act criticised by Cook's co-star Dudley Moore when he appeared on *Parkinson*. The 1970s, too, saw much wiping of old black-and-white shows because it was thought viewers who had recently paid for a colour TV licence would never want to see them again. The ITV channels took even less care of their old programmes, being unwilling to pay to store or insure them. The critic T. C. Worsley rightly called television 'the ephemeral art'.[66]

Those who took television seriously as an art form fretted often about its impermanence. Dennis Potter still felt a sense of paralysing anticlimax as the end credits rolled on each of his television plays, even though he knew more people had watched them than would have seen Agatha Christie's *The Mousetrap* in its entire West End run. 'The pictures flow on easy as tapwater,' he wrote. 'A play which has taken months to write, characters who have leapt up gibbering in your mind when you are trying to sleep, ideas which have simmered feverishly in your blood like a virus – all used up, all at once, all gone.' In his often dyspeptic television reviews in the *New Statesman* and the *Sunday Times*, Potter returned to the same theme: the TV was becoming nothing more than a domestic appliance for passing the time, 'a box that can be plugged into the same socket as a hairdryer or a coffee perculator'.[67] In an age before archiving, he worried about the fragile connection between writer and viewer, desperately wanting television to be a more enduring medium to justify the effort he put into his work.

Before the domestication of the video recorder, there was an industry of records and books based on television programmes, especially comedy – probably because, if shared humour does affirm membership of a group as Bergson claimed, that group may want something more concrete to hold on to than the fading memory of laughter. The first Monty Python film, *And Now for Something Completely Different ...* (1971), was a compilation of re-shot television highlights, aimed at the American market, but it did better business in the UK because viewers wanted to see their favourite sketches again. On their first theatre tour in 1971, the team noted that audiences preferred what they knew to new material, and greeted sketches recycled from television with applause after their first few lines, like rock fans cheering the opening bars of a song. Comedy fans accumulated cultural capital among their peers by knowing routines off by heart, as did troubadours before the arrival of the printing press. Perhaps the Dead

Parrot sketch would never have become seminal in a world populated by the domestic video recorder, because there would have been less playground or common room cachet in being able to recite a sketch that was purchasable and replayable.

BBC Television's fortieth anniversary in 1976 had prompted a round of introspection about the medium and the showing of many old programmes, in the first major attempt by television to explore its own history. That same year the BBC reached an agreement with the actors' union Equity and the technicians' unions which allowed them to present more of this kind of archive material. (The unions had feared that repeating shows indefinitely would cut down on new productions and put actors and technicians out of work.) When the BBC finally set up its Film and Videotape Library in 1978 in response to the Annan Report's call for proper archiving, it coincided happily with the arrival of home video recorders which were starting to open up new markets for old programmes. Suddenly television performers had the possibility of an artistic afterlife. Videotape began stacking along miles of shelving in the BBC's two vast warehouse hangars on Windmill Road in Brentford, close to the runway at Heathrow.

Television now had its own version of the library at Alexandria, and in years to come, when the BBC and the British Film Institute both launched appeals for missing material, romantic tales would be told of fans coming across lost material that had miraculously survived the scorched earth policies of the past. In 1983, two episodes of *Doctor Who* materialised in a basement of the Church of Latter Day Saints in Wandsworth. In 2001, nineteen cans of film of the lost second series of *Dad's Army* were discovered in a shed after being rescued years earlier from a skip outside Elstree studios. Two years later, an engineer was rummaging in a BBC tape archive at Kingswood Warren in Surrey when he came across a spool titled 'Opening of BBC2'. He played it and saw a man at a desk in a V-neck jumper and tie reading from cards: it was Gerald Priestland, in the Alexandra Palace newsroom, explaining that a massive power cut in west London had disrupted programmes. 'I ploughed on through every scrap of unedited Reuters tape they could feed me,' Priestland wrote later. 'After what seemed like an eternity of ad-libbing about Japanese fishery disputes and trains de-railed in Tunisia, I was taken off the air.' The disastrous launch of BBC2, which the corporation would probably have preferred to forget, could now be re-lived. Rumours thrive that other lost programmes exist and change hands between collectors – more missing *Doctor Who* episodes, the Beatles on *Juke Box Jury*, the classic 1961 sci-fi series *A for Andromeda* – but they have never resurfaced.[68]

While Morecambe and Wise's Christmas shows went out, though, this fascination with the television archive was only just emerging. They must have hoped their names would live on, while perhaps also fearing that they would go the way of Mr Pastry or Jewel and Warriss, early television's comedy stars who were now largely forgotten. 'When I'm gone, I'm gone,' Morecambe told his family after surviving a second heart attack in 1979. 'No point worrying about me, you know. But you will still watch the shows, won't you? If you don't, then it's all been for nothing.'

Those lobbying for better archiving argued that writers and performers were being made 'cynical or lazy by the essentially ephemeral nature of television' and would try harder if they knew their work had permanence. But the makers of the *Morecambe and Wise Show* were neither cynical nor lazy. John Ammonds and his successor, Ernest Maxin, rehearsed with Morecambe and Wise for at least five weeks before recording each show, and would carefully examine BBC audience reports in search of clues about how to improve things.[69]

A Christmas show would take Braben five weeks to write, working sixteen hour days, including weekends, pushing himself close to breakdown. In the back bedroom of his house in West Derby, Liverpool, where he kept his typewriter, he would clock on at 7.30 a.m. and see people in the street catching the bus to work. 'They weren't looking very happy at going to the factory or the shipyard,' he said, 'and I thought, some of them are saying to themselves, "Oh great, it's Morecambe and Wise tonight." That's what drove me on.' Privately, though, he felt they had created an impossible burden of expectation and that 'the *Morecambe and Wise Show*, for a lot of viewers, *was* Christmas. They were forgetting what Christmas was really all about.'[70]

Braben watched the show each Christmas Day, his whole body clenched with nervous tension, unplacated by the studio audience laughter. Morecambe was so full of fear-induced adrenalin before the Christmas shows that he came out in sties, got indigestion and developed a nervous itch in his ear. When he watched them with his family on Christmas night, he would cough or kick a nearby ash can with his foot to distract his audience from any slight fluffs left in the edit. And yet, investing enormous energy into a single television programme with no guarantee it would be remembered, Morecambe and Wise's gamble paid off. When Morecambe died of his third heart attack, in May 1984, thousands of people lined the streets of Harpenden for his funeral. An elderly woman in the crowd said, 'he was like someone you had known and loved all your life – a member of the family … And that funny little song … How did it go? That thing about sunshine and laughter and love. That was ever so nice. We'll never forget that …'[71]

Television ended the 1970s as it began, with blank screens. For most Britons, the industrial unrest of the now notorious 'winter of discontent' was sporadic, dispersed and endured only vicariously on the news. The one disruption that everyone noticed, though, was to the TV schedules. There was a virtual shutdown of both BBC channels in mid-December 1978 when unions resisted a plan to start BBC2 at the earlier time of 5.30 p.m., with the BBC quickly settling because it could not face the bleak prospect of its Christmas programmes being cancelled. Another strike in the spring of 1979 halted BBC outside broadcasts and the filming of other programmes, the most distressing upshot of which was the indefinite delaying of the final episode of *Fawlty Towers*. 'Should it matter one jot that *Fawlty Towers* fails to appear?' wrote one dissenting *Guardian* reader. 'Are the mass of people, after all, the helpless improvident "gammas" of Huxley's *Brave New World*? What manner of homo sapiens is evolving when it betrays all the symptoms of addiction, and is distressed when the drug known as pap is temporarily withdrawn?'[72]

There was now an unlikely addition to this mass of TV addicts: the previously hostile George Mackay Brown. He was finding it a source of distraction during his increasingly severe bouts of depression, a condition so linked with dark, isolated Orkney that islanders named it *Morbus Orcadensis*. In 1978, invited to appear in *Who's Who*, he put 'watching TV' in his list of recreations alongside reading and ale tasting. That autumn he noted with delight that old winter favourites like *Mastermind*, *The Good Life* and *All Creatures Great and Small* had returned and his mind was being 'fed full with shadows'. And he recounted his relief at getting hold of the *Radio Times* Christmas double issue from a Kirkwall friend after the Stromness paper shop had sold out and he had faced 'a bleak prospect of groping blindly about in a fog of programmes for a fortnight'.[73]

Now in his late fifties, Brown lived a frugal, monkish existence in his sparse council flat and left Orkney even more rarely. Television drew him out of this sometimes claustrophobic existence and offered a brief respite from his expansive imagination, steeped in the island's Viking past, introducing him to a less parochial, more contemporary reality. On Monday evenings he watched the BBC2 science programme *Horizon* so he could discuss immunology or extraterrestrial intelligence with his niece's scientist husband, Fraser Dixon, and his geologist nephew, John Flett Brown. He now conceded privately that he had over-egged his Luddite tirades against technology which were 'just a sort of stance', a rhetorical device used for contrast and effect. When Isobel Murray, an English lecturer at Aberdeen University, visited his flat and expressed surprise that he had a television at all, he replied weakly that 'the only concession I've made is that it is black and white, you see. I keep one step behind. I'm not in the vanguard of culture.' He certainly had no religious objection to television. For Brown, an attraction of Roman Catholicism, to which he had converted in 1961, was that, unlike the native Calvinism of what he called this 'Knox-ruined nation', it saw visual culture and music as augmenting the faith.[74]

In the spring of 1979, Brown found himself entranced by a series which, though presented by an atheist, resembled a theology in its celebration of life and the search for knowledge about it: David Attenborough's *Life on Earth*, which told the story of our evolution from primeval slime to late twentieth-century television-watching human. As controller of BBC2 in the late 1960s, Attenborough had inaugurated a new type of blockbuster colour documentary series, when he had commissioned Kenneth Clark's *Civilisation*. These had thirteen episodes which neatly filled three months, at a time when the schedules were always planned in quarters. 'Happily, when I sat down to survey geological time,' Attenborough reflected, 'the schedules of creation seemed also to be conveniently divided into thirteen parts.'[75] He insisted on presenting the series chronologically, beginning with the most basic organisms, although several BBC executives feared that all the interesting animals would come in the last few episodes, by which time viewers would have switched off. The fear proved unfounded. *Life on Earth* was both a sensual and educational experience, with haunting incidental music and groundbreaking footage of rarely seen creatures such as sea slugs, legless amphibians and coelacanths.

On 10 April, Brown watched the last episode in the lounge of Stromness's Braes hotel, specifically so he could view it in colour. The weather was wintry that night and Orkney's new BBC2 reception was poor, so a series conceived partly to show off high-fidelity colour kept disintegrating into kaleidoscopic patterns. Brown was also distracted by local women playing a darts match. But he still sat enthralled, sipping his beer, while Attenborough talked about a species of grasslands ape he called 'the compulsive communicators' who, having come down from the trees, had learned how to talk, paint and write. Brown's natural curiosity had won out over his acquired misanthropy, and he seemed finally willing to concede the lyrical, life-affirming potential of television. When the programme ended, he walked the few hundred yards home through the cold and rain, wondering 'what group of "homo sapiens" in a skin and wattle boat first had the courage to set foot on the bleak, black Orkneys, on such a night as this?'[76]

Brown does not seem to have been part of one of the most unlikely mass audiences of British television history, when at 10.20 p.m. on Tuesday 7 August 1979, about 16 million people watched Mike Leigh's *Abigail's Party*. It was a remarkable figure for the school holidays, and for a *Play for Today* which had been shown twice before, did not finish until just before midnight, and whose mise-en-scène seemed so unpromising: a dreadful suburban drinks party, dominated by the blowsy Beverley, smoking king-sized cigarettes and doling out cheese and pineapple nibbles.

The play mimicked the look of the 1970s domestic sitcom – the wallpaper of brown and orange swirls, the sunburst clock above the fake coal-effect fire, the padded leather suite – with background music provided by Beverley's favourite singer, Demis Roussos, a bearded, high vibrato Greek singer, dressed in a kaftan, who appeared often in light entertainment television specials. One man presumably not watching was Dennis Potter, who had reviewed the first TV showing in November 1977 as a play 'based on nothing more edifying than rancid disdain, for it was a prolonged jeer, twitching with genuine hatred, about the dreadful suburban tastes of the dreadful lower middle classes'.[77] Whether or not *Abigail's Party* was sneering at its viewers, as Potter suggested, it certainly dispensed with the easy, communal laughter of the 1970s sitcom and suspended its audience halfway between mortification and amusement.

The large audience for *Abigail's Party* had, however, been artificially inflated. At the beginning of August, commercial TV screens started to go blank, region by region. On 10 August a total walkout of technicians turned the whole of ITV into an apology caption. The shutdown lasted for eleven weeks, the longest in the history of British television. While Alan Sapper, hardline leader of the TV technicians' union, became briefly infamous for spoiling the nation's viewing, the landlady of the Maxwell Hotel, Orpington, said the strike had boosted her bar takings by £800 a week.[78]

For the first time, the *Radio Times* acknowledged the existence of ITV viewers on its letters page, as they complained about being 'forced' to watch BBC, suggesting that, more than twenty years after the arrival of commercial competition, some families still identified themselves as 'ITV' or 'BBC' households. Often unfairly, the BBC was seen as stuffy and middle-class, ITV as vulgar, brash and 'a bit council house'. 'We have been without ITV for a few days now, and believe me, what a boring time it has been,' wrote Mrs E. Jackson from Formby. 'You have two stations, I hope you never have any more.' D. J. Thompson from Blackpool said he had switched off the BBC and been 'thoroughly entertained by reading what might have been in *TV Times*'. Mrs Alys Quirk was among thousands who wrote directly to ITV to describe her withdrawal symptoms and complain about the stuffy BBC presenters and their 'forced smiles': 'I for one will never want to see BBC again.'[79]

ITV's ratings system measured a 'discernible number' of viewers (press leaks suggested over a million) tuning into the apology card played out each day from the Independent Broadcasting Authority's temporary national control centre at St Hilary near Cardiff. West Yorkshire Police, in an effort to make use of this captive audience, persuaded the IBA to vary the caption to read, 'We are sorry that ITV is still off the air. Here is a police message. If you think you could help to catch the Ripper please telephone …' The BBC, meanwhile, insisted that ninety-five per cent of ITV viewers were switching over to them, producing huge audiences, including 26 million for yet another repeat of the film *The Great Escape*.[80]

The large audiences would remain in the coming years but, subtly, the tone and ambience of primetime television was changing. *Abigail's Party*, with its lack of a laughter track, foreshadowed a less variety-oriented television comedy which did not demand that we all laughed at the same things. On *The Kenny Everett Video Show*, which had replaced *Opportunity Knocks* on Monday nights, the star, when not in character, wore a shirt and jeans and performed without a studio audience, with only a few gruff cameramen reacting to his jokes. For the comedian Stewart Lee, then aged ten and watching on a television in Solihull, 'the tinkling of genuine human laughs, however few, was a beautiful sound'.[81]

The light entertainment now remembered as the quintessence of 1970s TV had the ulterior motive of advertising the benefits of colour sets. The BBC in particular wanted people to buy the more expensive colour licences to offset the increased cost of making colour programmes. The hard selling of colour was led by the Miss World and Eurovision Song Contest spectaculars, and the star-with-guests specials hosted by stars like Lulu, Cliff Richard and Val Doonican, with their garish cerise backdrops and troupes of writhing dancers in sequins and tulle. By the end of the 1970s, though, colour television was the norm, and primetime programmes did not need to sell colour so energetically. A note of dry humour crept into primetime programmes, especially if they were hosted by the Irish presenter Terry Wogan, whose commentary on the Eurovision Song Contest genially subverted the whole charade, and who made much of the fact that the prizes on his quiz show, *Blankety Blank*, were rubbish: a mug tree, a plastic bicycle, a weekend in Reykjavik.

Perhaps there is even a relationship between improved heat insulation and changing styles of television around this time. Many families now had more than one TV set and the whole house was warmer: more than half Britain's 19 million homes had central heating, compared to a quarter at the start of the decade. Double glazing, only in ten per cent of homes by 1979, was about to experience a boom, thanks in part to a series of commercials featuring the Derbyshire farmer-turned-TV personality Ted Moult ('fit the best, fit Everest'), and by 1982 Britain was second only to West Germany in the amount of double glazing being installed.[82] TV programmes still attracted vast audiences. But they could not intuitively assume that they were speaking to a single family, crowding round the same set for social and actual warmth.

7

A BARRIER AGAINST
THE SILENCES

*And it was only a few days before Bert Tilsley died [on TV]
that our dog had got knocked over. My husband was sitting
on the settee watching Coronation Street. Tears streaming
down his face. I said, "What's the matter with you?" He said,
"I'm thinking of the dog with Bert Tilsley dying." Fancy
comparing the two. You've never seen anything like it. Tears
rolling down his face.*

Joyce, 42, *c.* 1986[1]

At the end of the late May Bank Holiday Monday in Britain in 1980,
the Dallas oil magnate, JR Ewing, was working late in his office
when an unseen hand poked round the door and shot him in the
chest with a revolver. A few minutes later, on the BBC *Nine O'Clock
News*, a reporter confirmed that Ewing had been critically wounded.
There was no shortage of people wanting to kill him: his alcoholic,
estranged wife Sue Ellen; his sworn business enemy Cliff Barnes; his
mistress and sister-in-law Kristin, who was carrying his baby and had
screamed 'I'll kill him' when JR had her arrested on a jumped-up
prostitution charge; and Lusty Dusty, Sue Ellen's ex-lover who was
thought to have died in a car crash but possibly hadn't. The next day,
thousands of people, most of them women, placed money on who

had shot JR, the surprise favourite being the theoretically posthumous Lusty Dusty at 6–4. The bookmaker William Hill took £50,000 in bets, more than it had made on most of the Bank Holiday races.[2]

When the first episode of *Dallas* had been shown in September 1978, the BBC seemed rather sheepish about it. 'Corn it may all be, but it is corn of the most compulsive sort,' said the *Radio Times*. The phrase 'wall to wall *Dallas*', evoked throughout the 1980s to suggest a nightmarish future swamped by cable and satellite television pap, was coined by Alasdair Milne, the BBC's director of programmes and then director general ultimately responsible for putting *Dallas* on British TV.[3] Even when it became the BBC's highest rated programme, Britons liked to believe that, unlike Americans, they watched it with a squint, finding it addictive but absurd. On his BBC Radio 2 breakfast show, Terry Wogan deployed *Dallas* as a running joke.

Another emigrant to the UK fed this flattering national self-image that British viewers knowingly enjoyed *Dallas* as kitsch. Since 1972, Clive James had written a television column for the back page of the *Observer*'s review section. Before James, TV criticism had received little attention as a literary form. While film and theatre reviews inhabited the present tense and addressed a potential audience, television critics reheated last night's schedule for the benefit of people who had already seen or would never see it. In the early days critics phoned in their copy late at night from their living rooms, having watched it at the same time as other viewers, which did not always encourage careful reflection. The more thoughtful reviewers, like Philip Purser, T. C. Worsley and Peter Black, had all previously been theatre critics and tended to focus on prestige programmes like single plays and documentaries, often looking down on the American imports, light entertainment shows and soap operas that most viewers watched.[4]

By the mid 1970s, cheaper video recording, assiduous lobbying by the *Sunday Times* critic Elkan Allan and the desire of television producers to have their work given more serious consideration began to force changes. The BBC started showing some programmes to critics before transmission; its preview day, usually a Friday, came to be known as 'Elkan's day'. Critics could now be more considered in their responses. James largely avoided the preview days or the little cinemas around London's Wardour Street requisitioned as TV viewing theatres, preferring to watch on a domestic television as his readers did. But writing for a Sunday newspaper, he had more time to hone his rococo, allusive style, which made his reviews creative works in themselves, often more artful than the programmes he was writing about. He did not originate the witty, epigrammatic television column – Bernard Levin, Nancy Banks-Smith and Alan Coren all predated him – but he turned it into a glamorous genre, becoming as important to his newspaper as Kenneth Tynan had been as its theatre critic a generation earlier. James's column was said to be worth an extra 10,000 on the *Observer*'s circulation.[5]

Ever since sailing to England from Australia in 1961, James had been fascinated by the relentless variety and ubiquity of British television. While studying at Cambridge, he would watch the whole evening's schedules in the Footlights clubroom, until the channels shut down. Starting out as a freelance writer in the late 1960s, he would channel-hop through the evening at his Swiss Cottage flat before settling down to write through the night.[6] When Karl Miller asked him to contribute a TV column to the *Listener*, he simply wrote about the programmes he was watching anyway. Borrowing a line from the seventeenth-century writer Thomas Browne, James called his first collection of TV criticism *Visions Before Midnight* (1977), an inspired title when television finished before the witching hour and was a fleeting apparition that had to be written about from memory. Without a video recorder, like most viewers at this time, James often had two sets running at once so as not to miss anything.

James wrote about the banal, everyday television that newspaper critics had traditionally ignored. Believing that, since watching television was now a near universal experience, he could dispense with plot summary, he packed in esoteric cultural references, quoting Rilke or Pater while reviewing *Charlie's Angels* or *The Incredible Hulk*. If the word had been in wide currency then, this stylistic promiscuity and eclectic mixing of high and low culture might have been called 'postmodern'. James preferred to cite John Keats's notion of negative capability, a way of being receptive to the multifarious nature of the world without bounding it with categories or judgements – a useful mindset, had Keats but known it, for the TV critic.[7]

James believed that, in all its chaotic diversity, British TV was 'an expanding labyrinth which Daedalus has long since forgotten he ever designed'. He had little patience with would-be moral censors like Mary Whitehouse who assumed that television had some directing, malign intention behind it. Television offered no answers or resolutions; it was an authorless, collective fiction too vast to generalise about or summarise. One of his favourite subjects was *Dallas* and its strange, riveting details, from its southern pronunciations (*prarlm* for problem, *lernch* for lunch) to the way that Sue Ellen moved her mouth in different directions to convey emotion. 'It washes my mind cleaner than ever before,' he wrote after the first few episodes. 'Try taking *Dallas* away from me and giving me some other product in exchange. I'll break both your arms.'[8]

It was not clear, though, that everyone in Britain watched *Dallas* as wryly. The Southfork women helped to create a fashion for shoulder pads and coiffeured hair, and the Ewings' habit of taking breakfast outside had, according to one study, contributed to the booming market for patio doors and furniture.[9] And at least some people were genuinely anxious to learn the identity of JR's killer for, in order that no one find out the ending in advance, the crucial episode had to be flown from Los Angeles to London in two boxes of film, escorted by private detectives and with an extra £120 being paid in order for the precious cargo to have its own passenger seat. The usual two-week gap between the American and British screening of episodes was compressed for this episode, although some British fans spent that morning's small hours listening to the radio bulletins giving the game away, as it was shown in America at 3 a.m. GMT.

Dallas police charged JR's attempted murderer on 22 November 1980 at 9.10 p.m. on BBC1. Her identity (Kristin, who had tried to frame Sue Ellen by hiding the gun in her closet) was an inevitable anticlimax. 'An imbecile curiosity has now compelled me to sit through two further boring episodes – mainly composed of hospital visits from his dreadful family and the drooling of his estranged wife,' wrote Alex James of East Moseley, Surrey, to the BBC's *Points of View*. 'I no longer care who shot JR. I only wish the public spirited assassin had been a better marksman, and that he or she had not wasted the remaining bullets in the revolver.'[10]

Television had never before been so much a subject of public discussion. As tabloid newspapers competed among themselves for a declining readership, they clung parasitically to the younger medium as a source of gossip. The *Sun* and the *Daily Mirror* now had double-page TV sections which became the most read part of the newspaper. Pre-publicity for programmes, from on-air trailers to newspaper previews, also became more visible. The arrival of the VHS tape having enabled bulk copying, one of the familiar features of the London landscape in the 1980s was the number of motorcycle couriers racing through the streets to deliver preview tapes to critics.[11] TV executives began referring to 'the *Dallas* effect': generating an audience for a show through news coverage, encouraging viewers to believe they would be missing out by not watching it.

But many programmes continued to attract intensely loyal audiences without being part of this kind of publicity buzz at all. While Britain was being introduced to JR Ewing, *Crossroads*, an ATV soap opera set in a Midlands motel, was quietly reaching its three thousandth episode. Because it had twice as many episodes per week as *Coronation Street*, it was now by far the longest story ever told in Britain, thousands of bit-part actors having walked through the motel lobby or mouthed pleasantries in the bar. Until they all synchronised watches on 1 April 1975, the different ITV regions often showed it out of synch, so *Crossroads* Christmases could happen in the summer and vice versa, which added to the sense that the motel existed at a wonky angle to the rest of the universe, unbounded by the linear tyranny of seasons and years. During the ITV strike of 1979, a small group of viewers had rung the ATV studios daily to ask what was happening at the motel while *Crossroads* was off air. By the end of the 1970s, its viewing figures exceeded 20 million, and it vied with *Coronation Street* as Britain's most popular programme, remarkable for a serial shown before many people had got home from work.

In June 1981, it did briefly make headlines. The *Daily Mirror* revealed that Noele Gordon, who had played the motel owner, Meg Mortimer, since the first episode, was to be axed. Charles Denton, director of programmes for Central Television, soon to take over the Midlands franchise from ATV, promised her demise would be 'absolutely spectacular' and 'even better than who shot JR'. Hundreds called the studios, pleading with the producers to change their minds. A more sanguine *Daily Star* invited readers to send in ideas about how Meg should be written out, and awarded a £25 prize for the suggestion that she be beaten to death with a frying pan. Pupils at Keir Hardie Junior School in Newham, east London, sent the *Crossroads* producer Jack Barton an illustrated book showing different ways in which Meg could be killed, from poisoning to drowning.[12]

Crossroads had long excited conflicting responses. Some of its assumed awfulness was folk legend perpetuated by non-viewers. The lobby telephone never did carry on ringing after it was answered, and not since the programme's earliest days, when it was filmed from a disused Aston cinema using theatre flats, had the walls of the set wobbled. Nor did the beanie-hatted innocent, Benny Hawkins, ever disappear for six months in search of a spanner, although Shughie McFee the motel chef did vanish for three years when, in order to save money, the kitchen set was dismantled. Recorded 'as live' with minimal rehearsal, *Crossroads* did contain fluffed lines, garbled crosstalk and continuity errors, though not as many as collective memory insists.

The serial's roots were in the romantic melodrama of repertory theatre, from where it inherited its clunky dialogue exposition and static staginess. Women walked round sofas and held on to them, or dabbed their eyes with the corners of handkerchiefs. Men gripped women's arms and looked deep into their eyes.

'We've said goodbye before, it's not too difficult.'

'Oh, why did you have to come home? I was perfectly happy. It's *over*, Hugh. It was over a long time ago. We've just been *daydreaming*.'

'Try *looking* at me when you say things like that.'

'Oh, I *hate* you!'

The cramped, internal sets and endless medium close-ups created a series of tableaux, more theatrical than televisual. The hard-of-hearing and non-native speakers did at least welcome another of its residues from local rep, the tendency of its actors to over-enunciate their lines. 'David Hunter [the motel manager], in particular, speaks so clearly that it is a great help to people like me,' wrote a Ugandan Asian immigrant to the *Daily Mirror* in 1978.[13]

'To criticize *Crossroads* is to criticize sliced white bread, or football or keg beer – you are made to feel it's class snobbism,' claimed the *Sunday Telegraph*. 'Unfortunately, the ordinary people are wrong, and the critic is right and *Crossroads* is bad, slack, inept and untruthful, even within its own miserable limits.' 'This serial is just about the most stunning, stupefying affront to intelligence and proper human values perpetrated on British television,' agreed the *Listener*. The programme's fiercest critic was the Independent Broadcasting Authority which was ultimately responsible for it being on air, and whose chairwoman, Lady Brigette Plowden, described it as 'distressingly popular'.[14] In 1980, the IBA ordered that the show be cut from four to three episodes a week (having already imposed a cut from five to four episodes in 1967) to improve its production values. On neither occasion was any improvement apparent. Even the ITV companies who broadcast *Crossroads* did not like it much, an attitude they betrayed by shunting it round the teatime schedules or putting it on so early that it clashed with the BBC children's programmes. In January 1981, ATV moved it from 6.30 p.m. to 6.05 p.m., angering many Midlands viewers who could no longer get home in time to watch it.

Around the emblematic awfulness of *Crossroads* hovered a more important and enduring argument between the guardians of public service 'quality' television, who had been in the ascendancy since the Pilkington Report of 1962, and the emergent champions of consumer populism. For everyone agreed that *Crossroads* was rubbish, except for its millions of viewers. As the critic Alexander Walker once wrote about the managing director of ATV who had first commissioned it, 'the only people who seem to like Lew Grade's shows seem to be people'.[15]

At the time of Meg's departure, Dorothy Hobson was researching *Crossroads* for her PhD at the Centre for Contemporary Cultural Studies at the University of Birmingham. The arrival of the video recorder had given a boost to the emerging discipline of media studies by allowing for the careful textual analysis of programmes. (In 1975, when the CCCS had begun a pioneering study of the magazine programme, *Nationwide*, they had to take it in turns to watch it together in each other's houses, making a sound tape and taking copious notes.)[16] Yet media studies had still to establish itself fully as a reputable academic subject. One wonders if Richard Hoggart, who retained a strong desire to distinguish between good and bad art, would have thought the study of a poorly regarded soap opera an appropriate subject for the research centre he had founded in the year that *Crossroads* began.

For Charlotte Brunsdon, who was also studying *Crossroads* at the CCCS, the defensiveness she felt about her research topic conflated in her mind with the anti-provincial attitudes of her metropolitan friends, who would say 'Poor you!' when she told them she lived in Birmingham. As Dorothy Hobson found, ATV viewers tended to identify with *Crossroads* characters because they were 'sort of close to Birmingham people ... not common, but unassuming'. Older Midlands viewers already knew and liked Noele Gordon because, in the early days of ATV, she presented many of its regional programmes, including over 2,000 performances of the popular daytime variety show *Lunch Box*, which ran from 1956 to 1964, and which once attracted a studio audience of 27,000 for an outside broadcast at Nottingham Forest's football ground.[17]

In 1958, the ATV Midlands controller, Philip Dorté, complained to its London office that 'Noel Gordon [*sic*], whose face and voice is so well known to every Midlands man, woman and child, is asked at Television House who she is and what she wants'.[18] ATV seemed more concerned with making and exporting networked shows than speaking for its region, which was in any case historically ill-defined. Lew Grade was said to care more about Birmingham, Alabama, than Birmingham, England, and a myth persisted that he had chosen the name 'ATV' because it sounded like 'ITV' in a Brummagem accent. Although Black Country vowels in *Crossroads* tended to emerge only from the mouths of peripheral characters like cooks and cleaners, Midlands viewers still prized *Crossroads* as one of the few programmes about their own region.

Crossroads, like most soaps, was easy to ridicule from afar. Its lines of dialogue in isolation sounded like things no one said in real life ('I don't know, Jill, but I intend to find out!') and its plots about poisonings, bigamy and unexploded bombs were absurd in summary. Spread over three or four episodes a week, though, the melodrama spaced itself out and weeks went by without much incident. (The most notoriously bizarre storyline, in which the cleaner Amy Turtle was accused of being a Russian spy, Amelia Turtlovski, was just a lighthearted subplot.) Most *Crossroads* characters were decent and stoical, trying to deal with ordinary problems as they came up, and the viewers Hobson met said they preferred this to the high emotional pitch of *Dallas*.[19] The serial's slowly accumulated familiarity made a scratched sideboard or a mildly rebellious teenager seem as meaningful on screen as they would be in the real world.

Crossroads formed a set of time-honoured late afternoon rituals: as the teatime commercials for Findus Crispy Pancakes or Birds Eye Potato Waffles faded out and the ATV fanfare sounded, the episode began with the nine-note motif that its composer Tony Hatch described as 'the call-sign which gets the family in front of the TV set',[20] followed by a slight pause before the strangely compelling main theme. At the end of each episode – after the distinctive closing credits, slightly unsteady caption cards crisscrossing up and sideways across the screen – came a final 'stop shot'. Designed to remind the audience what had happened in the final scene, perhaps adding a line of dialogue ('I'll never let her go, Barbara, never!'), it set up the cliff-hanger for the next episode.

Visiting the homes of women *Crossroads* viewers around Birmingham and watching the show with them, Hobson found that *Crossroads* held their full attention, despite being in a timeslot normally occupied by programmes which anticipated viewers dipping in and out as they made the tea or put young children to bed. Forty per cent of British homes now had more than one television and the second set was often a black-and-white portable kept in the kitchen. Hobson saw housewives watching the portable set while cooking or washing up and then hurriedly diving into the living room to view critical moments in colour, or just to see what someone was wearing.[21]

For these women whose lives were filled with amorphous, endless tasks such as housework and childcare, *Crossroads* offered a punctuation mark or caesura in the day. A young woman with a six-month-old baby who lived on the ninth floor of a Birmingham high-rise said she often looked out of the window and counted the cars passing along the road below. 'If you are so isolated that you resort to counting cars,' Hobson concluded, 'the importance of a television serial to "look forward to", even when it is less than perfect, does not seem so strange.'[22]

Not one of Hobson's interviewees commented on the programme's poor production values. Viewer surveys suggested that women were less likely than men to condemn soap operas as implausible or unrealistic, not because they were more credulous but because they simply filtered this information out. When Hobson watched the programme with her interviewees, the presence of another person seemed to sharpen their faculties and they would say, 'Well, it wasn't so good tonight,' when, as far as Hobson could tell, it was the same as ever. They could overlook hammy acting, shoddy camerawork and creaky scripts as long as they felt the inexorable momentum of the unending storyline.[23]

When Meg was axed from *Crossroads*, the *Birmingham Evening Mail* received hundreds of protest letters, a large number of which were from late middle-aged or elderly women in working-class areas like West Bromwich or Smethwick. For many of these women, Meg – with her carefully groomed hair, smart jackets and sitting room with sherry glasses, decanter and white telephone – suggested a precarious middle-class respectability to which they also aspired. One of the most common reasons for viewers to write to the ATV studios was to ask where they could buy Meg's wallpaper and curtains, and the most successful piece of promotional merchandise was a print of a painting that hung in her living room.[24]

At the Crossroads motel, romance was never tainted by sex, even the mildest curse was never uttered and no one smoked, it being against IBA rules at that hour. 'We like our middle-class image because it enables us to behave nicely and wear nice clothes which the public like to see,' Gordon said. 'We are told reliably that there is peace and quiet [in Northern Ireland] when *Crossroads* is on. And I think it is because people are leading such abnormal lives there that they look forward to switching on every night and seeing a more or less normal existence.' Hobson made a similar point about the axing of Meg, which was announced just before a summer of riots in Brixton, Liverpool, Birmingham and other English cities. *Crossroads*, which was on directly before or after news bulletins showing burning cars and buildings, suggested a reassuring normality and continuity that its viewers saw threatened by Meg's imminent departure.[25]

On the eve of bonfire night, another kind of blaze engulfed the television screens of *Crossroads* viewers: the motel was on fire, and a tremulous Meg was last seen staring at a bottle of tranquillisers after leaving a note to her daughter. As a plangent oboe piped an *Andante* version of the *Crossroads* theme, hundreds of fans, some in tears, called the switchboard to demand whether Meg had died in the fire. The producers had added to their anxiety by staging a fake funeral, both the *Sun* and ITN News showing pictures of undertakers removing a body from the motel's ashes. After being left dangling over the weekend, though, viewers discovered that Meg was alive and leaving on the *QE2* for America.

The viewers' pleas had reprieved her. 'The elderly people who lived for nothing else ... it was to them going to be a real bereavement,' conceded Jack Barton. After getting hundreds of thank you letters, he said he felt like a Home Secretary who had saved someone from the gallows. Peter Ling, co-creator and sometime writer of *Crossroads*, watched it every afternoon in Hastings, with his family, especially his daughter, Vicky, making fun of it. Once, while she and her father were walking on the pier, an elderly woman attendant recognised him. 'I am a widow and live by myself,' she told him. 'I have no family and I get very lonely, but every day I watch *Crossroads*. I live with Meg and all the others. They have become part of my family.' 'Daddy,' Ling's daughter said as they walked off, 'I'll never laugh at *Crossroads* again.'[26]

'I am watching my life ebbing away,' wrote Kenneth Williams in his diary on 28 November 1983. That evening he had been sitting with his octogenarian mother, Louie, in her flat across the hallway from his own, in a mansion block off London's Euston Road, watching *Coronation Street* and Thora Hird 'in some rubbish about a funeral parlour'. They had lived opposite each other like this for over a decade and, having always refused to own a television, Williams spent many hours watching his mother's set. Writing his diary late at night, he would often use it to complain about that evening's television, and his judgements on the primetime schedules of the 1970s and 1980s showed little patience for programmes now remembered as classics. *The Good Life* had 'not a laugh line in it'. *Porridge* was 'sickening and disgusting'. *The Two Ronnies* was a 'comedy formula' without any comedy, 'like watching the Japanese immaculately performing a Morris Dance'. On the rare occasions Williams found something he liked – Leonard Rossiter in *Rising Damp*, Telly Savalas's minimalist acting in *Kojak* or the 'sad & rugged courage' of Les Dawson – it was when this formulaic urge to please, this sense of obligatory collective enjoyment, was absent.

Williams's TV criticism was not disinterested. His television career had been in decline since his one-man series, *The Kenneth Williams Show*, had flopped in 1970, the man on the bacon counter at his local supermarket calling it 'rotten' and the janitor at his block of flats telling him cheerfully that it was 'a load of shit'.[27] By the early 1980s his TV appearances were mostly confined to chat shows and voice-overs for children's cartoons and commercials. In his diary, he veered restlessly between complaining that camp stars like John Inman and Larry Grayson had stolen his act and believing that it was all beneath him anyway.

A fiercely intelligent autodidact, Williams in the 1970s had been employed as a television critic for the *Radio Times*. 'It is the capacity for taking pains which I admire,' he wrote, opening his first monthly column. While his alternating fellow columnists, Jonathan Raban and Margaret Drabble, happily declared their love for *That's Life* or *The Goodies*, Williams wrote with self-conscious erudition about *Panorama* and *The Book Programme*. But at home he was obliged to watch the undemanding television his mother liked, occasionally conceding that its killing of time could be merciful. 'The fact remains,' he wrote, 'that the flickering screen in the room is a barrier against the silences & the embarrassment of mute interludes when conversation peters out.'[28]

Viewers like Kenneth Williams and his mother, watching mostly whatever came along, were supposed to be an endangered tribe. Television producers feared that the primetime audience was about to be shrunk severely by the video cassette recorder, an object that people were buying even in the middle of a recession. Domestic video recorders had arrived in Britain in the mid 1970s but had been slow to take off. According to the writer and broadcaster Derek Cooper, some of the earliest adopters were in the Presbyterian strongholds of the Western Isles, where Sunday viewing was a clear Sabbath breach but videotaping programmes to watch in midweek was more ambiguous, God's position on time-shifting being moot. Another early adopter was Tony Blackburn, who would record *Crossroads* each day and watch it the next morning over breakfast before going to the studio to do his Radio 1 show.[29]

Britons were still more likely to rent electronic equipment than to buy it, and this helped the video market grow at a time when it was shared by two incompatible Japanese systems, Sony's Betamax and JVC's VHS. In more *dirigiste* France, all imported VCRs had to clear customs at Poitiers and VCR owners had to pay an annual licence fee; in Thatcherite Britain there were no such restrictions against cheap Japanese imports. Applied to pop promos, TV shows and the domestic recorder, 'video' became one of the modish words of the early 1980s, endowed, along with related vocabulary like 'rewind' and 'freeze-frame', with connotations of contemporaneity just as colour television had been a decade earlier.

Even so, the television ratings for Christmas 1982 were shocking. They suggested that so many people were renting videos, playing with their new video games or recording programmes to watch later, that there were 6 million fewer viewers than in Christmas 1981. The audience figures for the sitcom *Last of the Summer Wine* had fallen mysteriously from 17 to 9.9 million. Manchester University held a symposium with the title 'Is broadcasting going off the air?' and Charles Denton said, 'We have search-parties out looking for audiences.'[30] But this supposedly vanishing audience was a blip, probably caused by a glitch in the ratings system which meant that if a viewer was video-recording a programme at the same time as watching it, the ratings meter thought the set was switched off.

By the end of 1983 a quarter of British homes had a video recorder, more than any other European country, but viewers mostly carried on viewing in real time; thirteen per cent of recorded television was never even watched. The TV critic Peter Fiddick suggested that VCRs helped to reduce 'television guilt', allowing people to record things they felt they should have watched without having to actually watch them. The timer switch for pre-recording was also notoriously difficult to work.

The sociologist Ann Gray asked a group of women in Dewsbury, West Yorkshire to colour-code their domestic gadgets: pink for feminine, blue for masculine and lilac for neither. While VCRs were lilac, the timer function was a deep blue – which is odd when, as Gray pointed out, women routinely operated the equally difficult time settings on washing machines.[31] The most likely explanation is that women simply did not care enough to work out how to use the timer because, against expectations, the video recorder had not turned viewers into energetic time shifters.

But there was another threat to the homogeneous mass audience, sitting down to watch the same programmes each evening. Ever since the Annan Report, the political mood had favoured breaking up the comfortable ITV–BBC duopoly and increasing viewer choice, an ambition helped along by the arrival of Channel 4 in 1982. When the Tories retained power on a landslide in 1983, they were bolder about placing free market economics at the heart of policy. The BBC's monopoly of the licence fee, which Margaret Thatcher preferred to call a 'compulsory levy' and a 'poll tax backed by criminal sanctions',[32] together with the Thatcherite perception of left-wing bias in the corporation, made it a likely candidate for the bracing discipline of market forces.

At the beginning of 1984, newspapers quoted 'ministerial sources' attacking the BBC's showing of an American mini-series which, unprecedentedly, they had promoted with a billboard campaign across the country announcing, '*The Thorn Birds* are coming on BBC1'. The informant was a Home Office minister, Douglas Hurd, who suggested, on the strength of his wife having seen the first episode, that the series was so awful that it might jeopardise the BBC's proposed licence fee increase.[33] A hostile press campaign against the BBC began, accompanied by that partly manufactured anger from its commercial rivals that was to become familiar in the coming years.

The Thorn Birds certainly satisfied the Thatcherite market imperative: after the end of the penultimate episode, in which Father Ralph de Bricassart broke his vow of chastity and made love to the heroine Meggie on a remote Australian beach, the Electricity Board reported an increase of 2200 megawatts, the biggest surge in the National Grid's history. 'The series was much criticised for wooden stereotyping of many characters, for thin writing and implausible melodrama and its placing in the schedules,' conceded the BBC handbook. 'But [it] had a narrative drive that proved compulsive. It drew enormous audiences.'[34] The controversy suggested that drawing a big audience was not enough on its own to justify the licence fee, for the most contentious thing about the series was its place in the schedules: it had clashed with the prestigious ITV series *Jewel in the Crown* and, more shockingly, the BBC's long-running current affairs programme, *Panorama*, had been dropped for its duration.

In this new environment in which broadcasters had to satisfy both the demand for high ratings and the more nebulous expectations of public service broadcasting, the art of the scheduler was crucial. Each channel now employed programme planners whose job was to sit in an office with clock grids of each quarter year, plotting shifts in mass viewing habits like generals in a war room planning troop manoeuvres. Horizontally they divided the thirteen weeks into series runs of six, seven and so on, and vertically they divvied up the broadcasting hours into time slots. Guided by programme synopses, audience research and ratings graphs, they then arranged the programmes, on sticky-backed coloured squares, along these grids in agreeable patterns, taking note of immovable objects like the news and certain received wisdoms about what went where. Early evening programmes were magazine-style, with short items that did not require viewers' full attention, to catch people coming in from work or eating their dinner. As viewers settled down after dinner, the primetime sitcoms and quiz shows followed. Serious programmes, like documentaries, arrived after nine, later-dining middle-class viewers having finished eating by then.

This delicate arrangement of an evening's entertainment was called 'vertical' scheduling and was fairly well known. More arcane,

and becoming more important, was 'horizontal' or 'jugular' scheduling, to compete with rival channels. The secret of this dark art was
that most viewers were, like Kenneth Williams and his mother, list-
less rather than carefully selective consumers. Even when the costs of
changing channels were minimal – and becoming more minimal with
the growing popularity of the infra-red TV remote control – there was
a carry-over effect from one show to the next, which today's propo-
nents of nudge economics would call a 'status quo bias'. Those invisible, unaccountable social engineers, the horizontal schedulers, were
thus able magically to induce inertia in millions of people, tempting
them with the next offering so they would carry on watching the same
channel for the whole evening.

The art of scheduling could be used to buoy up a less popular
programme, by 'hammocking' it between two more popular ones, so
that it benefited from 'inheritance' at the start (viewers staying tuned
to the same channel having tuned in for a previous programme) and
'pre-echo' at the end (viewers tuning in early to watch a favourite
programme, seeing the last bit of the preceding one and deciding to
watch it next week). ITV's current affairs series *World in Action* was
typically placed after an 8 p.m. comedy like *In Loving Memory* (the
'rubbish about a funeral parlour' that Kenneth Williams watched with
his mother), and before a popular drama like *Quincy* at 9 p.m. – a
mass exodus to BBC1 also being halted by the windfall of having
Panorama on the other side.

The recognised master of the scheduling arts was Lew Grade's
nephew, Michael Grade, appointed controller of BBC1 in 1984. Grade
had begun his career working on the *Daily Mirror* sports page and
compared television scheduling to arranging newspaper layout, presenting stories in attractive forms for maximum impact. He went on
to work as a showbusiness agent, where, like his uncle, he learned
to work out the running order on a variety bill, which again was
good training for scheduling. He first honed these skills directly in
the 1970s as head of light entertainment and then director of programmes at London Weekend Television. In theatre, you could try
out new ideas and unproven actors out of town before exposing them

to the West End. On LWT, a weekend channel that began at 7 p.m. on Friday evening, when viewers wanted to be entertained at the end of a working week, there was nowhere to hide the quirky or experimental. 'Every night on LWT was Saturday night at the London Palladium,' wrote Grade. 'There was no televisual equivalent of a wet Monday evening at the Hackney Empire.'[35]

Grade remembered one LWT programme with a salutary shudder: *Bruce Forsyth's Big Night*. In 1978 Forsyth, the star of the BBC's *Generation Game*, defected to LWT to present a lavish variety show which took up nearly two hours of Saturday primetime, with comic turns, star guests, audience participation games like Teletennis and Beat the Goalie, and the UK Disco Championships. 'We want to get away from the awful slot thinking which says that situation comedies have to be half an hour, and not a second longer,' one LWT executive said. 'It's a bit like the sports formula for Saturday afternoons – full of different kinds of goodies.' But the show was a famous failure, beaten easily in the ratings by the new *Generation Game* with Larry Grayson on BBC1. 'During the year the news was bad and the weather was worse,' argued the IBA's annual report. 'Many people turned to comedy and light entertainment with great expectations. Sometimes those expectations were realised. Sometimes they were not. The national press, in cynical and bitter mood, saw gloom everywhere. The most obvious victim was *Bruce's Big Night*.'[36] But Grade knew better than to blame the winter of discontent or the newspapers. Instead, this chastening episode convinced him of the need for tight scheduling, 'that awful slot thinking' in which an evening's entertainment had connected segments that built up to a climax like a multi-course gourmet meal.

In another of his comparisons, Grade likened the schedules to a supertanker, because the long gap between commissioning and broadcasting meant that changing course took time. So when he became controller of BBC1, he took the listings home and saw what could be done by tinkering with the arrangement of programmes that had already been commissioned. His first inspired tweak was moving *Tenko*, a drama series tracing the lives of a group of women from Singapore interned in a Japanese POW camp, from Thursday to Sunday night, increasing its audience from 5 to 11 million. He also told Robin Day, the presenter of *Question Time* on Thursday nights, not to close with his usual advice to 'sleep well' because this might dissuade viewers from staying up for the programme that followed. And he repeated the two episodes of the struggling soap opera *EastEnders* together on Sunday afternoons, thus boosting its ratings and achieving the '*Dallas* effect' of getting it talked about. Just over 30 million people watched its Christmas Day episode in 1986, the highest television audience of the decade. It was, wrote the *That's Life* presenter Esther Rantzen of Grade's scheduling skills, 'like watching an expert window dresser adjusting a bauble on a Christmas tree to make it shine'.[37]

Grade's carefully cultivated image, enhanced by his cigar and red braces, was that of an impresario who went with his intuitions rather than relying on what he called 'the mumbo-jumbo jargon' of concept testing and demographics. 'It smelt like a Sunday show,' he said after moving *Tenko*. 'It was just instinct.' In fact, Grade worked closely with Pamela Reiss from the BBC's Broadcasting Research Department and relied on research which showed that audiences were happy to watch more demanding drama later on Sunday night. In autumn 1984 this department questioned 1,500 viewers. Asked to write out last night's and tomorrow night's schedule on ITV and BBC1, it turned out that most could name only two programmes, one of which was the news. Grade decided that the schedules must have 'fixed time points that are almost like alarm clocks in viewers' minds'. The research showed that viewers thought naturally in hours and half hours. For years they had misread the unshakeable fixtures of Thursday evening, thinking that *Tomorrow's World* was on at 7 p.m. and that *Top of the Pops* followed at 7.30, when in fact they were both usually on five minutes before or after that. Grade insisted that, even though the international standards were twenty-five and fifty-five minutes to accommodate commercials, BBC programmes should now be made in half-hour and hour-long segments.[38]

Grade was also helped by a four-volume publication of Proustian proportions from the Broadcasting Research Department, *Daily Life in the 1980s*, which exhaustively examined the behaviour of Britons in the summer and winter of 1983–4, each volume containing over 600 pages of statistical tables. A 'scheduler's Bradshaw', as one critic called it, it carefully mapped the activities of every Briton over four years old (toddlers never having been counted statistically as viewers), in quarter hours, from 6 a.m. to 2.30 a.m. – so, for example, it could tell you how many five- to nine-year-old children were in sight of a television when *Crackerjack* was broadcast on Friday afternoon at 4.50 p.m., or exactly how many people were awake and available to view television at 9.30 p.m. in the winter (ninety-one per cent) and in the summer (sixty-nine per cent). There were 52.4 million people in the country over four years old and every winter night, about 25 million of them were sitting dutifully in front of a television, like Kenneth Williams and his mother. If you measured the total audience at any time between the peak hours of 6.30 p.m. and 10.30 p.m., it was always around this number.[39]

This broad mass of 25 million people had retained the desire to watch a wide range of programmes and there seemed to be a large element of randomness about their likes and dislikes. *Tenko* had initially been rejected by one BBC commissioner, its co-writer Jill Hyem revealed, because, he said, 'no one'll want to know about an all-woman cast looking their worst'. And yet its female-dominated, quotidian storylines about the rationing of sanitary towels, the non-delivery of Red Cross parcels or the organising of games of rounders proved to be absorbing when put in the right place in the week. 'I was impressed by your portrayal of women over 30 as human beings,' wrote one male viewer. 'Men usually find it easy to relate to a woman in her twenties, probably because their mothers were that age when they were young boys. We need to see older women more often if we are to perceive them as real people.'[40]

Another programme that showed how unexpected viewers' tastes could be was *One Man and His Dog*. It was presented by a Staffordshire-born naturalist, Phil Drabble, who had initially declined to take part because he thought it would make viewers 'drop off their perch with boredom'. Consisting largely of shepherds whistling and calling out commands ('Come by, Meg', 'Steady lass!') to a dog trying to get a bleating flock of sheep into a pen somewhere on a British hillside, it introduced viewers to this traditional rural skill and turned the border collie into a cult hero. By the mid 1980s it had a primetime audience of 8 million on Tuesday nights on BBC2, most of them town- and sofa-dwelling vicarious shepherds, the majority of them women.

Some programmes made little impression and then mysteriously struck a chord. *Only Fools and Horses*, a sitcom about unlicensed market traders living in a council block in Peckham, had first gone out on Tuesday nights in September 1981, attracting a modest BBC1 audience of under 8 million and many letters from viewers asking what the title meant. It was only when the second series was repeated in the summer of 1983, to fill a gap in the schedules during a BBC technicians' strike, that it began to emerge slowly as the most popular sitcom of the decade, adding new words to the common language like 'lovely jubbly' and 'plonker' (a word for the penis originating in 1960s London that, as often happens with penis synonyms, had become an innocent name for an idiot). Despite the choices offered by video and the remote control, viewers did not seem to behave like carefully discriminating consumers. Seemingly unglamorous dramas, obscure sports and underwhelming sitcoms could turn almost overnight into national obsessions. Grade was fond of quoting the wisdom of his former boss at LWT, Cyril Bennett, that 'hits are 90 per cent luck and 10 per cent accident'.[41]

Grade soon found to his cost that, once acquired, viewers' allegiances were hard to shift. In January 1985, Thames Television announced that it had bought the next series of *Dallas*, poaching it from the BBC. Grade retaliated by announcing that the BBC's remaining sixteen episodes would not be shown. *Dallas* was taken off air and replaced by repeats of *The Two Ronnies*. A Sheffield councillor presented a petition containing 3,000 signatures to Margaret Thatcher, asking her to help get the lost episodes back, and the *Sun* ran three editorials on the subject. 'Do we have to act like spoiled children,' another frustrated viewer, Spike Milligan, asked in a letter to the *Guardian*. 'Michael Grade is paid by public monies to put *Dallas* out *when the public want it*, and not withhold it to play "yaboo sucks to you" with Thames Television. Grow up.'[42] *Dallas* resumed on 27 March after Grade and the BBC backed down, a discomfiting moment which confirmed that the viewer remained anchored in peculiar loyalties and strange habits – further proof, if it were needed, of the indispensability of the scheduler.

One phenomenon encapsulated the mercurial nature of the television audience and how it could slowly and collectively be drawn into something seemingly unexciting: the cult of snooker. Without television, snooker would have been forever a minority sport because the largest audience that can be afforded any meaningful view of a snooker table is a couple of thousand. Until the late 1960s, it had been a subterranean working-class pastime, with a tiny professional élite eking out a living in dingy clubs and holiday camps, occasionally appearing on *Grandstand* as a filler between horse races or when rain stopped play in the cricket: usually a single frame, with the finish timed to coincide with the runners going down to the starting gate or the covers coming off. Numbered balls were meant to make the game intelligible to viewers watching in black and white, but were too small to read in long shot.

In the late 1960s, the *Grandstand* producer Philip Lewis was one of the first people in Birmingham to have a colour set for BBC2 programmes and, wondering which sport would be most enhanced by colour and easiest to film with the few colour cameras then available, he woke up one morning with the answer in his head. The single-frame tournament *Pot Black* began in the summer of 1969, in the week after the moon landing, and quickly became one of BBC2's most popular programmes, even though the vast majority of viewers were watching it in monochrome. The *Sunday Telegraph* compared the players favourably with the 'hysterical pooves of the football field'. The snooker commentator Ted Lowe, who helped to develop *Pot*

Black, required every player to sign a contract obliging him to wear a dinner suit. The first *Pot Black* champion, Ray Reardon, believed this helped to remove the stigma of seediness that had attached to snooker since the 1930s when the billiard halls were places where stolen goods changed hands and illegal gambling was rife. Lowe remained irritated that the profession's bad boy, Alex Higgins, on the strength of a doctor's note of dubious provenance, got away without wearing a bow tie.[43]

But the colour TV studio lights were a major technical obstacle to broadcasting the long game. The light glared off the balls and the heat was such that players lost pounds in weight and the Formica on the cushion rails burned their hands. During the 1976 world championship finals it became so hot that the players threatened to strike. But Nick Hunter, producing the championship for the BBC, could see on screen the reddened ends of Alex Higgins's fingers, bitten down through nerves, and was convinced that, if they could just sort out the lighting, snooker could provide a source of slowly absorbing psychological drama. Over the next two years, the BBC perfected a glare-free, shadowless canopy of lights that also reduced the heat on the table.[44]

The BBC began full daily coverage of the world championship in 1978. A little rectangular patch of baize at the Crucible Theatre in Sheffield held viewers' concentration for the next two weeks as two bow-tied duellists pushed twenty-two balls around it with long, tapered sticks. 'It could be a subversive experiment in mass hypnosis: millions of Britons transfixed before the shifting dots like rabbits facing a swaying weasel,' reflected Peter Fiddick. In 1979, viewers followed the dazzling progress of Terry Griffiths, a former postman from Llanelli who had learned to play during a postal strike, as he won the championship at his first attempt. The next year, the world championship competed for airtime with a six-day siege of the Iranian Embassy in London, with the climax of one interrupting that of the other. At 7.23 p.m. on 5 May, the novelist Frederick Forsyth was watching the final on BBC1 as it built to a suspenseful climax. 'Cliff Thorburn and Hurricane Higgins were tied at 17 frames each; the world crown hung on the 35th frame,' he wrote. 'Then the screen blanked and turned to a blizzard of white dots that eventually dissolved into a street scene. The language in my own sitting room went as blue as the sky outside.'[45]

Brian Wenham, the BBC2 controller, was a snooker fan and happily used it as an audience builder for the channel's more highbrow programmes. Wenham also gave generous time in his channel's schedules to his other great loves, classical music and opera, and perhaps snooker was not dissimilar: its pleasures were also incremental and demanded commitment from the viewer in order to overcome the dull or ponderous moments. Snooker filled up television's twilight hours, in the daytime and late into the night, when the game, interrupted only by the presenter David Vine's deep Devonian voice and the hushed, sparse commentary of 'whispering' Ted Lowe, had a sepulchral stillness.

Lowe had acquired his whisper at Leicester Square Hall in the early days of TV snooker in the 1950s, when he sat with the commentator Raymond Glendenning in the crowd, giving him expert tips not meant to be picked up by the microphone. By the 1980s, Lowe tended to speak less, on the assumption that viewers did not need to have the game explained so much. Once he collapsed during a match between Cliff Thorburn and Doug Mountjoy and was carried off on a stretcher while the reserve commentator Jack Karnehm was called, eight minutes of play passing without comment.[46] There were no complaints from viewers, so used were they to long stretches of silence, interspersed only with the metronomic scoring of the referee, occasional throat clearing from the audience and the sound of baked resin balls clacking against each other and plopping into holes.

Snooker was unhurried, unedited television. Whole minutes passed unproductively as players examined the balls from various angles, prepared to take a shot and thought better of it, instead furrowing their brows or scratching their cheeks. Jeremy Isaacs, head of Channel 4, believed the dyed green of the baize aided the sport's late-night popularity, because it was soothing to look at, with the balls travelling in neat parallel lines as they bounced off cushions. The smartly blazered referee would occasionally caress the balls with his white-gloved hands like a butler polishing the family silver. It was a case study in the fundamental meaninglessness of television and how it could draw people into a spectacle whose significance was entirely symbolic and circular, as futile as all sport ultimately is. 'The familiar ritual is as restful as watching waves break,' wrote the author Gordon Burn, 'and, miraculously, it is a tranquillity that can be piped, Mogadon in the ether, into the country's living rooms.'[47]

As players took it in turns at the table, the tiniest accidental glances or the mere friction of the baize could hand a match to an opponent. 'There is something fascinating about the game: the absolute precision required,' wrote George Mackay Brown in his council flat in Stromness, Orkney, where he had recently thrown out his 'Stone Age TV' and installed a colour set. 'The slight subtle touch of ball on ball; the wild foray that sets them in a scatter, helter-skelter, all over the green baize table. The moving colours themselves fascinate the eye ... It is exciting and soothing at the same time.' The author A. S. Byatt, who had loathed the group passions and intimate contact of competitive sport since her schooldays, became entranced by the beautiful geometry of snooker with its 'lines of force playing across a clear green screen, human dramas which were part of the lines of force, the suffering and exulting faces briefly picked out by the cameras'.[48] Like the TV wrestlers whom they had replaced in the nation's imaginings, snooker players had nicknames – Cliff 'the Grinder' Thorburn, Alex 'Hurricane' Higgins, 'Steady' Eddie Charlton, Jimmy 'Whirlwind' White – that conveyed their personalities in vivid shorthand. And there was something courtly and chivalrous about the way they would celebrate an opponent's 147 break or own up to a foul shot even if no one else had noticed. Clive James, a fan since the first series of *Pot Black*, thought that unlike other sports, in which gamesmanship was now routine, snooker confirmed Ludwig Wittgenstein's dictum that a game consisted of the rules by which it is played. Snooker, James reflected, was in essence 'two young men in black tie who would rather die than cheat'.[49]

In 1978, there were thirty-five hours of snooker on television; by 1985, 130 hours were given over just to the world championship in the spring, and there were seven or eight other major snooker tournaments a year on TV. But the 1985 World Championship turned out to be a dull tournament with few close games. The final, between Steve Davis and Dennis Taylor, looked like a mismatch from the start, although it did offer an intriguing personality clash. Davis, the reigning world champion, was known for his coolness and estuarine monotone, earning him the nickname 'the Romford Robot', with a certain alliterative licence since he was actually from Plumstead. His unremitting safety play, careful cue action and winning habit aroused little sympathy, which caused exasperation among those who saw it as a symptom of national defeatism. '[Davis] behaves as the British must behave if they are to maintain any position in the world,' wrote Brian Walden in the *Evening Standard*. 'Order, method, discipline, plus a stern control of eccentricity, is the passport to triumph in the modern world ... [But] the marvellously proficient Davis is clapped with some reluctance. Does this not prove what an essentially frivolous people we are?'[50]

Taylor was from Coalisland, a poor Catholic town in Tyrone and scene of the first civil rights march in 1968. Never world champion and now being eclipsed by younger players, Taylor also had specially designed, upside down glasses with enormous lenses, worn high on his face so he could look through the most optically exact part of the lens. Even in a decade in which outsized spectacles were fashionable, they made him look, according to 'Steady' Eddie Charlton, 'like Mickey Mouse with a welding shield on'.[51]

At 7.17 p.m. on the Saturday night of the final, Davis won the first frame of the evening session to take an 8–0 lead. 'Taylor looks three inches shorter,' said the commentator Clive Everton ruefully in the interval. 'His head sunk into his neck. Even if he gets a chance now, he won't be able to take it.' Viewers deserted the game in their droves, turning over to watch *The Price is Right* or *The Kenny Everett Television Show*. Then Taylor began winning games and viewers slowly returned as they heard the score was narrowing. By the end of the first day, Taylor had pegged Davis back to 7–9. At 11.15 on the Sunday night, he drew level with Davis for the first time, tying the frames at 17–17 to take the match into a final frame. Some viewers had switched on to BBC2 to see *Bleak House* and had carried on watching even though they had been told this was now postponed. After thirty minutes of edgy play, the score was 62–44 to Davis with four balls left on the table and Taylor needing all of them. He potted a tricky brown, blue and pink to ensure that a sport made for colour TV would enjoy its most mesmerising moment with two balls coloured black and white.

After a series of kamikaze attempts to pot the black, Taylor left Davis a fairly easy cut into the top pocket from close range. When Davis overcut it, Ted Lowe let out an astonished 'No!', more like an exhalation of breath than a word. The roar of the audience got louder as the white ball came to rest at the right angle for a half ball pot. This time, stretching a little to avoid using the rest, Taylor sank the black. It was 12.23 a.m., and 18.5 million people were still watching, the largest ever British TV audience after midnight.

In Coalisland, a huge crowd of people spilled out of Girvan's snooker hall, where they had been watching on television. Others poured out of houses, in dressing gowns and with children on their shoulders, and paraded around the town, or drove round the town square, sounding their horns. A few weeks later, a tiny, crumpled letter arrived at Taylor's father's house in Coalisland, from the Maze prison, after being scrunched up and smuggled out in someone's tooth: 'Dennis O chara, on behalf of all the republican POWs I'd like to thank you for scaring the life out off us!!? ... Some of the screws were not amused at you winning, and on Saturday they were like the cats who got the cream. However you fixed their wagons for them and at about 12.30 a.m. Monday morning there was a terrible din + banging round this camp as the lads got on to the doors, hammering to acknowledge your *fantastic* victory. *Maith thu a chara* [well done, my friend], it's a while since we've had an opportunity to "Bang" in such good news.' Later that year, October devotions in the Church of the Holy Trinity were specially rescheduled so Coalisland's Catholics could watch Taylor on *This is Your Life*.[52]

Snooker's slow decline as a televisual sport was as capricious and mysterious as its rise. After the black ball final, it never again captivated viewers in quite the same way. By watching the techniques of the game's best players on television, talented young players like Stephen Hendry, John Parrott and Alan McManus assimilated tactical lessons that once took a lifetime to learn. As these young players came through, frame times dropped dramatically. Counter-intuitively, this seemed to make the game less exciting. For, like Test cricket, the excitement of snooker had to be earned through the possibility of boredom and the sense that players might, when faced with the simple task of knocking balls into pockets on a flat, unchanging table, be gradually reduced to their last reserves of skill and nerve.

In the spring of 1985, the BBC launched its 'Domesday Project' to mark the 900th anniversary of the Domesday Book the following year. That summer, about 1 million people started work as surveyors, many of them children taken from 9,000 schools. The project divided the whole of Britain into 23,000 4 × 3 km areas called Domesday Squares or 'D-Blocks' in which the volunteer surveyors wrote about their local area and about their daily lives, the information being recorded on the BBC's own successful brand of microcomputer. The author of the teachers' guide for the project, Professor Ted Wragg of Exeter University, pointed out that schoolchildren had contributed to this sort of data gathering before, helping to sort the seeds that Darwin had brought back from his voyage in the Beagle, and working on the geographer Dudley Stamp's land use survey of the 1930s.[53]

Despite these high-minded precedents, a great number of the children in the Domesday Project simply wrote about watching TV. It was clear that, despite the arrival of the first, primitive computer games and the new presence of a video rental shop on every high street, children were still mostly captive customers watching what was put in front of them, from prosaic sitcoms like *Terry and June* and *Don't Wait Up*, to high-gloss soaps like *Dallas* and *Dynasty*. The Domesday entries, written by anonymous contributors asked to record what they thought would interest people reading in another thousand years, read as though written for a passing Venusian. 'A television is like a box run on electricity and when you switch it on you can watch films and sport and lots of other things,' said one young viewer. 'Television is one of the main entertainments in the Penistone area,' said another. 'To some people it has become a third parent, they become addicted to it.'[54]

Television was now eating up the last vacant hours in the schedules. An often cited concept in the new media studies was 'flow', a term coined by Raymond Williams. In 1972 Williams and his wife Joy were on their way to Stanford, where he was to take up a research fellowship for a year. Newly landed in the United States by boat, they spent a night watching TV in a Miami motel. They found themselves bemused by the grammar of American television in which programmes went into the incessant ad breaks without a pause, seamlessly and surreally. Television could run 'from the dinosaur loose in Los Angeles to the deep-voiced woman worrying about keeping her husband with her coffee to the Indians coming over the skyline and a girl in a restaurant in Paris suddenly running from her table to cry'.[55] After arriving at Stanford, Williams spent much of the year in his flat in Escondido Village watching and writing a book about television. On Californian TV the normal rules of scheduling had little purchase: you could watch movies from 6 a.m. into the small hours.

In America, Williams decided, watching television was a pursuit in its own right, almost unrelated to what was being watched. This was the state to which the medium aspired, insatiably occupying any blank moments in the schedules until it achieved the condition of uninterrupted 'flow'.[56] Television's natural instinct was simply to go on and on, to consume the infinite time stretching out in front of it, like those cartoons where Bugs Bunny is frantically laying down railway track so the train he is on can keep moving.

At the same time that Williams was arriving in Miami, ITV was responding to the end of restrictions on broadcasting hours by expanding its weekday afternoon programmes. BBC radio's daytime audiences declined sharply as listeners became viewers of the legal drama *Crown Court*, the rustic soap opera *Emmerdale Farm*, *The Indoor League*, in which people played dominoes, table football and shove halfpenny in pubs, and *Mr and Mrs*, which quizzed married couples on each other's quirks and rituals: 'What would your husband do if his trouser zip broke?' 'What is the waste paper basket in your bedroom made of?' Ian Trethowan, Radio 4's controller, worried that ITV now had 'an attractive pattern of afternoon entertainment, aimed particularly at housewives – the same audience at which Radios Two and Four had for years set their caps'.[57]

Until the arrival of breakfast television in 1983, however, British TV had mostly denied its uniqueness as a medium by dividing itself up into programmes that preserved the discrete categories of pre-TV culture, in the sense that they each belonged to a particular genre and viewers were expected to watch them from start to finish. Breakfast television was instead definitively televisual, its main organising principle being the clock in the corner of the screen. Items were only about four minutes long, the assumption being that people would dip in at any point and not watch for more than twenty minutes. The discordant mood shift, or what producers called 'light and shade', became routine, as items on keep fit and horoscopes ran straight into ones about alopecia and cancer, stitched together with a general tone of bright-eyed, muted concern ('The doctor said it was just a cyst, didn't he?') and slightly manic cheerfulness. Breakfast television, one BBC executive said, was about 'being nice to people'.[58]

The Australian Bruce Gyngell, who took over as managing director of ITV's breakfast franchise, TV-AM, in 1984, helped establish the tone for breakfast television and much of what followed it in the schedules. 'I set out to make TV-AM eternal summer,' he said, 'so that all those lost, lonely people would have a place in the world they could turn on and feel warm and bright.' On TV-AM's *Good Morning Britain*, the preferred style of furniture was a modified sofa, like an upholstered bench, to suggest informality while making guests sit up properly because, said Gyngell in one of many omniscient-sounding pronouncements, 'the hip-bone should never be lower than the knee-bone. Otherwise all you see is knees.'

The audience felt 'vulnerable' at breakfast time, he claimed, so the TV-AM set was in cheering pinks and yellows, male presenters wore patterned-knit V-necks and women pastel dresses. Early news bulletins were crisp, to attract a male audience. 'As the show moves on,' Gyngell explained, 'it becomes softer. By 8.30 it is mainly female. Between 8.30 and 8.40 it changes pace. The women have got the family off and like to relax.' Breakfast TV, he felt, should be sound-led to allow people to follow it while doing other things. 'Television has a grammar to it ... It's got to flow,' he said. 'This is one of the great problems of British television – they spend all their energy on the content, not enough on the form.'[59]

It took time for the mood and flavour of breakfast television, a triumph of form over content, to migrate to the rest of the day. There were still Zen-like moments of stillness and contemplation in the otherwise endless flow of programmes. Much airtime was filled with 'Test Card F', the little girl with an Alice band playing noughts and crosses on a blackboard easel who had occupied tens of thousands of hours of screentime since the arrival of colour TV in 1967. The accompanying music, by unknown session artists or little-known combos like the Stuttgart Studio Orchestra, the KPM All-Stars or Mr Popcorn's Band, had its unlikely fans, who hated it being dismissed as bland 'lift muzak'.

As a teenager, Bob Stanley would watch the test card solely for the music, and record it on C60 cassette tapes. For him it had a pleasingly furtive quality, for the card was not really meant to be watched and listened to, unless you were an engineer. Listening to the test card, he felt, had influenced the eclectic, soothing mix of kitsch pop, dance music and European synth instrumentals of his band Saint Etienne. Perhaps over-egging its import, he also detected the test card's influence in the work of groups like the Pale Fountains and Portishead and the 1990s lounge music boom.[60]

There were other dead hours, filled with programmes not designed for extended mass viewing: a long series of IBA engineering announcements 'for the radio and television trade' each morning, informing people that the Caradon transmitter was not on full power or reminding them to correctly polarise their television aerials; news and weather from the teletext service Ceefax, the pages changing languidly to accommodate even the slowest reader; and Open University programmes – which used to be shown on Saturday and Sunday mornings, but which now, with the growing use of the video recorder, had been shunted into the daytime and late night schedules – in which a lecturer explained velocity diagrams in engineering mechanics or dissected a sheep's brain.

This gentle-paced world disappeared on 27 October 1986, when BBC1's new daytime service began, with unbroken programming from breakfast to after school. ITV followed its example a year later, the IBA having refused to allow it to shift its schools programmes on to Channel 4 until the new channel's transmitters could reach every school in the land. Television now ran continuously from daybreak to midnight. The key insight from research undertaken by both channels on public attitudes to daytime TV was the feelings of guilt that watching it aroused, although this guilt was felt more in the affluent south-east than other regions, more among women (who saw it as distracting them from their domestic obligations) than men, and more in the morning than in the afternoon.[61]

This research influenced the scheduling pattern that developed, with the mornings given over to magazine programmes with a semi-educational slant and a sense that you could dip into them while doing something else. The afternoons had re-runs of American soaps or quiz shows shown at the same time each weekday, a technique borrowed from US television known as 'stripping' and designed to make viewing a daily habit. Ann Gray found that Dewsbury housewives guiltily combined watching daytime TV with housework, seeing it as a snatched treat or a reward for work completed. They caught Robert Kilroy-Silk's post-breakfast talk show between coming back from the school run and beginning the cleaning, or squeezed in the Napa Valley soap opera *Falcon Crest* between bringing the kids home from school and starting to make their tea.[62]

When broadcasters had lobbied for more hours in the daytime, they cited the deprived audience of housewives, shiftworkers and pensioners. No one mentioned unemployed people (or students, another group traditionally demonised as feckless and lazy). And yet the two great expansions in daytime television, in 1972 and 1986, both occurred, probably coincidentally, when unemployment reached unprecedented levels. In 1972, unemployment rose above a million for the first time since the 1930s, a then shocking statistic which led to Edward Heath being booed in the House of Commons; in 1986 it rose to over 3 million. In the great depression, jobless men had been highly visible: they queued up outside 'the labour', hung around on street corners or congregated in public libraries, and were often accused of repairing to the cinema immediately after collecting their dole money. But in the 1980s, as Ben Pimlott pointed out, unemployed people were 'nowhere to be seen: scattered through a hundred council estates, sitting in clubs, or slumped in front of television sets'. This, he felt, had contributed to the resigned acceptance of unemployment figures that would have been seen as intolerable a generation earlier.[63] Unemployed people were the hidden viewers of daytime television, unmentioned by advertisers, broadcasters or politicians.

Emerging 1980s bands often survived on the dole and inhabited a twilit world occupied in part by daytime TV. The songs of Nigel Blackwell, leader of the Birkenhead group Half Man Half Biscuit, are concerned, in the music critic Paul du Noyer's words, with 'people too educated to be on the dole but too luckless or lazy to be anywhere else. They take a witty revenge on the drivel of popular culture, without denying their fascination with it.'[64] Half Man Half Biscuit songs include dense allusions to pre-school programmes like *Trumpton* and the daytime television personalities of the era such as Una Stubbs and Lionel Blair (the team captains of the frenetic charades game *Give Us a Clue*) and the snooker referee Len Ganley.

Television now also began to colonise the night-time. The traditional closedown of programmes around midnight came with certain familiar rituals: ITV's epilogue from a vicar, the national anthem (a continuation of the patriotic tradition practised in cinemas and theatres), and the announcer's injunction to remember to switch off your set, followed by the high-pitched whine for those who had fallen asleep in front of it (necessary because of the propensity of the older valve televisions to overheat and catch fire). Even if people had a valid reason to be up after midnight, these nannyish rituals suggested, they were not to be encouraged to do so by television. But the Peacock Committee on Broadcasting, reporting in July 1986, drew attention to 'the non-occupied night-time hours' of the television wavelengths and concluded in über-Thatcherite mode that the unused airtime should simply be sold to the highest bidder. In 1987, fearing the government would franchise out these night-time hours to an outsider as they had done with breakfast television in 1983, several ITV regions began preemptively broadcasting through the whole night. Douglas Hurd, now the home secretary, accused them of exercising 'squatters' rights'.[65]

Watching this new ITV night-time service a couple of months after it started, the journalist Stephen Pile found himself 'plunged into a world as strange and exotic as anything Jacques Cousteau or Alice in Wonderland ever discovered'. The shows that punctuated these early hours were televisual Polyfilla: re-runs of *The Partridge Family* and *Batman*, old Hollywood 'B' movies, or phone-ins with callers discussing their personal problems with an on-screen psychiatrist. Nighttime TV was a world in which normal scheduling rules surrendered to surreal juxtapositions: a Hammer horror film like *Taste the Blood of Dracula* might be blithely followed by *50 Years On: More Newsreel Clips from 1937*, with monochrome footage of Henry Hall's farewell performance or a motorcycle scramble at Bagshot Heath. 'I staggered off to bed at 5.30 a.m., stunned,' wrote Pile. 'It was the most bizarre series of programmes I have seen in my entire life.'[66]

'Television knows no night. It is perpetual day,' mused the French cultural theorist Jean Baudrillard, an alien adrift in American motel rooms just as Raymond Williams had been, and marvelling at this ubiquity at a time when French TV still closed down around midnight. 'TV embodies our fear of the dark, of night, of the other side of things. It is the incessant light, the incessant lighting, which puts an end to the alternating round of day and night.' A persistent theme of Baudrillard's work was that our contemporary culture of postmodernity was one populated by the 'hyperreal', in the sense that endlessly replicated media images had merged with and displaced reality. Ours was a culture of the 'simulacrum', the copy that had supplanted the original and taken on a strange, self-generating life of its own.

Night-time television, a world of re-runs and jarring combinations with a weird, parallel relationship with waking reality, seemed definitively Baudrillardian. The twenty-four-hour schedules of America, he wrote, meant that televisions were often seen 'functioning like an hallucination in the empty rooms of houses or vacant hotel rooms … There is nothing more mysterious than a TV set left on in an empty room … It is as if another planet is communicating with you. Suddenly the TV reveals itself for what it really is: a video of another world, ultimately addressed to no one at all, delivering its images indifferently, indifferent to its own messages.'[67]

For all its incongruities, night-time television in Britain was an immediate success. Central TV's *Prisoner: Cell Block H*, an Australian series about life in a women's prison, had nearly a million viewers at 1 a.m. in the Midlands alone. The numbers watching in the long, insomniac stretch between 2 a.m. and 5 a.m. were much smaller – about 100,000 across Britain – but advertisers prized these cheap slots because late-night television appealed to the young, and young men in particular, who were traditionally hard to reach. Judging by its content, night-time TV seemed to be aimed at a community of oddballs, nonconformists, nighthawks, returning clubbers and distress purchasers who were prepared simply to watch the perpetual flow of television and see what came up from the vaults. But perhaps these viewers were also glimpsing the future of TV, one where its disposable content would matter less than its omnipresent occupation of the schedules.

Whereas peaktime TV was now acquiring a cultural memory through video, this kind of television had its hard drive wiped each day as though it had never been. While primetime shows referenced the passing of the seasons and years, the daytime and night-time shows existed only from one day to the next. Like the summertime Christmases at the Crossroads motel, they inhabited not the linear time of the real world but the recurring, self-contained time of television. And yet, because of their habit-forming regularity, these programmes could inspire great loyalty and affection in viewers. They drew their power from the fact that they mirrored the taken-for-granted, seemingly eternal nature of everyday life itself, what the French critic Maurice Blanchot called 'the inexhaustible, irrecusable, always unfinished daily'. As television filled up every hour of the day and night, it came to seem as natural and endless as daily life itself. 'The everyday is our portion of eternity,' Blanchot wrote. 'For in the everyday we are neither born nor do we die: hence the weight and the enigmatic force of everyday truth.'[68]

For many viewers, 4.30 p.m. each weekday was a point as fixed as a monastery's canonical hours. *Countdown*, the word and numbers game, had been the first show on Channel 4 when it launched on 2 November 1982. On that first Tuesday, 4.5 million people watched it; only 800,000 returned the next day, which its presenter, Richard Whiteley, later claimed as the biggest audience drop in television history.[69] Initially, Whiteley seemed ill at ease. 'I always feel so sorry for the little man who presents it,' said Mark, a student interviewed by Dorothy Hobson, now undertaking research on Channel 4. 'He looks as if he's not quite in control. He seems hesitant as to whether he should stop things.' But, slowly, he either grew into his role or his gaucheness became endearing. He began dressing in colourful jackets, reading out letters, addressing viewers as 'Ladies and Gentlemen of Countdownia', and delivering little homilies at the start of each show.

While its French parent programme, *Des Chiffres et des Lettres*, adopted computerised displays and touch screens, *Countdown* still used paper and felt tips, with the letters and numbers on linoleum tiles, so that even by the late 1980s its look was becoming appealingly retro. 'To the degree that he is influenced by play, man can check the monotony, determinism, and brutality of nature,' wrote the Dutch historian Johan Huizinga in his classic book about the human instinct for play, *Homo Ludens*. 'He learns to construct order, conceive economy, and establish equity.' *Countdown* fulfilled Huizinga's definition of play: its limits were finite, its rules were fixed, it was voluntary rather than a moral duty, its ethos was egalitarian and it was undertaken seriously but with an awareness that it was ultimately pointless, a way of simply enjoying and celebrating a moment in time. The winner of each series received the humble prize of a set of dictionaries and a *Countdown* teapot. Viewers played along with pen and paper; it appealed to the same instincts as Scrabble, crossword puzzles and word games, what George Orwell called 'the addiction to hobbies and spare-time occupations, the *privateness* of English life'.[70]

Presenting the Yorkshire regional programme *Calendar* alongside *Countdown*, Whiteley went on to appear over 10,000 times on TV, more than anyone except Carol Hersee, the daughter of a BBC engineer who appeared as the little girl in Test Card F. With its large clock and Alan Hawkshaw's ticking theme music counting down each thirty-second round, the show's metatheme was the passing of time itself, but its own time never ran out because there was always another round, another episode, another 'same time tomorrow'. On daytime television, where shows were stripped across a seemingly everlasting succession of weeks, the presenters gained a kind of immortality. 'You were my afternoon comfort blanket. You were my afternoon sit-down, between work and getting the supper ready,' wrote Helen Hooper in Friern Barnet after Whiteley died suddenly in 2005. 'You had only to see his face,' said Christina in London, 'to feel good, at home, in a human, kind, gentle space.'[71]

In 1985, Peter Collett, an experimental psychologist at the University of Oxford, later to become better known as one of the resident experts on *Big Brother*, conducted an experiment. He and his team built a box resembling an old 1950s television cabinet which contained a hidden, low-light video camera to record the activities of viewers in twenty homes over a week. Looking at the tapes, he found that people were in the room for only eighty per cent of the time the set was switched on. Even when they managed to stay in the same room as the TV, they only looked at it sixty-five per cent of the time. While 'watching' TV they also ate dinner, argued, listened to records, read, did homework or housework, kissed and hugged each other. From the viewing diaries they were also asked to keep, it was clear that they greatly overestimated how much attention they paid to the programmes.[72]

An ITV series in the spring of 1987, *Watching You Watching Us*, masochistically repeated this experiment, filming six families in front of two-way TV sets. One family spent an entire episode of *EastEnders* dividing up and eating a Chinese takeaway between themselves, Toby the terrier and Bozo the boxer. By the end of the programme, Bozo was the only one still in the room, and he was not watching very attentively. Another family left the room en masse as soon as *Crossroads* began, the entire episode flickering on alone without an audience. It was Baudrillard's vision of postmodernity, played out not in an American motel but an English living room. For unlike a cinema, where the lights go down and the projector starts whirring only when there is an audience in the auditorium, television carries on regardless of whether anyone is watching it. In their 1986 book *Uninvited Guests*, the sociologists Laurie Taylor and Bob Mullan discovered a number of viewers who put the set on as soon as they came into the house, as unthinkingly as they switched on the lights. 'If you turn the light on, you might as well turn the TV on,' said one. 'Might as well be on the same switch, really.'[73]

In *Watching You Watching Us*, even people who claimed to give the set their undivided attention turned out to be less attentive than they thought. Professor Geoffrey Gilbert, a biophysical scientist recently retired from Birmingham University, and his Hungarian wife, Lilo, at first stood out as role models of attentiveness. Each made a careful note of things they wanted to watch and then honed this list down to a final, smaller list. They insisted that they never had the TV on unless it commanded their full attention. As it turned out, though, she often shifted her gaze to the *Guardian* on her lap, and he was under the impression that *The Archers* was a TV programme. Collett's study made a similar discovery: although the presumption was that educated people watched more selectively and thoughtfully, they were actually almost as likely to be distracted as anyone else.[74]

In the 1970s, the former BBC television executive Stuart Hood had written a melancholy article for the *Listener* which stated that there were 'few experiences more salutary for the professional communicator than to have to watch television in a provincial hotel'. On one such occasion Hood had seen the absent-minded viewing of hotel guests interrupted by comings and goings from the bar and noise from the jukebox. As soon as the news was over, they rose and deserted the room 'like a flock of startled birds'. Now programme makers were confronted with the disquieting evidence that viewers behaved similarly even in their own living rooms. 'The inference that I wanted producers to take away,' wrote the BBC executive Will Wyatt when he saw Collett's research, 'was that you should not be afraid of giving a bit more information rather than a bit less, of reminding people of what had already been shown, of going out of your way to attract and retain attention.' Worried that viewers were paying insufficient attention to their programmes, programme makers invented a new televisual grammar that kept viewers awake by repeatedly telling them what they had just seen and what was coming up.

Others redoubled the efforts to search for the perfect technical fix that could precisely measure an audience that was drifting off into video viewing and zapping through channels on the remote. One such innovation was the 'passive people meter' which relied not on the unreliable viewer pressing a button when they were watching, as the old Tammeter had done, but on new image recognition technology to identify precisely which faces in the room were pointed at the TV set. The critic Ien Ang had a phrase for this quest to turn the elusive, intangible activity of TV viewing into a measurable entity: 'desperately seeking the audience'.[75]

Ludovic Kennedy, the presenter of the TV discussion programme *Did You See?*, thought that television made little lasting impression on its viewers. Since becoming one of the first ITN newsreaders in

1956, the high-born Kennedy had conveyed the impression of drift-ing absent-mindedly on to our screens having been, as one television critic put it, 'good enough to drop by to see if he can lend a hand while on his way to the club'. He had no illusions about how long he would be remembered, for he knew that good programmes might take months or even years to make, be on for an hour and then be almost instantly forgotten. Indeed, Kennedy had already forgotten much of the television on which he had appeared. While writing his memoirs he discovered from ITN records that he had interviewed Errol Flynn and Tennessee Williams, but had no recollection of meeting either of them. For Kennedy, the people who worried about television cor-rupting people's minds were confusing numbers with effect, and were assuming that a thing said on TV to millions of viewers had more resonance than something said by a friend one cared about.[76]

Kennedy's sceptical, liberal voice was out of kilter with much of the public discussion about television at the time, which seemed afflicted by a kind of moral monomania directed against the permis-sive society in general and homosexuality in particular. Two private members' bills in 1986 and 1987, by the Tory MPs Winston Church-ill and Gerald Howarth, tried and failed to bring television within the Obscene Publications Act. In the run up to Howarth's bill, Mary Whitehouse showed MPs extracts from *Sebastiane* (1975) and *Jubilee* (1977), two explicit films by the gay filmmaker Derek Jarman that had been shown late at night on Channel 4 in 1985, accompanied by a warning and a red triangle warning of adult content. Whitehouse also showed a notorious scene from Dennis Potter's drama series, *The Singing Detective*, shown in November 1986, of a boy watching his mother having sex with her lover in a wood.

When broadcast, the Derek Jarman films received a total of twenty complaints, compared with 300 protests about Channel 4's handling of the American Football results. *The Singing Detective*'s 'heaving bottom' scene inspired fewer than a hundred telephone calls, not all critical, and some of them before it was actually shown, the event having already been trailed in the newspapers. The series producer, Kenith Trodd, believed that Potter had leaked the story of the heaving bottom to the press beforehand, in the hope that it would help the series attract a bigger audience. If this is true, it seems to have worked, because the second half of the series run, after the heaving bottom appeared, added another 2 million viewers.[77]

Kennedy thought that television's real power came not in these intermittently shocking episodes but in its slow-burning, osmotic pervasiveness as it filled the schedules and slotted wordlessly into and around our daily routines. 'As a viewer I think of television as being comparable to a long train journey,' he wrote. 'As one gazes vacantly out of the window a succession of ever-changing images passes by ... For the essence of television is its ephemerality: it is a world of flickering images, each dying at the moment it is born ... survivors being pulled from wreckage, Miss World being crowned, one fish gobbling up another.' Amid the copious literature on television's baleful influence, he reflected, little attention had been paid to the most universal effect, its capacity to induce sleep. Kennedy had even once fallen asleep while *appearing* on television, during an interview with a particularly boring peer. 'I know of no other agency except alcohol which can so rapidly and effortlessly bring the head to the chest,' he wrote of TV, 'and the two combined are as good as any sleeping pill.'[78]

In the summer of 1988, Geoffrey Nowell-Smith of the British Film Institute announced a project inspired by the fiftieth anniversary of Mass Observation the previous year. Drawing on Mass Observation's tradition of day surveys, in which participants recorded everything they did on a single day, he conceived 'One Day in the Life of Television', which would document 'the impact of television on the life and culture of the nation on a single day: November 1'. The date, a Tuesday, had no special significance: it was chosen simply because it was far enough ahead to allow the event to be planned. The project would supply, as Mass Observation had intended to do when it was founded in the 1930s, first-person vividness rather than the dry empiricism of statistics, and give a sense of what viewers really thought, 'from the Surrey stockbroker to the unemployed labourer, from the children in a London tower block, to a miner's family in Yorkshire'.[79] The BFI handed out over 600,000 diary leaflets through bookshops, newsagents, libraries and supermarkets, with volunteers being asked to record what they watched and how they felt about it. About 7,000 schoolchildren and 11,000 adults completed diaries.

For many, the day's viewing began with breakfast TV. 'Jeremy Paxman, looking like a moose playing Noel Coward, is cheerfully putting the boot into a politician as usual,' wrote Thelma Sutton, a retired secretary in Woking, watching the BBC's *Breakfast Time*. Other diarists found Paxman 'opinionated, boorish, self-satisfied' and 'rude, ignorant and extremely unpleasant', or else they found him 'brilliantly incisive' and admired his 'lovely, wicked grin'. Thus began a pattern that continued for the rest of the day, with diarists tending to watch television as a confirmation of their own existing attitudes.

After breakfast television was over, Robert Kilroy-Silk walked on to the set of his discussion programme, *Day to Day*, and announced today's issue: marital rape. 'I felt that it was a bit too sensitive an issue to be tackled at 9.30 a.m.,' wrote David Green, aged fourteen, from Holywood, County Down, who like a lot of schoolchildren was on his half-term holiday. On ITV at 10.30 a.m. a magazine programme just a few weeks old began: *This Morning*, hosted by Richard Madeley and Judy Finnigan. Among diarists, the most intensely watched item in this programme was a segment on the season's new knitting colours. 'Day-time viewing must be the most socially unacceptable mass participation sin of the 1980s,' wrote Diana Hutchinson, a housewife from Stourport-on-Severn. 'We all watch, we all pretend we don't.'

After the lunchtime news came the day's most talked about show: *Neighbours*, a daily Australian soap bought in as a cheap import for the launch of the BBC's daytime schedules. If it seemed to resemble an antipodean reincarnation of *Crossroads*, that was because it was made by the same production team; it even had a similarly earwormish theme tune written by Tony Hatch. On 1 November, Nellie Mangel invited Harold Bishop to the church dance and the pregnant

Daphne felt unwell while minding the coffee shop – for the raw material on Melbourne's Ramsay Street, just as in the Crossroads motel, was small domestic incident. And yet it was the one show that diarists seemed to recall perfectly. Thousands wrote about it and tried to rationalise their watching of it. Among this latter group was the TV presenter, Roy Castle, who stopped work on his rockery to watch it, he wrote, in order to tell his daughter what had happened when she came home from school.[80]

Fourteen-year-old Justin Delap, a boarder at St Edward's School in Oxford, missed his lunch to get a seat in the television room, where almost his entire house had gathered to watch *Neighbours*. 'Had to watch the early showing of *Neighbours*,' wrote another diarist in Brighton. 'Have a board meeting of Sussex Opera this evening …' Students had a special affection for it, one Cardiff undergraduate describing the eyes turning to the screen in the student canteen when the theme tune started, 'as automatically as Pavlov's dogs used to salivate'. A Staffordshire Polytechnic student claimed the union cafeteria was losing so much money at lunchtime that they had installed a large TV to enable diners to watch *Neighbours*. Diarists noted that they now used phrases like 'g'day', 'what a wombat' and 'shot through', but made no mention of the rising inflexion that linguists call Australian Questioning Intonation, and which *Neighbours* surely helped to popularise.[81]

The diarists often seemed to view television distractedly through the distorting prism of their own anxieties. An unemployed Sheffield woman, Alison Fell, watched the afternoon film, *The Importance of Being Earnest*, with her partner and saw it as a metaphor for their failing relationship and that 'ludicrous thing' called love. 'This brilliant, polished gem of a work laughed at our misery from behind the glass,' she wrote. Stephen Pegg, a forty-year-old former teacher from Clevedon, Avon, watched the BBC2 schools programmes *Seeing and Doing* and *How We Used To Live* as a way of clinging to his previous life. Just a year earlier, after experiencing slight stiffness in one hand, he had been diagnosed with motor neurone disease. Now he was unable to speak, dress, feed or wash himself, but managed to type his diary with a head pointer on an electric typewriter. Television, he wrote 'is now an important part of my life, many of its images reminding me of recent normality'. Pegg later won the prize for the best diary, a chance to meet the stars of *EastEnders*.[82]

At 5.35 p.m. came the second sitting of *Neighbours*. Michael Grade had made this final virtuoso scheduling tweak before moving to Channel 4 earlier that year. Grade's teenage daughter had reported the frustration of her classmates at missing *Neighbours* after they had become addicted to it during the holidays. They found themselves watching it at lunchtime in the school computer laboratory. So Grade moved the repeat from 10 a.m. the following day to later on the same day. *Neighbours* nearly doubled its audience to over 20 million. The only active *Neighbours* refusenik among the diarists was a company secretary, Alan Dunn, who, arriving home from work at 5.50 p.m., hid in his car for ten minutes while his family watched it indoors.[83]

In HM Prison Lewes in Sussex, the 560 inmates were only allowed to watch TV in the evening association period between 5.45 p.m. and 8 p.m. Their thin televisual gruel comprised the end of *Neighbours*, the national and regional news and a quiz show called *Telly Addicts* with Noel Edmonds. Prisoners were often disgruntled but captive viewers. 'I don't like television anyway,' said one prison diarist, a long-term guest at Dartmoor. 'It's either bang-up or watch it, isn't it?' Two years earlier, there had been a riot at Dartmoor when a key episode of *EastEnders*, during which Michelle Fowler jilted Lofty Holloway at the altar, was ruined by poor reception. About sixty men in B wing smashed chairs, tables and light bulbs when the pictures returned, to reveal Lofty crying in his bedsit. Stephen Plaice, the writer-in-residence at Lewes Prison and later scriptwriter for *The Bill*, wrote that the ten-feet-high television screen in C wing was an 'Orwellian sight', looking over 'depressed cons, slouched in their low-slung armchairs, flooding them with bright images of an outside world some have not seen for more than two decades'.[84]

Viewers remained exercised about very particular details. A museum assistant from Wrexham, watching *A Question of Sport* at 8.30 p.m., was 'a bit disappointed with the pullover of question master

David Coleman, plain black', while eleven-year-old Master A. Heath-
cote of Chelmsford noted sadly that the BBC2 sitcom *Colin's Sand-
wich* had 'nothing to do with sandwiches'. The favourite primetime
programmes among the diarists were repeats: a ten-year-old episode
of *Rising Damp* and a thirteen-year-old *Fawlty Towers*. As the TV
audience fell off sharply, BBC1 still netted 6 million viewers for its
(second) repeat showing of *Meerkats United* at 10.25 p.m., a programme about these tiny southern African mongooses living in tight-
knit colonies, who solved childcare problems collectively and who
stood sentry in trees on strict rotation, sniffing the air and keeping
an eye out for predators while their friends foraged for insects and
lizards. 'Only by working as a team,' explained the narrator David
Attenborough, 'can they play on the hostile pitch of the southern
African desert.' Viewers seemed to love the programme less for this
perhaps unThatcherite message than for the meerkats' eerily human
faces, with their small noses and large eyes accentuated by surrounding patches of dark fur.[85] The BBC1 audience dropped drastically for
the TV discussion programme *Network* at 10.55 p.m., and still more
severely when a man from the Open University began lecturing them
about computer graphics. Well before midnight, almost everyone was
in bed.

The One Day project had aimed 'to reveal Britain's relationship with
its television service at a time when it is poised to change for ever'. A
bill to deregulate the television industry then going through parliament, finally enshrined in the 1990 Broadcasting Act, championed
the idea that consumers, not the ITV–BBC duopoly, should decide
what they watched, and that there should be more channels and more
television for them to choose from. But while they were often scath-
ing about the programmes available to them on four channels, few
diarists felt that deregulation would lead to better ones. 'Satellite and
cable, I firmly believe, will destroy television in this country,' wrote

Gareth Hughes, a sales executive from Newbridge, Gwent. 'Politicians and money moguls ... get their way and we, the poor plebs, suffer. I suppose that's democracy? ... What I want to know is, who among the British public wants all this satellite garbage?'[86]

In far-flung parts of Britain like the Scilly Isles, where the nearest cinema was in Penzance and bad weather often delayed the arrival of newspapers and post, diarists seemed particularly attached to their televisual routines and sceptical about change, as did those who watched TV in communal spaces like care homes, boarding schools and oil rigs. For Edward Street, lighthouse keeper on the Lizard, the most southerly point of mainland Britain, television was his only amusement, and he noted that in such isolation one could develop unusual interests. 'I was on one particular lighthouse where the three things we watched without fail were *Crossroads*, *Emmerdale Farm* and the *Financial Times* index,' he wrote. 'For some reason we'd become totally besotted with the *FT* index and so everything would stop as we sat down at the end of the midday news just to find out what the index was doing.'[87] The BFI project's sample was of course slanted in favour of people who cared enough about television to produce a diary about it. But it was clear that many felt television formed part of a collective national conversation and they enjoyed the sense that they were watching what others were watching, even if what most of them were watching was *Neighbours*.

Neighbours seemed to be as near to a communal culture as the nation possessed, bringing together people of different ages, social classes and ethnicity. The sociologist Marie Gillespie, doing fieldwork among Asian teenagers in Southall, found them to be avid fans, while their parents remained lukewarm about British television. Indian families had been early adopters of the video recorder, using it to view Bombay cinema, which they saw as a way of maintaining links with their country of origin and teaching their children its language and customs. Gillespie compared them to the *Gastarbeiter* Turkish community in West Germany, a similarly strong video-watching culture created out of a sense of marginalisation from the mainstream. By 1989, when about half of British homes had a video, eighty per cent of

Southall homes had one. Southall's Asian teenagers, though, were less likely to enjoy Bollywood films and had latched on to the all-white, suburban characters of *Neighbours*, using them as a way of talking indirectly about their own families, and the importance in Punjabi culture of family honour or *izzat*, which depended on the chastity of daughters. The gossipy character, Mrs Mangel, had entered their lingo ('Oh! She's a right Mangel!') to describe an interfering adult.[88]

Many viewers seemed to watch *Neighbours* without taking it seriously, or at least they excused their watching of it in these terms. Clive James's professionally flippant voice, accepting of kitsch and impatient of divisions between high and low culture, was now widely imitated. When his tenure at the *Observer* ended in 1982, other poets and novelists – Julian Barnes, William Boyd, Hugo Williams, Martin Amis, Peter Ackroyd, Adam Mars-Jones – started to be employed as television critics by newspapers and magazines. Dissecting popular culture was now a serious activity. The *Listener* had begun a guest column, *Schlockwatch*, in which contributors wrote about their weakness for popular television. Joan Bakewell commended the ITV guessing game, *Through the Keyhole*; George Melly sang the praises of the teenage quiz show *Blockbusters*; and Paul Theroux wrote of his fondness for *Coronation Street* and his delight at seeing a poster for *The Mosquito Coast*, the film of his novel, in Rita Fairclough's newsagents.[89]

The earnest *Crossroads* viewers whom Dorothy Hobson talked to in the early 1980s would not have understood this new, slyly populist tone. On Easter Monday 1988, after more than 4,500 episodes, *Crossroads* had come to an end, the motel closing its doors for the last time and Meg's daughter, Jill Chance, leaving her husband and driving off with her new man to found a new hotel. This time there was no stop shot at the end. On the mid-morning BBC television show *Open Air*, presenter Pattie Coldwell broke down during a live broadcast from the Midlands motel. 'I never thought I would be in tears over *Crossroads*,' she said, 'but I am.' Although *Crossroads* still had about 12 million viewers, its audience was disproportionately old and poor and thus unappealing to advertisers. 'We did a survey of what newspapers *Crossroads* viewers read,' said the producer William Smethurst, who had tried to rebrand the serial as *Crossroads, Kings Oak*. 'It was depressing. More of them read the *Daily Star*, which was going through its Daily Bonk phase, than the numbers who ever saw any of the quality papers. I realised there was no point in clever, funny writing if no one would appreciate it.'[90]

The elderly *Crossroads* fans who had written to the *Birmingham Evening Mail* about Meg's departure, fearful that they were being forgotten, had their fears vindicated. Commercial broadcasters now preferred to attract what they called 'ELVs' or 'elusive light viewers', such as teenagers and the young people with disposable incomes coveted by advertisers. When the ITV controller, Greg Dyke, dropped the Saturday afternoon wrestling in 1988, he said it was 'stuck in a timewarp' and 'personified the old English working class sitting round the telly, staring blankly'. A few months later ITV also cancelled the darts and bowls, and Channel 4 pulled snooker from its schedules, because these sports, too, had a relatively elderly audience.[91]

A quarter of Britain's television viewing was now done by the 8 million people over sixty-five. A third of them had hearing problems, and one in ten wore hearing aids, which made radio listening difficult; on a winter's evening ninety-five per cent watched TV. But this group of viewers was statistically invisible because the ratings system lumped over fifty-fives together, all 15 million of them, so as not to draw advertisers' attention to the fact that millions of their potential viewers were economically inactive pensioners. Over fifty-fives made up ten per cent of the audience for *Top of the Pops*, and eighteen per cent of the audience for *Blue Peter*. One and a half million of them watched the ITV cartoon, *Dangermouse*, half a million more than its target audience of four to nine year olds.[92]

Yet broadcasters behaved as though this most loyal group of viewers did not exist. The commercials populating daytime television, promoting denture fixant and walk-in baths, were the only real clue that they watched television at all. These older viewers were the ones who seemed most to welcome the filling out of the daytime schedules and the diurnal routines of daily quiz shows and regional news, the television that was now stripped across the week and existed in its own little bubble of recurring time. 'Television is an absolute boon for the lonely,' wrote Ivy Ryalls, a retired woman from Alvaston, Derbyshire, in her 'One Day' diary. 'At a flick of the switch one's rooms can be peopled. When my husband died 10 years ago, the loneliness was dreadful … I remember many sleepless nights and the utter relief when the sunrise opening of early morning television meant that there were other people awake in the world besides me.'[93]

8

THE AGE OF WARTS AND CARBUNCLES

Years ago I was walking down a street in a suburban town in the evening. The streets were empty, there was a feeling of dereliction. I passed this shop full of television sets, and I was on all of them. I thought 'Christ, that's awful.' I found it quite disturbing.

Melvyn Bragg[1]

The great historian of the English landscape, W. G. Hoskins, often complained of the despoliation of its countryside by soulless modernity. But there was one part of the modern world he admired. 'Goonhilly is one of the most marvellous sites in England,' he enthused in a BBC2 series, *Landscapes of England*, in May 1978.

What caps it all is the way that as you approach these immense saucers there are circular barrows – the burial mounds of Bronze Age men. It is the combination of these burial mounds four thousand years old and Goonhilly Earth Station which is to me a magnificent conjunction of the ancient world and the future. Goonhilly is obviously not just scenery: it is pure landscape and as deeply moving as any landscape fashioned a thousand or so years ago. Goonhilly at sunset, with no man in sight, silently listening all the time to the most remote signals. It is a scene that would have inspired Thomas Hardy.[2]

It is not surprising Hoskins made his peace with modernity here. The postwar phenomena he most hated, such as trunk roads, concrete airfields and bombing ranges, were all about noise and restless movement. But the architecture of television relies on the silent, invisible, quasi-magical radio wave. By the time Hoskins celebrated it, Goonhilly had become the largest satellite station on earth, with sixty huge, stainless steel mushrooms rising on their spindly bipods. They were so big and so many that Goonhilly had its own permanent team of painters who spent each day hanging like spiders on a metal web, priming and topcoating each dish with chlorinated rubber, to protect against rust and the ravages of the sea air. The names of the dishes – Uther, Lancelot, Guinevere, Percival, Pellinore – were grand reminders of the region's connections with Arthurian legend.

But Goonhilly's location on the extreme edge of England already mattered less in the age of geostationary satellites, which did not need to be tracked across the sky as they orbited the earth. In July 1969, when Goonhilly's engineers worked through the night to bring images of the moon landing to Britain, their technical triumph went unremarked, for in the few short years since Telstar, television from space had become a trick repeated to the point of banality. In July 1985, an enormous new dish, Merlin – known unofficially as the *Blue Peter*, which covered its official opening – carried the Live Aid concert to 2 billion people. But this was to be Goonhilly's last great triumph. As the first transatlantic broadcasts faded from memory, the nearby Telstar Café, on the lonely B3292 road crossing the Downs, renamed itself the Goonhilly Tea Rooms. In 2006, Goonhilly's satellite operations began to be wound down and outsourced to another earth station in Hertfordshire. Now, instead of coming from these far-off places on the edge of the nation, satellite television is centralised in order to cut costs.

But there is still something impressive about this patch of

heathland, with its curious confluence of the ancient and futuristic that Hoskins identified. It seems fitting that the 10,000-strong crowd assembled here in August 1999 were the only people in Britain to see the full solar eclipse, as the clouds covering the rest of the West Country miraculously parted just before the day turned dark, and birds roosted confusedly on the satellite dishes. The dishes, which sometimes share the skyline with Goonhilly's famous two-humped Bactrian camels carrying holidaymakers across the downs, are now being developed into a space-themed outreach centre with the potential to communicate with future piloted missions to Mars.

The satellite dish had already lost much of its space-age lustre when, a few weeks before Christmas 1988, some strange-looking objects began to appear on the outside walls of British houses. They were pointed heavenwards, not towards the star of Bethlehem, but towards a signal from the Astra satellite, which had just been launched from a rocket in a remote jungle clearing in Kourou, in the equatorial rain forests of French Guiana. White, round, about three feet wide and shaped like outsized frying pans, they resembled shrunken versions of the Goonhilly dishes. Advertisements for them drew on the imagery of rocket launches and cratered moonscapes familiar from science fiction movies and the Apollo missions. But now, as the space race had ended and the Cold War was petering out, satellites had become mundane; when stuck on the sides of houses the dishes looked incongruous and bizarre.

Satellite television used gigahertz frequencies, which terrestrial TV stations could not use because their very short wavelengths were absorbed by the earth's atmosphere. They worked from space because the signal went straight up and down and crossed only a short stretch of the atmosphere, but the dish had to be perfectly aimed so that its bowl could gather up the super-weak waves. The engineers who installed the dishes on the sides of houses would use a compass and meter to check they were pointing at the precise bit of sky where the invisible Astra satellite was, no bigger than a car and hovering 22,300 miles over the equator. If a dish was too casually adjusted in fine weather, it might give poor pictures in the wet because of 'rain fade', the absorption of waves by water in the atmosphere. British dishes had to face south-east to pick up the signals from Astra centred on mainland Europe. Prospective satellite television viewers were told to go out at 10.30 a.m. or 2 p.m. to see where the sun hit their house, which was where they would have to mount the dish. Often, to the regret of those who thought they could hide it in their backyard, it had to be stuck high on the house front, just below the eaves, so the satellite could see it clearly – and so could everyone else.

At first there were no more than a few thousand of these odd-looking contraptions in the whole of the country. When Rupert Murdoch's Sky television launched in February 1989, many high street shops were waiting to see what demand was like and had dishes just for display purposes. Audience numbers were sometimes only in three figures. If his audience got any smaller, the Sky News anchor John Stapleton said privately, he would be locked up for talking to himself.[3] Broadcast from a satellite registered in Luxembourg, Sky was exempt from Britain's media laws and the duties of a public service broadcaster and its schedules relied heavily on imitative or recycled shows stripped across the week. Electronic signals were being imprinted on to carrier waves, shot into space from giant aerial dishes to a two-tonne satellite spinning in geostationary orbit and then beamed back down to earth – a 44,600 mile trip – all so that a few thousand people could watch a recycled ITV quiz show, *Sale of the Century*, repeats of *General Hospital* and a talent show called *Keith Chegwin's Star Search*.

Gradually, though, more dishes sprouted under the eaves of houses as the audiences grew, and a row began to brew about the 'woks on the wall', as Liverpudlians named them after the hemispherical Chinese pan popularised by the TV chef Ken Hom. Astra's signal was concentrated on middle Europe, and Britons needed large dishes to gather up the waves from outer space, which became fainter the further north you got. Sky dishes in the south were two feet across, but north of Aberdeen they had to be three feet, and above that size, in Shetland or the Outer Hebrides, you needed planning permission.[4]

Underneath these arguments about the look and size of the dishes, other anxieties simmered. For the resilient British class system had infected even the seemingly private act of watching television. Cable television had been slow to take off in part because it was associated with the municipal piping in of television in tower blocks and council estates. By comparison, satellite dishes at first had an upmarket image because they were mostly owned by electronics enthusiasts and rich European expats wishing to watch television in their own language. Dishes appeared on the roofs of hotels such as the Dorchester on Park Lane, and Harrods had reported 'enormous interest' when it started selling them before Christmas 1985. By the following February they had sold eleven. 'For the status-conscious, a parabolic television antenna is what now piques the neighbours,' said *The Times* in 1986.[5] Sky, though, targeted its dishes at relatively prosperous working-class men, the upwardly mobile standard bearers of Thatcherite popular capitalism, who were known to be keen on new gadgetry and home entertainment. Impatient with aesthetic concerns which he viewed as disguised class snobbery, Rupert Murdoch saw the prominent white dishes not as an eyesore but a free advertisement.

One part of the country became particularly associated with the satellite dish. An unsigned newspaper profile on 7 October 1990, headed 'Mrs Thatcher's bruiser', had invented a new phrase: 'Essex man'. The profile was written by Simon Heffer, a resident of the county, who had conducted his anthropological fieldwork on commuter trains to and from Liverpool Street. Essex man was the child of parents who had been shipped out from the East End to new towns like Basildon and Harlow after the war. A bedrock of support for the new Tory Party, he was 'young, industrious, mildly brutish and culturally barren'. His recreations were 'drinking with his mates, watching sport on Sky television, playing with his car and thinking about (and occasionally attempting) sexual intercourse'. The accompanying illustration featured a muscly-necked young man in a sharp suit standing outside his ex-council house with a new car in the drive and a satellite dish on the roof.[6] Essex man was largely confined to inner Essex, a wobbly crescent of land stretching north and east of London from Enfield to Southend. Its spiritual and geographical epicentre was somewhere between Chingford, the constituency of the Tory MP Norman Tebbit, and Chigwell, home of Alan Sugar, the man Murdoch had entrusted to make his satellite dishes.

Appearing in the pages of the *Sunday Telegraph*, the profile of Essex man accurately reflected the squeamishness of some older Tories about the more vulgar manifestations of Thatcherism. He was the cartoonish resident of an imagined place, but one with just enough sociological verisimilitude to gain purchase in the public imagination. One of the images of social change in the 1980s was the sold-off council house and, along with the other signs of militant individualism on its exterior that marked out the homeowner from the tenant, from stone cladding to coaching lamps, was the satellite dish that many local councils forbade their tenants from erecting.

Satellite dish wars tended to be fiercest where the social classes mingled. Dishes on secluded detached houses, in new docklands apartments or indeed in the sprawling ex-council estates of inner Essex, were uncontentious. Dish battles were fought either within picturesque villages, where natives lived alongside blow-in commuters and second homers, or in gentrifying areas of urban terraces, particularly in London where rising house prices were forcing the middle classes to colonise places like Battersea, Stoke Newington and Hackney.[7] Here the relationship between the middle-class incomers and the established working-class residents was sometimes testy, as gentrifiers tended to worry about the aesthetic integrity of terraces being destroyed by piecemeal alterations like PVC windows and satellite dishes.

Dishes joined washing lines and willow herb as black marks in best-kept village competitions. 'We are now in danger of having forests of intrusive satellite dishes and other metalwork springing up across the rooftops of England,' the Council for the Protection of Rural England protested. 'I'd certainly think twice about buying a house if the next door neighbour had one of those filthy little carbuncles stuck up,' said

Auberon Waugh. 'Because what he's telling me is that he's the sort of incurious moron who lives on 24 hours a day drivel.' The *Guardian* called satellite dishes 'identified non-flying objects, staring motionlessly south-east like pilgrims at an electronic Mecca'. They told us we now lived in 'the age of warts and carbuncles: and programmes beamed in from on high to reassure us all of the benefits of being a nation of consumers rather than producers'.[8]

When Sky's rival, British Satellite Broadcasting, was about to launch, it took out full-page advertisements with a picture of a dinner plate, a reference to Sky's claim that its dishes would be no bigger than one. On the authority of the British Ceramics Manufacturers' Association, BSB stated that the average dinner plate was ten inches across. 'Dear Rupert,' the ad said, 'if your satellite dish is a dinner plate, you must eat whopping dinners.'[9] Unlike Sky, BSB did not have to share its satellite with continental Europe, but had its own British satellite, Marco Polo, whose signal was aimed straight at Manchester. So BSB's distinctive 'squarial' dishes really would be the size (although not the shape) of a dinner plate.

BSB launched inauspiciously on an April weekend in 1990, as day trippers packed coast roads during an unexpected heatwave, and most people indoors were watching BBC2 as Stephen Hendry beat Jimmy White to become world snooker champion. Although BSB promoted itself as a quality broadcaster, some of its initial offerings appeared to stretch this claim. They included *Wife of the Week*, which required wives to identify their husbands by their distorted voices; *Jupiter Moon*, a soap opera set on board a twenty-first-century spaceship polytechnic, soon nicknamed '*Crossroads* in Space'; and *Heil Honey, I'm Home!*, a spoof sitcom, which did not survive beyond its pilot, in which Adolf Hitler and Eva Braun live next door to a Jewish couple. BSB struggled to attract subscribers, and in November 1990 Sky effectively took it over in a merger. Its Marco Polo satellite became instant cosmic rubbish, left like Telstar to career uselessly round the earth in its eternal orbit. The odd BSB squarial can sometimes still be seen on the sides of houses, tilted towards the skies as though it hasn't given up hope of picking up a lost episode of *Jupiter Moon*.

In May and June 1990, Channel 4 screened a series called *The Television Village*. The previous spring, Granada Television, with the help of Manchester University's European Institute for the Media and students from Salford University and Preston Polytechnic, had brought the satellite television of the near future to a guinea pig group of sixty-five homes in the village of Waddington in Lancashire's Ribble Valley. For five weeks these homes received twenty-nine channels, from Sky and BSB to European imports. So that rows about ugly dishes did not complicate the villagers' attitudes, they ran a TV cable along a convenient brook running through the centre of the village. Granada also helped the villagers set up a local community station, Waddington Village Television. The Independent Broadcasting Authority lent them a small TV mast which was erected on soft ground next to a local farmer's pig slurry tip.[10]

Everyone in Waddington could receive the village channel, which broadcast each evening between 7 and 8 p.m. from the church hall, its badminton lines still visible. The evening programmes included cubs meetings, parish council sittings, music from the local barber shop singers and the vicar Alan Bailey giving his thoughts for the day. The only technical glitch came when sheep nibbled through the wires in the transmitter field. The village station gained ninety-five per cent of the available audience, beating not only the satellite channels but *EastEnders* and *Coronation Street* as well. People in neighbouring villages like Bashall Eaves and Grindleton adjusted their aerials to pick up the evening hour of WVTV.

Apart from a delegation of farmers who turned up at the Granada command centre at eight o'clock one evening to ask if the late-night porn could be shown earlier because they had go to bed before it started, the experiment suggested that people preferred programmes about their own community to glossier alternatives. At the end of the experiment, a panel of villagers interviewed David Waddington, the home secretary and local MP, in the village hall. One villager asked why they were getting more television when fewer people were watching it. 'It's a free country,' Waddington answered. What about all the rubbish on the satellite channels, a woman asked.

'If people are prepared to pay for rubbish, that's up to the people,' he replied.[11]

One satellite channel did, though, prove popular with the residents of Waddington: Sky Sports, which was broadcasting Serie A Italian football and re-runs of old FA Cup Finals. Viewing figures for television football had been declining since the late 1970s onwards, and hooliganism had cast a pall over the game, but England's excellent run in the 1990 World Cup had altered public perceptions of the sport, adding new fans and allowing existing ones to declare their interest more fervently. Karl Miller, after watching the semi-final between England and West Germany at his house in Chelsea, described the young midfielder Paul Gascoigne as 'strange-eyed, pink-faced, fair-haired, tense and upright, a priapic monolith in the Mediterranean sun – a marvellous equivocal sight'. When, in extra time, Gascoigne had to fight back tears after being booked for a foul which meant he would miss the final should England get to it, Miller protested that the tackled player had 'rolled about in a piece of German theatre that might have earned him a place in Goethe's *Walpurgisnacht*'.[12]

The game was decided by a new form of torment for England fans: a penalty shoot out. When Chris Waddle blasted the ball high over the bar to give Germany victory, the Electricity Board braced itself for a soar in demand. It was a summer evening and it had got dark during the match, and they feared a mass switching on of lights as soon as it was over. Instead, viewers were shocked into paralysis and it was not until eight minutes after Waddle's penalty that the demand for electricity surged to 2800 megawatts, beating the previous record set by *The Thorn Birds*.[13]

The day after the match, it became clear that what had most affected viewers had not been the penalty shoot out, but Gascoigne's tears. 'We can cry in public as long as we look like we are trying not to,' argues Tom Lutz in his book *Crying: A Natural and Cultural*

History of Tears. 'We can continue to issue those tearful demands we supposedly stopped making at the age of five or eight by employing conventional gestures that both disguise and display our weeping.' Like Gilbert Harding's frantically swallowed emotion on *Face to Face* thirty years earlier, Gascoigne's tears had this touching quality of being both hidden and revealed. Instead of crying when he was booked, he screwed up his face and gasped for breath, trying to conquer his emotions. He sobbed freely only after extra time, when the camera discovered him in a crowd of players being comforted by his manager Bobby Robson. John Moynihan noted that Gascoigne, whom he felt had played only sporadically well, had 'charmed a great many English female television-watchers with his wisecracks and tears, women, in many cases, who didn't know the difference between a football and a tangerine'.[14]

'Who is Gazza?' asked Mr Justice Harman in the high court that September, after Paul Gascoigne Ltd had applied for an injunction against an unauthorised biography. 'Paul Gascoigne is a very well-known footballer,' explained his barrister, Michael Silverleaf. 'As a result of his performance [in the World Cup] he has come to be very greatly recognised by the public in this country.' After establishing that it was possible that television had made Gazza even more famous than the Duke of Wellington after Waterloo, the judge concluded that, like the duke, Gazza had no legal protection against unwelcome biographers. 'Gascoigne became Gazza at the moment of the tears,' reflected Anthony Giddens, professor of sociology at Cambridge, in an essay in the *Times Higher Education Supplement*. 'Gazza's tears are not a nostalgic and self-pitying reaction to past glories lost … [they] are simultaneously comforting and disturbing, symbolising real achievement in a puzzling wider world in which, however, England's role has become distinctly problematic.'[15]

Football was not, of course, reinvented in one moment, and made the subject of such ambitious cultural semiotics, because of a single match on television. It had been gradually gaining middle-class viewers in the postwar era with the growth of TV coverage, while football grounds had remained mainly the preserve of the working classes. One of BBC2's most popular programmes in the 1960s was *Match of the Day*, which Mary Whitehouse stayed up every Saturday night to watch after her husband and two sons had gone to bed. Televised football developed its own visual and verbal lexicon which made it ever more unlike the experience of watching on the terraces. When the BBC first used the slow-motion 'action replay' after a near miss in the opening match of the 1966 World Cup between England and Uruguay, the duty office was inundated with calls asking if the match was live or recorded. The World Cup Final of that year gained the biggest audience in British television history: more than 32 million, an even more impressive figure when one considers that the game involved only one of the home nations and that it is probably an underestimate, since the collective watching in public places that occurs during big sports games does not register well in ratings systems.

But some worried that television was colonising and transforming British football just as it had done with American football. The ex-Spurs player Danny Blanchflower sincerely believed that televised football should be straight reportage, and that a boring match should be edited into equally boring highlights so as not to mislead the viewer. 'Television is the Moloch of the age, into whose vast, undifferentiated maw anything and everything can disappear,' agreed the journalist Brian Glanville. Editing was turning football into 'something other than it is, vulgarising it into a thing of goals, shots and goalmouth escapes'. And yet televised football could animate viewers like no other kind of television. When Charlie George struck the winning goal for Arsenal in the 1971 FA Cup Final, five-year-old Jason Cowley was returning from the sweet shop with his sister and walking past a window in a Harlow street. 'As the ball hit the back of the net it was as if a bomb had exploded inside the house, scattering bodies,' Cowley wrote later. 'If the windows weren't already open I'd have sworn the sound of the celebrations inside would have blown out the glass.'[16]

While the new scourge of hooliganism in the 1970s put many people off attending matches, the parallel universe of televised football achieved a new realism. Electronic cameras meant matches could be snappily edited, and on a colour set you could see everything beautifully, from churned-up goalmouths to the grass changing colour from late summer to spring. The *Match of the Day* presenter, Jimmy Hill, addressed the camera like an Open University lecturer, a textual critic revealing the game's subtext, spotlighting a key player, passing judgement on whether a goal was offside and castigating ungentlemanly play. In their early work of media studies, *Reading Television* (1978), John Fiske and John Hartley noted that the programme abstracted football from its open-air, partisan, proletarian messiness. '*Match of the Day* is not football,' they wrote, 'in the way that *Come Dancing* is not dancing.'[17]

Televised football brought in new, literate fans. Standing in for Clive James as the *Observer*'s television critic in August 1978, Martin Amis wrote about a whole weekend watching football, from *Football Focus* on Saturday lunchtime to *The Big Match* on Sunday afternoon. 'Intellectual football-lovers are a beleaguered crew,' he argued later, 'despised by intellectuals and football-lovers alike, who regard our addiction as affected, pseudo-proletarian, even faintly homosexual. We have adapted to this; we keep ourselves to ourselves – oh, how we have to cringe and hide!'[18] This confession appeared in the *London Review of Books*. Its editor Karl Miller – who, along with John Moynihan had been part of a group of trailblazing middle-class Sunday footballers, made up of writers, artists, actors and journalists, who had begun playing on Hyde Park in the late 1950s – often gave intellectuals like A. J. Ayer and Hans Keller the space to write about their fandom. So when Sky, buoyed by the success of the 1990 World Cup, latched on to televised football as a way of selling dishes, it was drawing on a slightly subterranean, cross-class interest in the game that had been developing, with interruptions, since at least the 1960s.

Sky had noticed the sharp rise in dish sales when they broadcast the Mike Tyson–Frank Bruno fight in February 1989, and England's progress to the Cricket World Cup final in March 1992. But as ITV's Greg Dyke prophesied, Britain's national game would be 'the biggest dish-driver of the lot'.[19] In May 1992 Sky paid £304 million, more than ten times the current rate, for the rights to televise live games in the newly formed Premier League. On the first Sky 'Super Sunday' that August, a single match between Nottingham Forest and Liverpool was padded out into five hours of television. Pitch inspections and shots of the referee getting changed in his dressing-room preceded the game. During it, pitchside cameras raced down the touchline with wingers or showed managers screaming ineffectually at players. After it, ex-footballer experts used electronic chalkboards to show how moves had developed. The Monday night game, inspired by the Monday night American football on US television, employed sumo wrestlers dressed in team colours, and cheerleaders, the 'Sky Strikers', as half-time distractions.

The televised Premier League became turbo capitalism in excelsis, a hyper-mercenary trade in which a small coterie of clubs secured much of the TV money for themselves and then proceeded to earn even more through merchandise and stock market flotations. Oddly, though, as clubs became detached from their localities, ruled by offshore interests and money markets, football's emotional landscape was enriched. This new mood had been anticipated in the 1990 World Cup, even before Gazza's tears. The BBC's opening credits for its coverage had shown slow motion, balletic images of footballers, including the agonised ecstasy of Marco Tardelli's goal celebration in the 1982 World Cup Final, over Luciano Pavarotti singing 'Nessun Dorma' from *Turandot*. New Order and the England squad's 1990 World Cup song, 'World in Motion', was a similarly heady concoction of optimism and nostalgia, which began with a sample from Kenneth Wolstenholme's BBC commentary at the end of the 1966 World Cup Final.

As the final goal went in, Wolstenholme had said: 'And here comes Hurst! He's got – some people are on the pitch. They think it's all over – it is now! It's four!' These words did not resonate immediately with viewers, no doubt because they were drowned out by millions of living room cheers, which was probably just as well, since they inconveniently drew attention to the fact that the goal should have been disallowed because there were spectators on the field. It was only when the whole game was repeated on BBC2 in August 1966 that their concision and neatness caught the public mood, and continued to do so over the years as the nation rued its failure to repeat its only footballing triumph. As a piece of Wolstenholme commentary, it was atypical. He was best known for his clipped RAF tones and meaningful silences, for he believed that words should merely annotate what was on screen. Wolstenholme's standard response when a player scored was 'it's a goal', a phrase so familiar to 1960s TV viewers that the Beatles, none of whom were football fans, sampled it on a loop for an alternative mix of the song 'Glass Onion', which later appeared on *Anthology 3*.

Over on ITV, only about 4 million viewers heard Hugh Johns's more prosaic celebration of the winning goal and Hurst's hat trick: 'Geoff Hurst goes forward. He might make it three. He has! He has! And that's it, that's it!' But Johns's voluble commentaries, delivered in a rich voice honed in theatre rep, coarsened by chain smoking and lubricated with Brain's Bitter, became the default style. David Coleman, who replaced Wolstenholme as the main BBC commentator for the 1970 World Cup, was similarly excitable, calling out players' names in ascending pitch and then, when the goal went in, finishing with a crescendo '1–0!' Sky's football commentary, a torrent of atmospheric shouting and interjections by 'summarisers', followed this school of commentary to its outer edges. Towards the end of his life, Wolstenholme became sick of the 'demeaning trivia' of the commentators, and would turn the sound down when watching a game.[20] But the best commentary, as his enduring eight words in 1966 showed, could provide a collective, emotional response to an event that lingered long in the memory.

Just as Sky began its Premier League coverage, Nick Hornby published his affecting and influential book about football fandom, *Fever Pitch*. Hornby's contention that 'the natural state of the football fan is bitter disappointment, no matter what the score' contrasted eloquently with satellite football's hype.[21] Grassroots fanzines and a raft of Hornby-influenced fan memoirs recalled the terraces of the 1970s as a sensual world of cigarette smoke, proximate bodies and BO, an implicit retort to the touchless, passive voyeurism of televised football. The Sky deal had also reinstated *Match of the Day*, as the BBC won back from ITV the rights to broadcast highlights, and a wave of nostalgia greeted the return of this late Saturday night fixture. In the mid 1990s the BBC broadcast *Match of the Seventies*, highlights of old editions of *Match of the Day* intercut with evocative 1970s music: a fascinating social document resurrecting all kinds of lost phenomena, from footballers' bushy sideburns to the standing crowds swaying like a single organism. Football, formerly associated with a lumpen masculinity, was now a way for men to think lyrically about longing, loss and the local and familial ties unravelled by globalisation and the free market. It became what literary theorists call a reverse discourse, a critique of the dominant culture that also validated it, for it allowed fans to carry on watching Premier League football on satellite television without feeling part of the relentless mercantilism of the modern game.

The received wisdom for years had been that television was slowly killing the live game. When *Match of the Day* began in August 1964, it was broadcast on BBC2 because the Football League was worried about its effect on crowd numbers, and only agreed to it being broadcast on a channel not then available outside London and which hardly anyone was watching. There had been a long-term decline in attendance since the late 1940s and a particularly sharp fall with the rise of colour television in the early 1970s. The historical pattern seemed clear, but the received wisdom turned out to be wrong. In the new satellite football era, match attendances remained buoyant as fans seemed quite prepared to pay inflated prices to watch live games they could see at home much more cheaply, or even to do both and pay twice over for the same product. As customers, they were as irrational and captive as the typical Hornbyesque narrator of the football fan memoir.

Satellite football created a new way of watching television. Walking through a town centre on Sunday afternoons or Monday evenings, you would see the coloured chalkboards outside pubs advertising live football and hear the mingled sounds of pub cheers and Martin Tyler's Sky commentary wafting through the open air. Enormous BBC plasma screens, twenty-five metres square, grew on stilts in city squares, where crowds would congregate for matches. Goal celebrations became part of public life, and a news footage cliché. A reporter would be sent to a bar for a big game, with the camera trained not on the screen but the supporters, showing them edging towards the screen, open-mouthed in anticipation at a goal chance and then erupting with joy or throwing back their heads in despair. Sometimes they would show the more subdued groans when the other side scored. Rarely in modern times had public life been given over to such self-abandoning extremes of anguish and euphoria.

Such public television was, of course, how Baird had once imagined the future of his invention. His former laboratory at 22 Frith Street in Soho was now an espresso bar with slatted metal chairs and tables spilling over on to the pavement, and much of its back wall was taken up by a huge TV screen which lit up the room when football matches, especially Italian ones, were shown. When a goal went in, the customers celebrated with a fervour that would have astonished the forty scientists from the Royal Institution who once queued up in evening dress along a narrow staircase in order to inspect a quivering image of the head of a ventriloquist's dummy.

The novelist Kingsley Amis did not have a subscription to Sky Sports. Apart from cricket and snooker he did not care for televised sport, especially, he wrote to his friend Philip Larkin, 'filthy soccer'.[22] And yet as he entered his seventies, watching television consumed much of his evening life. Always scared of flying and unable to drive, he now feared even everyday travel, including the Underground, and was afraid of being left on his own at night with nothing to occupy him. He lived with his first wife, Hilly, her husband Lord Kilmarnock and their son, on Regents Park Road in north London. Amis paid the mortgage and Hilly acted as his housekeeper, bringing him his suppers on a tray and sitting with him in front of the TV – a small, portable set, with an indoor aerial, which sat on top of a chest of drawers in Amis's bedroom.

For Amis, watching television was both a congenial evening routine and a way of affirming his political and cultural aesthetic. He believed the best fiction was narrative and character-driven, the best poetry was recitative and understandable, the best restaurant food was unpretentious and advertised on the menu in English, and the best television was soap operas, sitcoms and popular drama. Like Larkin, he got impatient over poetic pretension and artistic earnestness. 'You deduce from this that I now have a television set,' wrote Larkin to another friend, the English professor Brian Cox, in 1981, 'and find it rots the mind comfortably, but I don't as a rule watch "serious" things: sport, old films, Miss World are my level.' Both Amis and Larkin hated being bored, and had the intellectual self-confidence summarily to dismiss highbrow culture they found dull. Amis had got his first TV set in the mid 1950s and became immediately irritated with the hostile sociologising about it that he called 'Hoggart-wash', which dealt with 'the putative corruption of some inadequately visu-alised pools-telly-and-fish-and-chips Everyman', an attitude he saw as 'a protest made on behalf of others who are deemed too comatose or inarticulate to make it for themselves'.[23]

In his own, intermittent career as a TV critic for the *Observer* in the 1970s, Amis wrote freely and admiringly about the wrestling or *The Generation Game* but grudgingly and disobligingly about foreign films and documentary. In his column in the *Radio Times* he presented himself as an average, sensual man, a television-watching Sancho Panza torn between the nature programme *Bellamy's Britain* and going to the pub on a Sunday lunchtime, or between *The Marriage of Figaro* and *Kojak* on the other side. He was a firm fan of Benny Hill and *The Dick Emery Show*, of which he wrote that 'nothing disturbs the ordered calm of my household more than an attempt to prevent me from watching it, and people who ring me up while it's on have been known to burst into tears'.[24]

In the 1980s, Amis's populism became increasingly entwined with his support for the Thatcherite attack on liberal-professional élites, and his objection to a mentality he called 'sod the public' in the arts and service industries. He believed subsidies corrupted the relationship between artists and audiences and accused the Arts Council of funding 'plays without plots' and 'poems that are meaningless patterns of letters'. In a 1984 essay, 'Television and the intellectuals', Amis argued that the viewer also faced 'a semi-benign semi-conspiracy to foist on him what is thought to be good for him'. Television, he felt, should be an escape from such cultural nannyism: it should stick to what customers paid to see and the medium did best, such as sport, family sagas, crime and comedy series.[25]

Amis's television viewing may have been partly a sally in the culture wars of the Thatcher years, but there was no sense of position-taking about his two favourite programmes, *The Bill* and *Coronation Street*, which he followed devotedly. Amis had long believed that the novel needed to regenerate itself not through avant-garde experiment but by drawing on genre fiction, with its capacity for combining pleasingly familiar formulae with creative reinvention. Having already written a detective story (*The Riverside Villas Murder*, 1973) and an episode of the *Z Cars* follow-up, *Softly, Softly*, he was interested in crime drama long before a serial set in Sun Hill police station in the East End began in 1984, with its memorable staccato theme tune, 'Overkill', accompanied by wailing police sirens and an insistent saxophone riff.

The Bill was not strictly speaking a soap opera: its episodes were self-contained narratives, but with recurring characters, allowing viewers to dip in and out. Storylines were uncluttered, steering clear of the officers' private lives. One of the serial's unwritten rules was that a police officer appeared in every scene, allowing it to deal with adult themes before the 9 p.m. watershed, because the police generally arrived at the scene of a crime after the grisly stuff had already happened. Many of the characters felt like old friends: like Bob Cryer (Eric Richard), the eternally patient duty sergeant who had not been the same since he killed an armed robber who turned out to have an unloaded gun; loveable, crisp-quaffing failure DC 'Tosh' Lines (Kevin

Lloyd), with his scruffy moustache, crumpled suit and battered old Volvo; and Sun Hill's darling, Viv Martella (Nula Conwell), shockingly shot dead in 1993 by building society robbers.

According to a study of four Midlands prisons in the early 1990s, *The Bill* was the most popular programme among inmates, rivalled only by the rural soap opera *Emmerdale*. Between 1991 and 1996, the British Film Institute asked several hundred people to keep diaries of their television watching. The most popular programme with men, particularly those over sixty like Amis, was *The Bill*. When he died in 1995, Amis's daughter Sally kept her portion of his ashes in an urn, and when *The Bill* was on she would sit the urn next to her and watch it with him.[26]

Amis had watched *Coronation Street* from the start. Arguing in an article in the *TV Times* in 1964 that television was improving as the viewer who would watch anything became extinct, the main planks in his argument – which dutifully mentioned only ITV programmes in a publication that refused to acknowledge the existence of the other side – were *University Challenge*, *The Avengers* and *Coronation Street*. 'Must you be a moron to enjoy *Coronation Street*?', Amis mused, *à propos* those viewers who wrote to the character, Len Fairclough, threatening to beat him up if he did not change his ways. Amis answered himself in the negative, adding that 'Patricia Phoenix, who plays Elsie Tanner, must be one of the most beautiful women on television'. *Coronation Street* suggested to Amis that television's primitive phase was ending and 'that old glassy-eyed viewer, anchored in front of his set whatever is on it, is on the way out'.[27]

When *Coronation Street* began, it seemed to be rooted in the dark, monochromatic social realism that Amis professed to dislike. In 1963, at a village debating society in Hayfield, where its creator Tony Warren lived, one speaker blamed the programme for causing unemployment in the north, because its bleak imagery dissuaded businesses from investing in the region; another said it made viewers believe that 'northerners were peasant morons'. As late as 1974, an Oldham councillor called for the series to be scrapped, because 'people who see *Coronation Street* think we are all married to Hilda Ogdens, wear clogs and have outside loos'. But it had always had elements of human comedy, with pitch-perfect northern dialogue and deft character touches, and even its earliest programmes teased the edges of its everyday realism, including one memorable 1964 episode – broadcast just as Amis was defending the show in the *TV Times* – based on the plot of *High Noon*, with Len Fairclough as the sheriff. The arrival of colour in 1969 seemed to detach the soap definitively from its roots in the new wave northern social realism of the early 1960s. John Betjeman, another fan, saw it as Manchester's version of the most comic and warmest of Dickens's novels, *Pickwick Papers*.[28]

Actual streets like Coronation Street were already being demolished in great numbers when the programme began: a common sight in Salford was an entire row of houses marked with an X, under sentence of demolition. Granada soon had to build its own outdoor set, there being no suitable streets left near its Deansgate studios in which to film exteriors. The street used in the credits, Archie Street, nicknamed 'Coronarchie Street' by locals, was condemned in 1967 in Salford's last great slum clearance scheme and finally demolished in 1971, when Bernard Youens and Jean Alexander, who played Stan and Hilda Ogden, went along to pay their last respects, in character.[29]

Coronation Street was now an intertextual, mythic entity, having more relationship to the paintings of L. S. Lowry, the street photography of Shirley Baker or the plays of Shelagh Delaney than to any real Salford – although the famous opening credits, of huddled rooftops with television aerials, trees in blossom and a cat looking for a shady spot under a wall, were less sombre than these earlier visual representations. A diligent curator of this kind of self-conscious 'urban pastoral' (to borrow the historian Chris Waters's term) was Steven Morrissey, brought up in the *Coronation Street*-style terraces of Stretford and Moss Side, who would, as a teenager, unsuccessfully submit script ideas for the soap to Granada and who, in 1985, interviewed Pat Phoenix for the zeitgeisty style magazine *Blitz* as well as ensuring that she adorned the cover of the Smiths' single 'Shakespeare's Sister'.[30]

Even if the cobbled Coronation Street was now a parallel universe without a real world template, viewers still imagined it as a definite place, with so many tangled relationships and ancestral antagonisms that the serial had to employ its own full-time historian, Daran Little, to monitor the elongated backstories and maintain internal consistency. In the seemingly ephemeral genre of soap opera, *Coronation Street* had developed its own sophisticated rituals of commemoration. At the Granada Studios Tour in Deansgate, Manchester, which attracted 5,000 visitors a day, the main attraction was the *Street*'s outdoor set, built from bricks and tiles salvaged from Manchester demolitions. Tourists could walk along the cobbles, touch Jack and Vera Duckworth's ill-advised stone cladding at number 9 and look through the houses' letter boxes or windows where, disappointingly, they saw only a long empty space full of studio equipment, with an upper gallery for actors to appear at bedroom windows.

Kingsley Amis, who had always believed that art should craft a self-contained world of conscious artifice with only a glancing relationship to 'reality', was a natural fan of *Coronation Street*. One can imagine his response to the increasingly insistent criticism, voiced in a 1991 Channel 4 documentary, *J'Accuse ... Coronation Street* and subsequent comments by the chair of the Broadcasting Standards Council, Lord Rees-Mogg, that the *Street* failed to represent the multi-ethnic makeup of the real Salford.[31] While its BBC rival *East-Enders* engaged tenaciously with social issues like racism or homophobia, the *Street* spun its own alternative reality out of dry wit and near caricature.

'I never allowed the programme to become a platform for debate, moral or otherwise,' said the serial's long-running producer Bill Podmore who, although he had retired in 1988, had established this idea of the street as a kind of dramatic sitcom. 'I regard that as the province of documentary, not light entertainment.' In the early 1990s, these sitcom characters were in their prime: the brassy pub landlady

Bet Lynch, the winsome shop assistant Mavis Barlow, the squabbling but strangely uxorious Duckworths – Pickwickian characters all, but with a touching vulnerability. This period also saw the introduction of a character who would last only a few years but linger long in the memory: the barmaid Raquel Wolstenhulme, her film-star first name contrasting eloquently with her down-to-earth northern surname. Played with great subtlety and tenderness by Sarah Lancashire, she had, wrote Nancy Banks-Smith, an 'almost saintly idiocy' and was 'a rare creation, lovely, funny and incapable of unkindness … a wicket-splintering spin on dumb blondeness'.[32] Amis would surely have loved her.

With the TV volume turned up high, he would cheer the best bits of *Coronation Street* ('Bloody marvellous – you wouldn't want to change a word of that!') and boo his least favourite characters ('Get her off – I can't stand the sight of her!'). The poet and critic Neil Powell suggests that Amis's later novels betray the effects of his nights in front of the TV. *The Folks that Live on the Hill* (1988), for instance, feels like a soap opera, with subplots featuring minor characters interrupting the main action, and its denouement bringing the whole cast together in a pub not unlike the Rovers Return. Some of his later works, such as the novel *Difficulties with Girls* (1989), and his posthumously published guide to English usage, *The King's English* (1997), refer explicitly to *Coronation Street*. After primetime, Amis retired to bed reluctantly with a book, avoiding the late night arts programmes with their talking heads and 'crappy opinions'.[33]

The sociologist Zygmunt Bauman called them 'life strategies' or 'ingenious techniques of exorcism': the self-deluding subterfuges we use to deny the reality of our own mortality. The trick was to make 'the whole of life into a game of bridge-crossing … so that no bridge seems to loom ominously as the "ultimate" one … Nothing seems to vanish forever, "for good" – so that it cannot reappear again.'[34] It is doubtful that Amis would have had much patience with Bauman's speculative postmodern sociology, but he was certainly a man full of phobias and existential fears and this seems a fairly convincing explanation, at least in part, for his fondness for soap operas.

While Amis was watching *Coronation Street* in Regents Park Road, the poet Stephen Spender, his mobility curtailed after an accident while running for a bus, had become a devotee of *Neighbours*. At his home in St John's Wood, Spender also enjoyed a Newcastle-set crime series called *Spender*, about a plain-clothes detective with unorthodox methods. 'He seems to spend most of his time watching youths, who turn out to be drug addicts, pee in men's rooms where they do most of their illicit business,' Spender explained in a letter to the poet Alan Ross. 'He gets his kicks out of arresting them. It is quite well written and funny to those who share his name.'[35] A lifelong champion of modernism who was at the heart of the literary establishment, Spender seems a more unlikely fan than Amis of soap operas and crime dramas. 'The critical faculty is somehow suspended when people watch it,' reflected his son-in-law Barry Humphries on Spender's *Neighbours* habit. But perhaps it is not so unlikely. Spender, like Amis, was the right age to be watching television – older, less mobile people being, in the broadcasters' language, more 'available to view'. He was not alone in finding himself slowly and semi-accidentally drawn into television's formerly unfathomable rituals.

Soap operas now took up more of the viewing week. Several of the BFI's television diarists worried that their favourite programme would be axed if Thames lost out in the franchise auction of 1992,[36] but while Thames did lose the franchise, the new owner, Carlton, carried on commissioning *The Bill* and indeed switched it to three nights a week – not surprisingly, since it was so popular. By 1994, all three major British soaps, *Coronation Street*, *Brookside* and *East-Enders*, had also increased their number of episodes to three a week. Many people had feared that the auctioning off of ITV franchises, mostly to the highest bidder, would plunge the channel downmarket. But the most immediate effect seemed to be to increase the importance in the schedules of soap operas and popular dramas like *Inspector Morse, Soldier, Soldier* and *London's Burning* – the kind of uncomplicated lower-middlebrow consumerism that Kingsley Amis longed for.

And yet television was changing in subtler ways. Ratings were now an ever more precious currency, the data gathered silently from a few thousand homes by an unheard telephone call from a mainframe computer at the dead of night, and processed in time to deliver the rough viewing figures, or 'unconsolidated overnights', to the office computers of channel controllers the next morning before being emailed to their underlings. The new BBC director general, John Birt, was an advocate of the 'consumer-facing' ethos that had been transforming the public sector since the Thatcher era. For years the BBC's Broadcasting Research Department had been a separate fiefdom with little direct influence on programme making. Now the central planning and strategy units undertook audience research themselves and it began to shape commissioning and scheduling.

One type of research acquired its own demonology: the 'focus group', a cross-section of about eight people, invited to comment on existing or potential programmes in return for a small fee and some free pizza, perhaps with TV executives watching via a two-way mirror. The BBC's use of focus groups was partly political: a seemingly neutral, democratic research tool also embraced by political parties, they reinforced the BBC's sense of being answerable to its customers. But by the end of the millennium, the media had seized upon focus groups as a stick with which to beat both the New Labour government and the BBC. The focus group was now so associated with unimaginative conformity that the Rover 75 advertised itself with the slogan 'rejected by focus groups', although, as it turned out, it was also rejected by car buyers. When Michael Wearing resigned as the BBC's head of drama serials in 1998, he said that focus groups were used 'to placate a political loathing of anything in the arena of public service' and 'patronisingly reduce the audience to the role of passive consumer'. Terry Wogan described 'focus group' as 'the two most devalued words in television and the sooner they get away from them the better'.[37]

The focus group became something of a bogeyman, when it was really just part of a general cultural shift at the BBC to more management-level decision making. It is hard to calibrate exactly what effect focus groups had on the programmes being shown, since the results were rarely made public. When she looked at focus groups while doing fieldwork at the BBC in the mid 1990s, the anthropologist Georgina Born found that 'the quality of audience insights delivered was often achingly banal'.[38] Anticipating what viewers wanted seemed to remain a hazardous and unpredictable business, because people do not always behave like the carefully deliberating consumers that focus groups assume them to be, perhaps especially when they are sitting in front of a television. Since it is difficult to talk about the experience of watching TV hypothetically, and viewers do not necessarily know what they will like until they have seen it, many market-tested programmes remained curious failures. Others were equally curious successes.

In August 1994, BBC1 scheduled *Animal Hospital Week*, a programme set in an RSPCA hospital in Holloway, over a whole week. Its unlikely choice of host was the artist and children's entertainer Rolf Harris, who had been a familiar face on British television for more than forty years, but whose career appeared to be over after his cartoon show was dropped by ITV in 1993. On the Wednesday night, a young man brought in his father's alsatian, Floss, who could only walk a few steps before his back legs collapsed. When he was told that the dog had to be put down, the man buried his head in Harris's shoulder, and both of them cried. This seems to have had a dramatic impact on viewers, for the next day the show's audience rose sharply to 9.5 million.[39]

The Oxford English don Peter Conrad, after watching a pet owner being told his cat's cancer was inoperable, concluded that the programme was 'as gut-wrenching as *King Lear*'. When the new series of *Animal Hospital* in January 1995 was pitted against *The Bill* on Thursday evenings, it got over 11 million viewers against this seemingly impregnable megalith of the schedules. Viewers found themselves caring about the fate of a chicken found wandering lost around

Camden or a dog with a stick caught in its throat. Some BFI diarists insisted their pets enjoyed watching it as well.[40]

Animal Hospital ensured the success of a new type of programme: the docusoap. Competition for ratings and declining budgets meant that in-house and independent producers, vying for the same primetime slots, swooped eagerly on successful, repeatable formulae. An unexpected hit like *Animal Hospital* could produce a television scheduling version of chaos theory, creating a domino effect that transformed the whole of primetime. Here was a new form of documentary that was cheap, because new digital editing suites meant that long observational shooting could be easily stitched into a narrative, and which the BBC could even loosely define as educational. The commercialisation of broadcasting, rather than making television producers more responsive to the needs of viewer-consumers, had simply created a different set of mostly unintended market conditions.

Kingsley Amis's hated form of the documentary, which he associated with well-meaning liberalism that talked down to viewers, had been in long-term decline and most TV people thought it would be a victim of the new market. No documentary of any sort had made it into the top 100-rated television programmes of 1993.[41] But now the documentary was reborn as a soap opera of the mundane. In each episode of *Airport*, a programme about Heathrow, different aspects of airport logistics were parsed into narrative strands: four Norwegian women lost their luggage and were refusing to fly on to Oslo until BA found it; the airport photographer waited in vain to take a picture of a supermodel; and a man dressed in a Womble costume found that he could not travel unidentified for security reasons.

While *Airport* made a celebrity of a camply officious Ground Services Manager for Aeroflot called Jeremy Spake, *Driving School* brought national renown to a Welsh cleaner, Maureen Rees, who had to write 'L' and 'R' on her hands because she could not tell left from right, and whose most memorable moment was running over her husband's foot. The peaktime schedules, once full of quizzes and sitcoms, were colonised by a new genre, 'reality TV'. Few had predicted its popularity, and it is unlikely any focus group had ever expressed a preference for it.

'Personally I call her Delia, so totally has she taken on the nature of a family friend,' wrote Joan Bakewell in 1980, 'bright and neat, competent without being bossy, friendly without being familiar.' The woman with the fairly uncommon forename and the most common English surname was perhaps fated to be known by the former. By 2001, 'Delia' had entered Collins dictionary as both a noun and verb, from 'Delia dish' to 'doing a Delia'. Some of the hundreds of usages found in the Collins Bank of English included 'the anti-Delia, anti-Aga backlash' and a list of middle-class British institutions such as 'the Dordogne, dishwashers, Delia Smith and dyslexia'.[42] By then, Delia had earned her first-name fame for her magically galvanising effect on Britain's amateur cooks.

Television cookery programmes had long provided vivid proof of the power of television to transform daily habits. This was partly a symptom of culinary ignorance: in a country with more cooking expertise passed down through families, like France or Italy, food programmes did not wield so great an influence. In the early postwar years, the TV chef Philip Harben, cooking on a basic enamelled four-ring stove, probably had a greater impact on culinary standards than Elizabeth David, who did not start to be published in Penguin paperback until 1955 and who, well into the 1960s, was mainly a north London middle-class taste. Raymond Postgate, who in 1949 had proposed a Society for the Prevention of Cruelty to Food and in 1951 published the first *Good Food Guide*, praised Harben as 'one of the major influences towards good living in this country, and there is no country which needs it more'.[43]

In 1953, Harben had shown a still austere Britain how to cook the tail of the Dublin Bay Prawn, which he named 'scampi'. The next day fishmongers were swamped with orders they could not meet and soon many kinds of shellfish were being doused in batter and served as scampi in restaurants. Scottish fishing communities welcomed this example of television's mass influence even before they had sight of a TV screen themselves. By the early 1960s, scampi, mostly bound for the Midlands and the south, accounted for a third of the total catch at the fishing port of Ayr on the Firth of Clyde. Then, in 1974, Scottish fishermen blamed Fanny Cradock for a precipitous decline in the demand for prawns after she showed how to make ersatz scampi using monkfish. Cradock had replaced Harben as the BBC's main television chef in the mid 1950s, when he fell foul of the corporation by agreeing to sponsor a frying pan.[44]

When Peter Bazalgette began producing the programme *Food and Drink* in the early 1980s he noticed that large numbers of viewers were asking for the recipes. He realised that, because TV programmes moved along too quickly for the viewer to write things down, it created an inbuilt demand for information in more tangible form. And so he deployed the BBC's teletext service, Ceefax. Ceefax ('see facts') had been conceived in a Brompton Road pub in 1969 when BBC engineers met to work out how text could be hidden in the spare lines of the analogue TV signal to provide subtitles for deaf people. But Ceefax's founding editor, Colin McIntyre, saw that it could also be used to provide news and information, and accommodate 'the viewer who doesn't check his Pools till Tuesday, the man who wants waterways information, or the film fan who wants the details of a cast list'.

In the 1970s, Ceefax had few viewers, because the decoders needed to show it on television sets were expensive. But as Bazalgette took over on *Food and Drink*, Ceefax was just starting to be included as standard on newly bought televisions, and he used it to create another platform for the programme. In 1985, after *Food and Drink* demonstrated an apple corer and put the details on Ceefax, two factories had to be opened in the Far East for British orders. The next year, some of the ingredients for the programme's Oxtail soup recipe had to be shipped from Holland to meet demand.[45]

Ceefax, which simply involved teams of people typing information on to a screen, looked primitive even in the 1980s. McIntyre described it as a 'string and sealing wax operation', 'printed radio' and a 'bicycle in the technological age', and it was known in-house as the 'printed bicycle'.[46] But Bazalgette's use of it was a novel form of interaction with viewers, giving his programme a life beyond the broadcast itself. *Food and Drink* went on to pioneer the trend for television programmes to spawn commercial offshoots, such as BBC *Good Food* magazine, launched in 1989, and the BBC Good Food Show at the Birmingham National Exhibition Centre, first held in 1991. The show's centrepiece was the British Gas Celebrity Theatre, where television chefs such as Gary Rhodes and Michael Barry performed, before moving to the book stand to sign copies of their books. A chef might still have got into trouble with the BBC for sponsoring a frying pan. But there were more creative, roundabout ways of selling products and lifestyles to viewers than a straight pitch on the new shopping channels – especially on commercial and satellite television, where a general mood of celebratory consumerism led nicely into the ad breaks.

On 6 December 1990, in an edition of *Delia Smith's Christmas*, Smith showed viewers a recipe for chocolate truffle torte and pointed out that its key ingredient, liquid glucose, was available from chemists. Within days, Boots' West Country warehouse was emptied of its stock and two weeks later there was no liquid glucose to be had throughout Europe. According to an Aberdeen pharmacy, Charles Michie and Sons, Scottish chemists were caught 'with their breeks down'.[47] By the mid 1990s, Smith's ability to empty shelves simply by mentioning types of pie-topping lattice cutter or lemon squeezer was well known, but this still left the country ill-prepared for the great cranberry shortage of 1995. A previously minor berry known mainly for its medicinal qualities (until 1991, cranberry juice was available on NHS prescription to cure cystitis), its status was transformed by Smith's copious use of it in her series *Delia's Winter Collection*, which unhappily coincided with a poor cranberry harvest in America. 'It is murder,' said one beleaguered importer. 'We *must* have cranberries.'[48]

Television's effect on its viewers is endlessly conjectured but, since it takes place in millions of individual living rooms, remains essentially invisible and immeasurable. The Delia effect, by contrast, seemed to show this effect vividly, giving the workings of mass consumer society a narrative simplicity, a clear sense of cause and effect. Four or five million viewers watched a programme on BBC2 and the next day supermarket shelves emptied. In his 1999 book *Living on Thin Air*, the former New Labour adviser Charles Leadbeater argued that Delia Smith 'symbolises a vital aspect of the New Economy: the power of knowledge'. Leadbeater saw the boom in cookery books and TV chefs as 'a worldwide upgrade of the software which runs our kitchens', introducing us to food from around the world in a way that proved that 'globalisation is good for our palates'. And while a chocolate cake could only be eaten once, he pointed out, the same chocolate cake recipe could be endlessly replicated without anyone being worse off – rather like the new weightless economy which would be driven by the exchange of ideas and information. Leadbeater called it 'the thin-air business'.[49]

But there was nothing very ethereal or weightless about the Delia effect. With the relaxation of planning laws in the 1980s, supermarkets had grown in number and power, and the big stores learned to react quickly to trends through just-in-time distribution networks, tracking purchases through loyalty cards and till receipts and even Met Office data, which told them when to stock up on ice cream and salad, or hot water bottles and de-icer. *Delia's Winter Collection* tied in with a book of the same name which included a list of Sainsbury's stores at the back, and Smith's office warned supermarkets in advance to stock up on key ingredients. The publication of this book coincided with the withdrawal of major publishers from the 95-year-old Net Book Agreement, the arrangement by which all books were sold at full price, which had somehow managed to survive into the post-Thatcher era because publishers argued that mark-ups on bestsellers allowed them to subsidise loss makers. The collapse of the agreement allowed the big book chains and supermarkets to offer selected titles at huge discounts, and a new publishing phenomenon was born, the hardback bestseller, usually with a television tie-in. Between 1960 and 1995, Elizabeth David's most successful book, *French Provincial*

Cooking, sold just under 250,000 copies; by the end of 1995, *Delia's Winter Collection* had sold a million.[50]

Why Smith had such a devastating impact on supermarket shelves compared to other TV chefs is less clear. When she returned to television in 1990 after a decade-long career break writing Catholic devotional books, she retained a certain didacticism, a residue of the old cookery demos that used to be on television and which sat somewhat oddly with the style of the newer, hyperactive TV cooks like Keith Floyd and Gary Rhodes. Unlike them, Smith never ate her own food on camera: even when showing viewers how to eat spaghetti, by curling a single strand round a fork, she refused to lift it to her mouth. Writing in the *Times Literary Supplement*, a Cambridge English don, Eric Griffiths, related her style to Hegel's theory of the aesthetic, in which 'smell, taste, and touch remain excluded from the enjoyment of art'. In place of sensuous immediacy, Delia had 'regal self-control', a 'dowdy reticence' and an 'over-arching and point-instant grip of time'. 'Hegel would, on the whole, have approved of Delia Smith,' concluded Griffiths, 'and settled back after a day of wrestling with the Absolute to watch eagerly what she might think to do next with a cranberry.'[51]

One of the constants of postwar British cultural history is that each age persuades itself that it is becoming more informal and less elitist than the last. In the late 1990s the sociologist Alan Warde, drawing on the experiences of a thousand diners in London, Bristol and Preston, found that most of them rejected the highly structured, traditional model of the dinner party but quietly improvised on it, so there were still clear but silent rules at work, such as having no more than about eight people, or using cutlery and crockery reserved for such occasions.[52] When informality has its own tacit conventions like this, it is easy to imagine Smith playing an anxiety-alleviating role. Her recipes were clear, easy to follow, on-trend but not intimidatingly so and, with her naming of 'star' ingredients, she steered the average cook through the daunting superfluity of consumer choices.

'People could hardly go out to dinner with friends,' claims Smith's biographer, 'without being served up Delia's mixed-leaf Caesar salad, her chicken basque or the fromage frais cheesecake with strawberry sauce.'[53] But how many fromage frais cheesecakes or rillettes of duck with confit of cranberries were actually eaten at 1990s dinner parties remains unknown, because what people do around dinner tables leaves as little trace as what they do in front of their televisions.

'Our dreamscapes have become domesticated – we now look for fantasy and escape in our back gardens and on our dinner tables,' wrote Andy Medhurst in *Sight and Sound* in 1999. 'These are programmes where we're invited to prioritise home life, be knowledgeable consumers (but never seriously question the ethics of consumption), temper our daydreams with the acknowledgement that only hard work really delivers, learn just a little from feminism and pretend that only the middle classes exist.'[54] Medhurst was writing about a new type of lifestyle television, the makeover show, in which experts did up homes or gardens over a frenetic couple of days and showed them to the surprised and usually (but not always) pleased occupants.

'I love that *Changing Rooms*. I get loads of ideas from it – I can't wait to get out of here and decorate my own place,' said Tim, an inmate in a Midlands prison who described himself as a 'Christian heavy metal biker', and who sported a leather jacket over his prison uniform and numerous tattoos and piercings. 'I definitely want deep red, textured walls … I like Laurence Llewelyn-Bowen. I'd like to *be* Laurence Llewelyn-Bowen. I know he's a bit camp, but I'd model myself on him. He's cultured, he's stylish. Classy without being boring. That's how I want to be.' Llewelyn-Bowen was the *Changing Rooms* designer who, dressed in leather trousers, frock coats and jewel-toned shirts with outsized cuffs, dismissed the Victorian 'design-o-saurs' who had policed interior decoration and stopped ordinary people from expressing their tastes.[55]

While he was certainly well known, Llewelyn-Bowen's influence on domestic design was probably minimal compared to the BBC's

DIY expert of the 1950s and 1960s, Barry Bucknell, a home improvement modernist who recommended covering period features such as fireplaces and dust-collecting panelled doors with fibreboard. Bucknell received up to 35,000 letters a week from viewers and employed ten secretaries to sort through it. The eclectic, post-Bucknell 'retro' styles seen on *Changing Rooms* predated the programme. B&Q, the historian Raphael Samuel noted in 1994, was now full of 'archaicizing aids' like staircase spindles, damask wallpapers and ceramic tiles.[56] Llewelyn-Bowen was most renowned, in fact, for making contestants burst into tears with his garish designs. Favourite *Changing Room* techniques, such as stencilling, the rag-rolling of unsightly walls and the use of MDF (Medium Density Fibreboard) for architectural moulding effects, were employed so often on the programme that it probably hastened their journey into démodé visual clichés.

Gardeners, by nature people who are happy to wait for flowers to bloom and trees to mature, seemed particularly unconvinced by makeover programmes. Writing in *The Garden*, the Royal Horticultural Society's journal, gardening experts often criticised makeover shows, and readers' letters suggested that their opinions were widely shared. The *Gardeners' Question Time* presenter, Eric Robson, argued that celebrated gardens such as Sissinghurst and Stourhead would not now exist if our ancestors had behaved as we did, covering our little plots of land with container-grown shrubs, low-maintenance perennials and decking, which would 'soon be to gardens what avocado suites are to bathrooms'. Alan Titchmarsh, the presenter of *Ground Force*, at which Robson's animus was directed, countered that it aimed to 'appeal to and inspire those who would never dream of watching *Gardeners' World* and to whom the garden was a foreign country whose language and customs were beyond comprehension'.[57]

But gardening programmes had long stood for a different kind of populism, which believed in imparting esoteric knowledge to anyone prepared to make use of it by expending patient effort. Television gardeners had pioneered an unaffected, intimate way of talking to viewers. The owner of a hard mongrel rural accent forged mostly in the south Midlands, Percy Thrower could never work from a script so he always ad libbed, believing that the plant would tell him what it wanted him to say. Perhaps because viewers thus found it easy to identify with them, Thrower and other *Gardeners' World* presenters profoundly affected gardening trends. An unapologetic user of paraquat and DDT, Thrower curated the age of lawns and rosebeds; his successor, Geoff Hamilton, a jeans-wearing, muddy-kneed socialist and environmentalist, introduced them to the organic era, building his own garden in Rutland from wasteland, happily recycling egg cartons for seedlings and polythene from the dry cleaners for the greenhouse. Habit-loving gardener-viewers trusted these presenters and were suspicious of change. 'When you took over *Gardeners' World* from Geoff Hamilton my heart sank,' wrote a viewer to Alan Titchmarsh after his sudden assumption of presenting duties when Hamilton died of a heart attack in the summer of 1996. 'I have been watching you closely over the past few months. You'll do.'[58]

Ground Force seemed at first to have an equally striking effect on gardening trends. When Robert Pearcey, a painter and decorator, was convicted of stealing pebbles from the beach at Budleigh Salterton in Devon, the local mayor blamed *Ground Force* and its love of dry gardens full of shingle and stones. At Chesil Beach in Dorset, gardeners were sneaking on to the beach at night in search of plunder, armed with shovels and wheelbarrows. So many grey shale pebbles were taken from a shingle ridge at Crackington Haven on the Cornish coast that the cliff was in danger of collapse.

But the theft of stones to make rockeries had preceded *Ground Force*. Geoff Hamilton, to dissuade plunderers among *Gardeners' World* viewers, had shown them how to make rocks out of an artificial aggregate called Hypertufa. And it was *Gardeners' World*, rather than *Ground Force*, which had started the decking boom of the late 1990s. When Titchmarsh laid decking in his Hampshire garden on *Gardeners' World* (which he had christened Barleywood just before the copy deadline for the *Radio Times* that listed his first programme as presenter), and stained it deep blue, Cuprinol launched a preservative called 'Barleywood Blue' which became the bestselling colour for trellises and fences. The spread of decking in back gardens, so prevalent by the early 2000s that its stained wood effects could be seen from the new satellite imaging sites like Google Earth, was just part of a more general move, evident since the rise of the garden centre in the 1960s, towards seeing gardens as outdoor living rooms.[59]

In his next book, *Up the Down Escalator* (2002), Charles Leadbeater attributed the mushrooming of makeover programmes to a cult of 'inner escape' and a 'retreat into domesticity as an antidote to innovation and change'. 'The more our working lives seem to involve screens, computers and ephemera, the more we seem to like gardens, changing our rooms and cooking,' he wrote. 'Or perhaps it is simply that we like the *idea* of doing all these things and so we celebrate the possibility with glossy television programmes.'[60] Or perhaps lifestyle TV was not really about 'us' at all. Post-Thatcherite political culture tended to see the public as a single, apolitical entity – a mostly homogeneous, property-owning middle class, made up of 'ordinary taxpayers' and 'hard-working families'. In this quasi-mythical middle England, pop-psephological caricatures such as 'Mondeo Man', 'Worcester Woman' and 'Pebbledash People' lived. Here, uncomfortable divisions of class and wealth could be skirted over with more nebulous allusions to leisure and lifestyle. This was just the kind of England (and, occasionally, the rest of Britain) featured in makeover shows. It was suburban, family-focused and, above all, homeowning – since there wasn't much point making over a rented flat or bedsit.

Mostly, though, these makeover shows were about the economics of television. They were partly a product of new technology, for cameras had become smaller and lighter and it was now easy to film in living rooms and small gardens. Compressing activities that normally took much longer into neat little half hours of mild tension, false jeopardy and instant reaction, they also fitted a world in which more and more half-hour scheduling slots had to be filled cheaply. Medhurst called it 'the snowballing daytime-isation of evening TV'.[61] With more pressure to create replicable formats, the cheap, formulaic programmes that had filled the daytime schedules since the late 1980s were colonising primetime. These programmes then had an afterlife of repeats in the daytime, or on satellite and cable channels devoting themselves

solely to 'lifestyle', like the Carlton Food Network, Granada Sky Food
& Wine Channel or UK Living. Here, from breakfast into the middle
of the night, you could watch people cooking dinner, doing up spare
bedrooms and installing garden water features.

In the *Radio Times* in May 1996, Polly Toynbee derided the content of
daytime television. There was now, she pointed out, a varied audience
during the day: more people putting in shift hours or working from
home, early retired people and, with the mass expansion of higher
education in the 1990s, a new army of students with flexible hours.
But this was not reflected in daytime TV. 'Most of it looks cheap and
designed for no one in particular – perhaps some computerised cal-
culation of the lowest common denominator,' she complained. 'It
is a tepid, dishwater soup, without character or flavour, inhabiting
some cardboard world 20 years out of date, in some imaginary middle
suburbia.'

Toynbee conceded that were some exceptions, like the 'awful but
magic insanity' of *Supermarket Sweep*, an unrepentant paean to consumerism in which contestants in colour-coded sweatshirts pelted up
and down the aisles trying to cram food into their trolleys. It had
an audience of more than 3 million and was, according to the *New
Musical Express*, causing an epidemic of lateness for morning lectures among students. But mainly, Toynbee concluded, daytime television was 'Stupidvision – where most of the presenters look like they
have to pretend to be stupid because they think their audience is ... It
talks to the vacuum cleaner and the washing machine and the microwave, without much contact with the human brain.'[62]

Daytime viewers, at least those who expressed an opinion, agreed.
Toynbee invited *Radio Times* readers to send in their dream schedules
to replace the 'weary grunge of the past' and they wrote in asking
for repeats of classic dramas like *Poldark*, prestige documentary
series like *Civilisation* and the *Ascent of Man*, and lessons in foreign

languages, life drawing or how to play a musical instrument. 'Women and men felt that daytime TV was aimed at an imaginary housewife whom they had never met,' concluded the BFI's study based on the submissions of its television diarists. They felt guilty, 'like adulterers', about watching TV in the daytime. Young people in particular thought it was 'trivial and insulting to women' and men were embarrassed at watching what they thought was a female 'daytime ghetto'.[63]

The BFI study found that viewers were more likely to treat television as moving wallpaper when they were lonely or depressed. 'TV ... gives an air of colour, light, movement in the corner of the room which I can ignore at will but keeps at bay the very oppressive feeling of being alone,' wrote an elderly widow, living in remote rural Lancashire, for her television diary. An elderly man, also living alone, found television a comfort when feeling vulnerable or ill, and when he was particularly anxious he liked to watch the children's programme *Postman Pat*. During the period of the study, a teacher got divorced, lost her job and had a breakdown. She went from carefully choosing what to watch to sitting numbly in front of Saturday night shows like *Blind Date* and *Beadle's About*. The guilt people felt at relying on television as a 'visual anti-depressant' was exacerbated because so many of the programmes were now about cooking, gardening and decorating, activities undertaken vicariously through the TV screen. 'There is something unbearably poignant,' reflected Auberon Waugh, 'in the BBC's claim that 3.5 million people regularly watch a low-budget mid-afternoon cookery programme called *Ready Steady Cook*.'[64]

In January 1996, suffering from inoperable bowel cancer and coming stoically towards the end of his life, George Mackay Brown was housebound, with little energy even to read, and found himself watching great tranches of daytime television for the first time. 'On TV, there is a group of Australian families caught up in some perpetual string of dramas,' he told regular readers of his column in the *Orcadian*. 'It is called *Neighbours* and is very popular with young people. I'm glad that, in our little neighbourhood in Stromness, there are few of these heart-wrenchings and deceptions, rages and reconciliations ... I don't intend to watch it more ... The dialogue is not exactly spellbinding, nor is the Australian accent the most beautiful on this earth.'

Without identifying them by name, Brown also seems to have watched the high-octane, confessional American talk shows presented by Ricki Lake and Oprah Winfrey and their homegrown ITV equivalent Vanessa Feltz. Their culture of therapeutic excess and emotional incontinence must have seemed quite alien to this bard of Orkney. They discussed, he noted, 'things which most people hide away in their heart's core … out it all comes, and the audience loves it, and now and then somebody stands up and either upbraids or congratulates the person in the hot seat. And if the show seems to be flagging, there is a lady who keeps it going the way a conductor handles a choir or an orchestra; and the lurid pot begins to bubble again.'

It is sad to imagine Brown, the great chronicler of the silent weight of ritual, tradition and landscape, who believed that 'all relationships and all words end in solitude and in silence', ending his life watching shouty programmes with titles like 'I'm terrified of my own child' and 'Help! I married a love rat.' A small mercy is that the genre's exploitative nadir, *The Jerry Springer Show*, was at that time confined to the UK Living channel and Brown is unlikely to have seen it. 'I hope I won't be watching afternoon TV for very much longer,' he signed off his column.[65] He died in April, just three months later.

As television filled the schedules with the type of shows that Toynbee called Stupidvision, the end of the millennium saw a revival of the cultural jeremiads against television that had last enjoyed a serious vogue in the late 1950s. In 1996, David Burke, a New Jerseyite computer programmer living in Brighton, launched the British branch of the anti-television organisation, White Dot. While modern TVs switched off with what Thomas Hardy called 'an eyelid's soundless blink', White Dot was named after the tendency for older televisions to keep firing electrons after they were turned off, until the cathode ray cooled down, so they arrived all at once at the centre of the screen, creating a white dot that shrank into nothingness like a distant, imploding star.

White Dot's ambitious aim was to reduce all televisions to dead screens. Burke stood on a broken television set one morning near Westminster Abbey in front of a sign saying 'Get A Life' and read out an open letter to Prince Charles asking him not to televise his coronation, when it came round. Burke felt that, since his mother's coronation in 1953 had marked the start of widespread television viewing in the UK, a TV-free crowning of King Charles would have a nice historical symmetry. A few days later, Prince Charles's office replied, politely refusing his request.[66] Undaunted, White Dot organised an annual Turn Off TV Week and ritual events called *zócalo* (Mexican for 'town square') in which people sat outside their houses and chatted to each other instead of watching TV. It also promoted a universal remote control for turning off televisions in pubs. White Dot had some affinities with the Idler movement, associated with an eponymous magazine that advocated a life defined by neither the Protestant work ethic nor passive consumption. Tom Hodgkinson, editor and co-founder of *The Idler*, would later rail against the pernicious passivity engendered by television, banning it for his children and preferring to spend his own evenings chopping wood, brewing beer and beekeeping. Among the middle classes there was a revival of camping, festivals and other outdoor activities, an ethic of living an active life rather than a substitute one in front of the television.

The journalist Peter Hitchens thought the rot had set in with colour TV, which made even bad programmes look so enticing that the best storyteller could not compete with them. The unspoken secret of the 1990s was that television had become 'a free national child-minding service', he complained, as adults shamelessly used 'the flickering, braying, never-silent device to mesmerise the next generation, so that they can get on with their grown-up lives'. This was how millions of parents had found out about the death of Princess Diana, as their children switched on their 'electronic dripfeeds' one Sunday in August 1997 and, instead of cartoon wallpaper, got the news. 'To leave a child unsupervised in front of a television set,' Hitchens concluded, 'is no less dangerous than giving it neat gin, or putting it within reach of narcotics.'[67]

As in the late 1950s, the anti-television voices of the late 1990s crossed the political spectrum, for TV could be blamed both for the breakdown of family life and for selling the capitalist waking dream of aspirational consumerism. At a time when Prozac and other anti-depressants were raising awareness of mental illness as a medical condition, the psychotherapist Oliver James saw TV as the prime culprit in creating what he called 'the low serotonin society'. By overpromoting glamour and wealth and lowering reserves of self-esteem over the last half century, he believed, television had been 'the engine-room' of a 'psychic holocaust'.[68]

Around the time that George Mackay Brown was becoming belatedly acquainted with daytime TV, a small community in the Yorkshire Wolds, about twenty miles east of York, achieved brief renown for not watching TV at all. Thixendale, an isolated village of barely a hundred souls in the shelter of the six dales from which it took its name, was revealed by several newspapers to be the land that had managed to escape television for sixty years. The village lay in a steep-sided, dry valley reached by narrow country lanes and approached from every angle by chalk escarpments. Thixendale had long been used to being cut off by snow as these lanes became impassable in winter, and as television spread it found itself cut off from television as well. Unlike the harder rocks of the Yorkshire dales and moors, Wolds chalk is soft, so when glacial meltwater rushed across it at the end of the last ice age it created rounded peaks and deep valleys that the novelist Winifred Holtby called 'fold upon fold of the encircling hills, piled rich and golden beneath a tranquil sky'.[69] It also created a Bermuda triangle for the TV signal which now defended Thixendalians from *Supermarket Sweep* and *Ready Steady Cook*.

In the 1970s, one side of the main street got blurry BBC signals via a communal aerial and the odd ghostly apparition of ITV appeared during electrical storms. Then, on 2 January 1985, the old 405-line signal stopped, the government being anxious to find extra frequencies for the nascent mobile phone network. This rendered the old H-shaped aerials redundant, and the village was again televisionless. In the early 1990s villagers began to be doorstepped by satellite television reps, proffering free dishes and a year's free subscription if they would sign up.

The absence of television seemed to have helped Thixendale to forge a strong community spirit, and the thirty-odd local children learned to read more quickly than their friends from other villages. Then in June 1996 Thixendale held a festival, 'Life Without TV', which showcased the villagers' skills, such as pottery, tile-making and woodwork, that had flourished without television. But the proceeds, shared with the church roof fund, were used to pay for a new £10,000 hilltop aerial. Villagers paid an annual fee towards its upkeep and received a local newsletter, *Fuzzy Lines*, updating them on reception. But one afternoon in May 1999, just as the village's children were on their way home from school, there was a lightning storm. A thunderbolt zapped the aerial of one of the houses and ran along its shared cable, burning out the entire system, including fourteen of the village's television sets. Perhaps an Old Testament God was punishing the villagers for their presumption in wanting to watch *Changing Rooms*. 'I've never been able to get a decent picture,' said Charles Brader, a local farmer to whom the thunderbolt mattered little. 'But it really doesn't make much difference. It's like opening your post. Every now and then something interesting comes along but you still forget about it two minutes later.'[70]

The story of the last televisionless village in the kingdom was a neat one, but only partly true. There were still many other isolated hamlets and villages, mostly in parts of south Wales such as Carmarthenshire and Ceredigion, or the outer Western Isles of Scotland, without a TV signal. It was part of the lore of shipping that oil tankers went through the Minch between the Outer and Inner Hebrides, rather than skirting Harris and Lewis, because it was the only way to get a decent TV reception. Receiving a TV picture in these parts involved chance and luck. The Hebridean island of Iona had one because Penry Jones, a former head of religious broadcasting at ITV and BBC, retired there and managed to get the Glengorm mast on the Isle of Mull adjusted to take account of chinks in the hills, while also persuading the council to build a communal aerial on top of the only suitable building, the public toilet.[71]

One of the worst places in Britain for reception was, perhaps surprisingly, the centre of London, because of all the tall, steel-framed buildings with metallised windows that blocked the TV signal. While Thixendalians were clubbing together for a television aerial, almost 700 residents in a block of flats on the Isle of Dogs were launching a compensation claim against the London Docklands Development Corporation and Olympia and York, developers of the 800-foot Canary Wharf tower. For three years, from 1989 to 1992, until BBC engineers took pity on them and installed a booster mast, the residents had no reception. 'I like the soaps, especially *EastEnders*, even though it is not really like life in the East End,' said one of the complainants, Rose Humphries, a widow recovering from breast cancer. 'When the picture went, I had to keep telephoning my daughter to find out what happened next.' In 1997, after a series of appeals, the case reached the highest court in the land, the House of Lords. The law lords conceded that television was 'a great distraction and relief from the circumscribed nature of the lives of aged, lonely and bedridden people'. But they did not think the deprivation of television an 'actionable nuisance', especially since, as TV signals were invisible, developers could not be expected to know of their existence before putting up a building.[72]

Watching television may still not have been enshrined in law as a basic human right. But perhaps it did not need to be, for it was now available to anyone prepared to pay for a satellite dish. By the end of the television century, geostationary TV satellites could beam down on every square foot of land in the country. There were hundreds of satellite and cable channels, and many broadcast continually from morning to night, as did ITV and BBC1. Test Card F, the once ubiquitous girl with the Alice band who appeared when there was nothing on TV, had vanished from our screens, for there was no need of a screensaver when there always something on, even if it was only pages from Ceefax in the small hours on BBC2. The cathode ray Ancient Mariner carried on talking to its viewers whatever time it was, and whether or not it had anything to say.

9

A GLIMMER ON THE DULL GREY TUBE

Hundreds of millions of people thus spend time every day flipping from one channel to the next, editing their own montages based on chance whilst looking for the news programme or game show that takes their fancy ... Ours is the cult of the electronic fragment.

Robert Hughes[1]

'I first saw television when I was in my late teens. It made my heart *pound*,' said Dennis Potter in a lecture in Edinburgh in 1993. 'Here was a medium of great power, of potentially wondrous delights, that could slice through all the tedious hierarchies of the printed word and help to emancipate us from many of the stifling tyrannies of class and status and gutter-press ignorance.' Born in 1935, Potter was brought up in Berry Hill, a coalmining village in the Forest of Dean, which did not receive television until the opening of the Wenvoe transmitter in 1952, and so he came of age just as it was emerging as a mass domestic medium. His feelings about that 'little grey-faced monster squatting in our living rooms' remained conflicted throughout his life.[2]

These conflicted feelings were already evident when he began his career as a professional television watcher, a job he got through illness. After being hired as a *Daily Herald* reporter in 1961, his knees became painfully swollen, the early stages of the psoriatic arthropathy that afflicted him for the rest of his life, and he began to work from home as the paper's TV critic, watching in his Hammersmith flat and phoning in the copy late at night, his deadline meaning that he could only write about primetime shows. He was already a reluctant fan of the great popular serials and soap operas that emerged in the late 1950s to put a strain on the National Grid. His first TV column, in May 1962, a review of *Wagon Train*, revealed him to be an addict of the television western, 'the most productive folklore of all time'. And in his second, he confessed to being hooked on *Emergency – Ward 10*.[3]

A key moment in Potter's conversion into being a television writer came when he was hospitalised and wrote about the uncanny experience of watching this medical soap while being treated: 'Shimmering on the screen is the mythical, glamorised world of godlike doctors and nubile, toothpaste-smiling nurses. But the real world of bedpans and squeaking tea trolleys around one is far less like the cover of a glossy film magazine.' One of his earliest TV plays was *Emergency Ward 9* (1966), set in a seedy hospital a world away from Ward 10, where ATV's Lew Grade permitted the scriptwriters only five deaths per year.[4]

As Potter wrote his first plays, he was driven on by the knowledge that both coalminers and Oxford dons might be watching, that TV could offer a way of reaching both his parents and his university friends, unlike the middle-class medium of the theatre. Two-channel television could, he felt, satisfy his yearning for 'at least the possibility of a common culture'.[5] But he was also painfully aware that this shared televisual culture often served up undemanding pap, much of which he was forced to watch while bed-ridden in hospital. Potter had something of the lay preacher about him, making him both exasperated with and sympathetic to the viewers who used television as a soporific. 'I have often looked out of the train windows on the approaches to Paddington Station ... and at thickening dusk seen the tower blocks loom up,' he wrote in 1983 about the train journey he regularly made from his home in Ross-on-Wye to London. 'At almost every porthole in the gloomy blocks, floor upon floor upon floor, the lilac flicker of the television set comes from deep within the rooms

… Many old communities … have been broken apart, to be replaced with this flickering illusion of communality.'[6]

Potter's vision of a common culture, he came to see, had proved as elusive on television as it had in the rest of society. His own plays were mostly acclaimed but only intermittently reached large audiences. Even Potter's family thought his target audience in the Forest of Dean was puzzled and repelled by his work. 'To be quite honest, you see, I'm not awfully keen on his plays,' said Iris Hughes, Potter's former school teacher. 'They're not everybody's cup of tea, you know. And he did tend to run the forest down.' Potter grew disillusioned about his ability to reach a wide audience through television and dismissed the idea of a golden age when the whole nation was sitting around a set. Only when the TV was switched off, he reflected in his Edinburgh lecture, did it pick up 'a direct or true reflection of its viewers, subdued into a glimmer on its dull grey tube … The already aborted dream of a common culture … has long since been zapped into glistening fragments.'[7]

By the time Potter died in 1994, his vision that TV could create a common culture seemed not only dead, but unmourned. Many welcomed the end of communal viewing. 'For Huw Wheldon's generation the possibility of broadcasting attracting the whole nation to a common culture, like a village drinking from the same well, was a sustaining ideal,' said the television producer Tony Garnett in his 1996 Raymond Williams Memorial Lecture. 'It was also merely the social manifestation of the technology of the day.' Now Britain was in the vanguard of a new age of digital television, promising hundreds of new channels. Since the digital TV signal was condensed into binary code, it took up less space on the airwaves than analogue, and so consumer choice would no longer be artificially narrowed by the shortage of wavelengths. The outgoing BBC director general, John Birt, predicted that 'broadcasting will one day no longer be a shared cultural experience'.[8]

The independent television producer, Peter Bazalgette – the man behind many of the makeover shows and docusoaps that now filled the schedules, such as *Ready Steady Cook*, *Changing Rooms*, *Ground Force* and *Pet Rescue* – was a cheerleader for this new economy. Born in the year of the coronation, his memory of the common culture of the three-channel era was of a dull, monochrome world in which the screens went blank on Sundays to protect Evensong ('One wonders how many of the Pharisees who instituted such rules actually turned up for the Nunc Dimittis themselves'), well-meaning greybeards produced television plays that were really like filmed theatre, and Kenneth Clark's *Civilisation* – 'an almost mystical totem for the miserable brigade ... wheeled out frequently as an example of what we have lost' – had fewer than a million viewers. This broadcasting era, he felt, had been ruled by a BBC–ITV cartel, controlling the airwaves and imposing its tastes on the public. Now, in the new age of multiplying channels and digital recorders, viewers would be able to watch what they wanted, when they wanted.[9]

The new ideal was instant interactivity, just as it had been for those *Manchester Guardian*-reading would-be viewers in 1934 who thought that television would allow them to see distant places like Oberammergau or St Peter's Square in Rome. The twenty-first-century viewer would be able to crop the image on screen or zoom in on a detail, download films, order takeaways, check bank balances and book holidays from an armchair. In place of a common culture, the digital age offered a profusion of personal choice. A BBC advertisement for its new digital channels had Stephen Fry sitting at the dinner table with his television, asking it to 'pass the salt please, darling'.

The real viewer, however, remained inconveniently unconvinced by this brave new world of variety and abundance. So far Britons had largely resisted cable and satellite TV; it had only been a success because the minority that used these channels were willing to spend more on them than anyone had guessed, particularly for football. On 4 September 1998, with the whole nation returned from its summer holidays and back to work and school, and the BBC, Sky and ITV preparing to launch their new digital channels, most viewers were far more interested in a new ITV quiz show.

The host, Chris Tarrant, sat with the first contestant, a drama student called Graham Elwell, in the middle of a chrome and Perspex amphitheatre, and told him he was 'fifteen questions away from winning one million pounds'. Elwell sailed through the first question, correctly identifying the part of its body a woodpecker uses for pecking, for £100. As the stakes got higher, 140 tailor-made snatches of music subliminally built up tension like a film score, and intelligent light fixtures known as Vari-Lites that could change colour automatically, originally used by the rock group Genesis on their 1982 world tour, grew darker and dimmer. On £64,000, Elwell phoned a friend, his granddad, to ask him which country lay between Ghana and Benin. His granddad didn't know, and Elwell took the money.

Who Wants To Be a Millionaire? helped set the pattern for terrestrial TV's attempt to retain viewers in the digital age by returning television to the form in which Baird had first introduced it to viewers: a live, interactive spectacle. Thanks to a premium rate phone line for would-be contestants, it also turned this interactivity into a revenue stream. David Briggs, the show's co-deviser, correctly foresaw that it would encourage family members to call answers at the screen and castigate contestants for their ignorance, a phenomenon he called 'shoutability'. The first series ran every night of the week, building up momentum, and increasing the suspense by carrying answers to questions over the ad breaks. By the end of its ten-day run, two-thirds of British adults had seen it at least once.[10] A common culture that was supposed to have zapped into glistening fragments was continuing to form round the television set, as viewers found themselves unexpectedly exercised about what Kojak's first name was, or who presented the Channel 5 show *Naked Jungle* in the nude.

In the summer of 2000, a series of enigmatic billboard posters appeared throughout the country featuring nothing but a giant staring eye. The programme they promoted seemed to resemble a device for simply watching time unfold, rather like those webcams depicting mundane activities inside people's homes that now had cult followings on the internet. Almost every night for nine weeks, viewers could watch a group of young adults living in a purpose-built, space-age bungalow on Three Mills Island in east London, cut off from the world by the Bow Backs, a spaghetti junction of tributaries of the River Lea. Their every move recorded by cameras, the ten housemates talked, flirted, slept and argued over whether to put tofu on the weekly shopping list, before being voted out of the house in turn. The Geordie-accented narrator, Marcus Bentley, enhanced the sense of Beckettian uneventfulness with his lugubrious way of delivering lines like 'the housemates are in the living room, passing round the Jaffa Cakes' and 'to alleviate the boredom, Darren suggests they make farm animals out of potatoes'.

Once again, though, television demonstrated its ability to make viewers incrementally interested in the most apparently unpromising material. An engrossing drama developed involving one of the housemates, Nick Bateman, who was making up stories about himself and breaking the rules by writing notes to fellow contestants. Having uncovered his subterfuge, Bateman's housemates confronted him at a house meeting, at which he dissolved into tears and then left the house. Rumours of this showdown spread around the country via email. In high-tech offices, the only places with fast enough bandwidth to watch it, employees crowded round computer screens to watch a live transmission on the Channel 4 website, which had already become the most popular site in Europe, forcing some employers to turn off their internet connections to stop people accessing it. George Alagiah broke the story as the lead item on the BBC *One O'Clock News*: 'Nasty Nick falls foul of Big Brother. He's thrown out after being caught cheating ...' To those caught up in the story, Bateman's banal venality seemed like the intrigues of a modern-day Iago.

For others in that summer of the new millennium, *Big Brother* encapsulated the neurotic self-display of the modern media age. 'Camcorders and the internet have stolen our sense of shame, and soon the inhibited will be a minority,' argued Cosmo Landesman. 'The British are on the brink of becoming a nation of exhibitionists and voyeurs.' *Big Brother*, wrote the novelist Will Self, was 'a National Service of the ego. With its senseless and irrelevant democracy, its pitiful voyeurism, its decadence and counselling, *Big Brother* is bizarrely one of the least distorting of the lenses with which television currently regards our society.'[11]

Self's friend, J. G. Ballard, was more open-minded. His early short stories had actually anticipated reality TV. In 'Manhole 69' (1957), three men take part in a sleep deprivation experiment; under fierce arc lights, they are watched continually by scientists from a circular observation window, and descend disastrously into catatonia. In 'Thirteen to Centaurus' (1962), thirteen astronauts who think they are on a century-long flight to a distant planet are actually in a simulated spaceship in a vast hangar on earth, an experiment to test the psychological effects of space travel, watched by scientists on a line of closed-circuit TV screens. The public, who are following the experiment closely, 'are beginning to feel that there's something obscene about this human zoo; what began as a grand adventure of the spirit of Columbus, has become a grisly joke'. Ballard's scenarios were weirdly replicated in two Channel 4 *Big Brother*-inspired reality programmes: *Shattered* (2004), in which contestants competed for a prize fund of £100,000 by trying to stay awake for a week, and *Space Cadets* (2005), in which participants were tricked into thinking they were in a spaceship in low earth orbit. 'Sooner or later,' says the opportunistic TV documentarist Professor Sanger in Ballard's 1987 novel *The Day of Creation*, 'everything turns into television.'[12]

As usual, Ballard was more phlegmatic in life than on the page. Watching in his semi-detached house in Shepperton, he pronounced himself a fan of *Big Brother* while claiming only to have seen bits of it because his partner was addicted – and the fact that she voted 'something like 30 times one evening' led him to discount the huge voting figures on the grounds that people were just pressing the redial button. He was intrigued by its seemingly uncut actuality, although he would have preferred the people to be unaware they were being filmed, as in *The Truman Show*, while conceding that this was unethical. As Ballard told *Spike* magazine:

Most television is low-grade pap, it's so homogenised it's like mental toothpaste. But *Big Brother* is a slice of reality – or what passes for reality. It is like Tracey Emin's *My Bed*. If you focus on anything, however blank, in the right way, then you become obsessed by it. It's like those Andy Warhol films of eight hours of the Empire State Building or of somebody sleeping. Ordinary life viewed obsessively enough becomes interesting in its own right.[13]

Ever since the 1990 Broadcasting Act allowed Channel 4 to sell its own advertising, inclining it to broadcast what would sell it most effectively, it had aimed its programmes at young people. Although most *Big Brother* viewers were female, a large minority were the elusive young male viewers coveted by advertisers. Over fifty per cent of students watched it regularly. For all its apparent longueurs, watching *Big Brother* was an intense, involving experience. The series invited gossip and discussion, as viewers tried to decipher the housemates' social performances. Both tabloid and heavyweight newspapers, with ever declining circulations, devoted pages of comment to *Big Brother* to draw in readers. It did seem that, in the summer of 2000, almost everyone was talking about the goings-on in that sealed compound in east London.

Big Brother acquired a cultural symbolism that was much greater than its viewing figures, perhaps because it seemed to represent a *ne plus ultra*: television stripped to its barest essentials. The existential fear of wasting one's time on this earth with trivialities had long been at the heart of anxieties about watching TV, and *Big Brother* tapped into these anxieties because it was all about watching the passing of time – especially on the live web feed, where bored or insomniac viewers could look at housemates sunbathing or snoring. In the middle of these moments of torpor might come a strange piece of non-action, such as a housemate walking across the kitchen to open the fridge door, or sitting in silence pensively eating a chocolate biscuit.

Alongside this extreme mundanity came its opposite. For in the *Big Brother* house, life was lived at a higher emotional pitch than outside it. It compressed the normal arc of human relationships into several weeks and generated a great deal of shouting, moaning, bitching, hugging and crying. Crying is, as Charles Darwin wrote, one of the 'special expressions of man', something no other animal does (although he conceded that the jury was still out on the Indian elephant).[14] And yet it is usually done in public sparingly, so in the most public forum of all, television, it has had a peculiar force. After *Big Brother*, though, tears on television no longer drew their power, like Gilbert Harding's on *Face to Face* or Gazza's in the 1990 World Cup, from the desperate attempt by their shedders to conceal them. Perhaps one of the most significant, intangible legacies of reality TV was this undermining of stoicism, this sense that an adult shedding tears in public was an unremarkable thing. But this aspect of *Big Brother* only seems to have heightened the sense of estrangement of the ninety per cent of the population who were not watching it. On the night that Nick Bateman's eviction was broadcast, the show attracted a peak of 6 million viewers, around the same number as the current repeats of *Fawlty Towers* and *Tarrant on TV*.[15]

Big Brother was not, perhaps, such a radical departure as it at first seemed. In a sense, it was simply transferring to the naked ape and the human zoo that interest in looking at other species that had defined television from the beginning. Some of the earliest television stars were zoo animals, and the career of the most admired personality of the television age, David Attenborough, had been fashioned around such zoological scopophilia. In the mid 1980s, Laurie Taylor and Bob Mullan interviewed hundreds of viewers and found that Attenborough was the only TV personality not to attract any criticism. 'If there was one aspect of his appeal which stood out,' they wrote, 'it was the feeling that we – the viewers – had been privileged witnesses to the development of his interest: we had been drawn into this world by his genuine curiosity and then watched as he went about satisfying it.'[16]

The most memorable scene from Attenborough's series, *Life on Earth*, came in the penultimate episode, when he explained the closeness of homo sapiens to other apes by lying on the slopes of the Virunga volcanoes in Rwanda while a pack of the human race's non-TV-watching cousins, mountain gorillas, checked his scalp for fleas. Attenborough's hushed voice, much imitated by TV impressionists, exemplified the care he took not to alarm the animals, the assumption being that their privacy could be disturbed as long as they were not distressed. Soon cameras the size of a lipstick could be put inside a badger's warren, strapped on a bird's back or hidden in artificial stones named 'bouldercams'; low light cameras illuminated nocturnal animals; fibre-optic endoscopes filmed insects underground; and helicopter cameras steadied by gyroscopes could film an animal from half a mile away. Animals were seen mating, killing and being killed – things that viewers rarely saw other humans do on television, even on *Big Brother*.

'The whole proceeding seems to contain an unpleasant voyeuristic streak, verging on the pornographic,' wrote Ferdinand Mount about Attenborough's programmes. 'Isn't there something faintly repellent about a posse of cameramen training their sights on a python slowly swallowing an antelope or on a coot killing her surplus young – and then countless millions of us crowding round to watch the footage?'[17] But such dissenting voices were not only rare; they were the opposite of what most people felt. These nature spectaculars, particularly when fronted by Attenborough, were some of the most admired programmes on television. Homo sapiens is the only species curious about other species, and such curiosity is, mostly, a benign and touching quality – even if, as when it is aimed at the contestants on reality TV programmes, it merges with *schadenfreude*.

Attenborough might at one point have taken a different route, into the televised ethnography of which *Big Brother* was a coarsened version. In the early 1960s the BBC seconded him to study at the LSE under the ethnologist Raymond Firth and, as part of this arrangement, he came up with a number of programme ideas to examine human territoriality. He planned to take a wrecked car, park it in Mayfair and secretly film the reactions of residents; or to hide a camera in a hotel room to see how a guest marked his territory, by putting his pyjamas on the bed and so on. But Attenborough soon realised that for the experiment to be valid, people would need to be filmed unawares. 'Programmes could not be made in such a way,' he concluded. 'Human beings are not, after all, the same as other animals and television should not treat them as though they were.' *Life on Earth* did not end with the then voguish sermon about what a human-created mess the world was in, for Attenborough maintained that to pretend we were no different from other species was 'to carry modesty too far'.[18]

Attenborough's friend, Desmond Morris, did make the move from wildlife expert to anthropologist. A curator at London Zoo, he had begun hosting Granada's *Zoo Time* in 1958, but as his and the public's views about zoos changed, he resigned both posts and moved on to the zoological study of humans, notably in his bestselling 1967 book *The Naked Ape*. One of Morris's key theories was that modern urban life resembled being an inmate in a zoo; like caged animals, humans were protected from the dangers and discomforts of the natural world and were thus more likely to become neurotic and inward-looking. His 1977 TV programme, *Manwatching*, helped to popularise the study of body language and the tiny, involuntary displays of self he called 'social leakage'. One of *Manwatching*'s fans was a Dutch television producer, John de Mol, who in 1993, invited Morris to cooperate on the idea that became *Big Brother*.[19]

Morris declined, but the *Big Brother* house, particularly as reinvented for British audiences by Peter Bazalgette, certainly seemed Morris-inspired. While at London Zoo, Morris had inaugurated a special house for small nocturnal mammals. By using bright lighting at night and dimmer lighting during the day, he convinced the animals that day was night, so they were awake during the zoo's opening hours and visitors could see them at their most active. The *Big Brother* house was a similarly simulated environment with bright lighting on constantly in order to blur the division between night and day.

Morris had also devised tests for chimpanzees to stop them from becoming bored, and to provide entertainment for viewers of *Zoo Time*. If they passed, the chimps would receive tokens which they could use to buy raisins at a 'chimpomat' slot machine. To test whether apes had the precise aim of early hunting humans, Morris enlisted the help of Bruce Lacey (a performance artist responsible for inventing the weird props used for the comedian Michael Bentine's surreal television shows) to make a chimp coconut-shy with grapes. When the ball hit the grape, it rolled down a sloping panel, the chimp being able to collect it if he learned to push a rod through various holes.[20] Like Morris's chimps, the *Big Brother* housemates were set tasks, such as learning semaphore or how to ride a unicycle which, if completed, could win them a luxury shopping budget and other 'rewards'. Academic psychologists were on hand to interpret the housemates' body language, from flirting to passive aggression. With public opinion shifting against zoos, the pleasure of observing animals in captivity could now only be satisfied by watching consenting adults.

Morris had declined to participate in *Big Brother* but was a keen viewer. 'For a professional people-watcher like myself, *Big Brother* provides a feast of body language and social interaction,' he wrote. 'There is a never-ending supply of courtship rituals, confrontation displays and appeasement gestures as the housemates struggle to adjust to one another and to their isolation.' After a few series, though, he became disillusioned by the exploitative gimmickry of the show and the public hostility to the participants. Attenborough was also intrigued by *Big Brother* and its clones. 'Reality TV programmes are quite fascinating, a real social phenomenon,' he reflected. 'These programmes might seem like a big shift, but really they are about human nature and about registering your identity.'[21] He did not, however, think them a proper experiment, because the participants, unlike the animals on nature programmes, were aware of what was going on. Everyone, from watchers to watched, knew it was television.

A new type of scabrous, surreal TV criticism, pioneered by Jim Shelley in the *Guardian* and Victor Lewis-Smith in the *Evening Standard*, had by now emerged to satirise the trashily attention-seeking programmes of the multichannel era. In 1999, *TVGoHome*, a website of mock TV schedules which parodied the television listings style of the *Radio Times*, acquired a cult audience. The site's founder, Charlie Brooker, also began a TV column for the *Guardian* in 2000, with a much imitated, scatological style in which he dwelled mainly on the factory-produced television he called 'untertainment'. For Brooker, malignantly trite shows such as *Elimidate*, *So You Think You Want Bigger Boobs?*, *Celebrity Wife Swap* and *My Breasts Are Too Big* were a simple by-product of market conditions. 'Hundreds of channels, filling hundreds of hours,' he wrote. 'No wonder the majority of programmes are churned out like sausage meat: unloved swathes of videotape whose sole purpose is to bung up the schedule ... Most modern TV is uniformly nondescript, the equivalent of oxygen-flavoured gum.'[22]

In this new environment, good television carried on being made but seemed to be smarter, edgier and less needy in its search for the audience's approval. The first episode of the BBC sitcom, *The Office*, went out with no great fanfare on 9 July 2001, on a midsummer Monday evening after a rain-delayed Wimbledon final. Partly because it mimicked the then ubiquitous formula of the docusoap and had no laughter track, many viewers did not realise it was a comedy. The BBC chairman Gavyn Davies was an immediate fan, but his wife, Sue Nye, who ran the office of the Chancellor of the Exchequer, Gordon Brown, mistook it for a documentary. It got fewer than 1.5 million viewers; only one other new addition to BBC2's schedule that year scored lower in the BBC's audience appreciation index, and that was women's bowls. Not until the autumn of 2002, when the DVD came out and the second series was heavily promoted, did *The Office* come to be seen as a modern classic. Even then, while the first episode of the new run got 5.2 million viewers, 400,000 viewers had turned off by the end, and only 3.6 million came back for the next episode.[23]

Nowadays the understated performing style and atmosphere of *The Office* is the industry standard and the 'fourth wall' sitcom, performed in front of a live audience like a play on a proscenium stage, seems old-fashioned. But in 2001, *The Office*, while not the first comedy to dispense with background laughter, took some getting used to because it seemed almost to forget that its viewers were there. Where a comedy producer might once have ticked the script for studio audience laughs, *The Office* instead had long shots of an office worker yawning or feeding paper into a shredder. It also broke the sitcom convention that viewers would laugh at characters on the assumption that nothing too awful would happen to them. David Brent's decline and fall in the second series was a betrayal of this compact with viewers, who gradually realised they were laughing at something rather tragic. 'We are living in a new golden age, but this time it is the golden age of a much colder, cynical and more clique-ish kind of entertainment,' wrote Graham McCann, the biographer of Morecambe and Wise. 'For every viewer who savours each awk-wardly tender exchange between Tim and Dawn, and laughs aloud at the sheer awfulness of David Brent, there are several more who shake their heads and protest: "I don't get it."'[24]

Critics of the new digital era tended to focus on the threat to 'quality television', a peculiarly British term which has its origins in our tradition of public service broadcasting and the idea that it needs protecting from an unfettered market. There was even a 'Cam-paign for Quality Television', born in opposition to the selling off of ITV franchises to the highest bidder that was proposed in the late 1980s. Mobilising TV stars like Rowan Atkinson, Esther Rantzen and Michael Palin, it campaigned successfully for a 'quality thresh-old' which every applicant for an ITV franchise had to pass. In 1999, the Campaign for Quality Television published a paper whose title summed up its fear about the fate of what it was campaigning for: *A Shrinking Iceberg Slowly Travelling South*.

But despite quite a lot of evidence of untertainment on the ever-expanding number of digital channels, shows like *The Office* proved that 'quality television' was also thriving. Quality TV actually bene-fited from the multiplication of channels, for it could now have several lives, appearing on a main terrestrial channel, its sister digital chan-nels and on a DVD box set with extras. In his book *Everything Bad is Good for You*, the American critic Steven Johnson argued that this kind of quality television had to be complex to stand up to such rep-etition. Following a pattern set by *Hill Street Blues* as early as 1981, American drama series, such as *The Sopranos* and 24, now built up multi-stranded narratives and demanded more intellectual and emo-tional work from viewers. To gorge on a box set of *The West Wing*, watching several episodes in 'a single glorious wodge' that stretched deep into the night, was, wrote Clive James, 'like Bayreuth with snappier music'.[25]

The octogenarian Richard Hoggart, who had co-authored the Pilkington Report on Broadcasting forty years earlier, and whose ideas about creating a common culture through television had influenced Dennis Potter when he was beginning his career, now joined this argument about quality. Hoggart worried not so much that good programmes would stop being made, but that television was losing the sense of an empathetic common ground. After fifty years of consumer populism, he feared a new tyranny of cultural relativism, in which everything had its place and value judgements were seen as elitist and patronising. Reserving the right to criticise bad television, Hoggart evoked the example of Anton Chekhov, who once spoke with 'love and anger' to his own people: 'You live badly, my friends; it is shameful to live like that ...'[26]

In 2002 Hoggart complained, in language highly reminiscent of the Pilkington Report, about 'cheap and nasty offerings aimed at people who are assumed to be both insufficiently educated and ill-informed'. The quiz show *The Weakest Link*, whose presenter's putdowns had earned her the sobriquet 'The Queen of Mean', revealed a 'mindless, cruel competitiveness and a disguised or perhaps unconscious contempt in the makers for those at whom they are directed'. Meanwhile the new highbrow digital channel BBC4, whose most popular shows drew about 50,000 viewers, offered 'a little caviar for the snobs', allowing arts programmes to be ghettoised 'so that – like the celebrated daft pianist in a brothel – they may not know and so may cease to complain about what goes on elsewhere in the building'.[27]

This feared fragmentation of audiences did not, however, quite materialise. In his book *The Shock of the Old*, the historian David Edgerton argues that our understanding of historical progress is 'innovation-centric'. We think that technological change happens inexorably and in linear fashion. So we focus on exciting new inventions and underestimate how much they will have to struggle against the forces of habit and inertia in our daily lives, and how resilient older, still serviceable technologies often turn out to be. The American theorist of technology, John Seely Brown, gave the name 'endism' to this historical fallacy that new technologies like the internet would simply do away with older ones, like television.[28]

Words like 'digital' and 'new media' seem to belong inevitably to the future; 'analogue' and 'cathode ray' seem rooted in the past. And yet well into the new century, most Britons seemed unpersuaded by the choice offered by over 200 digital channels and carried on buying analogue televisions even when told they would soon be obsolete; and at the end of its first decade, forty years after the arrival of colour TV, 28,000 people still had a black-and-white TV licence. Notable among their number was the Labour MP Chris Mullin, who revealed he had been questioned by the *Daily Telegraph*, which uncovered the scandal of MP's expenses in 2009, about his claim for a £47 monochrome licence. He had owned his set for over thirty years, being averse to throwing away things that still worked. 'The *Telegraph* reports that I claimed for a black-and-white TV licence,' he wrote in his diary, 'which has been the subject of much amusement among colleagues, many of whom dwell in the world of plasma screens.'[29]

New Labour had come to power in 1997 extolling the consumer freedoms opened up by digital television and the internet. This commitment now began to conflict with a new anxiety germinating in the rioting of Asian youths in the summer of 2001 on the streets of Oldham, Bradford and Burnley, crystallising in an atmosphere of post-9/11 suspicion and coming to a head with the London tube bombings of July 2005. While tabloid newspapers adopted a strident language directed against newly arrived immigrants and asylum seekers, politicians talked less flammably about the promotion of 'community cohesion' and 'Britishness'. The home secretary, David Blunkett, set up citizenship and language tests for those applying for British passports, and exhorted Asian parents to speak English to their children at home.

One of the issues underlying these anxieties was the fragmenting of the television audience, for the most fertile markets for cable and satellite television had been Britain's 2.5 million British Asians. After late night programming aimed at minorities disappeared on mainstream channels in the 1990s as they went in search of the largest (or youngest) audiences, satellite channels like Zee TV, Alpha Bangla and Star TV, carrying the Indian subcontinent's most popular soaps, game shows and Bollywood movies, filled the gap. Young British Asians could now choose from dozens of channels speaking Urdu, Punjabi, Hindi or Bengali.

But the habit of communal viewing turned out to be more resilient than people had hoped or feared at the start of the digital era. Programmes like *Who Wants To Be a Millionaire?*, the celebrity ballroom dancing competition *Strictly Come Dancing* and the revived *Doctor Who* still brought millions of families together in front of the set on weekend nights. A 2006 government White Paper on the BBC recognised this shift and began to tweak the orthodoxy that the era of communal television watching was over. It now argued that the BBC should form part of the 'national glue', bringing people together in 'water-cooler moments', reflecting and reshaping national identity.[30]

The White Paper also rewarded the BBC for helping to rescue the government's digital policy after the calamitous failure of ITV Digital, a digital package known to terrestrial viewers through a series of commercials presented by the comedian Johnny Vegas and a knitted woollen monkey. While the ad was popular, and the replica monkeys given away free with a subscription were fetching hundreds of pounds on eBay, ITV Digital was not. Its reception problems were legendary; even opening a fridge door could knock out the signal. In 2002, its abandoned licences were relaunched as Freeview, a free service led by the BBC with only about thirty channels. It became the fastest new consumer technology to reach a million homes, ahead of the DVD player and PlayStation. Only eighteen months after its launch, around 3.5 million homes had it, with a bias towards the middle-aged and older. With viewers at last signing up to digital, the government could now begin to switch off the analogue signal, first launched at Alexandra Palace in 1936, so that the digital signal could be broadcast at full power across the country. Switching off analogue would also allow the government to sell off these frequencies to mobile phone and broadband companies. The BBC would play a vital role, said the White Paper, in 'building Digital Britain' just as it had first introduced Britons to black-and-white and colour TV.[31]

Labour MPs, however, feared that voters might punish them if the digital switchover did not work and left people without their favourite programmes in the run up to a general election. Worried about what they called the '*Coronation Street* bug', the government tested the waters at Ferryside and Llansteffan, two villages on opposite sides of the estuary of the River Tywi in Carmarthen Bay, served by the same tiny transmitter. On 30 March 2005, for around 500 homes and a few scattered beach chalets and static caravans, the analogue signal was switched off for the first time in Britain. Apart from a few unhappy residents hidden behind the Cliff, a wooded outcrop above Ferryside which the new signal couldn't get over, the villagers settled down to watch Wales lose to Austria at football on digital TV.

A little Cumbrian coastal outcrop, bounded by the Lake District on one side and the Irish Sea on the other, was the perfect place for the next and much bigger controlled experiment. Whitehaven had long been a televisual backwater. It had missed the coronation because it could not get television until the Isle of Man built a transmitter at the end of 1953. It did not have ITV until 1968, picked up Channel 4 six years late and still could not get Channel 5. One of the biggest firms in White-haven in the 1970s and 1980s had been the cable company British Relay, because analogue reception was so poor and homes on the new housing estate had no chimneys, which made fitting aerials difficult anyway.

A billboard in Whitehaven harbour with a countdown ticker, a giant blinking LED display, reminded people of the switchover's zero hour. The town's oldest resident, Florence Parnaby, aged 100, opened the official Digital Help Scheme shop, which, with an eye to an older demo-graphic, was giving away a pile of cassette tapes with an audio step-by-step guide, alongside a bowl of mint humbugs.[32] There was much local grumbling, particularly from the proprietors of Whitehaven's many guesthouses, who complained that they would have to convert multiple sets. But on the day of the switchover, hordes of people were seen emerging from the town's electrical shops with set-top boxes. In the early hours of 14 November 2007, the analogue signal disappeared, painlessly, while most of Whitehaven was sleeping. At 3.27 a.m., all the digital channels arrived, just in time for a repeat of *The Jeremy Kyle Show* on ITV1. The *Coronation Street* bug had proved as phantasmal as the Millennium Bug, its nomenclatural ancestor.

In the analogue era, television had depended on the power of the transmitter, and how far its radio waves could reach from the top of a hill. In the digital era, television was not so reliant on geography and landscape; as well as radiating from transmitters, it could live on internet catch-up sites and be downloaded on to laptops or mobile phones. Those raised in an analogue world were familiar with each medium's flawed attempt to transcribe a message from one physical object to another: the white noise of the radio, the hiss of the cassette tape, the crackle of stylus on scratched vinyl or the flicker of electrons against the back of the cathode ray tube were all part of the listening or viewing experience. But digital media stored information in binary ones and noughts that bore no telltale trace of whichever material objects were used to carry and decipher these abstract symbols. On a cathode ray tube, the numberless electrons had to be continually fired at the back of the phosphor-coated screen to make each millisecond of television picture and pull off the illusion of persistent vision, so no two televisual moments were exactly the same. On a digital television, each pixel was the product of binary code that could be endlessly decoded and revisited. Television no longer needed to move from one place to another at a unique moment in time. Now it seemed to come from nowhere and be everywhere, as omnipresent as the air.

Television was losing its connection with place. As the digital switchover happened gradually by ITV region, the disappearance of the analogue signal marked the effective demise of these regions, which had essentially been defined by the reach of the analogue transmitters.

This nationalisation of television, an unintended side effect of the digital revolution, passed largely without comment, probably because ITV's regions had been losing their identities for years anyway. Their in-vision announcers, a quaint throwback to the BBC years of McDonald Hobley and Sylvia Peters, had disappeared by the late 1980s, and their start-up themes had been rendered superfluous with the arrival of twenty-four-hour TV. Their proud idents and fanfares had given way to the cleaner, blander, corporate fonts of ITV. Finally, in the early 2000s, the visual identity of the regions vanished entirely into a set of branded idents for 'ITV1': gnomic visual poems showing people hugging trees, examining their beer bellies or falling asleep on trains.

Ironically, the ITV regions had enjoyed a brand loyalty of which the modern digital channels could only dream. Some Midlands viewers carried on referring to ITV as ATV, while in the Fens they still called it Anglia. These invented regions had taken on a tangible truth. Anglia had somehow united its vast catchment area into an imagined community, to the extent that other organisations, from Anglia Ruskin University to Anglia Railways, had copied its historically spurious name. The north-west remained defined by its ITV region, evoked often in the weather forecast ('a bit of a gloomy day in Granadaland'). Tyne Tees, according to the historian Richard Lewis, had played a crucial role in scripting a collective identity for that recent invention, the north-east.[33] But now the analogue signal was fading away, and the idea of the regions along with it.

ITV companies had long used their regional news programmes to forge an identity and lock viewers into their early evening schedules – especially in the early days of commercial television, when there was no BBC regional news programme until BBC Midlands began in 1964. These programmes were often appealingly untutored and amateurish. They were usually fronted by middle-aged men of long service who were given the time and space to develop their eccentricities. Mike Neville, the long-running presenter of the BBC's *Look North* and then Tyne Tees' *North East Tonight*, had begun his career as an announcer, where he developed the skill of filling in if a programme underran, what he called 'talking to a clock'.[34] Because he instinctively knew that five seconds equalled fifteen or twenty words, he became expert at weaving in extempore witticisms during breakdowns. The Durham folksinger Jez Lowe's song, 'Mike Neville Said It (So It Must Be True)', a poignant account of hearing about pit closures on the regional news, conveys the affection that Neville inspired in north-easterners, a sense that he was on their side against the world. In the song, Neville breaks the news that 'our mining days are through' as gently he can, before moving on to a story about a sheep that sings the blues, 'even though inside you know his heart was burning'.

Eric Wallace of Border's nightly *Lookaround*, known affectionately to locals (after the Cumbrian dialect words for 'news' and 'look') as 'Crack'n'deek-about', was almost as loved as Neville. The local-accented Wallace had worked on the programme since 1968 and often waylaid viewers with accounts of his early life working at Carr's biscuit factory in Carlisle. He had covered the warp and weft of the region's life, from UFO sightings on the Solway Firth to Lake Windermere's version of the Loch Ness Monster, from the Lockerbie disaster to the foot-and-mouth outbreak of 2001: long, heartbreaking interviews with distraught farmers who had been forced to burn all their cattle, conveying the region's distress in a way that the national news could not. Like his north-west counterpart, Tony Wilson, a Cambridge-educated polymath who founded the experimental Factory Records and the Haçienda nightclub while incongruously presenting *Granada Reports*, Wallace had an unlikely avant-garde hinterland: an aficionado of German expressionist cinema, he had directed a number of arthouse films including *I Can Lick Any Girl in the House* (1976) and *Stimmung* (1986).

But regional news was dying and in Cumbria, the first English region to switch over to digital, it was dying fastest. Just as Whitehaven was losing its analogue signal, ITV announced that Border and Tyne Tees would merge their regional news programmes. Had Wallace, who had died in 2004, still been presenting it, there would have been an even fiercer campaign against *Lookaround*'s axing. As it was, thousands of 'Save *Lookaround*' stickers and hours of petition-gathering outside the region's supermarkets failed to save it. On Shrove Tuesday, 24 February 2009, the long-serving presenter, Fiona Armstrong, seemed close to tears during the last ever edition from Carlisle as she made small talk with her co-host about making pancakes later on. The next day, the new super-regional news began broadcasting from a Gateshead business park, presented, as all regional programmes now seemed to be, with the bland professionalism of a rolling news channel. The big cities of the north-east now got the bulk of the news, and Workington AFC's football results would probably never be read out on TV again.

Intermittent mutterings had long been heard that television was a metropolitan medium which overlooked the country's rural fringes, mutterings which now became more insistent. The social divide between town and country was particularly fractious in the New Labour years, with many political arguments – on foxhunting, supermarkets, fuel prices, second homes – having this undeclared civil war at their heart. New Labour, associated with a north London metropolitan media class, insisted that people in the countryside had most to gain from digital television, because analogue reception was worse in rural areas and those in listed cottages could not always get planning permission for a satellite dish. The language was of digital 'exclusion', a New Labour catchword applied to everything from social deprivation to school expulsion to TV reception. Like other forms of New Labourite modernisation, the benefits of digital were assumed to be universal and apolitical; anyone clinging to analogue was 'excluded', left out of the inevitable march towards the future – a digital 'have-not', or, worse, a refusenik.

With low inflation and steady growth, these years were ones of prosperity for much of urban and suburban Britain, but they also coincided with a crisis in farming and rural communities, from foot and mouth to a longer-term problem of overproduction, with farmers relying heavily but barely subsisting on EU and government subsidies.

The Countryside Alliance, formed in 1997 to oppose an anticipated ban on hunting with dogs, sought to tap into this wider sense that a way of life was under threat and that the modern urbanites who bought meat wrapped in supermarket plastic did not understand the bucolic ways of life and death. Many rural people felt that their lives were unrepresented on television, particularly since the farming programmes that used to be on Sunday lunchtimes had all disappeared in the 1980s, an especially urbanite decade on television. 'You'd watch the burgeoning Channel 4 and it was all telling you about London,' recalled Darren Flook, born in 1971 in the industrial, coalmining countryside outside of Newcastle. 'It was sending out a signal to the entire country saying: leave your shitty villages and come and live here in wonderful media-land and you'll have a life of never-ending clubbing and glamour and wonderfulness.'[35]

This resentment about the neglect of rural life found a focus when, in 1999, the BBC cancelled One Man and His Dog. This programme, a kind of rustic, alfresco snooker that fashioned slow pleasures out of watching shepherds guide sheep into pens, had been an unexpected hit in the 1980s; but its viewing figures had dropped to under a million and it seemed to be coming to the end of its natural life. Its presenter Phil Drabble had already left the programme, saying 'it gets boring watching dogs chase stroppy sheep around the same sort of course'. But its cancellation coincided with a wider sense that television had forgotten the countryside. The culture secretary, Chris Smith, said it was a 'wonderful programme ... which I have watched with pleasure over the years' and axing it was a 'big mistake'. The Daily Telegraph began a campaign to reinstate One Man and His Dog, which was meant to culminate in a march of shepherds and their dogs on BBC Television Centre, although this never materialised. Robin Page, the show's presenter, accused Television Centre of being dominated by a 'metrocentric élite' with an 'inner-M25 mindset'.[36]

There were sporadic attempts to heal the growing sense of estrangement between town and country. In 2000, the BBC2 controller Jane Root, mindful of the protests about One Man and His Dog, commissioned Clarissa and the Countryman, in which the TV chef

Clarissa Dickson Wright and the Border farmer Johnny Scott travelled round talking to country people like gun-makers and shrimp-fishers. Its model was Jack Hargreaves's programme *Out of Town*, which had ended in 1982, just as 'out of town' was becoming a prefix for 'supermarket'. Evoking Hargreaves's example, the presenters intended their programme to help bridge the gulf of understanding between rural and urban viewers. Instead, it seemed to underline the divisions, getting good audiences but angering others with its coverage of fox hunting in the Cheviots and hare coursing in the Lancashire marshes. The ninety-year-old Barbara Castle complained in the House of Lords about the programme's claim that the banning of hunting would destroy rural life. 'To hear some people talk, you would think that none of us who supports a total ban on hunting with dogs had ever seen a blade of grass,' she said.[37]

On *Out of Town*, Jack Hargreaves had held together competing groups with an interest in rural life, such as second-home owners, blood sports enthusiasts, weekend anglers, environmentalists and self-sufficiency enthusiasts. His emollient personality helped, but so did the less fractious rural politics of the time. Dickson Wright, instead, had to be assigned her own special branch officer after receiving death threats from animal rights activists. The *Countryfile* presenter, Adam Henson, also received death threats after presenting a studiedly neutral report on a proposed badger cull. 'We are going to burn your children,' one of them said. Some rural viewers, meanwhile, felt that 'welly telly' like *Countryfile* and *Springwatch* presented the countryside as a playground refuge for urbanites rather than a living, working entity.[38]

In 2005, the Canadian writer Craig Taylor returned to the Suffolk village where Ronald Blythe had written *Akenfield* and Peter Hall had made the film of the same name, based loosely on Blythe's 1969 book. Shown on ITV one Sunday evening in January 1975, Hall's film drew 15 million viewers, twice the anticipated number. Despite a challenging score by Michael Tippett, improvised dialogue and some strong Suffolk dialect from the amateur cast ('I toowd yew that hehf ewr agoo'), it seems, in a period of stagflation and rising energy prices, to have left an impression on desensitised urban viewers attracted to the simpler life. The next day Peter Hall's taxi driver congratulated him on *Akenfield* on the way to the theatre, and Princess Margaret phoned him to say she didn't understand why anyone had complained it was hard to understand the dialect, because she hadn't found it hard at all. 'Though of course,' she added, 'one did grow up there, in Norfolk at any rate.'[39]

Craig Taylor noted that the broad Suffolk accent captured by Blythe and Hall had now been practically snuffed out by TV, making way for the estuarine vowels and glottal stops of south-eastern English, just as the young had also rejected the western rolled 'r' in the television era because of its country bumpkin associations. Dennis Potter, who had written in 1962 about his love of the Forest of Dean dialect – a rich mix of 'the speed and lilt of the Welsh borderland, the broad, lengthened vowel sounds and buttery emphases of the West country and many distinctive local words and rhythms of its own' – would have found a similar levelling effect in his homeland: not the sort of common culture he had craved.[40]

'People don't look at the fields now ... They're living urban lives in the countryside – not just here, but all over the place,' said one of Craig Taylor's interviewees in Akenfield, the 83-year-old Ronald Blythe himself. 'Because, after all is said and done, the same television programmes, same newscasters, same everything are seen by everyone in Britain, every night, from the Orkneys to Cornwall.' At nearby Otley Agricultural College, they were treating the spread of gardening makeover programmes as a recruiting tool and a source of jobs for their graduates. 'Horticulture,' the prospectus said, 'is the new rock'n'roll.'[41]

A year after Taylor went back to Akenfield, the broadcaster Eric Robson returned to his birthplace, Newcastleton, a Scottish village just a few miles from the English border. One evening, at the top of Holm Hill, the summit overlooking the village, he struck up a conversation with an elderly man, muffled against the cold, and told him about the book he was writing, on whether the border between the two countries still mattered. The only border that amounted to anything, the old man replied, was between STV's Loch Lomond-set soap opera *Take the High Road* and *Coronation Street*. 'Television has rubbed us all flat,' he said.[42]

Sheepdog trials were still shown on digital channels, and there was even the odd *One Man and His Dog* special on BBC2. But the rural people who were unhappy with the depiction of country life on television did not seem to want their interests hived off into specialist channels hidden away in the higher reaches of the channel numbers, seen only by those adventurous with the buttons on their remote controls. They wanted the main channels to convey the realities of rural life to themselves and others: television as common culture.

The television-watching nation seemed to be splintering in other directions. The voices in favour of Scottish independence had been rising in volume since the Thatcher era, when many Scots felt they had been forgotten by the south. The Gaelic music revival, led by bands and singers such as Runrig, Oi Polloi and Julie Fowlis, and reinforced by folk festivals like the Feis and the official use of Gaelic in the devolved Scottish parliament, had given the language a newly progressive image; and this parliament, now dominated by nationalists, was pressing for the BBC to spend more of its licence fee on Scottish programmes. And so, on 19 September 2008, the BBC inaugurated a Scottish Gaelic channel, Alba, the first mainstream channel to come entirely from Scotland. Its opening programme was *Eilbheas*, in which a Gaelic teenager assuages his loneliness on the Isle of Lewis by becoming friends with the ghost of Elvis Presley. In care homes in the Western Isles, free digital boxes were provided for the large number of elderly Gaelic speakers.

British television had always assumed, as the minimum commitment to its imagined and often imaginary national community of viewers, the sharing of a common language. While the combined forces of political devolution and digital television were now openly questioning this assumption, the issue had been simmering away since the late 1970s, when the Annan committee argued that television should give more of a voice to the regions. BBC Alba might never have happened if the Conservative home secretary, Willie Whitelaw, had got his way when, on 12 September 1979, he announced that the government would not be honouring its election pledge to establish a Welsh language TV channel. Plaid Cymru had lost seats in the election and the people of Wales had rejected a Welsh assembly in a referendum, and the new Tory government believed that Welsh nationalism was in retreat. But that Christmas, while watching *The Muppet Show* with his grandchildren, the leader of Plaid Cymru, Gwynfor Evans, hatched a plan for a grand gesture. On 3 May 1980, the 69-year-old Evans threatened to fast to the death unless the government agreed to a Welsh channel. Before the start of his fast on 5 October, Evans held a series of tearful rallies throughout Wales where he talked of his possible death.

Margaret Thatcher refused to give in to threats, but that September the more pragmatic Whitelaw, worried about the violence and unrest that might follow Evans's death, gave the go ahead for the fourth channel, Sianel Pedwar Cymru (S4C). On the Embankment wall opposite the House of Commons appeared the legend 'Gwynfor 1, Whitelaw 0'. Evans, motivated as much by his desire to revive Plaid Cymru and create a nationalist reawakening as his wish for a fourth channel, thought it a pity Whitelaw had surrendered so soon.[43]

Even after the arrival of S4C, the tensions persisted. HTV now rebranded itself as an English language channel for Welsh people and sought to win back the non-Welsh speaking viewers who had turned their aerials to England. 'HTV Wales speaks your kind of language,' said advertisements in Welsh newspapers in October 1982, a few days before the start of S4C, as HTV inaugurated its first English language soap opera, *Taff Acre*. But S4C, which became best known for its children's cartoons, *Super Ted* and *Fireman Sam*, and was often the subject of ridicule for its low ratings, does seem to have helped to halt the decline of Welsh. By the 1991 census, the number of Welsh speakers had stabilised and by 2001 it had increased to over a fifth of the population, a cultural revival also evident in bands such as Catatonia and Super Furry Animals and singers such as Cerys Matthews and Duffy, all of whom have sung in Welsh; and in S4C-funded Welsh language films such as the Oscar winning anti-war biopic *Hedd Wyn* (1992) and *Gadael Lenin* (*Leaving Lenin*, 1993). Some Welsh nationalists, however, felt that the language issue had distracted them from their broader political aims, and that the expansion of Welsh television provided a career path for the nation's intellectual élite, depriving their movement of its natural leaders. 'Talented people became part of the "intellywelshia",' suggested Gwynfor Evans's biographer, 'indulging themselves in the fashionable suburbs of west Cardiff, rather than leading "Plaid" back to "Welsh Wales".'[44]

For Scottish nationalists, as for the Welsh, television had turned from enemy to ally: having blamed it initially for eroding their local traditions and languages, they realised that it could be used to protect and develop them. But Scottish Gaelic was never as widespread as Welsh. Native speakers were mainly found in the Western Isles, which had suffered chronic economic decline and population loss for over a century. According to the 1981 census, there were only 82,000 Gaelic speakers, less than two per cent of Scots. The number of people who spoke only Gaelic had not been recorded since the 1971 census, when it was just 477.

Non-Gaelic speaking Scots were often ambivalent about Scottish programmes. 'The memory of *The White Heather Club* lingers on as if it were only yesterday,' wrote the film and television critic John Caughie in 1982, 'the voice of the Laird of Cowcaddens still rings in the ears, and although Hogmanay specials only happen once a year it takes at least twelve months to forget them.' When the BFI asked viewers to keep diaries in the early 1990s, it found that many Scots, from Dumfries and Galloway to the Shetlands, disliked the Scottish opt-out programmes, especially the Gaelic ones. 'I detest regional programmes ...' said a 21-year-old Beith woman, 'they are aimed at "teuchters" – the kilt wearing, Gaelic speaking minority.' 'Whilst I agree that there should be some Gaelic TV programmes,' said a 32-year-old Kilmarnock man, 'I feel that STV put a number of them on at peak viewing times. No one in the central belt of Scotland can understand a bloody word of them.' A study of articles and letters in Scottish newspapers in the late 1990s and early 2000s pointed to anti-Gaelic prejudice among non-Gaelic speaking Scots, who associated it with elderly, poor, Hebridean crofters.[45]

A Gaelic Television Fund created out of the 1990 Broadcasting Act, which added 200 more hours of Gaelic programmes a year on the BBC and STV, seemed to have had the effect of increasing the number of people learning Gaelic, especially in Glasgow and Edinburgh, but not fast enough to replace the dying native speakers. According to the 2001 census, the numbers of Gaelic speakers had fallen to 58,652, just over one per cent of the Scottish population. Scottish Gaelic did not deserve its own channel, wrote Allan Brown in the *Sunday Times*, because it was 'attuned to a distant, pre-technological world' and was 'a rural patois, a bonsai idiolect'.[46]

Every Saturday night, Alba showed a live Scottish Premier League football match, with Gaelic-only commentary. The Gaelic translation company Cainnt Cultural Services provided English-speaking viewers with some useful phrases, including *Tha e air a bhith air a h-uile pios feur* ('He's covered every blade of grass') and *Tha feum againn a toirt a h-uile game mar a thig e* ('We just have to take each game as it comes'). The Scottish historian Michael Fry, who saw the Gaelic revival as an exercise in wishful thinking and special pleading by lowland intellectuals, said that most viewers only watched Alba for the sport, and that 'the whole thing is being set up to make this channel appear more popular than it is ... You don't need Gaelic to watch football.'[47] By the end of 2008, though, the audience for Alba was about 400,000, nearly seven times the number of Gaelic speakers.

Perhaps one of the attractions of Alba was that it bore little sign of what the Scottish nationalist intellectual Tom Nairn called the 'vast tartan monster', that 'huge self-contained universe of *Kitsch*', from Hootenannies to shortbread tins, which he felt had reduced the national psyche to infantilism and sentimentality.[48] Instead, there were a few understated clarsachs and bagpipes and the beautiful Alba idents, with their traffic lights and cones bending towards the north star in the twilight; evocative glimpses of the far north, in sheepdog trials from Shetland or motoring programmes that test-drove cars on deserted Hebridean roads; and a blizzard of pleasing guttural noises punctuated by familiar words for which there was no Gaelic equivalent, like 'empowering' and 'exhilarating'. For non-Gaelic speakers, watching BBC Alba had something of the strange poetry of the shipping forecast, that radio broadcast listened to intently by millions of people who, not being on ships, are not its intended audience.

For it seemed that, even in the digital era when audiences were supposed to pick and choose programmes to fit their own consumer demographic, television still clung to the literal, agricultural sense of the word 'broadcast'. 'The parable of the sower celebrates broadcasting as an equitable mode of communication that leaves the harvest of meaning to the will and capacity of the recipient,' writes the philosopher John Durham Peters, in his book *Speaking into the Air*. 'Though much is thrown, little is caught. And the failure of germination is not necessarily something to lament.' Television viewing retained something of this unselective, ecumenical quality, so that Gaelic programmes broadcast into the democratic air might still form part of what Peters calls the 'cumulative intelligence of the universe'.[49]

One show still brought the nation together like no other: *The X Factor*. Since the beginning of the century, this type of reality TV talent show had been transforming Saturday night entertainment, helped by new fibre-optic technology and a device called a Digital Main Switching Unit which allowed thousands of phone votes to be registered simultaneously. On 9 February 2002, the night of the final of the talent show *Pop Idol*, British Telecom reported that 57 million calls, at 10p each, were made on 28,000 dedicated lines to vote for the finalists, Will Young and Gareth Gates, equal to one call for nearly every person in Britain. The writer and radio presenter Francine Stock described it as 'a kind of modern equivalent of the crowd response at a gladiatorial contest, but instead of using the thumbs up and thumbs down, we're using our dialling fingers'.[50]

Others, like Peter Bazalgette, noted that phone-in votes were engendering the kind of public engagement that was missing from politics. The turnout at the 2001 general election had been only 59 per cent, the lowest since the wartime election of 1918, and membership of political parties had declined, particularly among the young people who watched reality shows. It became a truism that more people voted on premium rate lines for reality show contestants than in general elections – although, as J. G. Ballard surmised, the truism was probably untrue, because many of these phone votes were made up of multiple calls by the same people. 'E-mail and mobile telephony have transformed the tenor of our lives ... But we still only vote for the government once every four years or so,' noted Bazalgette sadly. 'Our democracy is divorced from the rhythm of the age.'[51]

Researchers from the Universities of London, East London and Sheffield, after spending two years watching children play, concluded that these new reality shows were feeding into playground life. Inspired by Iona and Peter Opie's classic studies of children's playground and street games in the 1950s, which had documented the incorporation of advertising jingles and TV theme tunes into clapping and singing games, the researchers discovered playground games based on dance routines from *Britain's Got Talent*, *The Jeremy Kyle Show* and, especially, *The X Factor*. The playground researchers noticed one personality recurring constantly in children's roleplay: Simon Cowell, the charismatic, caustic svengali who was mobbed during public auditions held round the country, who frequently appeared in the dreams of women and children, and who could silence studio audiences with a regal wave of his hand. Interviews with first-time voters in East Anglia found that most thought Cowell 'a person of authority' whose success had earned him the right to be rude. 'He knows what he is talking about so he is someone who can say if you are crap,' said one. Several put the case for Cowell to be prime minister.[52]

The incumbent, Gordon Brown, let it be known that he was a fan of *The X Factor*, and had found time to write letters of congratulation or commiseration to the finalists. It seemed unlikely viewing for the child of a Kirkcaldy minister from whom he had inherited that ethical and intellectual seriousness that marks out the Church of Scotland ministry. The Free Church had a long-held hostility to television, one which seems to have deeply affected another minister's son, Lord Reith. After he left the BBC in 1938, the corporation presented Reith with a TV set, but he barely looked at it. His daughter, Marista Leishman, attributed this disaffection to his Presbyterianism. Her father, she wrote, 'looked out at television from the scarcely opened door of an unadorned Free Church building, the glass of its windows frosted and crinkled as a barrier between the worshippers within viewing the distractions of worldly matters without'.[53]

But perhaps Brown's viewing of *The X Factor* still carried a trace of his background as a son of the Manse. For instead of watching just for entertainment, he drew improving morals from it, and sought to link it to the New Labourite politics of individual aspiration, his vision of what he called 'an *X Factor* Britain'. 'These shows,' he said, 'are saying to people, "Look, if you've got a talent you don't have to know someone. You can just apply and we'll have a look at what you're like."' Just as *The X Factor* was unearthing untapped talent, we needed to 'eradicate failure across our education system' in order to 'unlock all the talents of all of the people'.[54]

This eagerness of politicians to discuss their television viewing was relatively new. 'None of our party leaders have television sets,' Tony Benn wrote in his diary in 1958. 'How can one lead a great party unless one keeps in touch with the people?' The then prime minister, Harold Macmillan, although an astute performer on TV, did not own a set and, as the member of a distinguished publishing family, feared it would take the place of books. Harold Wilson and James Callaghan made rather arch references to their viewing of *Coronation Street*, and Margaret Thatcher claimed to be a fan of the Whitehall sitcom *Yes, Minister* but barely watched anything, acquiring her sense of television as an inefficient, complacent industry from the size of the crews that came to interview her. Tony Blair was the first prime minister fully to embrace television viewing as shorthand for a contemporary and populist attitude, claiming to be a 'modern man' who came from the generation of 'the Beatles and colour TV', and revealing that *Pop Idol* was 'regular family viewing'.[55]

Post-New Labour politicians, forty-somethings who grew up during the now tenderly recalled age of three-channel colour television, talked freely of their watching habits. During the 2010 general election campaign, David Cameron told the *Radio Times* of his youthful enthusiasms for *Tiswas*, *Neighbours* and the daytime quiz show *Going for Gold*.[56] Several senior politicians claimed to enjoy *The X Factor*, and Tory strategists read its voting patterns as a way of gauging popular attitudes to people who worked in the public services, single mothers and asylum seekers – assuming, like Brown, that the show had something to teach them about democracy.

In fact, *The X Factor* was a grotesque caricature of democracy. It flattered viewers by reminding them constantly that the result was in their hands, while simultaneously getting them to pay to provide free product testing on new artists. It claimed to be empowering but was actually infantilising. The utopian promise of democratic interactivity held out at the start of the digital era was now reduced to a single phone call, a triumph of direct-line consumerism. Before viewers cast their votes, the show worked brazenly on their emotions through the sentimentality of the contestants' backstories, the casual pseudo-malice of the judges, and the baying audience at the Circus Maximus of the auditions, belittling the deluded souls who wrongly presumed themselves to have the X factor.

'Future generations,' the culture secretary Jeremy Hunt told the Royal Television Society, 'will learn more about us from what we watched on TV than from any historian. And looking at our media in 2010, they will conclude that it was deeply, desperately centralised.' Why, asked Hunt, did Birmingham, Alabama have eight local TV stations but Birmingham, England had none? He praised one of the few local channels, Witney TV, which had a policy of only covering positive news, from charity auctions to local fetes, as 'a hyper-local initiative that is helping to prove that the Big Society is alive and well in David Cameron's constituency'.[57]

The Big Society was one of the big policy phrases of the new coalition government, its aim being 'to create a climate that empowers local people and communities'. As an idea, the Big Society relied heavily on the positive connotations of the word 'local': local communities, local charities, local sourcing, local post offices, local television. But the recent history of these local stations was unpromising. Hunt invited a merchant banker, Nicholas Shott, to review the commercial prospects of local TV. His report found that the two dozen local stations formed since the 1996 Broadcasting Act, which allowed new channels to take out restricted service licences to broadcast on spare analogue frequencies, had met with 'limited success'.[58] This was mandarin understatement, for almost all these companies had failed to attract enough investors or advertisers and had stopped broadcasting.

The Isle of Wight's TV-12 channel, for example, coming from a converted caretaker's bungalow in the grounds of a Newport school, had filmed local bands playing in pubs and an amateur dramatic society, The Ferret Theatre Company, putting on plays. But it was replaced by Solent TV which, even after it diluted its local content with cheap imports such as *Futbol Mundial* and old black-and-white films, also went out of business. Lanarkshire TV, broadcasting from an old lunatic asylum near Kirk O'Shotts with a sign outside saying 'Brace yourself, Lanarkshire!', had a talent show called *Talented Lanarkshire*, a quiz night from Lanark Grammar School and a local constable appealing for witnesses in a small-scale version of *Crimewatch*. It was replaced by Thistle Television, which broadcast to a wider catchment area and interspersed this local material with Sky News and the QVC shopping channel. It too went bust.

The free market ethos that had governed the television industry since the 1990 Broadcasting Act treated viewers as rationally selective consumers – part of a general trend in cultural and political life. This ethos did not really see television watching as a collective activity;

instead, it saw the TV audience more as an accumulation of lots of individual consumer preferences. But this assumed that viewers always knew exactly what kind of television they liked before they watched it, as though they were choosing items from a supermarket aisle to put in their trolleys. When asked in consumer surveys, people did say they wanted more local news, and Waddington Village Television, that short-lived Granada experiment from the start of the satellite era, showed that very local TV could be surprisingly addictive. But in practice, when presented with the amateurish efforts of small stations trying to sustain themselves with low advertising revenue, viewers usually preferred to watch more lavishly produced network television.

That there was an untapped desire for local content among viewers was clear even from a national, primetime show like *The X Factor*. This started locally, with auditions held across the country, and regularly revealed the intensity of regional feeling, particularly in northern and Celtic areas. Two mediocre, tartan-tie wearing wedding singers from Ayr, the MacDonald Brothers, were kept in the show for weeks by millions of Scottish viewers who, as the letters page of the *Daily Record* attested, were considerably more exercised about their fate than about the survival of Gaelic language television. When the *America's Got Talent* judge Piers Morgan met Gordon Brown at the Treasury in November 2006, Brown expressed his irritation at the MacDonald Brothers' progress, saying 'they're giving Scotland a bad name'.[59] At the Liverpool auditions, the audience cheered contestants when they called out the names of the streets they lived in. Thousands of Northern Irish viewers complained when they could not get through on the phone lines to vote for Eoghan Quigg, a young singer from Dungiven in County Derry who had just been voted off the show – controversies about vote rigging being another recurrent aspect of the show's caricaturing of democracy.

And yet *The X Factor* was interested in the regions only insofar as they provided a provincial context from which the potential star could escape. Like Madame Bovary dreaming of Paris fashions or Chekhov's three sisters sighing for Moscow, those auditioning wished only to be allowed to make the journey to boot camp or the London finals, and receive the beneficence of the head judges. *The X Factor* used bountiful central budgets to create a televisual sensorium with spectacular pyrotechnics, tension-creating music and the basso profundo of Peter Dickson, whose grandiloquent, pause-laden introductions made his voice as recognisable to British viewers as Richard Dimbleby's had been half a century earlier. A familiar ritual thus played out each Saturday night in autumn, with the magical incantations 'calls cost 50p from landlines, mobile networks may vary' and 'please ask the bill-payer's permission' causing millions of thumbs to press urgently on keypads, and the closing of the phone lines conducted with the solemnity of a sacred rite. *Talented Lanarkshire* could never have matched this sense of theatre.

The habit of communal television watching had proved surprisingly resilient. Despite confident predictions at the start of the digital era about the end of 'linear viewing', most people still sat down each night and flicked through the channels to see what was on. As with video in the 1980s, catch-up sites and digital recorders had encouraged an element of time shifting but had not destroyed primetime or shared viewing. Some viewers were taking laptops to bed to watch programmes on the BBC iPlayer, or lying in with it at weekends, but otherwise the iPlayer had roughly the same peak hours as TV, with the same programmes being watched. And precisely because there was so much television available and so many ways of watching it, programme makers placed a high worth on family-centred, live television that would be watched and talked about across the nation.

The social networking site Twitter, with its improvised invention of the identifying hashtag, allowed vast virtual communities to meet to discuss shows while they were being broadcast: a universe of instant reaction and ongoing commentary, much of it inane and noisemaking, some of it funny and insightful. Television programmes began publishing these hashtags in their opening titles to encourage viewers to tweet; producers followed the feed to get free market research. People still seemed to seek that ephemeral, undemanding together-ness created by watching the same programmes. While governments carried on reciting the mantra of individual choice, television pointed to the residual longing for a collective national life.

Shows like *The X Factor* revived Dennis Potter's vision of televi-sion as a mass democratic form that could break through Britain's traditional class and educational barriers. For better or worse, they were probably now the nearest we had to a common culture. 'I sit in a first-class carriage on the Liverpool to Euston route,' complained the record producer Pete Waterman. 'You might think my fellow com-muters – businessmen, MPs, a clutch of lawyers and a smattering of City brokers – had better things to discuss on the two-hour journey. Our ailing economy perhaps, or the state of public transport? Appar-ently not. They witter endlessly about who's been ousted from [*The X Factor*] and whether they should have stayed put.' At a *Private Eye* lunch, the documentary filmmaker Adam Curtis and the former *Sunday Times* editor Andrew Neil were overheard having a prolonged and animated discussion – about who should win *The X Factor*.[60]

Potter would presumably have loathed *The X Factor*, although given the inbred contrarianism that led him to write occasional paeans of praise to *The Black and White Minstrel Show*, we cannot be sure. It is more likely that he would have been baffled and bewildered by it, and especially by the way it had become almost obligatory to watch and talk about it. Intelligent, literate people were now supposed to watch popular TV with savviness and sarcasm, not judgemental ear-nestness. Potter had high expectations of television and its viewers, which is why he felt so disappointed when it and they failed to live up to them. It is hard to imagine him viewing *The X Factor* with the requisite reserves of wry detachment and kitsch pleasure.

10

CLOSEDOWN

A friend has just given his television set to a surprised caller.
Is he a candidate for the calendar or for the social services?
He has turned the newscasters out, lock, stock and goodbye
smiles, and is master in his own house. We should try it. It is
a lay form of Trappism.

Ronald Blythe[1]

In the middle of March 1969, a severe ice storm hit the southern Pennines. At the top of Emley Moor, the spun metal stays of the television mast twanged and whistled in the wind and great clumps of ice fell off, denting parked cars and piercing the roofs of houses. Since being completed three years earlier, the mast had acquired an ugly reputation among the surrounding villagers, who called it 'the ice monster'. After receiving complaints from the council, the Independent Television Authority installed signs on approach roads and a flashing amber beacon on the mast to warn of ice falls. Muriel Truelove, before taking over as landlady of the nearby Three Acres Inn eight weeks earlier, anxiously paced out the distance between the mast and the pub to see whether the former would hit the latter if it ever fell down.[2]

At 5.01 p.m. on Wednesday 19 March, it did. A crash like a thunder crack could be heard for miles around. The top section of the mast, made of meshed steel girders clad in fibreglass, narrowly missed two cottages as it pitched into a field a third of a mile away. A Methodist chapel was sliced in two by one of the ice-laden, metal stays. Two men inside the building saw a cascade of ice hit the roof and then the stay come crashing through it. Silverwood Burt, a 68-year-old trustee of the chapel, was covered in plaster and woodwork, but was saved by the crash helmet he had borrowed for just such an eventuality. 'I dived under some seats in the classroom,' said the caretaker, Jeffrey Jessop. 'I laid there until it was all over, saying a lot of prayers.' The other stays whiplashed into the earth, with ten-feet-deep craters gouged in fields, and road surfaces where the wreckage fell smashed into tarmac fragments. The police closed all the roads to keep back sightseers who were crowding in through the fog, as breakdown crews hauled the debris away. 'The whole superb structure which dominated the West Riding as effectively as its transmissions dominated the county's TV screens, has been reduced to tangled metal by nothing more sinister than drizzle,' said the *Yorkshire Post*.[3]

When the mast came down, tens of thousands of the region's viewers, from the hill-shadowed villages of the West Riding to the coastal towns across the Yorkshire plain, were watching *Discotheque*, a children's pop show on ITV presented by Billy J. Kramer. Suddenly, a few minutes before a comedy show called *Do Not Adjust Your Set* was about to start, their screens disintegrated into static. As soon as the television went blank in the Leeds control room, the duty engineer's phone began ringing off the hook. Several callers demanded that the missed episode of *Coronation Street* be broadcast on BBC1 after closedown. Yorkshire TV's switchboard logged over 5,000 calls, mostly complaints about missing *Coronation Street* and *The Avengers*.[4] Over the next three days, seventeen Polish migrant workers put in eighteen-hour shifts in freezing 50 mph winds to build a temporary mast that covered most of the region, allowing Yorkshire TV to claw back its haemorrhaging advertising revenue. The only part of the original mast that survives now does service as Huddersfield sailing club's lookout tower, offering a panoramic view of the Boshaw Whams Reservoir.

By the end of the 1960s, the television set burbling away in the living room had come to signify normality and routine. The people who rang the Leeds duty engineer to complain about missing *Coronation Street* probably gave little thought as to how its radio waves reached them. Television had become a mundane piece of wizardry, something only really noticeable when it broke down or was interrupted. Historically, the most vociferous complaints from viewers have not been about sex, violence or bad language, but about when television stops for no apparent reason or their favourite programmes are cancelled or postponed. What viewers seem to demand most of television is that it carries on, like an ever-flowing stream. And, mostly, it does: a non-stop, decades-old technical miracle. The collapse of the Emley Moor mast was a brief reminder of how much we take television for granted and how much it depends on apparatus that might, at some point, come crashing down on our heads.

Some of the original TV masts, which caused so much excitement when they were built, such as Holme Moss and Kirk O'Shotts, have stopped sending out television signals and now transmit mobile phone conversations or digital radio. The nameless engineers who kept television going in these remote places have long since moved on to other masts, retired or died. The remaining masts are mostly unsung in our cultural mythology, with a few eccentric exceptions. The Mancunian post-punk funk band A Certain Ratio recorded a song about the Granada region's Winter Hill transmitter in 1981, which consists of thirteen minutes of stubbornly monotonous drumming and a techno motif of just two alternating notes, meant to imitate a TV signal.

The Yorkshire-born poet Simon Armitage once hymned the new 900-foot Emley Moor mast, a tapering, reinforced concrete tower completed in 1971, in a ten-minute visual poem for BBC2's *One Foot in the Past* series in 1993, and elsewhere described it as 'like the afterburn of a rocket disappearing into the clouds'. In a 1996 BBC2 documentary, *I Remember the Future*, the presenter, Jonathan Meades, stood at the bottom of this mast in order to give a sense of its height and surprising girth, and proclaimed it 'established by aliens in 1966 [*sic*] in order that 30 years later this film might reach you'. These 'punctuation marks of human supremacy,' he mused, belonged to 'that brief and far off parenthesis when Britain was modern', the third quarter of the twentieth century, when public architecture was 'self-celebratory, bloated, grandiose'.[5] No one, except the odd non-conformist like Meades, rhapsodises about TV masts any more.

While I was writing this book, the analogue signal slowly disappeared, region by region. One of the soundtracks to its writing was the constant repetition on the television and radio of the restful Welsh accent of the BBC newsreader Huw Edwards reminding me that my analogue television would soon be useless but that, if I were over seventy-five or registered disabled, I could get help. The technologically unschooled became reluctant students of the new vocabulary of the digibox and scart socket. At my local tip, I saw several dozen 'fat-screen' televisions piled up in a skip. In America they call it the Super Bowl effect, the mass dumping of old TVs as viewers upgrade to sleeker, better sets in time for the sporting event of the year. The digital switchover was the Super Bowl effect in extremis. On some of these old TVs, as their former owners had thrown them casually away, the cathode ray tube had become separated from its plastic housing. Seen in the raw, the tubes seemed suddenly bulky and primitive, a Victorian technology that had survived improbably into the present.

'They are so ubiquitous in life that their bodies in death litter our wastelands and edgelands,' the poets Paul Farley and Michael Symmons Roberts write in their book *Edgelands*, about the old televisions you see abandoned on peri-urban wasteland and landfill. 'And why does a dead TV's blank face resonate so much with us? Is this our image of oblivion?'[6] I have heard these clunky cubic sets end up on container ships bound for Nigeria, China and other countries unencumbered by legislation about the lead, strontium and other toxic substances inside them. There, ragpickers, usually young girls, plunder them for tiny amounts of precious metals like silver and caesium. They give no thought (and why should they?) to the zillions of electrons that have flickered and died on their phosphorescent tubes for the amusement and bemusement of distant others.

On 4 November 2009, on the same day the Winter Hill transmitter switched to digital, an exhibition opened at the Urbis gallery in Manchester, called 'Ghosts of Winter Hill'. Its conceit was that for half a century domestic life in Britain had been ruled by the TV set, and the north had helped to define this television era that was ending. 'The collectivisation of the nation through the conduit of television is no longer anything like so concentrated. In fact it's infinitely diluted,' said Phil Griffin, the co-curator. 'So, in some sense, I believe that one could argue that the television era is over.'[7] I went to the exhibition, a series of cutaway period sitting rooms looking out of place in Urbis's glassy, minimalist surroundings. There was a G-Plan 1950s room, an *Abigail's Party*-style 1970s room, a flatpack 1990s room, and in each of them was a contemporaneous television set, screening programmes from that decade that had come out of Manchester: *The Army Game*, *Top of the Pops* or *Cold Feet* played on a loop.

If the television era was over, though, it didn't feel like it. There were terrible warnings in Granadaland before the switchover that if we did not retune our sets all our programmes would disappear – the *Coronation Street* bug again – but I forgot to do anything, and when I turned the TV on the next day it had somehow righted itself and was all the same as usual. The programmes simply carried on as normal; there were no pomp-and-circumstance ceremonies from transmitter sites as there had been in the postwar era when analogue television arrived in a region. When London and the south-east switched over in April 2012, the Crystal Palace transmitter, the most important in the network with a range of over forty miles, did host a VIP event to mark the occasion. Interviewed by the BBC Radio 2 presenter Chris Evans on stage, Professor Brian Cox, whose own science programmes had been inspired by watching *Life on Earth* and Carl Sagan's *Cosmos* as a boy, went off-message by admitting a nostalgia for a four-channel world in which you could always 'find something to watch that you didn't know you liked'.[8]

As David Attenborough, whose career in television now spanned sixty years, hit a big red button, sonorous *X Factor*-style music boomed out. Beams of light representing the invisible digital TV signals were now supposed to shoot up the tower and radiate over London. But, in the middle of the wettest April on record, it was pouring down. The beams reached no further than Brixton and the spinning searchlight at the top was covered by low cloud. The switching off of the analogue signal, which had caused so much excitement when it arrived across the country, was thus fittingly anticlimactic. The few valedictions in the newspapers were all for Ceefax, that primitive version of the internet that would be lost in the analogue switchover. Journalists eulogised about its Lego-like coloured graphics and the excitement of following football games by staring at the slowly changing scores.

A few days after the Crystal Palace switchover, I went for a walk around my neighbourhood in the early evening. The houses here are *Coronation Street*-style terraces – like Granada's fictional street, they were built in 1902 and are named Coronation Villas to mark the accession of Edward VIII – and there are no walk-up steps to separate house from pavement. So as I passed each home, without even trying to look in, I could see televisions, mostly showing that now half-a-century-old programme, *Coronation Street*, through the bay windows. These TV screens are more detailed and smoothly moving than ever before, and they are as big and wide as wallcharts, magnifying the talking heads in the corner of the room so that shaving rash and undyed hair roots are visible. As usual, high-definition television is presented as our inevitable appointment with the progress we all wanted all along. But I wonder if humankind, like Gulliver inspecting the giant blemished faces of the Brobdingnagians, will be able to bear this much reality.

The televisions may be huge, but the people watching them remain as inscrutable as ever. We still know remarkably little about this *terra incognita*, the living room with the TV on. Who are these square-eyed spectres, hidden behind curtains or briefly glimpsed like this at lighting-up time? From its first incarnations, people feared that television would create supine, insular citizens. As early as 1930, the *Manchester Guardian* wondered whether, 'with all the stars of entertainment twinkling and chattering on the parlour wall', television would 'seal us up in a gaol of domesticity'.[9] The human shadows that we see through the windows of houses as we pass them, briefly illuminated by the flickering television screen, have sometimes seemed to resemble the cave dwellers in Plato's *Republic*, turning their backs on the cold light of the world in favour of their own illusory reality created by the silhouette of a fire playing on the back wall.

The media historians Daniel Dayan and Elihu Katz once compared the mass viewing of television to the *seder*, the Jewish ritual marking the start of Passover. Jews celebrate the *seder* in their own homes, which are open to extended family and sometimes strangers, and these millions of synchronised, homebound microevents take place around a symbolic centre, a sense that the Jewish diaspora is celebrating all at the same time. Dayan and Katz saw television as a similar kind of 'festive viewing', a powerful social chemistry bonding society together.[10] But on the whole, this has only been sporadically true, and even big events like the coronation and the moon landing, which Dayan and Katz focus on, have produced too wide a range of reactions to be compared to a religious ritual. Not everyone wants to be part of the armchair nation, and there is always something on the other side – or the off switch.

But even if they are not a virtual society organised as ritualistically as the *seder*, television viewers are surely more than just a collection of lots of atomised, a-collective individuals slumped in front of the box. If you were to magic your way into the countless British living rooms (not to mention oil rigs, prisons, lighthouses, hospitals, boarding schools, care homes ...) where television has been watched over tens of thousands of days, you would no doubt find some of those passive, Platonic cave dwellers. But you would also find millions of micro-communities, all doing similar things such as laughing, crying, arguing, querying ('who's he again?'), irritatedly 'shushing' those not watching as attentively as them, passing verdicts ('well, that wasn't up to much …') – but in individual, idiosyncratic ways that would seem as rich and varied as television itself.

As I walked past the houses, and heard the dying fall of *Coronation Street* dialogue from one house being picked up again by another as I passed it, I wondered about the fate of the analogue signal that would soon be no longer of this earth. When high fidelity television started in 1936, it began simultaneously broadcasting through space. For nearly eighty years these high frequency waves have been radiating into the skies at the speed of light, swept across our planet by its rotation. Imagine a huge, invisible mass of carrier waves, most of which we will never see again, at the leading edge of which, and already past several thousand stars by now, is the smooth, matinee idol voice of Leslie Mitchell saying 'Hello Radiolympia. Ladies and gentlemen, "Here's Looking at You".'

In 1976, Woodruff Sullivan of the University of Washington decided to work out just what the earth's radio leakage actually was. He concluded that, were sentient alien beings to exist, the thing most likely to indicate our presence to them, because of their number and the consistency of their frequencies, would be our television carrier waves.[11] At the time there was much excitement about the launching of Voyager I and II, the space probes sent off into the farthest reaches of the galaxy with a disc containing birdsong, music by Bach and Chuck Berry, pictures of the Sydney Opera House and the Pyramids and messages recorded in various languages ('Greetings to our friends in the stars. We wish that we will meet you someday') for the bemusement of hypothetical aliens. Sullivan simply pointed out the obvious: only light could make headway in the almost unimaginable distances of interstellar space, and so remnants of old television were far more likely to give our position away than those snail-slow Voyager aircrafts, which have only just left the outer reaches of our solar system, and will not pass another planet for another 40,000 years.

By collecting information about the thousands of television masts then in operation, Sullivan was able to speculate about the nature of the waves that would be picked up elsewhere. The weaker signals of the smaller masts would be masked by the pervasive interstellar static emitted throughout the universe known as cosmic microwave background radiation, some of which appears on a TV screen when it is not tuned into a channel (that random pattern of hyperactive dots the Scandinavians compare to warring ants). But the TV masts with the strongest power, then concentrated in western Europe, America and Japan, would be detectable above this galactic noise. Assuming they knew about the Doppler effect, the shift in frequency of an observed wave because the observer or the source has moved, an alien picking up these signals would be able to work out the size of our planet and perhaps seasonal changes – in winter, for example, fewer leaves on the trees would make the waves stronger.[12] And that would be before they even sat down to watch the programmes.

Just before Christmas 2011, NASA announced that its space telescope had discovered Kepler 22b, the first confirmed planet to orbit squarely within what scientists call the 'Goldilocks zone' of a Sun-like star, where temperatures would be just right to allow surface water throughout its orbit and thus sustain life. It is 600 light years away from earth, which means that in about 600 years' time, some civilised aliens on this earth-like planet, assuming they had managed to invent something resembling a cathode ray tube and a TV aerial, could be watching the current offerings on ITV2 or Sky Living and wondering if they really represent the summit of human creativity and achievement.

But perhaps even the most fatuous, banal TV will be viewed in a kindlier light from billions of miles away, reduced to what it is in essence: an imperfect attempt to make a human connection across empty space. Bad television is still a technical triumph, needing huge reserves of labour and skill, much of it unacknowledged, to bring it to us. And like all attempts at conversation, it is a leap into the dark, with no guarantee it will be heard or understood. Who has not turned on a TV programme and felt that the people who created it, even though they might occupy the same small patch of our planet, were basically cognitive aliens, tuned to a different mental wavelength from our own? And yet somehow, out of mere shapes and shadows made of electrons and pixels, television has sent us messages that we have managed to mould into meaning. It has spoken to us through the air and permeated our intimate lives, filling them with boredom and wonder, irritation and inspiration, dismay and delight.

NOTES

The following abbreviations have been used:
BBC WAC: BBC Written Archives Centre at Caversham, Reading
MOA: Mass Observation Archive at the University of Sussex
NA: National Archives at Kew

1. Switching on

1. David Jacobs, 'Matt Monro', *Oxford Dictionary of National Biography*, online edition.
2. D. J. Taylor, 'A funny thing happened', *Independent*, 29 March 2001; 'More child participation in new BBC TV programmes', *The Times*, 6 September 1973; David Oswell, *Television, Childhood, and the Home: A History of the Making of the Child Television Audience in Britain* (Oxford: Clarendon Press, 2002), p. 50.
3. Biddy Baxter, *Dear Blue Peter* (London: Short Books, 2008), p. 63.
4. Simon Garfield, *The Wrestling* (London: Faber, 1996), p. 89.
5. Roland Barthes, *Mythologies* (London: Vintage, 1993), p. 25.
6. Raymond Williams, *Culture and Society 1780–1950* (Harmondsworth: Penguin, 1961), p. 253.
7. A. A. Gill, 'Oh Lord, he's still stuck in the past', *Sunday Times*, 27 March 2005.
8. John Sutherland and Stephen Fender, *Love Sex Death & Words: Surprising Tales from a Year in Literature* (London: Icon, 2010), p. 432.
9. William Barkley, 'They've got it on the brain!', *Daily Express*, 16 November 1965; Philip Thody, *Don't Do It!: A Dictionary of the Forbidden* (New York: St Martin's Press, 1997), p. 154; letter from the

University of Essex Union to the BBC, 14 November 1965, BBC WAC, R41/279/1PCS.

10. Dominic Shellard, *Kenneth Tynan: A Life* (New Haven, CT: Yale University Press, 2003), p. 301.

11. 'Such a strange TV interview', *Daily Mirror*, 19 June 1956; Brum Henderson, *Brum: A Life in Television* (Belfast: Appletree Press, 2003), p. 72.

12. Letter from Kenneth E. Pottle to the BBC-3 producer, 19 November 1965, BBC WAC, R41/279/3PCS; Shellard, *Tynan*, p. 300; 'Housewives to defend liberal ideas', *Guardian*, 13 December 1965.

13. Shellard, *Tynan*, p. 301; Robert Robinson, *Skip All That: Memoirs* (London: Century, 1996), p. 127; Kingsley Amis, 'Swearing in decline?', *Guardian*, 17 November 1968.

14. Ed Harris, *Not in Front of the Telly: 75 Years of the BBC's Complaints Department* (Clifton-upon-Terne: Polperro Heritage Press, 2002), p. 100.

15. John Ellis, *Visible Fictions: Cinema, Television, Video* (London: Routledge and Kegan Paul, 1982), p. 5.

2. A waking dream

1. T. S. Eliot, 'The music of poetry', in *On Poetry and Poets* (London: Faber, 1957), p. 32.

2. Virginia Woolf, 'Oxford Street tide', in *The London Scene* (London: Snowbooks, 2004), pp. 27, 29.

3. Callisthenes, 'Television: first public demonstration', *The Times*, 24 March 1925.

4. John Durham Peters, *Speaking into the Air: A History of the Idea of Communication* (Chicago: University of Chicago Press, 1999), p. 29.

5. Lindy Woodhead, *Shopping, Seduction and Mr Selfridge* (London: Profile, 2007), p. 195; Callisthenes, 'Television'.

6. *The Race for Television*, Episode 2, Granada/ITV, 19 February 1985; Anthony Kamm and Malcolm Baird, *John Logie Baird: A Life* (Edinburgh: National Museums of Scotland Publishing, 2002), p. 58.

7. Gordon Honeycombe, *Selfridges: Seventy-Five Years: The Story of the Store 1909–1984* (London: Park Lane Press, 1984), p. 57.

8. R. W. Burns, *British Television: The Formative Years* (London: Peregrinus/Science Museum, 1986), p. 110.

9. Burns, *British Television*, p. 149.

10. Eric Linden, 'The first great love story of television', *TV Times*, 14 October 1955, 20–21.

11. W. L. Wraight, 'Reception of the B.B.C. 30-line television transmissions in Madeira', *Journal of the Television Society*, 2, 2 (June 1935), 27.

12. Russell W. Burns, *John Logie Baird: Television Pioneer* (London: The Institution of Electrical Engineers, 2000), p. 184.

13. Burns, *British Television*, p. 152; 'The week on the screen', *Manchester Guardian*, 19 July 1930.

14. Anthony Burgess, 'European culture: does it exist?', *Theatre Journal*, 43, 3 (October 1991), 302; Anthony Burgess, 'Takeover', *Listener*, 23 May 1963, 884.

15. Anthony Burgess, 'Return to reality', *Listener*, 5 December 1963, 956; Anthony Burgess, 'Why Benny is a king of comedy', *Guardian*, 1 December 1990.

16. Anthony Burgess, '1948: An old man interviewed', in *1985* (London: Hutchinson, 1978), p. 22.

17. Anthony Burgess, *Little Wilson and Big God* (London: Penguin, 1988), p. 103.

18. Burns, *British Television*, pp. 158–9; Kamm and Baird, *John Logie Baird*, p. 142.

19. Kamm and Baird, *John Logie Baird*, p. 147; Burns, *British Television*, p. 160.

20. Burns, *British Television*, p. 160; James Harding, 'George Robey', *Oxford Dictionary of National Biography*, online edition.

21. Dicky Howett, *Television Innovations: 50 Technological Developments* (Tiverton: Kelly, 2006), p. 81; *The Race for Television*, Episode 2, Granada/ITV, 19 February 1985; Bruce Norman, *Here's Looking at You: The Story of British Television 1908–1939* (London: BBC/Royal Television Society, 1984), p. 73.

22. Aldous Huxley, *Brave New World* (London: Vintage, 2007), pp. 174–6; Nicholas Murray, *Aldous Huxley: An English Intellectual* (London: Little, Brown, 2002), p. 432.

23. Ian McEwan, 'A medium of no importance', *Observer*, 31 July 1983.

24. Gordon Ross, *Television Jubilee: The Story of 25 Years of B.B.C. Television* (London: W. H. Allen, 1961), p. 25; Norman, *Here's Looking at You*, p. 90.

25. 'Experiments in television', *Observer*, 23 February 1936; Donald F. McLean, *Restoring Baird's Image* (London: Institution of Electrical Engineers, 2000), pp. xvi–xvii.

26. John Trenouth, 'Foreword', in McLean, *Restoring Baird's Image*, pp. xii–xiii.

27. Ross, *Television Jubilee*, p. 26; 'B.B.C. television troubles', *Daily Express*, 19 February 1934.

28. 'Seeing-in', *Manchester Guardian*, 16 May 1934.

29. Kingsley Wood, 'The Television Report: broadcast by the Postmaster-General on 31 January', *Listener*, 6 February 1935, 248; Leonard Miall, *Inside the BBC: British Broadcasting Characters* (London: Weidenfeld and Nicolson, 1994), p. 22; Burgess, 'An old man', p. 23.

30. 'What's in a name? £5 5s', *Daily Express*, 6 February 1935; Burns, *British Television*, p. 353.

31. Norman, *Here's Looking at You*, p. 109.

32. THB, 'Television and the Heaviside Layer', *Journal of the Television Society*, 1 (January 1931), p. 31.

33. 'Television "Adonis" found!', *Daily Mail*, 22 May 1936; Kenneth Baily, *Here's Television* (London: Vox Mundi, 1950), p. 7.

34. 'The arrival of television', *Observer*, 30 August 1936.

35. Robert Charles Alexander, *The Inventor of Stereo: The Life and Works of Alan Dower Blumlein* (Oxford: Focal Press, 1999), pp. 191–2.

36. 'Films televised to 'plane 4,000ft. up', *Daily Mirror*, 5 September 1936.

37. Norman, *Here's Looking at You*, p. 120.

38. L. Marsland Gander, 'BBC television handicaps', *Daily Telegraph*, 24 November 1936.

39. L. Marsland Gander, '*Picture Page* from both sides of the television screen', *Radio Times*, 13 January 1939, 6.

40. 'Appeal to owners of television sets', *Journal of the Television Society*, 2, 6 (December 1936), 219; Listener Research Section, 'Viewers and the television service, a report of an investigation of viewers' opinions in January 1937', 5 February 1937, BBC WAC, R9/9/1.

41. 'Television for the deaf – an experiment', *Journal of the Television Society*, 2, 8 (June 1937), 273.

42. 'What the viewers are saying', *Radio Times Television Supplement*, 26 March 1937, 5; Bernard Buckham, 'Television is no longer a novelty', *Daily Mirror*, 3 June 1937; Michael Barry, *From the Palace to the Grove* (London: Royal Television Society, 1992), p. 7.

43. Rene Cutforth, 'Fifty years of broadcasting, part four: television', *Listener*, 2 November 1972, 586.

44. 'The future of television', *Observer*, 23 May 1937; 'Television to-day', *BBC Handbook, 1938* (London: BBC, 1938), pp. 40, 42.

45. 'Television: Centre Court', *Listener*, 30 June 1937, 1297.

46. The Scanner, 'Big guns at the Palace', *Radio Times*, 4 November 1938, 17.

47. Jonah Barrington, 'Perfect television for two minutes', *Daily Express*, 13 November 1937.

48. 'Television boys show off their new lift', *Daily Express*, 18 February 1937; Jonah Barrington, 'Readers travel from as far as Land's End to see television', *Daily Express*, 17 August 1937; Jonah Barrington, *And Master of None* (London: W. Edwards, 1948), pp. 189–90.

49. 'Two years of television', *The Times*, 23 December 1938.

50. P. H., 'And this is how two reporters saw it', *Daily Express*, 24 February 1939.

51. Alan Hunter, 'Television is for the home', *Radio Times*, 10 February 1939, 10.

52. 'Phone "sees" man 106 miles away', *Daily Express*, 24 December 1938.

53. Morley interviewed in *Imagine: And Then There Was Television*, BBC1, 21 December 2006; Kate Dunn, *Do Not Adjust Your Set: The Early Days of Live Television* (London: John Murray, 2003), p. 27.

54. 'In praise of television', *Journal of the Television Society*, 3, 2 (1939), 49–50.

55. Bruce Forsyth, *Bruce: The Autobiography* (London: Sidgwick and Jackson, 2001), p. 3; Hermione Lee, *Virginia Woolf* (London: Vintage, 1997), p. 667.

56. Nigel Nicolson (ed.), *The Harold Nicolson Diaries 1907–1963* (London: Phoenix, 2005), pp. 182–3.

57. Ross McKibbin, *Classes and Cultures: England, 1918–1951* (Oxford: Oxford University Press, 1998), p. 15; 'Individual approach', *Listener*, 11 May 1939, 1015.

58. The Scanner, 'Club for television viewers?', *Radio Times*, 3 February 1939, 13; The Scanner, 'Au revoir to the king', *Radio Times*, 28 April 1939, 13.

59. 'Mr. Boar goes in for television', *Radio Times*, 24 February 1939, 6.

60. Baily, *Here's Television*, p. 18; The Scanner, 'Television is grand!', *Radio Times*, 7 July 1939, 18.

61. 'Views of viewers heard by the BBC', *The Times*, 27 June 1939.

62. Paddy Scannell, 'Public service broadcasting and modern life', in *Culture and Power: A Media, Culture & Society Reader*, eds Paddy Scannell, Philip Schlesinger and Colin Sparks (London: Sage, 1992), p. 330; Grace Wyndham Goldie, 'Television tea-party', *Listener*, 29 June 1939, 1368.

63. Ernest C. Thomson, 'Au revoir, television', in *BBC Handbook, 1940* (London: BBC, 1940), p. 53.

64. The Scanner, 'Television can take it!', *Radio Times*, 1 September 1939, 15.

65. 'Electrical and Musical Industries: television progress', *Observer*, 10 December 1939.

66. Thomson, 'Au revoir, television', p. 58.

3. A straight pencil-mark up the sky

1. Graham Payn and Sheridan Morley (eds), *The Noel Coward Diaries* (London: Weidenfeld and Nicolson, 1982), p. 77.

2. Patricia and Robert Malcolmson (eds), *Nella Last's Peace: The Postwar Diaries of Housewife, 49* (London: Profile, 2008), p. 31; 'Television service', *BBC Yearbook, 1947* (London: BBC, 1947), p. 77.

3. *Imagine: And Then There Was Television*, BBC1, 21 December 2006; Peter Sallis, *Fading into the Limelight* (London: Orion, 2006), p. 14.

4. Fay Schlesinger, 'Still in good working order, the television set made in 1936', *Daily Mail*, 20 July 2009; Anthony Kamm and Malcolm Baird, *John Logie Baird: A Life* (Edinburgh: National Museums of Scotland, 2002), pp. 363–4.

5. 'Case for television', *The Times*, 6 March 1947; Simon Garfield, *Our Hidden Lives: The Everyday Diaries of a Forgotten Britain 1945–1948* (London: Ebury Press, 2004), p. 477.

6. Richard Haynes, 'The BBC, austerity and broadcasting the 1948 Olympic Games', *International Journal of the History of Sport*, 27, 6 (April 2010), 1042–3.

7. Listener Research Department, 'Television: the "Viewers' Vote" scheme', 17 June 1948, BBC WAC, LT/48/1047; 'Television tastes', *Manchester Guardian*, 14 December 1950; Listener Research Department, 'Television: some points about the audience', BBC WAC, LT/48/1219.

8. Listener Research Department, 'Television Enquiry 1948, part 4, viewing', BBC WAC, LR/49/1260; *Mass-Observation's Panel on Television*, April 1949, MOA, File Report 3106, p. 5.

9. John Swift, *Adventures in Vision: The First Twenty-Five Years of Television* (London: John Lehmann, 1950), p. 132; Bob Phillips, *The 1948 Olympics: How London Rescued the Games* (Cheltenham: SportsBooks, 2007), p. xii.

10. Harold Hobson, 'The problem of personality', *Listener*, 1 June 1950, 962.

11. Leslie Hardern, *TV Inventors' Club* (London: Rockcliff, 1954), pp. 156–8.

12. 'Something for everybody?', *Manchester Guardian*, 17 September 1954; Joan Bush, 'What's your gadget?', *Picture Post*, 5 September 1953, 33; Hardern, *TV Inventors' Club*, p. 138.

13. Mike Ashley, *Starlight Man: The Extraordinary Life of Algernon Blackwood* (London: Constable, 2001), pp. 324–6, 334.

14. 'The dandy comes back to W.1', *Picture Post*, 7 June 1952, 28; Graham McCann, *Bounder! The Biography of Terry-Thomas* (London: Aurum, 2008), pp. 58, 60–62.

15. Su Holmes, *Entertaining Television: The BBC and Popular Television Culture in the 1950s* (Manchester: Manchester University Press, 2008), p. 83.

16. 'Lord Reith in conversation with Malcolm Muggeridge – part two', *Listener*, 7 December 1967, 744; C. A. Lejeune, 'Television', *Observer*, 31 December 1950.

17. '"Television mast a hazard" to planes', *Manchester Guardian*, 16 December 1949.

18. 'Television for 6,000,000 more', *Manchester Guardian*, 14 December 1949; Norman Collins, 'This thing called television', *Radio Times*, 9 December 1949, 6.

19. Kenneth Baily, *Here's Television* (London: Vox Mundi, 1950), p. 67; Norman Collins, 'Preface: Getting to know the place', in *London Belongs to Me* (London: Collins, 1945), p. 8.

20. Leonard Marsland Gander, *Television for All* (London: Alba Books, 1950), p. 39.

21. Collins, 'This thing called television', 6.

22. T. S. Eliot, 'The television habit', *The Times*, 20 December 1950; Norman Collins, 'Anxiety typical of every age', *The Times*, 23 December 1950.

23. 'Television's new venture', *Manchester Guardian*, 19 December 1949.

24. 'Wariness about television', *Manchester Guardian*, 20 December 1949.

25. 'Television's new station', *Manchester Guardian*, 19 December 1949; 'TV dealers brought from bed by rush to buy sets', *Daily Mirror*, 19 December 1949.

26. Steven Barnett, *Games and Sets: The Changing Face of Sport on Television* (London: BFI, 1990), p. 12; 'The fans hunted TV aerials', *Daily Mirror*, 26 September 1951.

27. Fyfe Robertson, 'We were wrong about television', *Picture Post*, 10 February 1951, 24.

28. 'A Wellsian world in the heart of the hills', *Manchester Guardian*, 11 October 1951.

29. Leonard Mosley, 'I've run into TV's top fans', *Daily Express*, 30 October 1951; Leonard Mosley, 'A fig for crooning cockneys!', *Daily Express*, 10 October 1951.

30. 'Professor and the "tangible terror"', *Daily Mirror*, 26 January 1952; '"Tangible terror" of television: a warning to Scotland', *Manchester Guardian*, 26 January 1952; Robert Armstrong, 'Kirk O'Shotts', *TV Mirror*, 1 May 1954, 21.

31. Hansard, HC Deb, 30 July 1949, vol. 467, col. 2940.

32. David Kynaston, *Austerity Britain 1945–51* (London: Bloomsbury, 2007), p. 585; 'Fascinating possibilities of TV medium', *Glasgow Herald*, 14 March 1952.

33. 'Television comes to Scotland', *Glasgow Herald*, 15 March 1952; David Pat Walker, *The BBC in Scotland: The First Fifty Years*

(Edinburgh: Luath Press, 2011), p. 188; 'Excellent reception', *Glasgow Herald*, 15 March 1952.

34. Richard Whiteley, *Himoff! The Memoirs of a TV Matinée Idle* (London: Orion, 2000), p. 12.

35. 'Obituary: Gerald Campion', *Independent*, 13 July 2002; Hansard, HC Deb, 15 May 1952, vol. 500, col. 1638.

36. Audience Research Department, 'Viewer research report: *Café Continental* – 28th February 1953', 11 March 1953, BBC WAC, LE VR/53/100; 'Hélène Cordet', *TV Mirror*, 10 October 1953, 16.

37. Whiteley, *Himoff!*, pp. 17, 12.

38. Tony Currie, *The Radio Times Story* (Tiverton: Kelly Publications, 2001), pp. 77, 79.

39. John Davies, *Broadcasting and the BBC in Wales* (Cardiff: University of Wales Press, 1994), pp. 203–4.

40. Norman Shacklady and Martin Ellen (eds), *On Air: A History of BBC Transmission* (Orpington: Wavechange Books, 2003), p. 123.

41. Nick Clarke, *The Shadow of a Nation: How Celebrity Destroyed Britain* (London: Phoenix, 2004), pp. 24, 19, 30, 295.

42. D. R. Thorpe, *Supermac: The Life of Harold Macmillan* (London: Chatto and Windus, 2010), p. 276; Reginald Pound, 'The King's funeral', *Listener*, 21 February 1952, 318; Henrik Örnebring, 'Writing the history of television audiences: the coronation in the Mass-Observation Archive', in Helen Wheatley (ed.), *Re-Viewing Television History: Critical Issues in Television Historiography* (London: I. B. Tauris, 2007), p. 176.

43. Cassandra, *Daily Mirror*, 22 October 1952, 7; 'Archbishop does not like TV', *Irish Times*, 12 September 1952.

44. Ben Pimlott, *The Queen: A Biography of Elizabeth II* (London: HarperCollins, 1996), pp. 205, 190–91; Peter Hennessy, *Having it So Good: Britain in the Fifties* (London: Penguin, 2007), p. 242; Leonard Miall, *Inside the BBC: British Broadcasting Characters* (London: Weidenfeld and Nicolson, 1994), p. 162.

45. Gillian McIntosh, *The Force of Culture: Unionist Identities in Twentieth-Century Ireland* (Cork: Cork University Press, 1999), pp. 120, 122.

46. Natasha Vall, *Cultural Region: North East England 1945–2000* (Manchester: Manchester University Press, 2011), p. 39.

47. John Moynihan, *The Soccer Syndrome: From the Primeval Forties* (London: MacGibbon and Kee, 1966), pp. 75–9.

48. Martin Johnes and Gavin Mellor, 'The 1953 FA Cup Final: modernity and tradition in British culture', *Contemporary British History*, 20, 2 (June 2006), 271.

49. Clarke, *Shadow of a Nation*, p. 43.

50. 'Seven hours of comfort', *Manchester Guardian*, 3 June 1953; 'Our London correspondence', *Manchester Guardian*, 3 June 1953.

51. Kynaston, *Family Britain*, p. 299; Harry Hopkins, *The New Look: A Social History of the Forties and Fifties in Britain* (London: Secker and Warburg, 1963), p. 295; '20,000,000 saw Abbey service', *Manchester Guardian*, 13 June 1953; Philip Ziegler, *Crown and People* (London: Collins, 1978), p. 115; 'Television at Finsbury Drive, Bradford', 2 June 1953, MOA, SxMOA1/2/69/6/C/8; 'TV eyes and procession feet', *Daily Herald*, 30 May 1953.

52. Örnebring, 'Writing the history', pp. 177, 181–2.

53. 'Looks like a chair, actually it's a lavatory', *A Night in with Alan Bennett*, BBC2, 5 July 1992.

54. 'Coronation 1953 – children's essays', MOA, SxMOA1/2/69/3/D/8. The boy's name has been changed in accordance with the MOA's policy of protecting anonymity.

55. Örnebring, 'Writing the history', p. 179; Ziegler, *Crown and People*, p. 118.

56. Örnebring, 'Writing the history', pp. 178–9; Ziegler, *Crown and People*, p. 122; Joan Bakewell, *The Centre of the Bed* (London: Sceptre, 2004), p. 94; Joan Bakewell, 'Diary', *New Statesman*, 7 April 2003, 8.

57. Miall, *Inside the BBC*, p. 190.

58. Arthur Bryant, 'Our notebook', *London Illustrated News*, 29 May 1954, 898.

59. '20,000,000 saw Abbey service'; '2 June 1953 – coronation day', in Kenneth Baily (ed.), *Television Annual for 1954* (London: Odhams, 1954), p. 68.

60. 'Viewers' views', *Radio Times*, 12 June 1953, 44; Ziegler, *Crown and People*, p. 104.

61. 'The year's retail trade', *The Times*, 29 December 1953.

62. '"Sign" of the television age', *TV Mirror*, 12 September 1953, 7.

63. John Moore, 'TV in our village', *TV Mirror*, 12 September 1953, 7, 22.

64. 'Hessary Tor not the only site for Western TV mast', *Manchester Guardian*, 1 October 1953; Dartmoor Preservation Association, 'Preliminary memorandum on the proposal of the British Broadcasting Corporation to establish a 750-ft television mast and installations at North Hessary Tor, Dartmoor', 10 December 1951, NA, COU 1/454; Mrs Sylvia Sayer to H. M. Abrahams, 25 November 1952, NA, COU 1/454.

65. Mrs Aimee Havard to Sir David Maxwell Fife, 29 December 1953, NA, BD 24/200.

66. 'TV aerial put up in garden', *Manchester Guardian*, 15 July 1952; 'Booster sets today and tomorrow', *Isle of Man Examiner*, 18 December 1953.

67. Walker, *The BBC in Scotland*, p. 191.

68. George Best, *Blessed: The Autobiography* (London: Ebury, 2002), pp. 24–6.

69. Philip Norman, *Babycham Night: A Boyhood at the end of the Pier* (London: Pan, 2004), pp. 133, 148–9.

70. Norman, *Babycham Night*, p. 263.

71. David Bret, *The Real Gracie Fields: The Authorised Biography* (London: JR Books, 2010), p. 1; 'Looking around, the Palace gets the new TV', *TV Times*, 20 September 1955, 17; Roy Blackman, 'Teletecs', *Daily Mirror*, 11 April 1960.

72. Jonathan Dimbleby, *The Prince of Wales* (London: Warner Books, 1995), p. 160.

4. The pale flicker of the Lime Grove light

1. J. B. Priestley, *Thoughts in the Wilderness* (London: Heinemann, 1957), pp. 194, 196.

2. Gilbert Harding, *Along My Line* (London: Putnam, 1953), p. 191; Wallace Reyburn, *Gilbert Harding: A Candid Portrayal* (Brighton: Angus and Robertson, 1978), p. 55; Andy Medhurst, 'Every wart and pustule: Gilbert Harding and television stardom', in John Corner (ed.), *Popular Television in Britain* (London: BFI, 1991), p. 62.

3. 'Fascinating possibilities of TV medium', *Glasgow Herald*, 14 March 1952; Isobel Barnett, 'Life has many "lines"', *TV Mirror*, 11 December

1954, 19; Peter Black, *Mirror in the Corner: People's Television* (London: Hutchinson, 1972), p. 26; *The Magic Rectangle*, BBC1, 18 November 1986.

4. 'Mr Harding may have been over-fortified', *Manchester Guardian*, 8 December 1952.

5. Harding, *Along My Line*, p. 199.

6. H. T. Himmelweit, A. N. Oppenheim and P. Vince, *Television and the Child: An Empirical Study of the Effect of Television on the Young* (Oxford: Oxford University Press, 1958), p. 161.

7. Ross McKibbin, *Classes and Cultures: England, 1918–1951* (Oxford: Oxford University Press, 1998), p. 531; see also p. 98.

8. *TV Mirror*, 5 December 1953, 3; A. J. P. Taylor, 'Let's be rude!', *Daily Herald*, 30 May 1953.

9. Stephen Grenfell (ed.), *Gilbert Harding: By His Friends* (London: André Deutsch, 1961), p. 121; Craig Raine, *T. S. Eliot* (Oxford: Oxford University Press, 2006), p. xiii; Gilbert Harding, *Master of None* (London: Putnam, 1958), p. 13; Reyburn, *Gilbert Harding*, p. 93; *The Magic Rectangle*, BBC1, 18 November 1986.

10. 'Gilbert Harding's notebook', *Picture Post*, 7 November 1953, 52.

11. 'Gilbert Harding's notebook', *Picture Post*, 9 January 1954, 37.

12. John Humphrys, *Devil's Advocate* (London: Hutchinson, 1999), p. 160.

13. 'Gilbert Harding's notebook', *Picture Post*, 19 December 1953, 52; 'Gilbert Harding's notebook', *Picture Post*, 12 June 1954, 11.

14. 'Gilbert Harding's notebook', *Picture Post*, 27 February 1954, 54; 'Gilbert Harding's notebook', *Picture Post*, 12 March 1955, 44; 'Christian name complex', *Manchester Guardian*, 23 January 1952; Brian Harrison, *Seeking a Role: The United Kingdom, 1951–1970* (Oxford: Clarendon Press, 2009), p. 492.

15. Mark Lewisohn, *Funny Peculiar: The True Story of Benny Hill* (London: Pan, 2003), pp. 174, 176, 178, 206.

16. Su Holmes, *Entertaining Television: The BBC and Popular Television Culture in the 1950s* (Manchester: Manchester University Press, 2008), pp. 84–5; Brian Tesler, 'The things they "Ask Pickles"', *TV Mirror*, 10 July 1954, 9.

17. Himmelweit *et al.*, *Television and the Child*, pp. 147, 149; 'Gilbert Harding's notebook', *Picture Post*, 4 December 1954, 9; Hansard, HL

Deb, 25 November 1953, vol. 184, col. 521; Brian Pullan with Michelle Abendstern, *A History of the University of Manchester, 1951–1973* (Manchester: Manchester University Press, 2000), p. 51.

18. Peter Black, 'A generation ago', *Listener*, 4 September 1969, 308.

19. Joan Gilbert, 'Tele-Talk', *Picture Post*, 17 October 1953, 36; David Attenborough, *Life on Air: Memoirs of a Broadcaster* (London: BBC, 2002), p. 20; Jacquetta Hawkes, *Adventurer in Archaeology: The Biography of Sir Mortimer Wheeler* (London: Weidenfeld and Nicolson, 1982), p. 299.

20. Paul Johnstone, *Buried Treasure* (London: Phoenix House, 1957), p. 101.

21. 'Obituary: Mr Paul Johnstone', *The Times*, 17 March 1976; Paul Jordan, 'Archaeology and television', in *Antiquity and Man: Essays in Honour of Glyn Daniel*, eds John D. Evans, Barry Cunliffe and Colin Renfrew (London: Thames and Hudson, 1981), p. 209; Glyn Daniel, *Some Small Harvest: The Memoirs of Glyn Daniel* (London: Thames and Hudson, 1986), pp. 268, 365.

22. Attenborough, *Life on Air*, p. 46; Audience Research Department, 'Audience research report: *Zoo Quest*, Friday 9th November 1956', 3 December 1956, BBC WAC, VR/56/587.

23. McKibbin, *Classes and Cultures*, pp. 410–11; Douglas Brent, '*Dancing Club* versus "The Creep"', *TV Mirror*, 1 May 1954, 23.

24. David Kynaston, *Family Britain 1951–57* (London: Bloomsbury, 2009), p. 198; 'Saturday night at the Palais', *The Economist*, 14 February 1953, 401; Elisabeth Maxwell, *A Mind of My Own: My Life with Robert Maxwell* (London: HarperCollins, 1994), p. 227.

25. '1984: Wife dies as she watches', *Daily Express*, 14 December 1954.

26. Daniel Lea, 'Horror comics and highbrow sadism: televising George Orwell in the 1950s', *Literature and History*, 19, 1 (April 2010), 71; John Rodden, *George Orwell: The Politics of Literary Reputation* (New Brunswick, NJ: Transaction, 2002), p. 279.

27. John Sutherland, *Magic Moments* (London: Profile, 2008), p. 118.

28. Hansard, HC Deb, 20 January 1954, vol. 522, col. 987; Joanna Bornat, *Oral History, Health and Welfare* (London: Routledge, 1999), p. 59; Roger Storey, *Gilbert Harding By His Private Secretary* (London: Barrie and Rockcliff, 1961), p. 13.

29. 'Driver "forced from car"', *Manchester Guardian*, 18 December 1954.

30. Pam Ayres, *The Necessary Aptitude: A Memoir* (London: Ebury, 2011), pp. 113–14; 'TV not as bad as it is painted', *Manchester Guardian*, 1 September 1956.

31. Himmelweit *et al.*, *Television and the Child*, p. 202; Jean Baggott, *The Girl on the Wall: One Life's Rich Tapestry* (London: Icon, 2009), pp. 267–8.

32. *TV Mirror*, 6 March 1954, 25; 'Rediffusion Television Survey 1955', MOA, SxMOA1/2/45/2/C.

33. George Howard, 'Pirates', *TV Mirror*, 20 February 1954, 10–11; 'Tracking down TV "pirates"', *Manchester Guardian*, 11 September 1954.

34. Tony Currie, *A Concise History of British Television 1930–2000* (Tiverton: Kelly Publications, 2000), p. 36; Christopher Green with Carol Clerk, *Hughie and Paula: The Tangled Lives of Hughie Green and Paula Yates* (London: Robson, 2004), p. 112.

35. Iona and Peter Opie, *Children's Games with Things* (Oxford: Oxford University Press, 1997), p. 213.

36. Denis Norden, *Coming to You Live! Behind-the-Screen Memories of Forties and Fifties Television* (London: Methuen, 1985), pp. 181–2; Jeremy Black, *Britain since the Seventies: Politics and Society in the Consumer Age* (London: Reaktion, 2004), p. 27; 'Seven years of TV commercials', *Guardian*, 23 March 1962.

37. Mary Hill, 'And now it's television in the morning', *TV Times*, 20 September 1955, 14.

38. Iona and Peter Opie, *The Lore and Language of Schoolchildren* (Oxford: Oxford University Press, 1959), p. 116.

39. Head of Television Design (Richard Levin) to CP Tel, 11 May 1955, BBC WAC, T16/156.

40. 'Television as part of everyday life', *The Times*, 6 September 1955.

41. Harry Hopkins, *The New Look: A Social History of the Forties and Fifties in Britain* (London: Secker and Warburg, 1963), p. 414.

42. Michael Davie, 'ITV: The Pit or the Pendulum?', *Observer*, 4 December 1955.

43. Richard Hoggart, *The Uses of Literacy: Aspects of Working-Class Life* (London: Penguin, 2009), p. 157; Ronald Hilborne, 'The great god TAM', *Tribune*, 1 October 1965.

44. Clifford Davis, '2,000,000 hear TV – but don't see it', *Daily Mirror*, 24 October 1955; 'Stranger than truth', *Punch*, 14 August 1957, 172; Hopkins, *The New Look*, p. 414.

45. Kenneth Clark, *The Other Half: A Self-Portrait* (London: Harper and Row, 1977), pp. 147, 208.

46. 'When "the telly" is one of the family ...', *Daily Mirror*, 14 February 1956; 'The astonishing story behind ... TELEMANIA', *Daily Mirror*, 13 February 1956; G. A. Rose, 'Television angina', *British Medical Journal*, 5120 (21 February 1959), 506.

47. Geoffrey Gorer, 'Television in our lives', *Sunday Times*, 13 April 1958; Geoffrey Gorer, 'TV and the growing child', *Sunday Times*, 4 May 1958; Geoffrey Gorer, 'Notes on television', 20 October 1957, MOA, SxMs52/1/7/3/2/1.

48. Geoffrey Gorer, 'Television in our lives – is it a drug or a stimulant?', *Sunday Times*, 20 April 1958; Gorer, 'Television in our lives', 13 April 1958; Enid Blyton to Geoffrey Gorer, 13 April 1958, MOA, SxMs52/1/7/3/2/1.

49. Asa Briggs, *The History of Broadcasting in the United Kingdom, Volume V: Competition 1955–1974* (Oxford: Oxford University Press, 1995), p. 148; Ruth Miller, 'Spare the television and you won't spoil the child', *Daily Telegraph*, 6 February 1958; Bevis Hillier, *Betjeman: The Bonus of Laughter* (London: John Murray, 2004), pp. 6–7.

50. Brian Jackson and Dennis Marsden, *Education and the Working Class* (London: Ark, 1986), p. 77.

51. C. A. R. Crosland, *The Future of Socialism* (London: Jonathan Cape, 1964), p. 355; Lawrence Black, 'Whose finger on the button? British TV and the politics of cultural control', *Historical Journal of Film, Radio and Television*, 25, 4 (October 2005), 567.

52. Dennis Potter, *The Changing Forest: Life in the Forest of Dean Today* (London: Minerva, 1996), pp. 113, 9; Humphrey Carpenter, *Dennis Potter: The Authorised Biography* (London: Faber, 1998), p. 103.

53. Michael Young and Peter Willmott, *Family and Kinship in East London* (Harmondsworth: Penguin, 1962), p. 143.

54. Philip Ziegler, *Crown and People* (London: Collins, 1978), p. 118.

55. 'A hundred music-halls closed since the war', *The Times*, 28 January 1959; 'Repertory theatres', *Manchester Guardian*, 5 October 1953; Baz Kershaw, 'British theatre, 1940–2002: an introduction', in Kershaw

(ed.), *The Cambridge History of British Theatre, Volume 3: Since 1895* (Cambridge: Cambridge University Press, 2004), p. 297; Timothy West, *A Moment Towards the End of the Play* (London: Nick Hern Books, 2001), p. 37.

56. Philip Hope-Wallace, 'Shortening the theatre front', *Manchester Guardian*, 26 February 1955; Kershaw, 'British theatre, 1940–2002', p. 297; Irene Shubik, *Play for Today: The Evolution of Television Drama* (Manchester: Manchester University Press, 2000), p. 77.

57. Reyburn, *Gilbert Harding*, p. 59; Claire Langhamer, *Women's Leisure in England, 1920–1960* (Manchester: Manchester University Press, 2000), p. 41; Caroline Brown, 'The fascination of knitting', *Guardian*, 30 December 1959; Mary Townsend Dunn, 'The effects of TV', *Sunday Times*, 20 April 1958.

58. Geoffrey Gorer, 'Home life, habits and hobbies', *Sunday Times*, 27 April 1958; Leonard Miall, 'Monday nights at Lime Grove', in Miall (ed.), *Richard Dimbleby, Broadcaster: By His Colleagues* (London: BBC, 1966), p. 101; Gorer, 'Television in our lives', 13 April 1958; William Empson to Geoffrey Gorer, 14 April 1958, MOA, SxMs52/1/7/3/2/1.

59. The Pythons, *The Pythons: The Autobiography* (London: Orion, 2005), p. 74.

60. Michael Frayn, 'The long and the short and the curl', *Guardian*, 14 October 1959; Philip Norman, *Buddy: The Biography* (London: Macmillan, 1996), p. 224.

61. Gorer, 'TV and the growing child'; Peter Hennessy, *Having It So Good: Britain in the Fifties* (London: Penguin, 2007), p. 108.

62. Jeremy Mynott, *Birdscapes: Birds in Our Imagination and Experience* (Princeton, NJ: Princeton University Press, 2009), p. 298.

63. ABC Telefusion Presentation, 'Down with Aerials!', *c*. 1960, britishpathe.com (accessed 4 September 2011); Ralph Edwards, 'Television aerials', *The Times*, 31 May 1960; *Desert Island Discs*, BBC Radio 4, 2 July 2000.

64. Malcolm Bradbury, *All Dressed Up and Nowhere to Go* (London: Picador, 2000), pp. 178–9, 101, 106.

65. Harold Evans, *My Paper Chase* (London: Abacus, 2010), p. 168; 'Commercial TV in the north', *Manchester Guardian*, 6 October 1955; Denis Forman, *Persona Granada: Some Memories of Sidney Bernstein*

and the Early Years of Independent Television (London: André
Deutsch, 1997), p. 51; Julia Hallam, 'Introduction: the development of
commercial TV in Britain', in John Finch (ed.), *Granada Television:
The First Generation* (Manchester: Manchester University Press, 2003),
p. 20.

66. 'Television: some thoughts, some views and a dream', *The Economist*,
    16 March 1963, 995.

67. Forman, *Persona Granada*, p. 51.

68. Forman, *Persona Granada*, p. 64; Tom Harrisson, 'Television at Bolton
    and Borneo', 15 July 1960, MOA, SxMOA1/5/19/65/I/5.

69. Harry Elton, 'The programme committee and *Coronation Street*',
    in Finch (ed.), *Granada TV*, p. 101; Richard Whiteley, *Himoff! The
    Memoirs of a TV Matinée Idle* (London: Orion, 2000), p. 34; Deborah
    Ross, 'Richard Whiteley – No taste, no style, no shame. No contest',
    Independent, 15 February 1999.

70. Jamie Medhurst, *A History of Independent Television in Wales*
    (Cardiff: University of Wales Press, 2010), pp. 34, 62, 105.

71. Natasha Vall, *Cultural Region: North East England 1945–2000*
    (Manchester: Manchester University Press, 2011), p. 4; Geoff Phillips,
    Memories of Tyne Tees Television (Durham: GP Electronic Services,
    1998), pp. 48, 143.

72. Dick Joice, *Full Circle* (Woodbridge: Boydell, 1991), pp. 141, 167–71.

73. 'How to land a peak audience', *Observer*, 19 March 1967.

74. Colin Willock, 'TV in the country', *Observer*, 19 February 1967.

75. Brum Henderson, *Brum: A Life in Television* (Belfast: Appletree Press,
    2003), pp. 75, 66–8.

76. Vall, *Cultural Region*, p. 44; Phillips, *Memories of Tyne Tees
    Television*, pp. 94, 140.

77. Vall, *Cultural Region*, pp. 40–41, 45, 7.

78. Antony Brown, *Tyne Tees Television: The First 20 Years: A Portrait*
    (Newcastle: Tyne Tees Television, 1978), p. 6; Henderson, *Brum*, p. 77.

79. Mary Crozier, 'Tyneside's tough television', *Guardian*, 8 June 1960;
    Mary Crozier, 'Anglia Television', *Guardian*, 11 July 1960; Joice, *Full
    Circle*, pp. 176–7.

80. 'Rush order of TV masts', *Irish Times*, 27 May 1953; Jeremy Lewis,
    Playing for Time (London: Flamingo, 1988), p. 34.

81. J. L. Judd to Gordon-Brown, 27 June 1961, NA, HO 284/72; A. D. Gordon-Brown to J. L. Judd, 18 July 1961, NA, HO 284/72.

82. Andrew Mulligan, 'Pirates in the British channel', *Observer*, 11 July 1965; John Ardagh, *The New France: A Society in Transition 1945–1973* (Harmondsworth: Pelican, 1973), pp. 607, 619; 'British TV seen in New York', *Manchester Guardian*, 26 October 1956.

83. Sir George Barnes, 'BBC Television: a national service', *Radio Times*, 16 September 1955, 3.

84. 'Sooan Sids', *Orkney Herald*, 18 October 1955.

85. 'What the Pier Head is saying', *Orkney Herald*, 15 November 1955.

86. Islandman, 'Look out, it's coming', *Orkney Herald*, 2 February 1954.

87. 'Sooan Sids', *Orkney Herald*, 31 December 1957.

88. Howard Hazell, *The Orcadian Book of the 20th Century* (Kirkwall: Orcadian Ltd, 2000), p. 217.

89. Reyburn, *Harding*, pp. 97–8; Grenfell (ed.), *Gilbert Harding: By His Friends*, p. 183.

90. Reyburn, *Harding*, pp. 60, 90.

91. Reyburn, *Harding*, p. 51; 'Dimbleby's dip', *Guardian*, 21 January 1960.

92. Jonathan Dimbleby, *Richard Dimbleby* (London: Hodder and Stoughton, 1975), pp. 295, 321–2.

93. Richard Lindley, *Panorama: 50 Years of Pride and Paranoia* (London: Politico's, 2002), p. 152.

94. 'Harding back – for two minutes', *Daily Mirror*, 19 March 1955; John Freeman, 'The captive viewer', *New Statesman*, 28 May 1960, 782; Jack Tinker, *The Television Barons* (London: Quartet, 1980), p. 173.

95. Hugh Burnett, 'Producing *Face to Face*', *Radio Times*, 16 September 1960, 13; Grenfell (ed.), *Gilbert Harding: By His Friends*, p. 139.

96. Audience Research Department, 'Audience research report: *Face to Face*: Gilbert Harding and John Freeman, Sunday 18th September 1960', 7 October 1960, BBC WAC, R9/7/48.

97. Holmes, *Entertaining Television*, p. 195; Hugh Burnett, *Face to Face* (London: Jonathan Cape, 1964), p. 3; *Radio Times*, 16 September 1960, 15.

98. Holmes, *Entertaining Television*, pp. 177–8; Douglas Warth, *Daily Herald*, 19 February 1958; James Thomas, 'The cruel keyhole', *Daily Express*, 19 February 1958.

99. Reginald Pound, 'Critic on the hearth', *Listener*, 25 November 1954, 928; 'This Is Your Life', *Manchester Guardian*, 4 February 1958; 'The very moment he said it', *Daily Express*, 17 November 1960; Merrick Winn, 'Should Harding have said it?', *Daily Express*, 20 September 1960.

100. Reyburn, *Harding*, p. 119; 'Mr. Gilbert Harding dies suddenly', *The Times*, 17 November 1960; 'Gilbert Harding dies on steps of BBC', *Daily Express*, 17 November 1960.

101. 'Mr Gilbert Harding', *Glasgow Herald*, 18 December 1953; 'Gilbert Harding ordered to bed', *The Bulletin*, 5 September 1953; Grenfell (ed.), *Gilbert Harding: By His Friends*, pp. 22, 24.

102. Stephen Grenfell, 'Foreword', in *Gilbert Harding: By His Friends*, p. 12; Brian Masters, *Getting Personal: A Biographer's Memoir* (London: Constable, 2002), p. 94.

103. Miall, *Inside the BBC*, p. 59; 'Richard Dimbleby – 30 years of broadcasting', *Listener*, 18 September 1975, 365; Lindley, *Panorama*, p. 166.

104. Reyburn, *Harding*, p. 120; John D. W. Greene and John R. Hodges, 'Identification of famous faces and famous names in early Alzheimer's disease', *Brain*, 119, 1 (February 1996), 111, 128.

105. Hansard, HC Deb, 8 May 1961, vol. 640, col. 182–3.

106. 'Television plain or purled', *The Economist*, 26 August 1961, 812.

107. Gorer, 'Television in our lives', 13 April 1958; Gorer, 'Television in our lives', 20 April 1958; Himmelweit *et al.*, *Television and the Child*, p. 12; Iona and Peter Opie, *The Lore and Language of Schoolchildren*, p. 118.

108. Harrisson, 'Television at Bolton and Borneo'.

109. Hansard, HC Deb, 2 May 1962, vol. 658, col. 1062; Richard Dyer, *Only Entertainment* (London: Routledge, 1992), p. 14.

5. The invisible focus of a million eyes

1. Brian Winston, *Messages: Free Expression, Media and the West from Gutenberg to Google* (Abingdon: Routledge, 2005), p. 357.

2. H. T. Himmelweit, A. N. Oppenheim and P. Vince, *Television and the Child: An Empirical Study of the Effect of Television on the Young* (Oxford: Oxford University Press, 1958), pp. 181–3; Griff Rhys Jones, *Semi-Detached* (London: Penguin, 2007), p. 20.

3. Burton Paulu, *Television and Radio in the United Kingdom* (Minneapolis: University of Minnesota Press, 1981), p. 342; 'TV Children's Hour hits power supply', *Daily Mirror*, 11 December 1954.

4. *New Scientist*, 19 July 1962, 129.

5. 'Double view of Test on Duke's TV', *Guardian*, 7 July 1961.

6. 'TV complaints brought home to minister', *The Times*, 24 April 1961.

7. Mary Crozier, 'All the fun of the air at Earls Court', *Guardian*, 22 August 1962; Edwin Morgan, 'Unscrambling the waves at Goonhilly', in Ken Cockburn and Alec Finlay (eds), *The Order of Things: Scottish Sound, Pattern and Concrete Poetry* (Edinburgh: Polygon, 2001), p. 35.

8. John Repsch, *The Legendary Joe Meek: The Telstar Man* (London: Cherry Red, 2000), pp. 17, 19–20.

9. Repsch, *The Legendary Joe Meek*, pp. 144–5.

10. Marshall McLuhan, *Understanding Media: The Extensions of Man* (London: Routledge, 2001), pp. 87, 336.

11. Maurice Richardson, 'Worms turn on Early Bird', *Observer*, 9 May 1965; Michael Billington, 'Notable feat of organization', *The Times*, 26 June 1967.

12. *Report of the Committee on Broadcasting, 1960* (London: HMSO, 1962), pp. 33, 35; 'Instant television', *Guardian*, 7 July 1962.

13. Richard Hoggart, *The Uses of Literacy: Aspects of Working-Class Life* (London: Penguin, 2009), p. 286; Simon Hoggart, 'Foreword', in Hoggart, *The Uses of Literacy*, p. vi.

14. Merlin, 'Mainly about people', *Sunday Times*, 11 September 1960; Richard Hoggart, 'The uses of television', in *Speaking to Each Other, Volume 1: About Society* (London: Chatto and Windus, 1970), p. 157; Richard Hoggart, 'When the telly clock goes back', *Observer*, 12 August 1962.

15. Richard Hoggart, *An Imagined Life: Life and Times, Volume III: 1959–91* (Oxford: Oxford University Press, 1993), p. 134; Humphrey Carpenter, *A Great Silly Grin: The British Satire Boom in the 1960s* (Cambridge, MA: Da Capo Press, 2003), pp. 212, 242.

16. Carpenter, *A Great Silly Grin*, p. 235; David Frost, *An Autobiography, Part 1: From Congregations to Audiences* (London: HarperCollins, 1993), p. 95.

17. Maurice Richardson, '*TW3*: inside story', *Observer*, 29 September 1963; Frost, *An Autobiography*, p. 70.

18. Richard Hoggart, *Mass Media in a Mass Society* (London: Continuum, 2006), p. 109; *Desert Island Discs*, BBC Radio 4, 15 October 1995; John Ardagh, 'TV satire is rage of the sixth', *Observer*, 10 March 1963.

19. Carpenter, *A Great Silly Grin*, p. 272; 'Eton boys admire "The Avengers"', *The Times*, 3 March 1964.

20. Pharic MacLaren, '*Between the Lines*', *Radio Times*, 23 April 1964, 51; Michael Tracey, 'Greene, Mrs Whitehouse and the BBC', *Observer*, 14 August 1983.

21. Hoggart, 'The uses of television', p. 158; '300,000 sign petition for cleaner television', *Guardian*, 24 April 1965; Lawrence Black, *Redefining British Politics: Culture, Consumerism and Participation, 1954–70* (Houndmills: Palgrave Macmillan, 2010), p. 115.

22. Joan Bakewell, *The Centre of the Bed* (London: Sceptre, 2004), pp. 180–81; Kenneth Robinson, 'Took it from here', *The Listener*, 16 August 1979, 210.

23. '"Cathy Come Home" to be repeated', *The Times*, 21 December 1966; Michael Tracey and David Morrison, *Whitehouse* (Basingstoke: Macmillan, 1979), p. 71; 'Audience of critics urged for second showing of "Cathy"', *Guardian*, 11 January 1967.

24. Black, *Redefining British Politics*, pp. 105, 112, 108; Alisdair Farley, 'Portrait of a lobby', *Listener*, 19 June 1967, 845–6; Mary Whitehouse, 'Rawness and truth on TV', *Financial Times*, 8 December 1966.

25. 'Close-up of the TV viewer', *Guardian*, 3 September 1964; 'Close view of the average viewer', *The Times*, 3 September 1964.

26. Kenneth Adam, 'A stretch towards happiness', *Radio Times*, 16 April 1964, 4; 'Poll shows few BBC-2 viewers', *The Times*, 9 June 1964.

27. 'University exploration of popular culture', *The Times*, 6 June 1963.

28. Barry Miles, *In the Sixties* (London: Jonathan Cape, 2002), p. 1; G. G. Eastwood, 'Newspapers and colour magazines', *Guardian*, 23 November 1961.

29. Anthony Burgess, 'Television', *Listener*, 27 July 1967, 123; Anthony Burgess, *You've Had Your Time* (London: Penguin, 1991), p. 105.

30. Kenneth Adam, 'American television: "The coloured marquee"', *Listener*, 29 June 1967, 850.

31. Memorandum by the Postmaster General, Cabinet Committee on Broadcasting Colour Television, 1965, NA, HO 256/387.

32. Richard Wagner, 'Colour TV switch-on tomorrow', *The Times*, 30 June 1967.

33. Adam, 'American television'; 'BBC colour TV in December', *Guardian*, 21 April 1967; Attenborough, 'American lesson is that ambition pays', *The Times*, 16 November 1967.

34. Nicholas Garnham, 'Bright and beautiful', *Listener*, 18 July 1968, 81; John Boorman, *Adventures of a Suburban Boy* (London: Faber, 2004), p. 98; 'Colour TV is hard on the teeth', *The Times*, 27 September 1967.

35. Peter Black, 'Occasions in colour', *Listener*, 28 March 1968, 418; Garnham, 'Bright and beautiful'; William Hardcastle, 'Getting colour', *Listener*, 27 June 1968, 846.

36. Timothy O'Sullivan, *Percy Thrower: A Biography* (London: Sidgwick and Jackson, 1989), p. 115.

37. Clifford Davis, 'At the big off it's 750–1 against colour', *Daily Mirror*, 2 December 1967; Ronald Faux, 'Western Islanders tune in to colour television', *The Times*, 20 July 1976.

38. 'TV salesmen look to the hills', *The Times*, 3 April 1964; Derek Cooper, *Skye* (London: Routledge and Kegan Paul, 1970), p. 138.

39. David Pat Walker, *The BBC in Scotland: The First Fifty Years* (Edinburgh: Luath Press, 2011), p. 240.

40. Cooper, *Skye*, pp. 138–9.

41. Kim Twatt, *Straight from the Horse's Mouth: The Orkney Herald, 1950–1961: The Paper and its People* (Kirkwall: Orcadian Ltd, 1996), p. 155.

42. Rob Young, *Electric Eden: Unearthing Britain's Visionary Music* (London: Faber, 2010), p. 34; Edwin Ardener, '"Remote areas" – some theoretical considerations', in *The Voice of Prophecy and Other Essays*, ed. Malcolm Chapman (Oxford: Berghahn, 2007), p. 219.

43. Iain Crichton Smith, 'Real people in a real place', in *Towards the Human: Selected Essays* (Edinburgh: Macdonald/Saltire Society, 1986), p. 17.

44. Paul Gilchrist, 'Reality TV on the rock face – climbing the Old Man of Hoy', *Sport in History*, 27, 1 (March 2007), 49; Dougal Haston, *In High Places* (Edinburgh: Canongate, 2003), p. 95.

45. Carol Osborne, 'An extraordinary Joe: the working-class climber as hero', in Stephen Wagg and Dave Russell (eds), *Sporting Heroes*

of the North (Newcastle: Northumbria Press, 2010), p. 61; Simon Thompson, *Unjustifiable Risk: The Story of British Climbing* (Milnthorpe: Cicerone Press, 2010), p. 231.

46. Tom Patey, 'The professionals', in *One Man's Mountains* (Edinburgh: Canongate, 1997), p. 225.

47. A. Kenneth MacKenzie, 'Points from the post', *Radio Times*, 20 July 1967, 2; Chris Bonington, *The Next Horizon* (London: Weidenfeld and Nicolson, 2001), p. 202; Gilchrist, 'Reality TV on the rock face', 58.

48. Patey, 'The professionals', pp. 217–18; Irene Shubik, *Play for Today: The Evolution of Television Drama* (Manchester: Manchester University Press, 2000), p. 161.

49. 'TV viewpoint on the Beatles', *Daily Mirror*, 30 December 1967; Kenelm Jenour, 'Beatles' mystery tour baffles viewers', *Daily Mirror*, 27 December 1967.

50. Garth and Carol Tucker, 'The Beatles' film', *Listener*, 18 January 1968, 84.

51. 'Second class viewers', *The Times*, 12 January 1967; Malcolm Muggeridge, 'Story behind the saga', *Observer*, 18 June 1967.

52. A. Boydell, 'Forsyte enchantment', *The Times*, 6 March 1969; Tracy Hargreaves, '"There's no place like home": history and tradition in *The Forsyte Saga* and the BBC', *Journal of British Cinema and Television*, 6, 1 (May 2009), 39.

53. Stanley Reynolds, 'The Forsytes on *Late Night Line-Up*', *Guardian*, 12 February 1969; Anne Chisholm, 'Why in mid-whirl of the permissive society, as we swing into the '70s ...', *Radio Times*, 8 January 1970, 55.

54. 'Television and church work', *Manchester Guardian*, 17 January 1952; Gordon Ross, *Television Jubilee: The Story of 25 Years of B.B.C. Television* (London: W. H. Allen, 1961), p. 115; Lewis Chester, *All My Shows Are Great: The Life of Lew Grade* (London: Aurum, 2010), pp. 105–6; 'Epilogue', *Guardian*, 9 May 1966.

55. Hugh McLeod, *The Religious Crisis of the 1960s* (Oxford: Oxford University Press, 2007), p. 72; Mary Whitehouse, *Who Does She Think She Is?* (London: New English Library, 1971), p. 46.

56. David W. James, 'The Forsyte threat', *The Times*, 12 September 1968; Rowland Hill, 'The Forsyte threat', *The Times*, 17 September

1968; A. N. Wilson, *Our Times: The Age of Elizabeth II* (London: Hutchinson, 2008), pp. 123–4.

57. Simon Schama, 'No Downers in "Downton"', *Newsweek*, 16 January 2012, 12; Ronald Blythe, *The Bookman's Tale* (Norwich: Canterbury Press, 2009), p. 88.

58. Bernard Davies, 'Non-swinging youth', *New Society*, 3 July 1969, 8.

59. Ronald Blythe, *Akenfield: Portrait of an English Village* (Harmondsworth: Penguin, 1972), pp. 98, 237, 91, 241, 140, 142.

60. J. G. Ballard, *Miracles of Life: Shanghai to Shepperton: An Autobiography* (London: Fourth Estate, 2008), p. 226.

61. J. G. Ballard, 'Escapement', in Ballard, *The Complete Short Stories: Volume 1* (London: Harper Perennial, 2006), p. 17.

62. Bea Ballard, 'J. G. Ballard', *Observer*, 13 December 2009; Bea Ballard, 'Daddy saw such horrors as a boy in a prison camp …', *Daily Mail*, 18 June 2011; John Baxter, *The Inner Man: The Life of J. G. Ballard* (London: Weidenfeld and Nicolson, 2011), p. 27.

63. Ballard, *Miracles of Life*, p. 226.

64. Raymond Williams, 'A new way of seeing', in *Raymond Williams on Television: Selected Writings*, ed. Alan O'Connor (London: Routledge, 1989), p. 48.

65. Fred Inglis, *Raymond Williams* (London: Routledge, 1998), pp. 223–4; '"Hostility" by minister', *Guardian*, 10 April 1961.

66. Raymond Williams, 'Watching from elsewhere', in *Raymond Williams on Television*, p. 67.

67. Patrick Moore, *The Autobiography* (Stroud: Sutton, 2003), p. 67.

68. Audience Research Department, 'Audience research report, *Omnibus: An Entertainment for Moon-Night: So What If It's Just Green Cheese?*, 20th July 1969', 26 August 1969, BBC WAC, R9/7/100.

69. Christopher Hitchens, *Hitch-22: A Memoir* (London: Atlantic Books, 2010), pp. 210–11; Michael Palin, *Diaries 1969–1979: The Python Years* (London: Phoenix, 2007), p. 5.

70. 'You write …', *Radio Times*, 31 July 1969, 2; Paul Trynka, *Starman: David Bowie: The Definitive Biography* (London: Sphere, 2010), p. 100; Peter Doggett, *The Man Who Sold the World: David Bowie and the 1970s* (London: The Bodley Head, 2011), p. 53.

71. Doggett, *The Man Who Sold the World*, p. 55; Trynka, *Starman*, p. 100.

72. Henry Raynor, 'Reality through the spectrum', *The Times*, 15 November 1969.

73. Peter Black, 'New dimension for the viewer', *Illustrated London News*, 7 November 1970, 18.

74. Martin Sherwood, 'Visit to a small planet', *New Scientist*, 8 July 1971, 85.

75. George Melly, 'Losing out on the lunar drama', *Observer*, 23 November 1969; George Melly, 'Flogging one's wonder', *Observer*, 1 June 1969.

76. Adam, 'American television'; Stanley Reynolds, 'Television', *Guardian*, 6 July 1967.

77. Peter Nichols, *Diaries, 1969–1977* (London: Nick Hern Books, 2000), p. 60.

6. The dance of irrelevant shadows

1. Irene Shubik, *Play for Today: The Evolution of Television Drama* (Manchester: Manchester University Press, 2000), p. 163.

2. Michael Palin, *Diaries 1969–1979: The Python Years* (London: Phoenix, 2007), p. 15.

3. Geoffrey Giuliano, *Dark Horse: The Life and Art of George Harrison* (Cambridge, MA: Da Capo Press, 1997), p. 223; Joshua M. Greene, *Here Comes the Sun: The Spiritual and Musical Journey of George Harrison* (London: Bantam, 2006), p. 230.

4. Laura Mulvey and Margarita Jiminez, 'The spectacle is vulnerable: Miss World, 1970', in Laura Mulvey, *Visual and Other Pleasures* (Basingstoke: Macmillan, 1989), p. 5.

5. 'Germaine Greer', *Listener*, 21 January 1971, 79.

6. Christopher Hitchens, 'Credibility politics: sado-monetarist economics', in *For the Sake of Argument: Essays and Minority Reports* (London: Verso, 1993), p. 162.

7. *BBC Annual Report and Accounts, 1969–70* (London: BBC, 1970), p. 25; *BBC Annual Report and Accounts, 1970–1* (London: BBC, 1971), p. 21.

8. 'Watching TV is favourite attraction of tourists', *Guardian*, 14 October 1970; Anthony Sampson, 'Doing our own thing', *Observer*, 12 July 1970; Anthony Sampson, *New Anatomy of Britain* (London: Hodder and Stoughton, 1971), p. 427.

9. Central Statistical Office, *Social Trends*, No. 3, 1972 (London: HMSO, 1972), p. 103; Milton Shulman, *The Ravenous Eye: The Impact of the Fifth Factor* (London: Cassell, 1973), p. 1.

10. Ernest Dewhurst, 'Granada viewers are now good listeners', *Guardian*, 9 June 1970.

11. Auberon Waugh, 'Welcome to Ruritania', *Time*, 26 November 1973, 48; James Lees-Milne, *Diaries, 1971–1983* (London: John Murray, 2008), p. 118.

12. Simon Hoggart, 'Labour derides clamp on TV', *Guardian*, 26 January 1974; Andrew Roth, *Heath and the Heathmen* (London: Routledge and Kegan Paul, 1972), p. 213; Keith Waterhouse, 'The light fantastic', *Daily Mirror*, 14 January 1974.

13. Peter Fiddick, 'The interesting thing is that people are relieved of some awful frustration …', *Guardian*, 28 January 1974.

14. David Butler and Dennis Kavanagh, *The British General Election of February 1974* (London: Macmillan, 1974), p. 67.

15. Rex Cathcart, *The Most Contrary Region: The BBC in Northern Ireland 1924–1984* (Belfast: Blackstaff, 1984), p. 257.

16. Andrew McKinney, *Our Jimmy: A Celebration of James Young* (Belfast: Brehon Press, 2003), p. 114; Jonathan Bardon, *Beyond the Studio: A History of BBC Northern Ireland* (Belfast: Blackstaff Press, 2000), p. 86.

17. Pat Loughrey, 'Culture and identity: the BBC's role in Northern Ireland', in Martin McLoone (ed.), *Broadcasting in a Divided Community: Seventy Years of the BBC in Northern Ireland* (Belfast: Institute of Irish Studies, Queen's University of Belfast, 1996), p. 70; McKinney, *Our Jimmy*, pp. 118, 123.

18. Burton Paulu, *Television and Radio in the United Kingdom* (Minneapolis: University of Minnesota Press, 1981), p. 351; Henri Bergson, *Laughter: An Essay on the Meaning of the Comic* (Rockville, MD: Arc Manor, 2008), p. 11; Katharine Whitehorn, 'Coachloads of clappers', *Observer*, 10 March 1974.

19. Leon Hunt, *British Low Culture: From Safari Suits to Sexploitation* (London: Routledge, 1998), p. 53; Francis Bennion, 'Laugh at thy neighbour', *New Society*, 31 July 1975, 256; John Twitchin (ed.), *The Black and White Media Book: Handbook for the Study of Racism and Television* (Stoke on Trent: Trentham, 1990), p. 124.

20. Kenneth Williams, 'Preview', *Radio Times*, 27 September – 3 October 1975, 15; David Croft, *You Have Been Watching … The Autobiography of David Croft* (London: BBC Books, 2004), p. 193.

21. Peter Kane, 'A Goodies fan dies laughing', *Daily Mirror*, 29 March 1975; Brian Viner, *Nice to See It, To See It, Nice: The 1970s in Front of the Telly* (London: Simon and Schuster, 2009), p. 12; Palin, *Diaries*, pp. 282, 290.

22. Jimmy Perry, *A Stupid Boy* (London: Arrow, 2003), p. 105; Audience Research Department, 'Audience research report, *Dad's Army*, Wednesday, 31st July, 1968', 16 August 1968, BBC WAC, VR/68/461; Penny Summerfield and Corinna Peniston-Bird, *Contesting Home Defence: Men, Women and the Home Guard in the Second World War* (Manchester: Manchester University Press, 2007), pp. 191–2.

23. Perry, *A Stupid Boy*, p. 176; Shelina Zahra Janmohamed, *Love in a Headscarf* (London: Aurum, 2009), p. 33.

24. Ruvani Ranasinha, *South Asian Writers in Twentieth-Century Britain: Culture in Translation* (Oxford: Oxford University Press, 2007), p. 222; Philip Howard, 'Immigrants in Southall form a tightly knit community', *The Times*, 9 June 1976.

25. Peter Fiddick, 'It is on the cards that 1976 will prove to be the year the box lobby lost its grip', *Guardian*, 5 April 1976; Kenneth Gosling, 'Colour TV sets outnumber black-and-white', *The Times*, 12 October 1976; '1-in-5 dole scroungers, says MP', *Guardian*, 12 July 1976; Michael Parkin, 'The benefit of the doubt', *Guardian*, 3 January 1977.

26. George Mackay Brown, 'The last ballad', *Listener*, 20 June 1968, 800.

27. Maggie Fergusson, *George Mackay Brown: The Life* (London: John Murray, 2007), p. 182; Ron Ferguson, *George Mackay Brown: The Wound and the Gift* (Edinburgh: Saint Andrew Press, 2011), p. 164; Mackay Brown, 'The last ballad', 801.

28. George Mackay Brown, *An Orkney Tapestry* (London: Quartet Books, 1973), pp. 20, 50–51; Mackay Brown, 'The last ballad', 800.

29. George Mackay Brown, *Letters from Hamnavoe* (London: Steve Savage, 2002), pp. 91, 87.

30. George Mackay Brown, *Under Brinkie's Brae* (London: Steve Savage, 2003), p. 56; George Mackay Brown, *Rockpools and Daffodils: An Orcadian Diary 1979–1991* (Edinburgh: Gordon Wright Publishing, 1992), p. 119; Brown, *Letters from Hamnavoe*, p. 119.

31. Brown, *Letters from Hamnavoe*, pp. 144–5.

32. Brown, *Under Brinkie's Brae*, p. 22.

33. Tom Stoppard, 'Preview', *Radio Times*, 7 November 1974, 5; D. J. Enright, 'Quick brown fox', *Listener*, 15 March 1973, 326.

34. 'So who's afraid of Dr Who?', *Daily Mirror*, 22 January 1975; Nancy Mills, 'The man Who is', *Guardian*, 4 September 1976; James Chapman, *Inside the Tardis: The Worlds of Doctor Who: A Cultural History* (London: I. B. Tauris, 2006), pp. 99, 114.

35. Richard North, 'Nice to see you – to see you, nice', *Listener*, 23 December 1976, 805.

36. Bruce Forsyth, *Bruce: The Autobiography* (London: Sidgwick and Jackson, 2001), p. 11.

37. Joanne Turney, *The Culture of Knitting* (Oxford: Berg, 2009), p. 38; Hilary Kingsley and Geoff Tibballs, *Box of Delights: The Golden Years of Television* (London: Macmillan, 1989), p. 158.

38. 'TV fury over rock boot filth', *Daily Mirror*, 2 December 1976.

39. Jonathan Ross, *Why Do I Say These Things* (London: Bantam, 2008), pp. 259–60; Greil Marcus, *Lipstick Traces: A Secret History of the Twentieth Century* (Cambridge, MA: Harvard University Press, 1989), p. 3.

40. Simon Frith, 'Look! Hear! The uneasy relationship of music and television', *Popular Music*, 21, 3 (October 2002), 279; Paulu, *Television and Radio in the United Kingdom*, p. 309.

41. Marc Spitz, *David Bowie: A Biography* (London: Aurum, 2010), p. 194.

42. Dylan Jones, *When Ziggy Played Guitar: David Bowie and Four Minutes That Shook the World* (London: Preface, 2012), pp. 1–2, 136–7.

43. Boy George, *Take It Like a Man: The Autobiography of Boy George* (London: Pan, 1995), p. 61; Dave Rimmer, *New Romantics: The Look* (London: Omnibus Press, 2003), pp. 102–3.

44. Paul Baker, *Polari: The Lost Language of Gay Men* (London: Routledge, 2002), p. 117.

45. Dick Emery, *In Character* (London: Robson Books, 1973), p. 84.

46. Andy Medhurst, *A National Joke: Popular Comedy and English Cultural Identity* (Abingdon: Routledge, 2007), p. 86; Baker, *Polari*, p. 118.

NOTES

47. Home Office, *Report of the Committee on the Future of Broadcasting* (London: HMSO, 1977), p. 58; Jonathan Raban, 'Preview', *Radio Times*, 11 July 1974, 5.

48. David Hendy, *Life on Air: A History of Radio Four* (Oxford: Oxford University Press, 2007), p. 243; D. A. N. Jones, 'Spokesmen and professionals', *Listener*, 28 October 1976, 551.

49. Michael Barrett, 'Enabling communication – a fourth function for television?', *Learning, Media and Technology*, 5, 1 (Spring 1979), 19.

50. Barrett, 'Enabling communication', 19; Home Office, *Report of the Committee on the Future of Broadcasting*, p. 293.

51. Antony Brown, *Tyne Tees Television: The First 20 Years: A Portrait* (Newcastle: Tyne Tees Television, 1978), p. 26.

52. *A Knight on the Box: 40 Years of Anglia Television* (Norwich: Anglia Television, 1999), p. 67.

53. Colin Willock, 'How to land a peak audience', *Observer*, 19 March 1967.

54. Jimmy Reid, 'Does the lens put us truly in the picture?', *Glasgow Herald*, 24 January 1981; George Harrison, 'Foreword', in *I Me Mine* (London: Phoenix, 2004), p. 11.

55. Brown, *Tyne Tees Television*, p. 48; Home Office, *Report of the Committee on the Future of Broadcasting*, p. 355.

56. Russell Harty, 'Shadow across the screen', in Brian Wenham (ed.), *The Third Age of Broadcasting* (London: Faber, 1982), p. 134.

57. Dave Lane, *Winter Hill Scrapbook* (Knutsford: Dave Lane, 2007), p. 72.

58. 'Welsh viewers prefer "Z Cars"', *Guardian*, 1 February 1964; 'Welsh language TV at peak time attacked', *The Times*, 31 August 1973; 'Dubbing for roots', *The Economist*, 7 October 1978, 30; Jamie Medhurst, *A History of Independent Television in Wales* (Cardiff: University of Wales Press, 2010), p. 172.

59. *Parkinson*, BBC1, 28 November 1971; John Davies, *Broadcasting and the BBC in Wales* (Cardiff: University of Wales Press, 1994), p. 298; Medhurst, *A History of Independent Television in Wales*, pp. 171–2.

60. Asa Briggs, *The History of Broadcasting in the United Kingdom, Volume V: Competition 1955–1974* (Oxford: Oxford University Press, 1995), p. 949; J. A. R. Pimlott, *The Englishman's Christmas: A Social*

History (Hassocks: Harvester Press, 1978), p. 170; Jonathan Coe, *The Rotters' Club* (London: Penguin, 2002), p. 274.

61. Paul Dacre, 'Why I want to cut the comedy', *Daily Express*, 28 December 1973.

62. John Peel, 'What's so funny', *Listener*, 7 July 1977, 6; James Thomas, 'Was it all worth it?', *Daily Express*, 28 December 1977.

63. Peter Fiddick, 'BBC steals march on Christmas viewing', *Guardian*, 6 December 1977; 'Britain's most watched TV' at bfi.org.uk/features/mostwatched/1970s.html (accessed 9 January 2009).

64. Graham McCann, *Morecambe & Wise* (London: Fourth Estate, 1999), p. 140.

65. John McGrath, *A Good Night Out: Popular Theatre: Audience, Class and Form* (London: Eyre Methuen, 1981), p. 56; Maria DiCenzo, *The Politics of Alternative Theatre in Britain, 1968–1990: The Case of 7:84 (Scotland)* (Cambridge: Cambridge University Press, 1996), p. 143.

66. Harry Thompson, *Peter Cook: A Biography* (London: Sceptre, 1998), pp. xi–xii; T. C. Worsley, *Television: The Ephemeral Art* (London: Alan Ross, 1970).

67. Humphrey Carpenter, *Dennis Potter: The Authorised Biography* (London: Faber, 1998), p. 202; Dennis Potter, 'Poisonous gas', *New Statesman*, 28 May 1976, 725.

68. Gerald Priestland, *Something Understood: An Autobiography* (London: André Deutsch, 1986), p. 206; Dick Fiddy, *Missing Believed Wiped* (London: BFI, 2001), p. 10.

69. McCann, *Morecambe & Wise*, p. 311; Steve Bryant, *The Television Heritage: Television Archiving Now and in an Uncertain Future* (London: BFI, 1989), p. 17; Graham McCann, 'Duo in the crown', *Observer*, 20 December 1998.

70. Stephen Smith, 'Bringing back the sunshine', *Evening Standard*, 15 November 2001; Paddy Shennan, 'Is Xmas telly a turn-off?', *Liverpool Echo*, 8 December 2003.

71. Dacre, 'Why I want to cut the comedy'; McCann, *Morecambe & Wise*, p. 231; 'Does that mean there'll be no more magic?', *Daily Mirror*, 29 May 1984.

72. N. Ratcliffe, *Guardian*, 14 March 1979.

73. Fergusson, *George Mackay Brown*, 249; Brown, *Under Brinkie's Brae*, pp. 173, 125.

74. Fergusson, *George Mackay Brown*, 249; Ferguson, *George Mackay Brown*, pp. 245, 250–51, 116.

75. David Attenborough, *Life on Air: Memoirs of a Broadcaster* (London: BBC, 2002), p. 280.

76. Brown, *Under Brinkie's Brae*, p. 206.

77. Dennis Potter, 'Trampling the mud to the wall', *Sunday Times*, 6 November 1977.

78. Kevin O'Lone, 'BBC? It drives you to drink!', *Daily Mirror*, 5 September 1979.

79. Viner, *Nice to See It, To See It, Nice*, p. 65; Letters, *Radio Times*, 8–14 September 1979, p. 83; Michael Parkin, 'And lo, ITV did rise from the dead', *Guardian*, 25 October 1979.

80. Stanley Reynolds, 'Tellyless in Camberwell', *Guardian*, 1 September 1979; Keith Waterhouse, 'All on the card', *Daily Mirror*, 11 October 1979; 'ITV viewers do switch over, BBC claims', *Guardian*, 17 September 1979.

81. Stewart Lee, 'And now this …', *Guardian*, 15 July 1995.

82. Peter Hooper, 'Where has central heating gone wrong?', *Guardian*, 7 October 1971; Stephen Games, 'Is your central heating really necessary?', *Guardian*, 14 September 1982; 'Double-glazing also cuts the bills', *Guardian*, 2 April 1982; Nick Cole, 'Save it – with insulation and double glazing', *Guardian*, 3 March 1979.

7. A barrier against the silences

1. Laurie Taylor and Bob Mullan, *Uninvited Guests: The Intimate Secrets of Television and Radio* (London: Chatto and Windus, 1986), p. 44.

2. 'Wives rush to bet on J.R.', *Daily Mirror*, 27 May 1980.

3. Mick Brown, 'Oil in the family', *Radio Times*, 2–8 September 1978, 14; Jane Root, *Open the Box* (London: Comedia, 1986), p. 55.

4. Paul Rixon, *TV Critics and Popular Culture: A History of British Television Criticism* (London: I. B. Tauris, 2011), pp. 56–7.

5. Mike Poole, 'The cult of the generalist: British television criticism 1936–83', *Screen*, 25, 2 (March 1984), 55.

6. Clive James, *North Face of Soho: More Unreliable Memoirs, Volume IV* (London: Picador, 2006), p. 46.

7. Clive James, *Visions Before Midnight: Television Criticism from the Observer 1972–76* (London: Jonathan Cape, 1977), p. 14.

8. Clive James, *The Crystal Bucket: Television Criticism from the Observer 1976–79* (London: Jonathan Cape, 1981), p. 13; Clive James, 'The Pinter sisters', *Observer*, 24 September 1978.

9. Taylor and Mullan, *Uninvited Guests*, p. 21.

10. Barry Took (ed.), *Points of View* (London: BBC, 1981), pp. 12–13.

11. John Ellis, 'TV pages', in Bob Franklin (ed.), *Pulling Newspapers Apart: Analysing Print Journalism* (Abingdon: Routledge, 2008), p. 236.

12. Clifford Davis, 'Noele Gordon sacked!', *Daily Mirror*, 22 June 1981; Dorothy Hobson, *Crossroads: The Drama of a Soap Opera* (London: Methuen, 1982), pp. 18, 15; Rosalie Horner, 'All cloak and dagger as we wait for Meg to peg out', *Daily Express*, 22 October 1981.

13. 'Who's cross about *Crossroads*?', *Daily Mirror*, 1 November 1978.

14. *Sunday Telegraph*, 6 April 1975, quoted in Charlotte Brunsdon, *Screen Tastes: Soap Opera to Satellite Dishes* (London: Routledge, 1997), p. 22; Jack Waterman, '"Crossroads" – en route to nowhere', *Listener*, 15 January 1976, 48; Michael Grade interviewed by Philip Dodd on *Nightwaves*, BBC Radio 3, 21 February 2011.

15. Hobson, *Crossroads*, p. 49; Lewis Chester, *All My Shows Are Great: The Life of Lew Grade* (London: Aurum, 2010), p. 119.

16. Charlotte Brunsdon and David Morley, 'Introduction', in *The Nationwide Television Studies* (London: Routledge, 1999), p. 4.

17. Charlotte Brunsdon, *The Feminist, the Housewife, and the Soap Opera* (Oxford: Oxford University Press, 2000), p. 10; Hobson, *Crossroads*, p. 119; John W. Pettinger, *From Dawn Till Dusk: A History of Independent Television in the Midlands* (Studley: Brewin Books, 2007), p. 71.

18. Pettinger, *From Dawn Till Dusk*, p. 64.

19. Hobson, *Crossroads*, p. 120.

20. Tony Hatch, 'The *Crossroads* theme tune' at crossroadsnetwork. co.uk/oldsite/themetune.htm (accessed 11 June 2011).

21. Robert Low, '"Down-market" BBC for Breakfast TV', *Observer*, 2 January 1983; Hobson, *Crossroads*, p. 113.

22. Hobson, *Crossroads*, p. 117.

23. Hobson, *Crossroads*, pp. 108, 118.

24. Hobson, *Crossroads*, p. 139; Brunsdon, *The Feminist, the Housewife, and the Soap Opera*, p. 80.

25. Ray Gosling, 'Friends and neighbours', *Listener*, 12 January 1978, 47–8; Hobson, *Crossroads*, p. 146.

26. Hobson, *Crossroads*, pp. 172–3; 'Obituary: Peter Ling', *Daily Telegraph*, 3 October 2006.

27. *The Kenneth Williams Diaries*, ed. Russell Davies (London: HarperCollins, 1994), pp. 686, 492, 505, 771, 475, 250–51.

28. Christopher Stevens, *Born Brilliant: The Life of Kenneth Williams* (London: John Murray, 2010), pp. 311, 293; *The Kenneth Williams Diaries*, pp. 533, 681.

29. Derek Cooper, *Hebridean Connection* (London: Routledge and Kegan Paul, 1977), p. 21; 'Top of the Pops for Tony', *Daily Mirror*, 31 October 1978.

30. Kenneth Gosling, 'Christmas TV viewing shows big decline', *The Times*, 11 January 1983; Peter Lennon, 'How will the liberated viewer swing?', *Listener*, 3 March 1983, 5.

31. Michael Poole, 'Failing to rate', *Listener*, 9 February 1984, 14; Robin Stringer, 'Recorded TV is often never seen', *The Times*, 1 February 1984; Peter Fiddick, 'TV's missing millions', *Guardian*, 11 February 1983; Ann Gray, *Video Playtime: The Gendering of a Leisure Technology* (London: Routledge, 1992), p. 169.

32. Chris Horrie and Steve Clarke, *Fuzzy Monsters: Fear and Loathing at the BBC* (London: Heinemann, 1994), p. xiv.

33. Michael Tracey, *The Decline and Fall of Public Service Broadcasting* (Oxford: Oxford University Press, 1998), p. 108.

34. Nancy Banks-Smith, 'Blessed release', *Guardian*, 23 January 1984; *BBC Annual Report and Handbook 1984* (London: BBC, 1984), p. 285.

35. Michael Grade, *It Seemed Like a Good Idea at the Time* (London: Macmillan, 1999), p. 92.

36. James Murray, 'The Forsyth saga', *Daily Express*, 7 October 1978; Rosalie Horner, 'Press blamed for Brucie flop', *Daily Express*, 9 November 1979.

37. Mihir Bose, *Michael Grade: Screening the Image* (London: Virgin, 1992), pp. 157, 165; Esther Rantzen, 'The tough TV lessons Michael has taught me', *Mail on Sunday*, 4 April 2004.

38. Michael Grade, 'What TV in US taught me', *Observer*, 26 August 1984; Bose, *Michael Grade*, pp. 159–60, 162–3; Grade, *It Seemed Like a Good Idea*, p. 186.

39. Peter Anghelides, 'Overrated ratings', *Listener*, 22 January 1987, 28; *Daily Life in the 1980s, Vol. 1: Broadcast Media Use and Associated Activities, Summer 1983* (London: BBC Data, 1984), p. 3; Bose, *Michael Grade*, p. 159.

40. Jill Hyem, 'Entering the arena: writing for television', in Helen Baehr and Gillian Dyer (eds), *Boxed In: Women and Television* (London: Pandora, 1987), pp. 153–4.

41. Phil Drabble, *A Voice in the Wilderness* (London: Pelham Books, 1991), p. 86; Graham McCann, *Only Fools and Horses: The Untold Story of Britain's Favourite Comedy* (Edinburgh: Canongate, 2011), pp. 94, 126; *Michael Grade: On the Box*, Episode 1: *New Dawn*, BBC Radio 2, 2 April 2012.

42. Bose, *Michael Grade*, pp. 172–3; Spike Milligan, 'Soap bubbles', *Guardian*, 28 January 1985.

43. Donald Trelford, *Snookered* (London: Faber, 1986), p. 75; Mike Cable, 'Ray, reared on snooker', *Radio Times*, 31 January 1974, 6; Gordon Burn, *Pocket Money: Bad-Boys, Business-Heads and Boom-Time Snooker* (London: Mandarin, 1992), pp. 166–7.

44. Trelford, *Snookered*, pp. 67–8, 78–9.

45. Peter Fiddick, 'Top of the pots, the new television spectacular', *Guardian*, 29 April 1978; Frederick Forsyth, 'Foreword', in Pete Scholey, *Who Dares Wins: Special Forces Heroes of the SAS* (Oxford: Osprey Publishing, 2008), p. 11.

46. Trelford, *Snookered*, pp. 72–3.

47. Trelford, *Snookered*, p. 33; Gordon Burn, 'There's nothing normal about snooker', *Listener*, 28 April 1983, 7.

48. George Mackay Brown, *Rockpools and Daffodils: An Orcadian Diary 1979–1991* (Edinburgh: Gordon Wright Publishing, 1992), pp. 120, 146; A. S. Byatt, 'I was a Wembley virgin', *Observer*, 30 June 1996.

49. Clive James, *A Point of View* (London: Picador, 2011), p. 324.

50. Burn, *Pocket Money*, pp. 29, 65.

51. Mordecai Richler, *On Snooker* (London: Yellow Jersey Press, 2001), p. 49.

52. Trelford, *Snookered*, p. 187; Eamonn Andrews, 'Taylormade on cue', *Catholic Herald*, 15 November 1985.

53. Sarah Boseley, 'Domesday 900 Project: kids' stuff of which history is made', *Guardian*, 7 February 1986.

54. 'Television Programmes', 1986, D-block GB-320000–540000; 'Television', 1986, D-block GB-424000–402000, BBC Domesday Reloaded Site at bbc.co.uk/history/domesday (accessed 9 January 2012).

55. Raymond Williams, 'Impressions of U.S. television', in *Raymond Williams on Television: Selected Writings*, ed. Alan O'Connor (London: Routledge, 1989), p. 25.

56. Raymond Williams, *Television: Technology and Cultural Form*, ed. Ederyn Williams (London: Routledge, 1990), pp. 78–118.

57. David Hendy, *Life on Air: A History of Radio Four* (Oxford: Oxford University Press, 2007), p. 140.

58. Peter Fiddick, 'A breakfast toast with jam on both sides', *Guardian*, 16 July 1983.

59. Lynn Barber, 'The vision of Bruce', *Independent on Sunday*, 18 August 1991; Maggie Brown, 'Not everyone's cup of tea', *Independent*, 24 February 1993; Andrew Lycett, 'The day of the panther', *The Times*, 26 August 1987.

60. Bob Stanley, 'The test card: when a girl and a clown ruled the airwaves', *Guardian*, 23 April 2012.

61. Roger Laughton, 'Guilt … is watching it before lunch', *Guardian*, 5 January 1987; Taylor and Mullan, *Uninvited Guests*, p. 196.

62. Gray, *Video Playtime*, pp. 39–40.

63. Ben Pimlott, 'One nation, one sickness', *Guardian*, 30 September 1985.

64. Paul du Noyer, *Liverpool: Wondrous Place: Music from the Cavern to the Capital of Culture* (London: Virgin, 2007), p. 204.

65. Paul Bonner with Lesley Aston, *Independent Television in Britain, Vol. 5: ITV and the IBA 1981–92* (Houndmills: Macmillan, 1998), p. 135.

66. Stephen Pile, 'Stuck on the tube after midnight', *Sunday Times*, 27 September 1987.

67. Jean Baudrillard, *Cool Memories* (London: Verso, 1990), p. 169; Jean Baudrillard, *America* (London: Verso, 1988), p. 50.

68. Maurice Blanchot, 'Everyday speech', *Yale French Studies*, 73 (1987), 13, 20.

69. Dorothy Hobson, *Channel 4: The Early Years and the Jeremy Isaacs Legacy* (London: I. B. Tauris, 2007), p. 152; Deborah Ross, 'Richard Whiteley – No taste, no style, no shame. No contest', *Independent*, 15 February 1999.

70. Johan Huizinga, *Homo Ludens: A Study of the Play Element in Culture* (Boston: Beacon Press, 1955), p. 58; George Orwell, 'The lion and the unicorn: socialism and the English genius', in *The Collected Essays, Journalism and Letters of George Orwell, Volume 2: My Country Right or Left 1940–1943*, eds Sonia Orwell and Ian Angus (Harmondsworth: Penguin, 1970), p. 77.

71. 'Richard Whiteley: Your tributes', at news.bbc.co.uk/1/hi/talking_point/4635131.stm (accessed 11 April 2010).

72. Peter Collett and Roger Lamb, *Watching People Watching Television: Final Report to the I.B.A.* (Department of Experimental Psychology, University of Oxford, February 1986), p. 1.

73. Taylor and Mullan, *Uninvited Guests*, p. 182.

74. Collett and Lamb, *Watching People*, p. 15.

75. Stuart Hood, 'As seen in the television lounge in a provincial hotel', *Listener*, 18 May 1972, 663; Will Wyatt, 'Television beyond the millennium', in Peter Day (ed.), *The Search for Extraterrestrial Life: Essays on Science and Technology from the Royal Institution* (Oxford: Clarendon Press, 1998), p. 107; Ien Ang, *Desperately Seeking the Audience* (London: Routledge, 1991).

76. Ludovic Kennedy, *On My Way to the Club* (London: Fontana, 1990), pp. 5, 402, 240, 404.

77. Farrah Anwar, 'Under the knife', *Guardian*, 20 March 1986; Jonathan Miller, 'BBC deny sexy TV storm', *The Times*, 2 December 1986; Humphrey Carpenter, *Dennis Potter: The Authorised Biography* (London: Faber, 1998), pp. 455–6.

78. Kennedy, *On My Way to the Club*, p. 404.

79. '*Broadcast* reviews the various aspects of the BFI's One Day in the Life of Television experiment', *Broadcast*, 25 November 1988, 21; 'Millions sought for TV survey' (press release), Angus Calder Papers, MOA, SxMOA28/10/5.

80. Sean Day-Lewis, *One Day in the Life of Television* (London: Grafton/ BFI, 1989), pp. 18–22, 63, 53, xv, 133.

81. Bob Woffinden, 'One day wonders', *Listener*, 26 October 1989, 26; Day-Lewis, *One Day in the Life*, pp. 134–6.

82. Day-Lewis, *One Day in the Life*, p. 186, 395; Stephen Pegg, 'A day in our television life', *Guardian*, 29 May 1989.

83. Day-Lewis, *One Day in the Life*, p. 216.

84. *One Day in the Life of Television*, ITV, 1 November 1989; Shyama Perera, 'TV jilting starts Dartmoor trouble', *Guardian*, 2 October 1986; Day-Lewis, *One Day in the Life*, p. 383.

85. Day-Lewis, *One Day in the Life*, pp. 298, 324.

86. 'Millions sought for TV survey'; Day-Lewis, *One Day in the Life*, p. 377.

87. Day-Lewis, *One Day in the Life*, p. 191.

88. Marie Gillespie, 'Technology and tradition: audio-visual culture among South-Asian families in west London', *Cultural Studies*, 3, 2 (May 1989), 226–8; Marie Gillespie, *Television, Ethnicity and Cultural Change* (London: Routledge, 1995), p. 152.

89. Joan Bakewell, '*Through the Keyhole*', *Listener*, 16 June 1988, 50; George Melly, '*Blockbusters*', *Listener*, 28 April 1988, 50; Paul Theroux, '*Coronation Street*', *Listener*, 31 March 1988, 50.

90. Ken Irwin, 'Pattie's tears for axed soap', *Daily Mirror*, 29 March 1988; Paul Cornell, Martin Day and Keith Topping, *The Guinness Book of Classic British TV* (London: Guinness Publishing, 1983), p. 43.

91. Simon Garfield, *The Wrestling* (London: Faber and Faber, 1996), p. 145; Alan Tomlinson, 'Introduction: consumer culture and the aura of the commodity', in Tomlinson (ed.), *Consumption, Identity, & Style: Marketing, Meanings, and the Packaging of Pleasure* (London: Routledge, 1990), pp. 32–4.

92. Samantha Cook, 'The elderly: a particularly valuable service', in Janet Willis and Tana Wollen (ed.), *The Neglected Audience* (London: BFI, 1990), pp. 46–7; Taylor and Mullan, *Uninvited Guests*, 29.

93. Day-Lewis, *One Day in the Life of Television*, p. 387.

8. The age of warts and carbuncles

1. Lynda Lee-Potter, 'I do know passion, but this is no autobiography', *Daily Mail*, 11 June 1990.

2. W. G. Hoskins, *One Man's England* (London: BBC, 1978), p. 74.

3. Peter Chippindale and Suzanne Franks, *Dished!: The Rise and Fall of British Satellite Broadcasting* (London: Simon and Schuster, 1991), p. 193.

4. Chippindale and Franks, *Dished!*, pp. 60, 64.

5. Michael Watts, 'Spectrum: a dish for TV gluttons', *The Times*, 18 February 1986.

6. 'Mrs Thatcher's bruiser', *Sunday Telegraph*, 7 October 1990.

7. Charlotte Brunsdon, *Screen Tastes: Soap Opera to Satellite Dishes* (London: Routledge, 1997), p. 159.

8. Patrick O'Hanlon and Richard Evans, 'Sky launch boosts sale of dishes', *The Times*, 4 February 1989; Chippindale and Franks, *Dished!*, p. 239; 'Leading article: dishing the carbuncles', *Guardian*, 14 July 1990.

9. Chippindale and Franks, *Dished!*, p. 64.

10. Raymond Fitzwalter, *The Dream that Died: The Rise and Fall of ITV* (Leicester: Matador, 2008), pp. 86–7.

11. Fitzwalter, *The Dream that Died*, p. 87; Peter Paterson, 'Weak links in the chain gang', *Daily Mail*, 20 June 1990.

12. Karl Miller, 'Diary', *London Review of Books*, 26 July 1990, 21.

13. Lin Jenkins, 'Patriotic football fervour collapses at home and on the violent streets', *The Times*, 5 July 1990.

14. Tom Lutz, *Crying in Public: The Natural and Cultural History of Tears* (New York: Norton, 2001), p. 295; John Moynihan, 'World Cup passions', *London Review of Books*, 30 August 1990, 2.

15. Ian Hamilton, *Gazza Italia* (London: Granta, 1994), pp. 63–4; Anthony Giddens, 'Gazza's goal slump', *Times Higher Education Supplement*, 21 December 1990, 11.

16. Brian Glanville, 'Kick-off for the Moloch', *Listener*, 19 December 1974, 835; Jason Cowley, *The Last Game: Love, Death and Football* (London: Pocket Books, 2009), p. 42.

17. John Fiske and John Hartley, *Reading Television* (London: Routledge, 1989), p. 145.

18. Martin Amis, 'The sporting week', *Observer*, 27 August 1978; Martin Amis, 'Football mad', *London Review of Books*, 3 December 1981, 23.

19. Richard Lander, 'Why Sky is over the moon', *Independent*, 11 March 1992.

20. Jeevan Vasagar and Jon Brodkin, 'Kenneth Wolstenholme dies at 81', *Guardian*, 27 March 2002.

21. Nick Hornby, *Fever Pitch: A Fan's Life* (London: Victor Gollancz, 1992), p. 20.

22. Kingsley Amis to Philip Larkin, 14 October 1985, in *The Letters of Kingsley Amis*, ed. Zachary Leader (London: HarperCollins, 2000), p. 1009.

23. Philip Larkin to C. B. Cox, 13 January 1981, in *Selected Letters of Philip Larkin 1940–1985*, ed. Anthony Thwaite (London: Faber, 1992), p. 637; Kingsley Amis, 'Lone voices', in *What Became of Jane Austen?: And Other Questions* (London: Jonathan Cape, 1970), p. 160.

24. Kingsley Amis, 'Preview', *Radio Times*, 14 November 1974, 5.

25. Kingsley Amis, 'An arts policy?', in *The Amis Collection: Selected Non-Fiction 1954–1990* (Harmondsworth: Penguin, 1991), p. 248; Kingsley Amis, 'Television and the intellectuals', in *The Amis Collection*, pp. 257–8; Kingsley Amis, 'Sod the public: a consumer's guide', in *The Amis Collection*, p. 239.

26. Yvonne Jewkes, 'The use of media in constructing identities in the masculine environment of men's prisons', *European Journal of Communication*, 17, 2 (June 2002), 220; Duncan Petrie, 'Critical discourse and the television audience', in Duncan Petrie and Janet Willis (eds), *Television and the Household: Reports from the BFI's Audience Tracking Study* (London: BFI, 1995), p. 105; Zachary Leader, *The Life of Kingsley Amis* (London: Jonathan Cape, 2006), p. 812.

27. Kingsley Amis, 'Looking in is looking up', *TV Times*, 7 February 1964, 7.

28. 'Coronation Street the home of peasant morons?', *Guardian*, 31 January 1963; Dave Russell, *Looking North: Northern England and the National Imagination* (Manchester: Manchester University Press, 2004), p. 200; Elizabeth Walton, 'And many happy Rovers Return', *The Times*, 25 November 1985.

29. 'The truth about Coronation Street', *Daily Mirror*, 6 August 1971.

30. Chris Waters, 'Representations of everyday life: L. S. Lowry and the landscape of memory in postwar Britain', *Representations*, 65 (Winter 1999), 131; David Bret, *Morrissey: Scandal and Passion* (London: Robson Books, 2004), pp. 7, 65.

31. Georgina Henry, 'Top soap washes too white for TV watchdog', *Guardian*, 15 October 1992.

32. Vera Gottlieb, '*Brookside*: "Damon's YTS comes to an end" (Barry Woodward): paradoxes and contradictions', in George W. Brandt (ed.), *British Television Drama in the 1980s* (Cambridge: Cambridge University Press, 1993), p. 53; Nancy Banks-Smith, 'Feather-brained wedding', *Guardian*, 15 August 2009; Nancy Banks-Smith, 'Like her or Kuala Lumpur', *Guardian*, 14 November 1996.

33. Neil Powell, *Amis & Sons: Two Literary Generations* (London: Macmillan, 2008), p. 233; Kingsley Amis, *Difficulties with Girls* (London: Penguin, 1989), p. 266; Kingsley Amis, *The King's English* (London: Penguin, 2011), p. 189; Eric Jacobs, *Kingsley Amis: A Biography* (London: Hodder and Stoughton, 1995), p. 15.

34. Zygmunt Bauman, *Mortality, Immortality and Other Life Strategies* (Cambridge: Polity, 1992), p. 173.

35. Mark Lawson, 'Life can be spooky in the fourth person', *Independent*, 14 November 1991; John Sutherland, *Stephen Spender: The Authorized Biography* (London: Viking, 2002), p. 543.

36. Petrie, 'Critical discourse and the television audience', p. 106.

37. Michael Wearing, 'What about real life, Mr Birt?', *Independent*, 28 August 1998; Thomas Quinn, 'Wogan hits out at BBC', *Daily Mirror*, 17 November 1999.

38. Georgina Born, *Uncertain Vision: Birt, Dyke and the Reinvention of the BBC* (London: Secker and Warburg, 2004), p. 287.

39. Rolf Harris, *My Autobiography: Can You Tell What It is Yet?* (London: Corgi, 2002), p. 359.

40. Peter Conrad, 'See no chimps …', *Observer*, 19 October 1997; John Ellis, 'Scheduling: the last creative act in television?', *Media, Culture and Society*, 22, 1 (January 2000), 32; Gauntlett and Hill, *TV Living*, p. 48.

41. John Ellis, 'Documentary and truth on television: the crisis of 1999', in Alan Rosenthal and John Corner (eds), *New Challenges for Documentary* (Manchester: Manchester University Press, 2005), p. 343.

42. Joan Bakewell, 'Delia Smith, BBC2', *The Times*, 15 March 1980; John Ezard, 'Delia finds the recipe for long-lasting fame', *Guardian*, 3 December 2001.

43. 'Postgate calling', *TV Mirror*, 2 January 1954, 22.

44. 'The empty lobster pots', *Financial Times*, 8 August 1962; 'New taste for scampi brings Scots fishing prosperity', *The Times*, 6 August 1962; Alan Davidson, *The Oxford Companion to Food* (Oxford: Oxford University Press, 2006), p. 789; Alison Bowyer, *Delia Smith: The Biography* (London: André Deutsch, 1999), p. 90.

45. Emily Green, 'First, catch your bandwagon', *Independent on Sunday*, 10 November 1996; Cathy Newman, 'Celebrity endorsement proves recipe for success', *Financial Times*, 23 November 1998.

46. Bob Chaundy, 'Obituary: Colin McIntyre', *Guardian*, 12 June 2012.

47. Bowyer, *Delia Smith*, pp. 153–4.

48. Bowyer, *Delia Smith*, p. 174.

49. Charles Leadbeater, 'Delianomics', *Mail on Sunday*, 12 December 1999; Charles Leadbeater, *Living on Thin Air: The New Economy* (London: Penguin, 1999), pp. 28–30.

50. Bowyer, *Delia Smith*, pp. 189, 174; Green, 'First, catch your bandwagon'.

51. Eric Griffiths, 'Hegel's winter collection', *Times Literary Supplement*, 8 March 1996, 20–21.

52. Alan Warde and Lydia Martens, *Eating Out: Social Differentiation, Consumption and Pleasure* (Cambridge: Cambridge University Press, 2000), pp. 58–61.

53. Bowyer, *Delia Smith*, p. 161.

54. Andy Medhurst, 'Day for night', *Sight and Sound*, 26, 6 (June 1999), 27.

55. Jewkes, 'The use of media in constructing identities', 215; Deborah Cohen, *Household Gods: The British and their Possessions* (New Haven, CT: Yale University Press, 2006), p. 207.

56. Hilary Kingsley and Geoff Tibballs, *Box of Delights: The Golden Years of Television* (London: Macmillan, 1989), p. 36; Raphael Samuel, *Theatres of Memory, Volume 1: Past and Present in Contemporary Culture* (London: Verso, 1994), p. 72.

57. Michael Leapman, 'The Mel Gibson of the potting shed meets his mulcher', *Independent*, 21 September 1997; Sue Arnold, 'These days you can't see the trees for the wood', *Independent*, 10 April 2004; Eric Robson, 'Why I loathe TV garden makeovers', *Daily Mail*, 10

April 2004; Alan Titchmarsh, *Knave of Spades: Growing Pains of a Gardener* (London: Hodder and Stoughton, 2010), p. 274.

58. Titchmarsh, *Knave of Spades*, p. 273.

59. Gay Search, *Gardeners' World Through the Years* (London: Carlton Books, 2006), pp. 65–6.

60. Charles Leadbeater, *Up the Down Escalator: Why the Global Pessimists are Wrong* (London: Viking, 2002), pp. 65–6.

61. Medhurst, 'Day for night', p. 26.

62. Justine Picardie, 'Dale Winton, the king of the aisles', *Independent*, 8 January 1995; Polly Toynbee, 'Most daytime TV is a tepid dishwater soup', *Radio Times*, 11–17 May 1996, 14.

63. Letters, *Radio Times*, 1–7 June 1996, 119; Gauntlett and Hill, *TV Living*, pp. 245, 288, 222–3.

64. Janet Willis, 'Staying in touch: television and the over-seventies', in Petrie and Willis (eds), *Television and the Household*, p. 38; Gauntlett and Hill, *TV Living*, pp. 107–8; Auberon Waugh, 'Creating new jobs', *Daily Telegraph*, 8 February 1997.

65. George Mackay Brown, *The First Wash of Spring* (London: Steve Savage, 2006), pp. 240–42.

66. Gerard Gilbert, 'Make your own entertainment', *Independent*, 20 April 1998.

67. Peter Hitchens, *The Abolition of Britain* (London: Quartet, 2000), pp. 142, 146; Peter Hitchens, *Monday Morning Blues* (London: Quartet, 2000), pp. 49–50.

68. Oliver James, *Britain on the Couch: Treating the Low Serotonin Society* (London: Arrow, 1998), p. 29; Oliver James, 'It keeps them quiet now but ...', *Observer*, 29 November 1998.

69. Winifred Holtby, *Anderby Wold* (London: Virago, 1981), p. 239.

70. Mark Rowe, 'Eighteen months of TV ends in a flash', *Independent on Sunday*, 23 May 1999.

71. Sean Day-Lewis, 'Langham Diary', *Listener*, 8 December 1983, 20.

72. Alexandra Frean, 'Viewers have no right to watch TV, say law lords', *The Times*, 25 April 1997.

9. A glimmer on the dull grey tube

1. Robert Hughes, *The Shock of the New* (London: Thames and Hudson, 1991), p. 345.

NOTES

2. Dennis Potter, *Seeing the Blossom: Two Interviews and a Lecture* (London: Faber, 1994), p. 55; Dennis Potter, 'Hurrah for the gogglebox', *Daily Herald*, 31 August 1962.

3. Humphrey Carpenter, *Dennis Potter: The Authorised Biography* (London: Faber, 1998), p. 123.

4. Carpenter, *Dennis Potter*, p. 133; Lewis Chester, *All My Shows Are Great: The Life of Lew Grade* (London, Aurum, 2010), p. 94.

5. *Arena*, BBC2, 30 January 1987.

6. Dennis Potter, 'Some sort of preface ...', in *Blue Remembered Hills and Other Plays* (London: Faber and Faber, 1986), pp. 28–9.

7. W. Stephen Gilbert, *Fight and Kick and Bite: The Life and Work of Dennis Potter* (London: Hodder and Stoughton, 1995), pp. 44–5; Potter, *Seeing the Blossom*, pp. 52–4.

8. Tony Garnett, 'Notes for the Raymond Williams Memorial Lecture', *Critical Quarterly*, 40, 3 (October 1998), 33–4; Chris Barrie, 'Pay TV warning for "all live sport and top shows"', *Guardian*, 6 November 1998.

9. Peter Bazalgette, 'Golden age? This is it', *Guardian*, 19 November 2001; Peter Bazalgette, 'TV totalitarianism is dead. Power to the digital people!', *Observer*, 30 November 2003.

10. Chris Tarrant, *Millionaire Moments* (London: Time Warner, 2002), p. 6; Mike Wayne, '*Who Wants To Be a Millionaire?* Contextual analysis and the endgame of public service television', in Dan Fleming (ed.), *Formations: A 21st Century Media Studies Textbook* (Manchester: Manchester University Press, 2000), pp. 209–10.

11. Cosmo Landesman, 'Not so much Big Brother as the little exhibitionists', *Sunday Times*, 23 July 2000; Will Self, 'It's National Service for navel-gazers', *Independent*, 20 August 2000.

12. J. G. Ballard, 'Thirteen to Centaurus', in Ballard, *The Complete Short Stories: Volume 1* (London: Harper Perennial, 2006), p. 447; J .G. Ballard, *The Day of Creation* (New York: Liveright, 2012), p. 64.

13. John Baxter, *The Inner Man: The Life of J. G. Ballard* (London: Weidenfeld and Nicolson, 2011), pp. 306–7.

14. Charles Darwin, *The Expression of the Emotions in Man and Animals*, ed. Francis Darwin (Cambridge: Cambridge University Press, 2009), pp. 154, 175.

15. Christopher Dunkley, 'That's enough of the navel-gazing', *Financial Times*, 23 August 2000, 16.

16. Laurie Taylor and Bob Mullan, *Uninvited Guests: The Intimate Secrets of Television and Radio* (London: Chatto and Windus, 1986), p. 62.

17. Ferdinand Mount, *Full Circle: How the Classical World Came Back to Us* (London: Simon and Schuster, 2010), p. 206; see also Brett Mills, 'Television wildlife documentaries and animals' right to privacy', *Continuum*, 24, 2 (April 2010), 193–202.

18. David Attenborough, *Life on Air: Memoirs of a Broadcaster* (London: BBC, 2002), pp. 187–8; Elaine Morgan, 'The greatest story ever told', *Radio Times*, 13–19 January 1979, 77.

19. Desmond Morris, 'The day of reckoning', *Guardian*, 15 September 2000.

20. 'Active life for zoo animals', *New Scientist*, 29 June 1961, 773; Desmond Morris, *Watching: Encounters with Humans and Other Animals* (London: Little Books, 2006), pp. 171–2.

21. Desmond Morris, 'Oh, Brother!', *Daily Mail*, 31 May 2005; Desmond Morris, 'Rumbled in the jungle', *Daily Telegraph*, 18 November 2006; Jenny Johnson, 'Nicest man on the planet?', *Daily Mail*, 31 May 2006.

22. Charlie Brooker, *Screen Burn* (London: Faber and Faber, 2005), pp. 17, 276–7.

23. James Harding, 'Davies has a bad week at the office', *Financial Times*, 16 March 2002; Ben Walters, *The Office* (London: BFI, 2005), pp. 40, 45.

24. Graham McCann, 'You never had it so good or so funny', *Financial Times*, 13 November 2002.

25. Steven Johnson, *Everything Bad is Good For You: Why Popular Culture is Making Us Smarter* (London: Penguin, 2006), pp. 65–6; Clive James, 'Fantasy in the West Wing', in *The Meaning of Recognition: New Essays 2001–2005* (London: Picador, 2006), p. 32.

26. Richard Hoggart, *An Imagined Life: Life and Times, Volume 3: 1959–91* (Oxford: Oxford University Press, 1993), p. 26.

27. Richard Hoggart, 'Dumb and dumber', *Guardian*, 14 March 2002.

28. David Edgerton, *The Shock of the Old: Technology and Global History Since 1900* (London: Profile, 2006), p. xii; John Seely Brown

and Paul Duguid, *The Social Life of Information* (Cambridge, MA: Harvard Business School Press, 2002), p. 16.

29. Urmee Khan, 'Nearly 30,000 homes in the UK still have black-and-white TVs', *Daily Telegraph*, 14 November 2009; Chris Mullin, *Decline & Fall: Diaries 2005–2010* (London: Profile, 2011), p. 334.

30. Department for Culture, Media and Sport, *A Public Service for All: The BBC in the Digital Age* (London: The Stationery Office, 2006), p. 16.

31. Paul Smith, 'The politics of television policy: The case of digital switchover in the United Kingdom', *International Journal of Digital Television*, 2, 1 (January 2011), 42; Department for Culture, *A Public Service for All*, p. 4.

32. Emily Dugan, 'Cumbrian town paves the way for television's big switchover to digital', *Independent*, 16 October 2007.

33. A. J. Pollard, 'Introduction', in Christian D. Liddy and Richard H. Britnell (eds), *North-East England in the Later Middle Ages* (Woodbridge: Boydell, 2005), p. 3.

34. Geoff Phillips, *Memories of Tyne Tees Television* (Durham: GP Electronic Services, 1998), p. 51.

35. Craig Taylor, *Londoners: The Days and Nights of London Now – As Told by Those Who Love It, Hate It, Live It, Left It and Long for It* (London: Granta, 2011), p. 255.

36. 'One Man quits, fed up with sheepdogs', *Daily Mail*, 27 September 1993; Anne Evans, 'Minister backs sheepdog show', *Observer*, 21 February 1999; Anne Evans and Peter Hooley, 'Smith cultivates dropped collies', *Observer*, 21 February 1999; Robin Page, 'Come bye and see us – sheep are back on TV', *Mail on Sunday*, 9 December 2007; Julia Stuart, 'One Man and His Dog', *Independent*, 24 March 2001.

37. Hansard, HL Deb, 12 March 2001, vol. 623, col. 539.

38. Louise Gray, 'Adam Henson receives death threats over badger cull', *Daily Telegraph*, 9 May 2011.

39. Rob Young, *Electric Eden: Unearthing Britain's Visionary Music* (London: Faber, 2010), p. 410; Peter Hall, *Diaries*, ed. John Goodwin (London: Oberon, 2000), p. 154.

40. Dennis Potter, *The Changing Forest: Life in the Forest of Dean Today* (London: Minerva, 1996), p. 2.

41. Craig Taylor, *Return to Akenfield: Portrait of an English Village in the 21st Century* (London: Granta, 2007), pp. 227, 112.

42. Eric Robson, *The Border Line* (London: Frances Lincoln, 2006), p. 61.

43. Rhys Evans, *Gwynfor Evans: A Portrait of a Patriot* (Tal-y-bont: Y Lolfa, 2008), pp. 407, 413, 428.

44. Jamie Medhurst, *A History of Independent Television in Wales* (Cardiff: University of Wales Press, 2010), p. 175; Evans, *Gwynfor Evans*, p. 428.

45. John Caughie, 'Scottish television: what would it look like?', in Colin McArthur (ed.), *Scotch Reels: Scotland in Cinema and Television* (London: BFI, 1982), p. 120; Duncan Petrie, 'Television in Scotland: audience and cultural identity', in Duncan Petrie and Janet Willis (eds), *Television and the Household: Reports from the BFI's Audience Tracking Study* (London: BFI, 1995), p. 87; Wilson McLeod, 'Gaelic in the New Scotland: politics, rhetoric and public discourse', *Journal on Ethnopolitics and Minority Issues*, 2, 2 (Summer 2001), 11–12.

46. Allan Brown, 'BBC Alba shows power of Gaelic lobby', *Sunday Times*, 5 October 2008.

47. Andrew Tolmie, 'Cho tin ris a pearraid', *Daily Mail*, 18 February 2008; Kathleen Nutt, 'Gaelic TV station loses a third of its viewers', *Sunday Times*, 1 February 2009.

48. Tom Nairn, *The Break-Up of Britain: Crisis and Neo-Nationalism* (Altona, Victoria: Common Ground, 2003), p. 150.

49. John Durham Peters, *Speaking into the Air: A History of the Idea of Communication* (Chicago: University of Chicago Press, 1999), pp. 52, 155.

50. Sheila Whitely, *Too Much Too Young: Popular Music, Age and Gender* (London: Routledge, 2005), p. 173; 'Telescope technical know-how helps give TV audience star-maker power', *PR Newswire Europe*, 8 February 2002.

51. Peter Bazalgette, 'Foreword', in Stephen Coleman, *A Tale of Two Houses: The House of Commons, the Big Brother House and the People at Home* (London: Hansard Society, 2003), p. 3.

52. Institute of Education, University of London, University of Sheffield, University of East London and British Library, *Children's Playground Games and Songs in the New Media Age 2009–2011: Project Report* (2011), pp. 13, 21; Sanna Inthorn and John Street, '"Simon Cowell for

prime minister"? Young citizens' attitudes towards celebrity politics',
Media, Culture and Society, 33, 3 (April 2011), 6.

53. Marista Leishman, *My Father: Lord Reith of the BBC* (Edinburgh:
Saint Andrew Press, 2006), pp. 112–13.

54. Ned Temko, 'Brown outlines his vision for an "X Factor" Britain',
Observer, 5 November 2006; Jonathan Freedland, 'Inspired by TV,
Brown gets the X factor', *Guardian*, 13 February 2008; Gordon Brown,
'We'll use our schools to break down class barriers', *Observer*, 10
February 2008.

55. Tony Benn, *Years of Hope: Diaries, Letters and Papers, 1940–1962*
(London: Hutchinson, 1994), p. 567; Peter Hitchens, *The Abolition of
Britain* (London: Quartet, 2000), p. 7; Adam Sherwin, 'Phone lines go
quiet as the Idol bubble pops', *The Times*, 20 December 2003.

56. David Cameron, 'I am pro-BBC', *Evening Standard*, 27 April 2010.

57. Jeremy Hunt, Speech at the Royal Television Society, London, 28
September 2010.

58. *Commercially Viable Local Television in the UK: A Review by
Nicholas Shott for the Secretary of State for Culture, Olympics, Media
and Sport* (December 2010), p. 12.

59. Piers Morgan, *Misadventures of a Big Mouth Brit* (London: Random
House, 2010), p. 10.

60. Pete Waterman, 'Why I refuse to watch X Factor', *Daily Mail*, 11
December 2009; Adam MacQueen, *Private Eye: The First 50 Years*
(London: Private Eye, 2011), p. 168.

10. Closedown

1. Ronald Blythe, *Word from Wormingford: A Parish Year* (Norwich:
Canterbury Press, 2007), p. 49.

2. 'How Emley Moor's giant crashed', *Yorkshire Post*, 20 March 1969.

3. 'Yorkshire's giant TV mast crashes on village', *Yorkshire Post*, 20
March 1969; Malcolm Barker, 'Ice crushes the TV monster', *Yorkshire
Post*, 20 March 1969.

4. 'YTV could be back tonight', *Yorkshire Post*, 21 March 1969; 'ITV
back soon for 4m viewers', *Yorkshire Post*, 21 March 1969.

5. Simon Armitage, *All Points North* (London: Penguin, 1999), p. 22;
Jonathan Meades, *Even Further Abroad: I Remember the Future*,
BBC2, 15 February 1996.

6. Paul Farley and Michael Symmons Roberts, *Edgelands: Journeys into England's True Wilderness* (London: Jonathan Cape, 2011), p. 159.

7. 'Manchester on TV: Ghosts of Winter Hill' at news.bbc.co.uk/local/manchester/low/people_and_places/arts_and_culture/newsid_8332000/8332589.stm (accessed 13 March 2009).

8. Rosie Millard, 'Do not adjust your mindset', *The Times*, 21 April 2012.

9. 'Seen and heard', *Manchester Guardian*, 1 April 1930.

10. Daniel Dayan and Elihu Katz, *Media Events: The Live Broadcasting of History* (Cambridge, MA: Harvard University Press, 1992), p. 1.

11. Jonathan Eberhart, 'Giving ourselves away', *Science News*, 113, 9 (4 March 1978), 138–9.

12. Jean Heidmann, *Extraterrestrial Intelligence* (Cambridge: Cambridge University Press, 1997), pp. 174–5.

ACKNOWLEDGEMENTS

During some of the writing and research for this book I held a British Academy Mid-Career Research Fellowship, and I am grateful to the British Academy for this support, which freed me from teaching and administrative duties and provided funding to visit archives. The Mass Observation material quoted in the book is reproduced with the permission of the Trustees of the Mass Observation Archive, and is copyright © the Trustees of the Mass Observation Archive. The material from the BBC's Written Archives is reproduced with permission of the BBC and is copyright © the BBC. Jessica Scantlebury at the Mass Observation Archive at Sussex and Louise North at the BBC Written Archives at Caversham were particularly helpful in retrieving material for me and dealing with my queries. Jez Lowe kindly allowed me to quote some words from his song 'Mike Neville Said It (So It Must Be True)', which are copyright © Jez Lowe/Lowelife Music. I would like to thank the following people for reading draft material or offering ideas, information and other assistance: Jim Barnard, Michel Byrne, Jo Croft, Ross Dawson, Alice Ferrebe, Elspeth Graham, Colin Harrison, Jackie Kelly, Liam Moran, Michael Moran, Wynn Moran, Glenda Norquay, Joanna Price, Amber Regis, Helen Rogers, Gerry Smyth, Karolina Sutton, Kate Walchester and Andy Young. Tony Rogers and Paul Thompson helpfully pointed out factual errors which I have revised for the paperback edition. Penny Gardiner and Penny Daniel took enormous care in preparing the manuscript for publication. And, as usual, this book has been immeasurably improved by the work of my wonderful editor, Daniel Crewe.

PICTURE CREDITS

1. Family watching television, 1954. Daily Herald Archive/SSPL/Getty Images.
2. Poster advertising John Logie Baird's demonstration of television at the London Coliseum, July 1930. Museum of Hastings.
3. Max Hastings and friends watching television, Kensington, 1950. Max Hastings.
4. Frances Day, Jerry Desmonde, Elizabeth Allen and Gilbert Harding on *What's My Line?*, 29 August 1951. BBC/Corbis.
5. A woman adjusts her TV set, 1960s. Mary Evans Picture Library.
6. Carole Hersee, daughter of test card designer George Hersee, posing for a new version of Test Card F at the Thames studios in Teddington, 10 March 1969. Ian Tyas/Keystone/Getty Images.
7. Richard Whiteley and Carol Vorderman on *Countdown*, 1980s. Granada Archives. ITV/Rex Features.
8. Delia Smith, 1971. David Reed/Corbis.
9. Jade Goody being interviewed on the big screen after her eviction from the *Big Brother* house, 26 July 2002. Press Association.
10. Stacked Old Televisions, 2011. Lindsay Blair Brown. www.lindsayblairbrown.com.

INDEX